Contents

Introduction to the Escort

The Escort was first introduced in 1968. Since then the range has been increased to include estate car versions and 'hotted-up' models. The basic construction and mechanical components of all models are similar but reference should be made to the Specifications Section at the beginning of each chapter to obtain details of minor variations between the different models.

Automatic transmission is available as an optional extra on all 1300 cc models except Sport, GT or 1300E. (It was once available on 1100 cc models also.)

The following brief descriptions will serve to identify the various models in the Escort range:

Basic 1100

Features include drum brakes all round, dynamo charge, cross-ply tyres.

1100L

Features include drum brakes all round, radial tyres and more luxurious interior.

1300L

Similar to 1100L except of course for larger engine. Opening rear quarterlights.

1300XL

Features include drum brakes all round, radial tyres, heated rear window, alternator, opening rear quarterlights, full instrumentation and luxury interior trim.

Sport

Features include twin-choke Weber carburettor, high lift camshaft, larger valves, four branch exhaust manifold. Front disc and rear drum brakes with servo assistance. 5 inch width sports type road wheels and flared front wheel arches, full instrumentation.

GT

Similar to the Sport model but with more luxurious XL style finish to the interior. Four door version discontinued April 1973.

1300E

This model was introduced in March 1973 combining the features of the Sport and GT versions except that it has a vinyl covered roof and special radiator grille, heated rear window and alternator, plus other differences and refinements.

Estate cars

Equipment and trim follows generally that of the saloons according to type (L, XL). The 1300 versions have front disc brakes and servo assistance and the XL version has a heated rear window and alternator.

Modifications to the equipment specifications of all models in the Escort range are continuous. 1974 models are equipped with radial tyres and alternators as standard.

Ford Escort 2-door Saloon

Ford Escort GT Saloon

Ford Escort 1100L

Ford Escort 1300E (4-door)

Ford Escort Estate (1300 X L)

Ford Escort XL

Ford Escort 1300 (Sport)

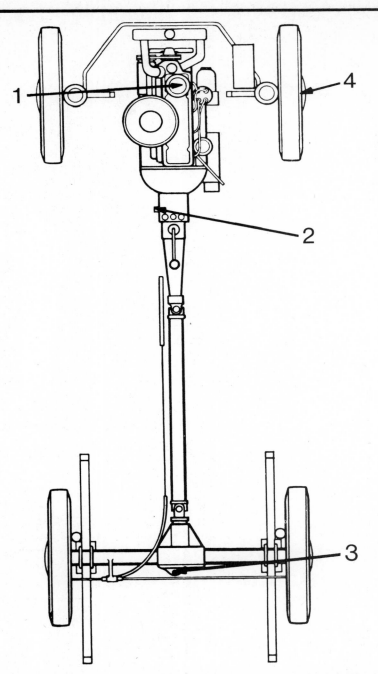

Lubrication chart and recommended lubricants

Components	Castrol Product
1 Engine...	Castrol GTX
2 Gearbox - Manual	Castrol Hypoy Light EP 80
- Automatic	Castrol TQF
3 Rear axle	Castrol Hypoy B EP 90
4 Front wheel bearings	Castrol LM Grease

Note: The above recommendations are general and intended for guidance only. Lubrication requirements vary from territory to territory. Consult the operators handbook supplied with your car.

Buying spare parts and vehicle identification numbers

Buying spare parts

Spare parts are available from many sources, for example: Ford garages, other garages and accessory shops, and motor factors. Our advice regarding spare part sources is as follows:

Officially appointed Ford garages - This is the best source of parts which are peculiar to your car and are otherwise not generally available (eg complete cylinder heads, internal gearbox components, badges, interior trim etc). It is also the only place at which you should buy parts if your car is still under warranty - non-Ford components may invalidate the warranty. To be sure of obtaining the correct parts it will always be necessary to give the storeman your car's vehicle identification number, and if possible, to take the 'old' part along for positive identification. Remember that many parts are available on a factory exchange scheme - any parts returned should always be clean! It obviously makes good sense to go straight to the specialists on your car for this type of part for they are best equipped to supply you.

Other garages and accessory shops - These are often very good places to buy materials and components needed for the maintenance of your car (eg oil filters, spark plugs, bulbs, fan belts, oils and greases, touch-up paint, filler paste etc). They also sell general accessories, usually have convenient opening hours, charge lower prices and can often be found not far from home.

Motor factors - Good factors will stock all of the more important components which wear out relatively quickly (eg clutch components, pistons, valves, exhaust systems, brake cylinders/pipes/hoses/seals/shoes and pads etc). Motor factors will often provide new or reconditioned components on a part exchange basis - this can save a considerable amount of money.

Vehicle identification numbers

Although many individual parts, and in some cases sub-assemblies, fit a number of different models it is dangerous to assume that just because they look the same, they are the same. Differences are not always easy to detect except by serial numbers. Make sure therefore, that the appropriate identity number for the model or sub-assembly is known and quoted when a spare part is ordered.

The illustrations on page 13 show the two vehicle identification plates - one of which will be attached to the inner wing on the right-hand side of the engine compartment. A key to the coding used on these plates is provided on page 13.

When buying a replacement part from a Ford dealer, decide which category that part fits into (eg, engine, trim, joint etc.) Then record the relevant number from the vehicle identification plate. Quote this number and the vehicle number to the storeman; he will then be able to provide you with the correct part for your individual vehicle.

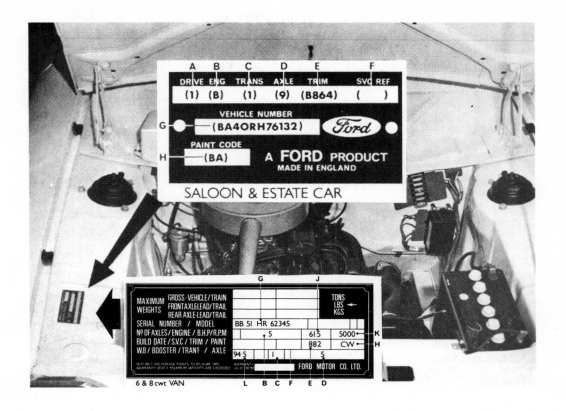

Coding key to vehicle identification plate

A   Type of drive

R or 1   Right hand drive   L or 2   Left hand drive

B   Engine type

B   1100 cc HC   S   1300 cc HC
C   1100 cc LC   T   1300 cc LC
R   1300 GT

C   Transmission

1   Floor change   7   Automatic

D   Rear axle

Heavy duty   Except heavy duty
A   3.777 : 1   2   3.900 : 1
B   4.125 : 1   4   4.125 : 1
C   4.444 : 1   4   4.444 : 1
D   3.900 : 1   9   3.777

E   Trim

the code indicates the colour and type of the original materials used.

F   SVC

indicates when a vehicle is moved from the factory of origin for assembly at another.

G   Vehicle number

consists of a combination of letters and numbers, referring to factories, body type and sequence number etc and can be interpreted by a Ford dealer.

H   Paint code

consists of letters indicating colours and type of original paint, and this can be interpreted by a Ford dealer.

J   (Van only)

gross maximum bhp.

K   (Van only)

engine speed at which maximum bhp available.

L   (Van only)

vehicle wheelbase in inches.

Routine maintenance

The maintenance instructions listed below are basically those recommended by the manufacturer. They are supplemented by additional maintenance tasks which, through practical experience, the author recommends should be carried out at the intervals suggested. Figure numbers correspond with paragraph numbers. Where no illustration is shown, refer to chapter indicated.

Weekly or every 250 miles (400 km)

1 **Check the level of the engine oil:** With the vehicle standing on level ground, withdraw the dipstick, wipe it with a piece of non-fluffy cloth, re-insert it and then withdraw it again - read off the oil level. Keep the oil level between the 'MIN' and 'MAX' marks.

2 **Check the battery electrolyte level:** This should be maintained at a level just above the tops of the plates by the addition of distilled water only.

3 **Check the coolant level in the radiator:** Add soft water if necessary to bring the level to within not more than ½ inch (12.7 mm) of the bottom of the filler neck.

4 **Check the fluid level in the automatic transmission unit (where fitted):** This must be checked with the oil hot after at least 5 miles (8 km) road running. With the engine ticking over, place selector in 'P'. Switch off the engine and wait two minutes for the oil to drain from the filler tube. Withdraw the dipstick, wipe, insert and then withdraw and read off the level. Top up to the 'Full' mark with recommended fluid.

5 **Check the brake reservoir fluid level:** Wipe any dirt from mark with recommended fluid taken from a sealed tin. With dual circuit braking systems, keep reservoir level above dividing baffle.

6 **Top up windscreen washer fluid container:** Add a recommended quantity of washer cleaning fluid to the water as a grease solvent and to prevent freezing.

7 **Check tyre pressures (including the spare):** Check when tyres are cold and inflate as necessary to pressures given in Specifications, Chapter 11.

Six monthly or every 6000 miles (10,000 km)

8 **Drain engine oil and renew filter** (Chapter 1).
9 **Lubricate dynamo rear bearing (where fitted).**
10 **Clean spark plugs and set gap** (Chapter 4).
11 **Clean and adjust (or renew) distributor contact points.**
12 **Check and adjust if necessary carburettor idling and mixture** (Chapter 3).
13 **Check engine oil filler cap and emission control valve.**
14 **Check and adjust valve clearances (hot).**
15 **Check fan belt tension and adjust if necessary.**
16 **Clean fuel pump screen or separate fuel line filter.**
17 **Check manual gearbox oil level:** Remove the plug on the side of the casing and inject oil of the recommended grade until it begins to run out. Refit the plug. Draining of the gearbox is not specified by Ford and no drain plug is provided.
18 **Check rear axle oil level:** Remove the plug from the rear of the casing and inject oil until it begins to run out. Refit the plug. Draining of the rear axle is not specified by Ford and no drain plug is provided.
19 **Check tightness of rear road spring U bolt nuts.**
20 **Adjust drum brakes and check linings for wear.**
21 **Check front disc brakes for pad wear.**
22 **Check brake flexible hoses for deterioration** (Chapter 9).
23 **Check all cooling system hoses for deterioration** (Chapter 2).
24 **Check exhaust system for damage or leaks** (Chapter 3).
25 **Check steering ball joints for wear or damaged rubber dust excluders** (Chapter 11).
26 **Check steering gear rubber bellows for deterioration.**
27 **Check clutch free movement and adjust if necessary** (Chapter 5).
28 **Oil all engine controls, door hinges and locks etc.**
29 **Check condition of steering shaft flexible coupling and renew if necessary.**

RM1. Check the level of the engine oil

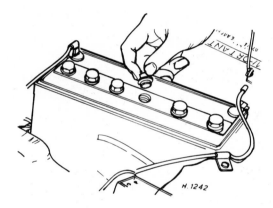

RM2. Check the level of the battery electrolyte

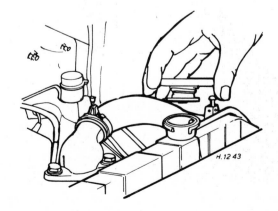

RM3. Check the coolant level in the radiator

Eighteen monthly or every 18,000 miles (29,000 km)

30 Renew air cleaner element.
31 Renew brake servo air filter (where servo fitted) (Chapter 9).

Every 30,000 miles (48,000 km)

32 Clean, repack with grease and adjust front wheel bearings.

Every 40,000 miles (64,000 km)

33 Renew all flexible brake hoses, cylinder seals and hydraulic fluid within the system (Chapter 9).

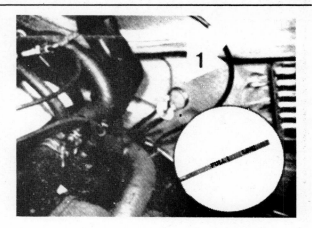

RM4. Check level of fluid in the automatic transmission unit

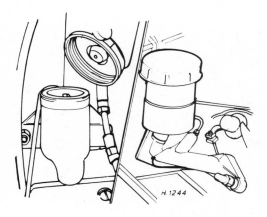

RM5. Check the brake reservoir fluid level

RM6. Top up the windscreen washer fluid reservoir

RM7. Check tyre pressure

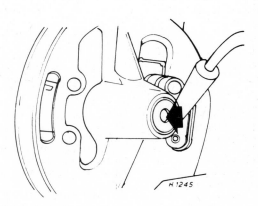

RM9. Lubricate dynamo rear bearing

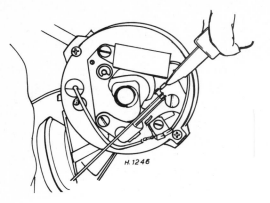

RM11. Adjust (or renew) distributor contact points

RM13. Check emission control valve

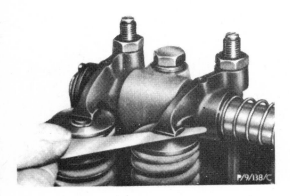

RM14. Check and adjust valve clearances (hot)

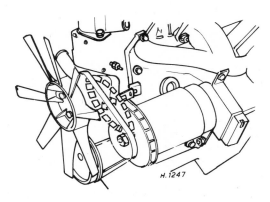

RM15. Check fan belt tension and adjust if necessary

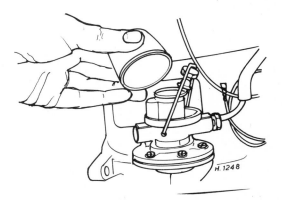

RM16. Clean fuel pump screen or separate fuel line filter

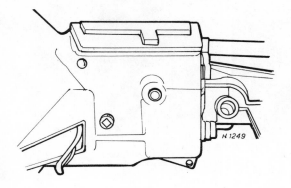

RM17. **Check manual gearbox oil level**

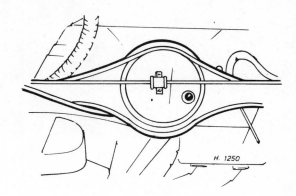

RM18. **Check rear axle oil level**

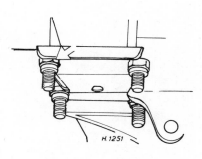

RM19. **Check tightness of rear spring U-bolt nuts**

RM20. **Check adjustment of drum brakes and check for wear**

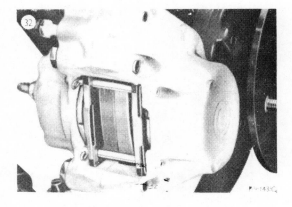

RM21. **Check front disc pads for wear**

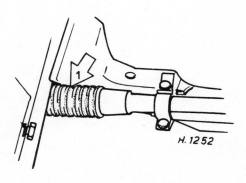

RM26. **Check steering gear rubber bellows for deterioration**

RM27. Check clutch free movement

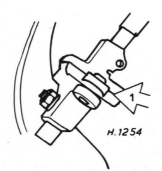

RM29. Check condition of steering shaft flexible coupling

H.1254

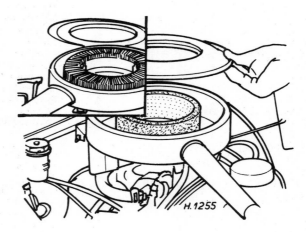

RM30. Renew air cleaner element

H.1255

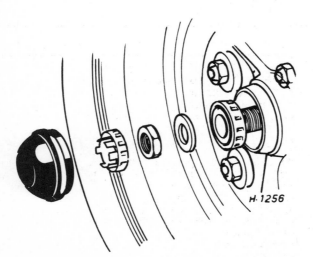

RM32. Clean, repack with grease and adjust front wheel bearings

H.1256

Chapter 1 Engine

Contents

Specifications

1100 cc models

Type	4 cylinder in line pushrod operation ohv
Bore	3.1881 in. (80.978 mm)
Stroke	2.098 in. (53.29 mm)
Cubic capacity	1098 cc (67.0 cu. in.)
Compression ratio - High C	9.0 to 1
- Low C	8.0 to 1
Compression pressure - High C	165 lb/sq in. (11.60 kg/cm^2) at 360 rev/min.
- Low C	154 lb/sq in. (10.80 kg/cm^2) at 360 rev/min.
Maximum bhp - High C	49.5 (net) at 5,500 rev/min
- Low C	47.0 (net) at 5,500 rev/min
Maximum torque - High C	58.5 lb/ft (8.12 kg.m) - net at 3,000 rev/min.
- Low C	54.5 lb/ft (7.52 kg.m) - net at 3,000 rev/min.
Engine idle speed - Optimum	580 to 620 rev/min
Location of No 1 cylinder	Next to radiator
Firing order	1 - 2 - 4 - 3
Engine mountings	3 point rubber bonded

Camshaft and camshaft bearings

Camshaft drive	Single roller chain from crankshaft
Camshaft bearings	Three white metal replaceable bushes, steel backed
Bearing oversize available	0.020 in. (0.513 mm) oversize on O.D. Standard I.D.
Camshaft journal diameter	1.6925 to 1.6940 in. (42.989 to 43.028 mm)
Camshaft bearing internal diameter	1.5615 to 1.5620 in. (39.662 to 39.675 mm)
Diametrical bearing clearance	0.001 to 0.0023 in. (0.025 to 0.058 mm)
Endfloat	0.0025 to 0.0075 in. (0.064 to 0.191 mm)
End thrust	Taken by camshaft retaining plate
Thrust plate thickness	0.176 to 0.178 in. (4.47 to 4.52 mm)
Maximum cam lift - Inlet	0.2108 in. (5.350 mm)
- Exhaust	0.2176 in. (5.523 mm)
Cam heel to toe dimensions - Inlet	1.3308 in. (33.802 mm)
- Exhaust	1.3176 in. (33.467 mm)
Timing chain	Single roller, 46 links

Connecting rods and big and small end bearings

Connecting rod - type	'H' section steel forging
Length between centres	4.324 to 4.326 in. (109.83 to 109.88 mm)
Big end bearings - type	Shell
Big end bearings - material	Steel backed copper/lead, lead/bronze or aluminium/tin
Big end bore	2.0825 to 2.0830 in. (52.896 to 52.908 mm)
Bearing liner wall thickness	0.0719 to 0.07225 in. (1.8269 to 1.8347 mm)
Effective bearing length	0.83 to 0.87 in. (21.1 to 22.1 mm)
Crankpin to bearing clearance	0.0005 to 0.0020 in. (0.013 to 0.051 mm)
Crankpin journal diameter	1.9368 to 1.9376 in (49.20 to 49.21)
Endfloat on crankpin	0.004 to 0.010 in. (0.10 to 0.25 mm)
Undersize bearings available	-0.002, -0.010, -0.020, -0.030, -0.040 in.
	(-0.05, -0.25, -0.51, -0.76, -1.02 mm)
Small end bush - type	Steel backed bronze
Small end bush internal diameter:	
Grade - white...	0.8121 to 0.8122 in. (20.627 to 20.630 mm)
- red	0.8122 to 0.8123 in. (20.630 to 20.632 mm)
- yellow	0.8123 to 0.8124 in. (20.632 to 20.635 mm)
- blue	0.8124 to 0.8125 in. (20.635 to 20.638 mm)

Crankshaft and main bearings

Number of bearings	5
Main bearing journal diameter - Blue	2.1253 to 2.1257 in. (53.893 to 53.993 mm)
- Red	2.1257 to 2.1261 in. (53.993 to 54.003 mm)
- Green	2.1153 to 2.1157 in. (53.729 to 53.739 mm)
- Yellow	2.1157 to 0.1161 in. (53.739 to 53.749 mm)
Regrind diameters - 0.010 in. (0.25 mm)	2.1152 to 2.1157 in. (53.726 to 53.739 mm)
- 0.020 in. (0.51 mm)	2.1055 to 2.1060 in. (53.480 to 53.492 mm)
- 0.030 in. (0.76 mm)	2.0955 to 2.0960 in. (53.226 to 53.238 mm)
Main journal length - Front	1.219 to 1.239 in. (30.96 to 31.47 mm)
- Centre	1.247 to 1.249 in. (31.67 to 31.73 mm)
- Rear	1.308 to 1.318 in. (33.22 to 33.48 mm)
- Intermediates	1.273 to 1.283 in. (32.33 to 32.59 mm)
Crankshaft end thrust	Taken thrust washers at centre main bearing
Crankshaft end float	0.003 to 0.011 in. (0.08 to 0.28 mm)
Thrust washers	Steel back, white metal semi-circular
Thrust washer thickness	0.091 to 0.093 in. (2.31 to 2.36 mm)
Main bearing material	Steel backed white metal liners
Main bearing clearance	0.0005 to 0.0020 in. (0.013 to 0.015 mm)
Undersize bearings available	-0.002, -0.010, -0.020, -0.030, -0.040
	(-0.05, -0.25, -0.51, -0.76, -1.02 mm)
Spigot bearing bore	0.8252 to 0.8264 in. (20.96 to 20.99 mm)

Cylinder block

Type	Cylinder cast integral with top half of crankcase
Standard cylinder bore diameter (graded)	
0	3.1869 to 3.1872 in. (80.948 to 80.955 mm)
1	3.1872 to 3.1875 in. (80.955 to 80.963 mm)
2	3.1875 to 3.1878 in. (80.963 to 80.970 mm)
3	3.1878 to 3.1881 in. (80.970 to 80.978 mm)
4	3.1881 to 3.1884 in. (80.978 to 80.986 mm)
5	3.1884 to 3.1887 in. (80.986 to 80.993 mm)
6	3.1887 to 3.1890 in. (80.993 to 81.001 mm)
7	3.1890 to 3.1893 in. (81.001 to 81.008 mm)
Cylinder liner availability	
Standard and 0.020 in. (0.51 mm) oversize on o.d.	
Bore for liner insertion	3.3115 to 3.3125 in. (84.112 to 84.138 mm)
Height, sump face to head face	7.224 to 7.229 in. (183.49 to 183.62 mm)
Oversize bores - First	0.0025 in. (0.064 mm)
- Max	0.030 in. (0.76 mm)

Gudgeon pin

Type	Fully floating, retained by end circlips
Material	Machined seamless steel tubing
Length	2.80 to 2.81 in. (71.1 to 71.4 mm)
Fit in piston	0.0001 to 0.0003 in. (0.003 to 0.008 mm)
Fit in small end bush	0.0001 to 0.0003 in. (0.003 to 0.008 mm)

Pistons

Type	Aluminium alloy tin plate, solid skirt with thermal slots
Number of rings	3. Two compression, one oil control
Clearance in cylinder	0.0013 to 0.0019 in. (0.033 to 0.048 mm)
Piston diameter (graded for similar bore gradings)	
0	3.1853 to 3.1856 in. (80.906 to 80.914 mm)
1	3.1856 to 3.1859 in. (80.914 to 80.922 mm)
2	3.1859 to 3.1862 in. (80.922 to 80.929 mm)
3	3.1862 to 3.1865 in. (80.929 to 80.937 mm)
4	3.1865 to 3.1868 in. (80.937 to 80.945 mm)
5	3.1868 to 3.1871 in. (80.945 to 80.952 mm)
6	3.1871 to 3.1874 in. (80.952 to 80.960 mm)
7	3.1874 to 3.1877 in. (80.960 to 80.968 mm)
Width of ring grooves:-	
Compression rings	0.0796 to 0.0816 in. (2.022 to 2.073 mm)
Oil control ring	0.1568 to 0.1598 in. (3.983 to 4.059 mm)
Gudgeon pin bore	Graded
Grade W	0.8120 to 0.8121 in. (20.625 to 20.627 mm)
One spot	0.8117 to 0.8118 in. (20.617 to 20.620 mm)
Two spot	0.8118 to 0.8119 in. (20.620 to 20.622 mm)
Three spot	0.8119 to 0.8120 in. (20.622 to 20.625 mm)
Piston oversizes available	+0.0025, +0.015, +0.030 in.
	(+0.064, +0.38, +0.76 mm)
Clearance (block face and piston crown) at T.D.C	0.005 to 0.023 in. (0.13 to 0.58 mm)

Piston rings

Top compression ring	Tapered, cast iron, chrome plated
Width	0.077 to 0.078 in. (1.96 to 1.98 mm)
Gap (fitted in bore)	0.009 to 0.014 in. (0.23 to 0.36 mm)
Groove clearance	0.0016 to 0.0036 in. (0.041 to 0.091 mm)
Lower compression ring	Cast iron, stepped lower face
Width	0.077 to 0.078 in. (1.96 to 1.98 mm)
Gap (fitted in bore)	0.009 to 0.014 in. (0.23 to 0.36 mm)
Groove clearance	0.0016 to 0.0036 in. (0.041 to 0.091 mm)
Oil control ring	Cast iron slotted
Width	0.155 to 0.156 in. (3.94 to 3.96 mm)
Gap (fitted in bore)	0.009 to 0.014 in. (0.23 to 0.36 mm)
Groove clearance	0.0018 to 0.0038 in. (0.046 to 0.097 mm)

Tappets

Type	Barrel with flat base
Stem diameter	0.4360 to 0.4365 in. (11.072 to 11.085 mm)
Length	1.85 in. (47.0 mm)

Rocker gear

Rocker shaft diameter	0.623 to 0.624 in. (15.83 to 15.85 mm)
Rocker arm bore	0.625 to 0.6265 in. (15.88 to 15.913 mm)
Shaft clearance in rocker	0.001 to 0.0035 in. (0.03 to 0.089 mm)
Rocker arm ratio	1.54 to 1

Cylinder head

Type	Cast iron with vertical valves
Port arrangement	Opposed separate inlet and exhaust ports
Number of ports - Exhaust	4
- Inlet	4

Valves

Head diameter - Inlet	1.405 to 1.415 in. (35.69 to 35.94 mm)
- Exhaust	1.240 to 1.250 in. (31.50 to 31.75 mm)
Valve seat angle	45° to 45° 15'
Valve seat width - Inlet	1/16 in. (1.59 mm)
- Exhaust	5/64 in. (1.98 mm)
Stem diameter - Inlet	0.3095 to 0.3105 in. (7.861 to 7.887 mm)
- Exhaust	0.3086 to 0.3096 in. (7.838 to 7.864 mm)
Stem to guide clearance - Inlet	0.0008 to 0.0030 in. (0.020 to 0.080 mm)
- Exhaust	0.0017 to 0.0039 in. (0.043 to 0.099 mm)

Valve length - Inlet ... ...   4.377 in. (111.18 mm)
         - Exhaust ... ...   4.368 in. (110.95 mm)
Valve life - Inlet ... ...   0.314 in. (7.97 mm)
         - Exhaust ... ...   0.334 in. (8.48 mm)
Valve stem to rocker arm clearances
     Cold - Inlet ... ...   0.008 to 0.010 in (0.20 to 0.25 mm)
          - Exhaust ... ...   0.018 to 0.020 in (0.46 to 0.51 mm)
     Hot - Inlet ... ...   0.010 in (0.25 mm)
          - Exhaust ... ...   0.017 in (0.43 mm)

Valve guides
     Type ... ...   Machined in cylinder head, guide bushes available
     Bore for guide bushes ... ...   0.4383 to 0.4391 in. (11.133 to 11.153 mm)
     Valve guide inside diameter ... ...   0.3113 to 0.3125 in. (7.907 to 7.938 mm)

Valve timing
     Inlet valve - Opens ... ...   17° BTDC
              - Closes ... ...   51° ABDC
     Exhaust valve - Opens ... ...   51° BBDC
                - Closes ... ...   17° ATDC
     Timing marks ... ...   Lines on camshaft and crankshaft sprockets

Valve springs
     Type ... ...   Single valve springs
     Free length ... ...   1.48 in. (37.6 mm)
     Fitted length (valve closed) ... ...   1.263 in. (32.08 mm)
     Load at fitted length ... ...   44 to 49 lbs. (19.96 to 22.23 kg)
     Total number of coils   6

Flywheel and starter ring gear (manual gearbox)
     Type (ring gear) ... ...   Shrunk-on
     Number of teeth (inertia type starter)   110
                  (pre-engaged starter) 132
     Ring gear fitting temperature ... ...   600°F (316°C)
     Spigot bearing material ... ...   Sintered bronze

Lubrication system
     Type ... ...   Wet sump, pressure and splash. Metered jet to timing chain, controlled feed to rocker shaft from camshaft front journal.
     Oil filter ... ...   Full flow with replaceable element
     Oil filter capacity ... ...   2/3rds pint (0.8 US pint, 0.38 litre)
     Sump capacity ... ...   (Early) 6.4 pints (7.6 US pints, 3.6 litres)
                                                        (Late) 5.72 pints (6.86 US pints, 3.25 litres)
     Oil pump type ... ...   Eccentric rotor or sliding vane
     Eccentric rotor type:-
     Capacity ... ...   2 galls per min (2.4 US gals, 9.085 litres) at 2,000 rpm
     Pump body bore diameter ... ...   0.500 to 0.501 in. (12.70 to 12.73 mm)
     Drive shaft diameter ... ...   0.498 to 0.4985 in. (12.65 to 12.66 mm)
     Drive shaft to body clearance ... ...   0.0015 to 0.003 in. (0.038 to 0.076 mm)
     Inner and outer rotor clearance ... ...   0.006 in. (0.15 mm) maximum
     Outer rotor and housing clearance ... ...   0.010 in. (0.25 mm) maximum
     Inner and outer rotor endfloat ... ...   0.005 in. (0.13 mm) maximum
     Sliding vane type:-
     Capacity ... ...   2.8 galls per min (3.36 US gals, 12.719 litres) at 2,000 rpm
     Pump body bore diameter ... ...   0.500 to 0.501 in. (12.70 to 12.73 mm)
     Drive shaft diameter ... ...   0.498 to 0.4985 in. (12.65 to 12.66 mm)
     Drive shaft to body clearance ... ...   0.0015 to 0.003 in. (0.038 to 0.076 mm)
     Vane clearance in rotor ... ...   0.005 in. (0.13 mm) maximum
     Rotor and vane endfloat ... ...   0.005 in. (0.13 mm) maximum
     Normal oil pressure ... ...   35 to 40 lb/sq in. (2.46 to 2.81 kg/cm^2)

1300 cc models
     Apart from the following differences, the specification is as for 1100 cc models

     Cubic capacity ... ...   1298 cc (79.2 cu in)
     Stroke ... ...   2.480 in. (62.99 mm)
     Maximum power (net) (9 : 1) ... ...   58 bhp at 5,000 rev/min
                       (8 : 1) ... ...   53.5 bhp at 5,000 rev/min
     Maximum torque (net) (9 : 1) ... ...   71.5 lb/ft (9.8 kg/m) at 2500 rev/min
                        (8 : 1) ... ...   68.0 lb/ft (9.4 kg/m) at 2500 rev/min

Connecting rod big end and small end bearings
     Length between centres ... ...   4.133 to 4.135 in. (104.98 to 105.03 mm)

Pistons

Piston clearance in cylinder bore	0.0019 to 0.0025 in. (0.048 to 0.064 mm)
Piston diameters (graded)	
0	3.1847 to 3.1850 in. (80.891 to 80.399 mm)
1	3.1850 to 3.1853 in. (80.899 to 80.907 mm)
2	3.1853 to 3.1856 in. (80.907 to 80.914 mm)
3	3.1856 to 3.1859 in. (80.914 to 80.922 mm)
4	3.1859 to 3.1862 in. (80.922 to 80.930 mm)
5	3.1862 to 3.1865 in. (80.930 to 80.937 mm)
6	3.1865 to 3.1868 in. (80.937 to 80.945 mm)
7	3.1868 to 3.1871 in. (80.945 to 80.952 mm)
Valve length - Inlet	4.277 in. (108.64 mm)
- Exhaust	4.268 in. (108.41 mm)

1300 (GT/Sport/1300E) models

Apart from the following differences, the specification is as for 1100 cc models

Cubic capacity	1298 cc (79.2 cu in)
Stroke	2.480 in. (62.99 mm)
Compression ratio	9.2 : 1
Maximum power (net)	71 bhp at 6,000 rev/min
Maximum torque (net)	70.0 lb/ft (9.6 kg/m) at 4,300 rev/min
Idling speed	680 to 720 rev/min

Camshaft and camshaft bearings

Maximum cam lift - Inlet	0.2309 in. (5.865 mm)
- Exhaust	0.2321 in. (5.905 mm)
Cam heel to toe dimension - Inlet	1.3109 in. (33.277 mm)
- Exhaust	1.3121 in. (33.327 mm)

Connecting rod big end and small end bearings

Length between centres	4.133 to 4.135 in. (104.98 to 105.03 mm)
Main bearings	Steel back, copper/lead or lead/bronze

Pistons

Piston clearance in cylinder bore	0.0019 to 0.0025 in. (0.048 to 0.064 mm)
Piston diameters (graded)	
As for 1300	

Valves

Valve head diameter - Inlet	1.497 to 1.507 in. (38.02 to 38.28 mm)
Valve length - Inlet	4.277 in. (108.64 mm)
- Exhaust	4.268 in. (108.41 mm)
Valve stem to rocker arm clearances	
Cold - Inlet	0.011 to 0.013 in (0.28 to 0.33 mm)
- Exhaust	0.021 to 0.023 in (0.53 to 0.58 mm)
Hot - Inlet	0.012 in (0.31 mm)
- Exhaust	0.022 in (0.56 mm)
Valve lift - Inlet	0.341 in. (8.66 mm)
- Exhaust	0.337 in. (8.56 mm)
Valve timing :	
Inlet opens	27° BTDC
Inlet closes	65° ABDC
Exhaust opens	65° BBDC
Exhaust closes	27° ATDC

Torque wrench settings

Big end bolts	30 to 35 lb/ft (4.15 to 4.84 kg.m)
Cylinder head nuts	65 to 70 lb/ft (8.98 to 9.67 kg.m)
Crankshaft pulley bolt	24 to 28 lb/ft (3.32 to 3.87 kg.m)
Camshaft thrust plate bolts...	2.5 to 3.5 lb/ft (0.35 to 0.48 kg.m)
Camshaft sprocket bolts	12 to 15 lb/ft (1.66 to 2.07 kg.m)
Chain tensioner to cylinder block	5 to 7 lb/ft (0.69 to 0.97 kg.m)
Engine front cover	5 to 7 lb/ft (0.69 to 0.97 kg.m)
Flywheel securing bolts	45 to 50 lb/ft (6.22 to 6.91 kg.m)
Main bearing bolts	65 to 70 lb/ft (8.98 to 9.67 kg.m)
Manifold bolts and nuts	15 to 18 lb/ft (2.07 to 2.49 kg.m)
Oil filter centre bolt	12 to 15 lb/ft (1.66 to 2.07 kg.m)
Oil pump bolts	12 to 15 lb/ft (1.66 to 2.07 kg.m)
Rear oil seal retainer bolts	12 to 16 lb/ft (1.66 to 2.07 kg.m)
Rocker shaft bolts	17 to 22 lb/ft (2.35 to 3.04 kg.m)
Rocker cover screws	2.5 to 3.5 lb/ft (0.35 to 0.48 kg.m)
Sump bolts	6 to 8 lb/ft (0.83 to 1.11 kg.m)
Sump drain plug	20 to 25 lb/ft (2.76 to 3.46 kg.m)
Tappet adjusting screw locknut	8 to 12 lb/ft (1.11 to 1.66 kg.m)
Bellhousing or converter housing to engine bolts	30 lb/ft (4.14 kg/m)

1 General description

The Escort range of vehicles comprises two and four door saloons and estate cars fitted with either the 1100 (1098 cc) or 1300 (1298 cc) engine. Automatic transmission is optionally available but only in conjunction with the 1300 cc power unit (not Sport, GT or 1300E).

A specially tuned version has been available since the range was first introduced and dependent upon the sales promotion image to be created in the particular year of manufacture, it may be designated Sport, GT or 1300E. These higher performance models are based on the 1298 cc power unit and vary in mechanical specification through various engine, carburation and final drive modifications. Body detail, interior trim and equipment specifications are more comprehensive in these tuned models.

The bore on both capacity engines is identical, the variations in capacity being achieved by different crankshaft strokes. All units are identical in design and differ only in the size of some of the components used eg block, connecting rods and pistons.

Two valves per cylinder are mounted vertically in the cast iron cylinder head and run in integral valve guides. They are operated by rocker arms, pushrods and tappets from the camshaft which is located at the base of the cylinder bores in the right hand side of the engine. The correct valve stem to rocker arm pad clearance can be obtained by the adjusting screws in the ends of the rocker arms. The valves fitted to the GT/Sport/1300E cylinder head are larger than on the standard 1298 cc engine in the interests of improved performance.

A crossflow cylinder head is used with four inlet ports on the right hand side and four exhaust on the left. High or low compression ratios may be used.

The cylinder block and the upper half of the crankcase are cast together. The open half of the crankcase is closed by a pressed steel sump.

The pistons are made from anodised aluminium alloy with solid skirts. Two compression rings and a slotted oil control ring are fitted. The gudgeon pin is retained in the little end of the connecting rod by circlips. The combustion chamber is machined in the piston crown and a different piston is used for each engine capacity and compression ratio. The connecting rod bearings are all steel backed and may be of copper/lead, lead/bronze, or aluminium/tin.

At the front of the engine a single chain drives the camshaft via the camshaft and crankshaft chain wheels which are enclosed in a pressed steel cover.

The chain is tensioned automatically by a snail cam which bears against a pivoted tensioner arm. This presses against the non-driving side of the chain so avoiding any lash or rattle.

The camshaft is supported by three renewable bearings located directly in the cylinder block. End float is controlled by a plate bolted to the front of the cylinder block and positioned between the front bearing journal and the chain wheel flange. GT/Sport/1300E models are fitted with a camshaft with higher lift and more overlap than standard.

The statically and dynamically balanced cast iron crankshaft is supported by five renewable thinwall shell main bearings which are in turn supported by substantial webs which form part of the crankcase. Crankshaft endfloat is controlled by semi-circular thrust washers located on each side of the centre main bearings. The main bearings fitted are of white metal except on the GT/Sport/1300E when they are of copper/lead or lead/bronze.

The centrifugal water pump and radiator cooling fan are driven, together with the generator, from the crankshaft pulley wheel by a flexible belt. The distributor is mounted toward the front of the right hand side of the cylinder block and advances and retards the ignition timing by mechanical and vacuum means. The distributor is driven at half crankshaft speed from a skew gear on the camshaft.

The oil pump is mounted externally on the right hand side of the engine under the distributor and is driven by a short shaft from the same skew gear on the camshaft as for the distributor

and may be of eccentric bi-rotor or sliding vane type.

Bolted to the flange on the end of the crankshaft is the flywheel to which is bolted in turn the clutch. Attached to the rear of the engine is the gearbox bellhousing.

2 Major operations possible with engine in vehicle

The following major operations can be carried out to the engine with it in place in the bodyframe. Removal and replacement of the:
   1 *Cylinder head assembly*
   2 *Oil pump*
   3 *Engine front mountings*
   4 *Engine/gearbox rear mounting.*

3 Major operations requiring engine removal

The following major operations can be carried out with the engine out of the bodyframe and on the bench or floor. Removal and replacement of the:
   1 *Main bearings*
   2 *Crankshaft*
   3 *Flywheel*
   4 *Crankshaft rear bearing oil seal*
   5 *Camshaft*
   6 *Sump*
   7 *Big-end bearings*
   8 *Pistons and connecting rods*
   9 *Timing chain and gears*

4 Method of engine removal

The engine complete with gearbox can be lifted as a unit from the engine compartment. Alternatively, the engine and gearbox can be split at the front of the bellhousing, a stand or jack placed under the gearbox to provide additional support, and the engine lifted out. The easiest method of engine removal is to remove the engine leaving the gearbox in place in the car. If the engine and gearbox are removed as a unit they have to be lifted out at a very steep angle which can be difficult.

5 Engine removal without gearbox or automatic transmission unit

1 Before commencing operations, it is essential to have a good hoist, and two strong axle stands if an inspection pit is not available. Engine removal will be much easier if you have a friend to help you.
2 Open the bonnet and pull off the windscreen washer tube from the pipe at the rear of the bonnet.
3 Undo the two bolts and washers from the bonnet side of each of the two hinges (photo).
4 Lift off the bonnet and stand it safely out of the way.
5 Remove the radiator cap and if the cooling system contains anti-freeze, place two bowls under the engine to catch the coolant.
6 Open the radiator drain plug and the one located on the left hand side of the engine block.
7 Drain the engine oil into a suitable container.
8 Remove the battery from the engine compartment by unscrewing the butterfly nut which secures the battery case clamp (photo) and disconnecting the two battery leads.
9 Remove the air cleaner by unscrewing the centre bolt (photo) and disconnecting the support bracket from the inlet manifold.
10 Remove the engine oil dipstick and detach the dipstick tube extension from the air cleaner body.
11 Detach the leads from the CB and SW terminals of the ignition coil and mark them for subsequent reconnection.

5.3 Removing bonnet hinge bolt

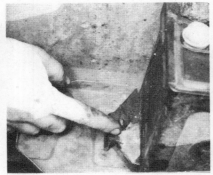
5.8 Removing battery clamp

5.9 Unscrewing air cleaner centre bolt

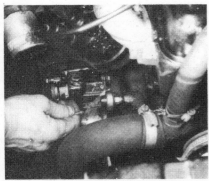
5.14 Disconnecting oil pressure switch

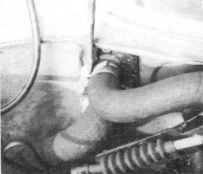
5.16 Disconnecting upper heater hose

5.18 Disconnecting radiator top hose

5.19 Removing radiator

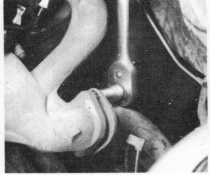
5.20 Uncoupling exhaust pipe from manifold

5.22 Disconnecting fuel pipe from pump

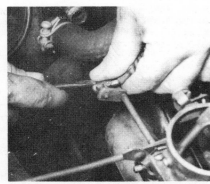
5.23 Disconnecting throttle control rod

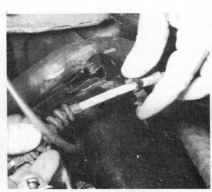
5.24 Removing throttle arm clip

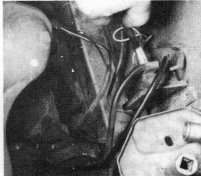
5.26 Location of starter solenoid switch

5.28 Unscrewing a clutch bellhousing to engine bolt

5.29 Removing coil bracket

5.30 Removing engine front mounting bolts

5.31 Hoisting the engine out

12 Disconnect the central HT lead from the coil (this may be a screwed or plug-in type connection) and after slackening the clamp screw, remove the coil.
13 From the rear of the generator detach the leads by pulling off the spade connectors (dynamo) or plug connector (alternator).
14 Disconnect the lead from the oil pressure switch which is located just below, and forward of, the distributor (photo).
15 Disconnect the lead from the water temperature transmitter unit.
16 Disconnect the upper heater hose at its engine rear bulkhead connection (photo).
17 Disconnect the heater hose from its connection adjacent to the carburettor.
18 Disconnect the radiator top hose from the thermostat housing outlet (photo).
19 Disconnect the radiator bottom hose from the water pump inlet and then remove the radiator side securing bolts and lift it out of the engine compartment with the hoses attached (photo).
20 Unscrew the two nuts which connect the exhaust manifold to the downpipe (photo).
21 Disconnect the earth strap from the left hand side of the cylinder block.
22 Disconnect the fuel inlet pipe at the fuel pump. Unless the level in the fuel tank is very low, plug the pipe to prevent loss (photo).
23 Pull down the spring-loaded connector and release the ball jointed throttle lever from the accelerator rod (photo).
24 Remove the clip from the throttle actuating arm (photo).
25 Detach the inner and outer choke control cables (manually operated choke).
26 On vehicles equipped with inertia type starter motors, unscrew the nut which secures the lead to the solenoid switch. This is mounted adjacent to the battery tray (photo). With pre-engaged type starter motors, disconnect the lead from the terminal on the motor end plate.
27 Unscrew and remove the sump shield.

On vehicles equipped with manual gearboxes
28 Unscrew the bolts which secure the clutch bellhousing to the engine crankcase. The starter motor is retained by these bolts and it should be removed at the same time (photo).
29 Remove the coil mounting bracket (photo).
30 Using slings and a suitable hoist, take the weight of the engine so that the bolts can be removed from the two engine front mountings (photo).
31 Position a jack under the gearbox and then raise both the hoist and the jack together until the top of the bellhousing is almost touching the underside of the body floor. Now pull the engine forward until the clutch assembly clears the splined first motion shaft of the gearbox. On no account allow the weight of the engine to hang upon the first motion shaft while it is still engaged with the clutch mechanism. Once clear, tilt the engine at an angle of 45º and lift it from the engine compartment (photo).
32 Check that no loose nuts and bolts have been left in the empty engine compartment. Lightly screw any nuts or bolts back from where they were removed or place them where they will not become lost.

On vehicles equipped with automatic transmission
33 Disconnect the downshift cable from its rocker cover support bracket and from the throttle linkage. Disconnect the water hoses from the automatic choke.
34 Remove the upper four bolts securing the torque converter housing to the engine crankcase.
35 Remove the coil mounting bracket.
36 Using slings and a suitable hoist, take the weight of the engine so that the bolts can be removed from the two engine front mountings.
37 Position a jack under the automatic transmission oil pan (use a block of wood to prevent distortion of the oil pan) and raise both hoist and jack together until the top of the converter housing is almost touching the body floor.
38 Unscrew each of the crankshaft drive plate to torque converter securing bolts. These are accessible, one at a time, through either the starter motor aperture or the lower semi-circular cover plate on the torque converter housing. The crankshaft will have to be rotated to bring each bolt into view.
39 Pull the engine forward and lift it out of the engine compartment in a similar manner to that already described for vehicles with manually operated gearboxes.

6 Engine removal with gearbox or automatic transmission unit

1 Carry out operations 1 to 25 in the preceding Section.
2 Mark the edges of the propeller shaft rear driving flange and the rear axle pinion flange and remove the four connecting bolts. Pull the propeller shaft slightly forward and then downward and pull it from engagement with the gearbox mainshaft rear end.
3 Jack up the front of the car and fit stands. It is now necessary to remove the gear lever. From inside the car lift up the gear lever gaiter and then remove the circlip in the spring.

Fig. 1.1. Cut-away view of Escort engine

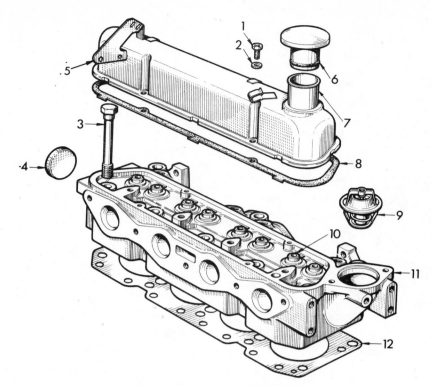

Fig. 1.2. Cylinder head major components

1 Rocker cover bolt	4 Core plug	7 Rocker cover	10 Valve guide
2 Washer	5 Throttle control support	8 Gasket	11 Cylinder head
3 Cylinder head bolt	bracket	9 Thermostat	12 Cylinder head gasket
	6 Oil filler/breather		

4 Bend back the lock tab and with a pair of mole grips or similar across the flats, undo the plastic dome nut and lift out the gear lever from the car.

5 From under the car disconnect the clutch cable from the clutch release arm. To do this it is necessary to loosen the clutch cable at the adjuster on the rear bulkhead or at the clutch bell-housing dependent upon its location, so that with the cable loose it can be pushed ½ inch backward from the release arm. This brings the narrow portion of the cable into line with the slot in the end of the release arm from which it can be detached.

6 Free the speedometer cable from the gearbox extension housing by extracting the circlip which holds the cable in place.

7 From under the car, remove the crossmember which supports the gearbox. To do this first place a jack (preferably of the trolley type) under the gearbox; undo the two bolts at each end of the gearbox crossmember, and with a socket spanner undo the sunken bolt in the centre of the crossmember.

8 Remove the crossmember and jack, and then remove the stands from the front of the car and lower the front to its normal height.

9 Attach a lifting chain or a strong rope round the engine, and take the weight on suitable lifting tackle. Place the rope as far forward as practicable as the engine will have to come out at a fairly steep angle.

10 Undo the bolt on each side which holds the front engine mounting in place.

11 If a trolley jack is available it is helpful to position it under the gearbox so the gearbox rolls forward with the jack. Pull the power unit forward at the same time lifting it on the hoist. As the gearbox tilts oil will run out of the rear of the gearbox extension. When the gearbox is clear of the gearbox tunnel lift the power unit out of the car with the hoist at an angle of

approximately 30º to the horizontal.

12 **On vehicles equipped with automatic transmission**, the procedure is similar to that already described but the following additional operations must be carried out.

13 Drain the automatic transmission fluid and retain for refilling the unit.

14 Disconnect the leads from the starter inhibitor switch. The switch is located on the left hand side of the transmission housing and the two larger terminals are the reversing light terminals.

15 Disconnect the speed selector linkage by removing the split pin and clevis pin at the selector arm on the side of the transmission unit and the support bracket.

Note: Where a propeller shaft is fitted having a centre bearing, the removal procedure is similar to that described in paragraph 2 except that the two centre bearing securing bolts must first be withdrawn.

7 Dismantling the engine - general

1 It is best to mount the engine on a dismantling stand but if one is not available, then stand the engine on a strong bench so as to be at a comfortable working height.

2 During the dismantling process the greatest care should be taken to keep the exposed parts free from dirt. As an aid to achieving this, it is a sound scheme to thoroughly clean down the outside of the engine, removing all traces of oil and congealed dirt.

3 Use paraffin or a good grease solvent such as Gunk. The latter compound will make the job much easier, as, after the solvent has been applied and allowed to stand for a time, a vigorous jet of water will wash off the solvent and all the grease

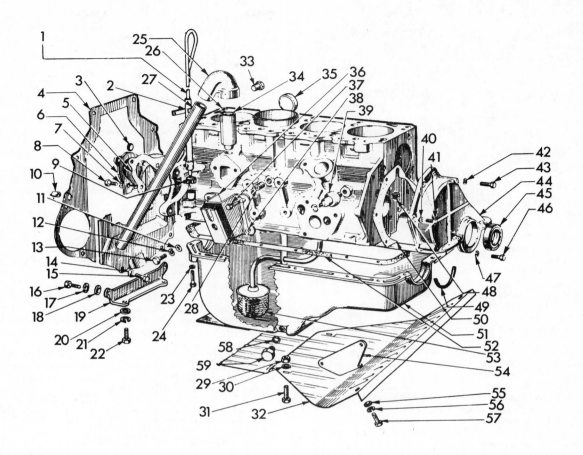

Fig. 1.3. Crankcase and sump - component parts

1 Dipstick
2 Dipstick tube
3 Plug
4 Engine endplate
5 Gasket
6 Camshaft end cover
7 Locking washer
8 Bolt
9 Dipstick tube retaining clip
10 Dowel
11 Washer
12 Locking washer
13 Bolt
14 Washer
15 Bolt
16 Bolt
17 Locking washer
18 Washer
19 Angle bracket

20 Washer
21 Locking washer
22 Bolt
23 Washer
24 Bolt
25 Breather elbow
26 Cylinder block
27 Breather tube
28 Plug
29 Nut
30 Washer
31 Bolt
32 Shield
33 Plug
34 Breather valve
35 Core plug
36 Mounting bracket
37 Bolt
38 Tab washer

39 Low oil pressure warning
   switch
40 Locking washer
41 Bolt
42 Locking washer
43 Bolt
44 Timing chain cover
45 Oil seal
46 Bolt
47 Locking washer
48 Plug
49 Seal
50 Gasket
51 Sump
52 Gasket
53 Oil pump pick-up filter
54 Bracket
55 Washer
56 Locking washer
57 Bolt
58 Washer
59 Sump drain plug

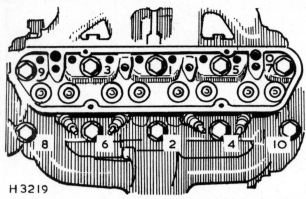

Fig. 1.4. Cylinder head bolt tightening sequence diagram

and filth. If the dirt is thick and deeply embedded, work the solvent into it with a stiff paintbrush.

4   Finally wipe down the exterior of the engine with a rag and only then, when it is quite clean, should the dismantling process begin. As the engine is stripped, clean each part in a bath of paraffin or petrol.

5   Never immerse parts with oilways in paraffin, ie the crankshaft, but to clean wipe down carefully with a petrol dampened rag. Oilways can be cleaned out with wire. If an air line is present all parts can be blown dry and the oilways blown through as an added precaution.

6   Re-use of old engine gaskets is a false economy and can give rise to oil and water leaks, if nothing worse. To avoid the possibility of trouble after the engine has been reassembled ALWAYS use new gaskets throughout.

7   Do not throw the old gaskets away as it sometimes happens that an immediate replacement cannot be found and the old gasket is then very useful as a template. Hang up the old gaskets as they are removed on a suitable hook or nail.

8   To strip the engine it is best to work from the top down. The sump provides a firm base on which the engine can be supported in an upright position. When the stage where the sump must be removed is reached, the engine can be turned on its side and all other work carried out with it in this position.

9   Wherever possible, replace nuts, bolts and washers finger-tight from wherever they were removed. This helps avoid later loss and muddle. If they cannot be replaced then lay them out in such a fashion that it is clear from where they came.

10   If the engine was removed in unit with the gearbox separate them by undoing the nuts and bolts which hold the bellhousing to the engine endplate.

11   Also undo the bolts holding the starter motor in place and lift off the motor.

12   Carefully pull the gearbox and bellhousing from the engine to separate them.

8   Removing ancillary engine components

1   Before basic engine dismantling begins the engine should be stripped of all its ancillary components. These items should also be removed if a factory exchange reconditioned unit is being purchased. The items comprise:

Dynamo or alternator and brackets
Water pump and thermostat housing
Starter motor
Distributor and spark plugs
Inlet and exhaust manifold and carburettor
Fuel pump and fuel pipes
Oil filter and dipstick
Oil filler cap
Clutch assembly (Chapter 5)
Engine mountings
Oil pressure sender unit

Oil separator unit (positive crankcase ventilation systems only)

2   Without exception all these items can be removed with the engine in the car if it is merely an individual item which requires attention. (It is necessary to remove the gearbox if the clutch is to be renewed with the engine in position).

3   Remove the generator after undoing the nuts and bolts which secure it in place. Remove the generator securing straps.

4   Remove the distributor by disconnecting the vacuum pipe, unscrew the single bolt at the clamp plate and lift out the distributor.

5   Remove the oil pump and filter assembly by unscrewing the three securing bolts with their lockwashers.

6   Unscrew the two bolts securing the fuel pump.

7   Unscrew the oil pressure gauge unit or the oil pressure sender unit, depending on model.

8   Remove the inlet and exhaust manifolds together with the carburettor by undoing the bolts and nuts which hold the units in place.

9   Unbolt the securing bolts of the water elbow and lift out the thermostat.

10   Bend back the tab lockwashers where fitted and undo the bolts which hold the water pump and engine mountings in place.

11   Undo the bolts holding the clutch cover flange to the flywheel a third of a turn each in a diagonal sequence, repeating until the clutch and driven plate can be lifted off.

12   Loosen the clamp securing the rubber tube from the oil separator unit to the inlet manifold and pull off the tube (where a positive crankcase ventilation system is fitted). Remove the oil separator located on the fuel pump mounting pad by carefully prising it off.

13   On early 1100 and 1300 models an open ventilation system consisting of an oil filler cap breather and a road draught tube is fitted. The tube is secured by one or two clutch housing bolts.

14   The engine is now stripped of ancillary components and ready for major dismantling to begin.

9   Cylinder head - removal

1   Undo the four screw headed bolts and flat washers which hold the flange of the rocker cover to the cylinder head and lift off the rocker cover and gasket.

2   Unscrew the four rocker shaft pedestal bolts evenly and remove together with their washers.

3   Lift off the rocker assembly as one unit.

4   Remove the pushrods, keeping them in the relative order in which they were removed. The easiest way to do this is to push them through a sheet of thick paper or thin card in the correct sequence.

5   Undo the cylinder head bolts half a turn at a time in the reverse order shown in Fig 1.4. When all the bolts are no longer under tension they may be unscrewed from the cylinder head one at a time.

6   The cylinder head can now be removed by lifting upward. If the head is jammed, try to rock it to break the seal. Under no circumstances try to prise it apart from the block with a screwdriver or cold chisel as damage may be done to the faces of the head or block. If the head will not readily free, turn the engine over by the flywheel as the compression in the cylinders will often break the cylinder head joint. If this fails to work, strike the head sharply with a plastic headed hammer, or with a wooden hammer, or with a metal hammer with an interposed piece of wood to cushion the blows. Under no circumstances hit the head directly with a metal hammer as this may cause the iron casting to fracture. Several sharp taps with the hammer at the same time pulling upward should free the head.

7   Do not lay the cylinder head face downward unless the plugs have been removed as they protrude and can be easily damaged.

8   The operations described in this Section can equally well be carried out with the engine in or out of the vehicle but with the latter, the cooling system must be drained, the battery disconnected and all attachments to the cylinder head removed as described in the appropriate paragraphs of Section 5.

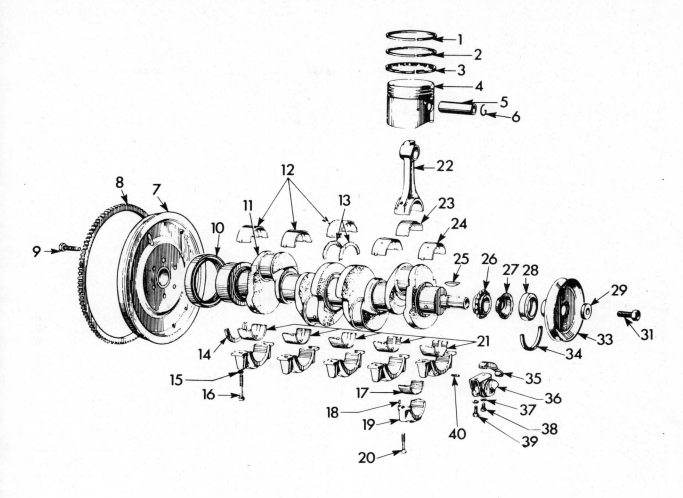

Fig. 1.5. Crankshaft and piston - component parts

1 Piston ring (compression)	11 Crankshaft	21 Main bearing shells	31 Bolt
2 Piston ring (compression)	12 Main bearing shells	22 Connecting rod	33 Crankshaft pulley
3 Piston ring (oil control)	13 Thrust washers	23 Big end shell	34 Seal
4 Piston	14 Seal	24 Main bearing shell	35 Timing chain tensioner
5 Gudgeon pin	15 Spring washer	25 Woodruff key	36 Tensioner ratchet assembly
6 Circlip	16 Set screw	26 Timing chain sprocket	37 Spring washer
7 Flywheel	17 Big end bearing shell	27 Oil thrower	38 Screw
8 Starter - ring gear	18 Dowel	28 Oil seal	39 Screw
9 Bolt	19 Big end bearing cap	29 Spacer	40 Swivel pin
10 Oil seal	20 Set screw		

10 Valve removal

1 The valves can be removed from the cylinder head by compressing each spring in turn with a valve spring compressor until the two halves of the collets can be removed. Release the compressor and remove the spring and spring retainer.

2 If, when the valve spring compressor is screwed down, the valve spring retaining cap refuses to free to expose the split collet, do not continue to screw down on the compressor as there is a likelihood of damaging it.

3 Gently tap the top of the tool directly over the cap with a light hammer. This will free the cap. To avoid the compressor jumping off the valve spring retaining cap when it is tapped, hold the compressor firmly in position with one hand.

4 Slide the rubber oil control seal off the top of each inlet valve stem and then drop out each valve through the combustion chamber.

5 It is essential that the valves are kept in their correct sequence unless they are so badly worn that they are to be renewed. If they are going to be kept and used again, place them in a sheet of card having eight holes numbered 1 to 8 corresponding with the relative positions the valves were in when originally installed. Also keep the valve springs, washers and collets in their original sequence.

11 Dismantling the rocker assembly

1 Pull out the split pin from each end of the rocker shaft and remove the flat washer, crimped spring washer and the remaining flat washer.

2 The rocker arms, rocker pedestals, and distance springs can now be slid off the end of the shaft.

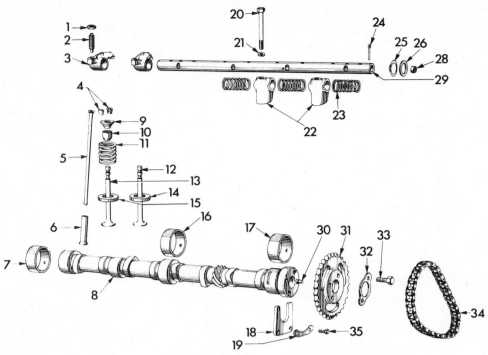

Fig. 1.6. Camshaft, valves and rocker gear - component parts

1 Nut	10 Valve stem seal	19 Tab washer	28 Plug
2 Rocker arm adjusting screw	11 Valve spring	20 Bolt	29 Rocker shaft
3 Rocker arm	12 Valve	21 Spring washer	30 Dowel pin
4 Valve collets	13 Valve	22 Rocker pedestals	31 Timing chain sprocket
5 Pushrod	14 Insert	23 Rocker arm spacer springs	32 Tab washer
6 Cam follower	15 Insert	24 Split pin	33 Bolt
7 Camshaft bearings	16 Centre camshaft bearing	25 Spacer	34 Timing chain
8 Camshaft	17 Front camshaft bearing	26 Shim	35 Bolt
9 Spring retainer	18 Camshaft thrust plate		

12 Timing cover, gearwheel and chain - removal

1 The timing cover cannot be removed until the sump has been removed, which necessitates removal of the engine from the car (see Section 14).

2 Unscrew the bolt from the centre of the crankshaft pulley. The best way to do this is to fit a ring spanner and then to give it a sharp blow with a club hammer in an anticlockwise direction. Alternatively, with manual gearbox vehicles, engage a gear and apply the handbrake fully to prevent the engine turning when the spanner is turned. On vehicles equipped with automatic transmission, remove the starter motor and jam the ring gear with a large screwdriver or cold chisel.

3 The crankshaft pulley wheel may pull off quite easily. If not, place two large screwdrivers behind the wheel at 180º to each other, and carefully lever off the wheel. It is preferable to use a proper pulley extractor if this is available, but large screwdrivers or tyre levers are quite suitable, providing care is taken not to damage the pulley flange.

4 Undo the bolts which hold the timing cover in place, noting that four sump bolts must also be removed before the cover can be taken off.

5 Check the chain for wear by measuring how much it can be depressed. More than ½ inch (12.5 mm) means a new chain must be fitted on reassembly.

6 With the timing cover off, take off the oil thrower. Note that the concave side faces outward.

7 With a drift or screwdriver tap back the tabs on the lockwasher under the two camshaft gearwheel retaining bolts and undo the bolts.

8 To remove the camshaft and crankshaft timing wheels complete with chain, ease each wheel forward a little at a time levering behind each gear wheel in turn with two large screwdrivers at 180º to each other. If the gear wheels are locked solid then it will be necessary to use a proper gear wheel and pulley extractor, and if one is available this should be used in preference to screwdrivers. With both gear wheels safely off, remove the Woodruff key from the crankshaft with a pair of pliers.

13 Camshaft - removal

1 The camshaft can only be removed from the engine when the engine is removed from the vehicle.

2 With the engine inverted and sump, rocker gear, pushrods, timing cover, oil pump, gearwheels and timing chain removed, take off the chain tensioner and arm.

3 Knock back the lockwasher tabs from the two bolts which hold the U shaped camshaft retainer in place behind the camshaft flange and slide out the retainer.

4 Rotate the camshaft so that the tappets are fully home and

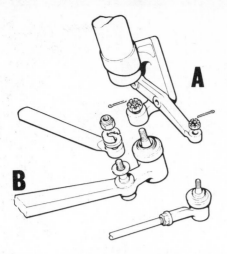

Fig. 1.7. Right-hand suspension components disconnected prior to sump removal (engine in vehicle)

A Strut   B Track control arm

Fig. 1.8. Method of numbering connecting rods (arrowed) and main bearing caps

then withdraw the camshaft from the cylinder block. Take great care that the cam lobe peaks do not damage the camshaft bearings as the shaft is pulled forward.

14 Sump - removal

1   The removal of the sump is not considered to be a practicable proposition whilst the engine is in the car, because of the necessity to detach steering, suspension and chassis components. If the engine has been removed from the car, after detaching it from the gearbox, the procedure is as follows.
2   Ensure that the starter motor is detached from the engine.
3   Unscrew the sump securing bolts and remove the sump. Use a penknife to cut around the joint if it is stuck.

4   Remove the cork strips from the timing cover and rear oil seal carrier, then thoroughly clean all the mating surfaces of the sump flange and engine crankcase.

15 Piston, connecting rod and big end bearing - removal

1   The pistons and connecting rods can only be removed with the engine out of the car.
2   With the cylinder head and sump removed, undo the big end retaining bolts.
3   The connecting rods and pistons are lifted out through the top of the cylinder block.
4   Remove the big end caps, one at a time, noting that they are numbered 1 to 4 with matched cap numbers, so that exact refitting will be facilitated (Fig 1.8).
5   Keep the original shell bearings with each connecting rod. Should the big end caps be difficult to remove, then they may be tapped gently using a plastic faced mallet.
6   The shell bearings may be removed from the big end caps and the connecting rods by pressing them at a point opposite to their grooves.
7   As each piston/connecting rod assembly is withdrawn, mark it so that it will be returned to its original bore. Temporarily refit the big end caps to the connecting rods to reduce the risk of mixing them up.

16 Gudgeon pin - removal

1   To remove the gudgeon pin to free the piston from the connecting rod, remove one of the circlips at either end of the pin with a pair of circlip pliers.
2   Press out the pin from the rod and piston with your finger.
3   If the pin shows reluctance to move, then on no account force it out, as this could damage the piston. Immerse the piston in a pan of boiling water for three minutes. On removal the expansion of the aluminium should allow the gudgeon pin to slide out easily.
4   Ensure that each gudgeon pin is kept with the piston from which it was removed for exact refitting.

17 Piston ring - removal

1   To remove the piston rings, slide them carefully over the top of the piston, taking care not to scratch the aluminium alloy. Never slide them off the bottom of the piston skirt. It is very easy to break the iron piston rings if they are pulled off roughly so this operation should be done with extreme caution. It is useful to employ three strips of thin metal or feeler gauges to act as guides to assist the rings to pass over the empty grooves and to prevent them from dropping in.
2   Lift one end of the piston ring to be removed out of its groove and insert the end of the feeler gauge under it.
3   Turn the feeler gauges slowly round the piston and as the ring comes out of its groove apply slight upward pressure so that it rests on the land above. It can then be eased off the piston.

18 Flywheel removal - manual gearbox

1   Remove the clutch (Chapter 5).
2   No lock tabs are fitted under the six bolts which hold the flywheel to the flywheel flange on the rear of the crankshaft.
3   Unscrew the bolts and remove them.
4   Lift the flywheel away from the crankshaft flange.
Note: Some difficulty may be experienced in removing the bolts by the rotation of the crankshaft every time pressure is put on

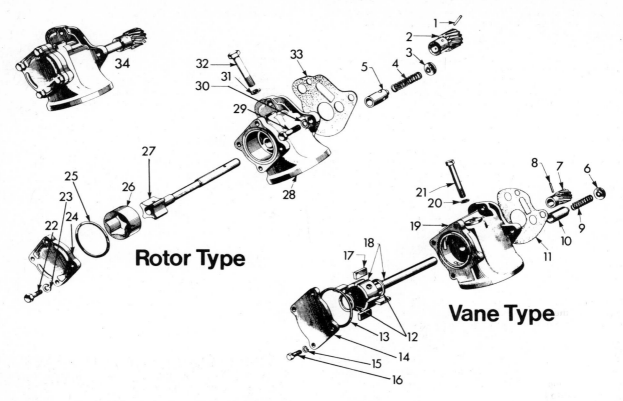

Fig. 1.9. Types of oil pump - component parts

1 Locking pin	10 Relief valve plunger	19 Pump assembly	27 Rotor shaft
2 Oil pump drive gear	11 Gasket	20 Spring washer	28 Pump body
3 Oil pressure relief valve retainer	12 Spacer	21 Bolt	29 Bolt
4 Relief valve spring	13 Oil pump cover sealing ring	22 Bolt	30 Spring washer
5 Relief valve plunger	14 Cover	23 Spring washer	31 Spring washer
6 Oil pressure relief valve retainer	15 Spring washer	24 Cover	32 Securing bolt
7 Oil pump drive gear	16 Bolt	25 Sealing ring	33 Gasket
8 Locking pin	17 Rotor blade	26 Rotor	34 Complete pump assembly
9 Relief valve spring	18 Rotor and shaft assembly		

the spanner. To lock the crankshaft in position while the bolts are removed, wedge a block of wood between the crankshaft and the side of the block inside the crankcase.

19 Drive plate removal - automatic transmission

1 The drive plate is attached to the crankshaft rear flange by six bolts and a locking plate.
2 When removing it, note the reinforcing plate and spacer.

20 Main bearings and crankshaft - removal

1 Unscrew each of the ten bolts securing the five crankshaft main bearing caps and remove them.
2 Remove each main bearing cap in turn noting that they are numbered 1 to 5 with a matching number on the crankcase so that there can be no confusion when refitting regarding sequence or orientation.
3 Remove the semicircular thrust washers fitted either side of the centre main bearing.
4 Lift the crankshaft from the crankcase and then withdraw the shell bearing halves from the crankcase.

21 Timing chain tensioner - removal

1 Undo the two bolts and washers which hold the timing chain tensioner in place. Lift off the tensioner.
2 Pull the timing chain tensioner arm off its hinge pin on the front of the block.

22 Lubrication system

1 A forced feed system of lubrication is fitted with oil circulated round the engine by a pump drawing from the sump below the block.
2 The full flow filter and oil pump assembly is mounted externally on the right hand side of the cylinder block. The pump is driven by means of a short shaft and skew gear off the camshaft.
3 Oil reaches the pump via a tube pressed into the cylinder block sump face. Initial filtration is provided by a spring loaded gauze on the end of the tube. Drillings in the block carry the oil under pressure to the main and big end bearings. Oil at a reduced pressure is fed to the valve and rocker gear and the timing chain and gearwheels.

4   One of two types of oil pump may be fitted. The eccentric bi-rotor type can be identified by four recesses cast in the cover whereas the vane type cover is flat. The pumps are directly interchangeable.

23 Oil filter - removal and refitting

1   A full-flow type oil filter is located adjacent to the oil pump on the right hand side of the engine block.

2   Early type filter bowls are retained by a long centre bolt but 1970 models onward have a disposable type in which the cartridge screws into the cover assembly.

3   Unscrew either the centre bolt or the cartridge according to type and lift it away. The bowl type will contain the element and both types will be full of oil. Place a bowl under the filter during this operation to catch the oil which will inevitably be spilt.

4   With the centre bolt type filter, throw the old filter element away and thoroughly clean the filter bowl, the bolt and associated parts with petrol and when perfectly clean, wipe dry with a non-fluffy rag.

5   A rubber sealing ring is located in a groove round the head of the oil filter and forms an effective leak-proof joint between the filter head and the filter bowl. A new rubber sealing ring is supplied with each new filter element.

6   Carefully prise out the old sealing ring from the locating groove. If the ring has become hard and is difficult to move, take great care not to damage the sides of the sealing ring groove.

7   With the old ring removed, fit the new ring (photo) in the groove at four equidistant points and press it home a segment at a time. Do not insert the ring at just one point and work round the groove pressing it home as, using this method, it is easy to stretch the ring and be left with a small loop of rubber which will not fit into the locating groove.

8   Offer up the bowl to the rubber sealing ring and before finally tightening down the centre bolt, check that the lip of the filter bowl is resting squarely on the rubber sealing ring and is not offset and off the ring. If the bowl is not seating properly, rotate it until it is.

9   Tighten down the centre bolt and run the engine to check the bowl for leaks.

10   With cartridge type filters, a new sealing ring is located in the face of the cartridge. Screw it home hand tight.

24 Oil pump - servicing

1   If the oil pump is worn it is best to purchase an exchange reconditioned unit as a good oil pump is at the very heart of long engine life. Generally speaking, an exchange or overhauled pump should be fitted at a major engine reconditioning. If it is wished to overhaul the oil pump, detach the pump and filter unit from the cylinder block, and remove the filter body and element or cartridge, according to type.

2   Unscrew and remove the four bolts and lockwashers which secure the oil pump cover and remove the cover. Lift out the O ring seal from the groove in the pump body.

Eccentric bi-rotor type pumps

3   Check the clearance between the inner and outer rotors with a feeler gauge (Fig 1.11). This should not exceed 0.006 inch (0.15 mm).

4   Check the clearance between the outer rotor and the pump body (Fig 1.12). This should not exceed 0.010 inch (0.25 mm).

Rotary vane type pump

5   Check the clearances as indicated (Fig 1.13).

All pumps

6   Check the end float of both types of pump by placing a straight edge across the open face of the pump casing and measuring the gap between its lower edge and the face of the

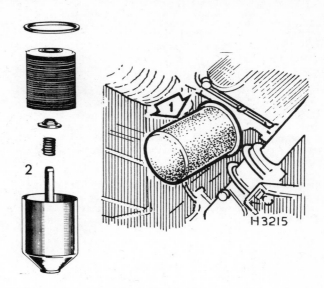

Fig. 1.10. Early and late types of oil filter

1   Disposable cartridge type   2   Centre bolt fixing type

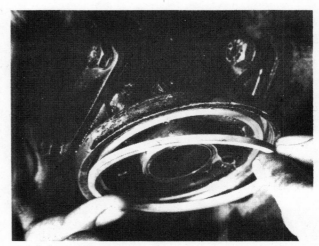

23.7 Fitting a new oil filter sealing ring

rotor. This should not exceed 0.005 inch (0.1270 mm) (Fig 1.14).

7   Replacement rotors are only supplied as a matched pair so that if the clearance is excessive, a new rotor assembly must be fitted. When it is necessary to renew the rotors, drive out the pin securing the skew gear and pull the gear from the shaft. Remove the inner rotor and drive shaft and withdraw the outer rotor. Install the outer rotor with the chamfered end towards the pump body.

8   Fit the inner rotor and drive shaft assembly, position the skew gear and install the pin. Tap over each end of the pin to prevent it loosening in service. Position a new O ring in the groove in the pump body, fit the end plate in position and secure with the fout bolts and lockwashers.

9   Refit the oil pump assembly together with a new gasket and secure in place with three bolts and lockwashers.

25 Crankcase ventilation systems - description and servicing

1   On early 1100 engines an open crankcase ventilation system consisting of a breather in the oil filler cap, a road draught tube, and a gauze oil trap in the crankcase outlet tube is fitted as standard.

2   On later 1100 and all 1300 engines a semi-closed positive ventilation system is fitted. A breather valve in the oil filler cap allows air to enter as required. Crankcase fumes travel out through an oil separator and emission control valve, and then via a connecting tube back into the inlet manifold. In this way the majority of crankcase fumes are burnt during the combustion process in the cylinder.

3   With the simple fume outlet draught tube, no regular maintenance is required but it is a good idea to remove it from the crankcase once a year and to wash it thoroughly with paraffin to ensure that the gauze filter is not blocked.

4   With the emission control type system, clean the valve and rocker box cover breather cap every 18,000 miles (29,000 km). To remove the valve, disconnect the hose and then pull it from its grommet in the oil separator box.

5   Dismantle the valve by removing the circlip (1) and extracting the seal, valve and spring (2) from the valve body (3) (Fig 1.18).

6   Wash and clean all components in petrol to remove sludge or deposits, and renew the rubber components if they have deteriorated.

7   Reassembly and refitting are reversals of removal and dismantling procedures.

26 Engine front mountings - removal and installation

1   With time the bonded rubber insulators, one on each of the front mountings, will perish causing undue vibration and noise from the engine. Severe juddering when reversing or when moving off from rest is also likely and is a further sign of worn mounting rubbers.

2   The front mounting rubber insulators can be changed with the engine in the car.

3   Apply the handbrake firmly, jack up the front of the car, and place stands under the front of the car.

4   Lower the jack, take off the engine sump shield where fitted, and place the jack under the sump to take the weight of the engine.

5   Undo the large bolt which holds each of the engine mountings to the body crossmember. Then knock back the locking tabs and undo the four bolts holding each of the engine mountings in place.

6   Fit new mountings using new tab washers and tighten the four bolts down and bend up the locking tabs.

7   Screw in the bolts which connect the mountings to each side of the crossmember.

8   Lower the vehicle.

27 Examination and renovation - general

With the engine stripped down and all parts thoroughly cleaned, it is now time to examine everything for wear. The following items should be checked and where necessary renewed or renovated as described in the following Sections.

28 Crankshaft - examination and renovation

1   Examine the crankpin and main journal surfaces for signs of scoring or scratches. Check the ovality of the crankpins at different positions with a micrometer. If more than 0.001 inch (0.0254 mm) out of round, the crankpins will have to be reground. They will also have to be reground if there are any scores or scratches present. Also check the journals in the same fashion.

2   If it is necessary to regrind the crankshaft and fit new bearings, your local Ford garage or engineering works will be able to decide how much metal to grind off and the size of new

Fig. 1.11. Measuring clearance between inner and outer oil pump rotors

Fig. 1.12. Measuring clearance between outer rotor and oil pump body

Fig. 1.13. Measuring clearance between rotor and rotary valve type oil pump body

Fig. 1.14. Measuring oil pump rotor end-float

bearing shells.

29 Big end and main bearings - examination and renovation

1   Big end bearing failure is accompanied by a knocking from

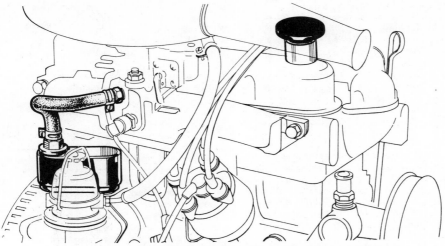

Fig. 1.15. Crankcase ventilation system fitted to later 1100 and all 1300 models

the crankcase, and a slight drop in oil pressure. Main bearing failure is accompanied by vibration which can be quite severe as the engine speed rises. Inspect the big ends, main bearings, and thrust washers for signs of general wear, scoring, pitting and scratches. The bearings should be matt grey in colour. With lead-indium bearings, should a trace of copper colour be noticed, the bearings are badly worn as the lead bearing material has worn away to expose the indium underlay. Renew the bearings if they are in this condition or if there is any sign of scoring or pitting.

2   The undersizes available are designed to correspond with the regrind sizes, ie −0.010 inch (0.2540 mm) bearings are correct for a crankshaft reground −0.010 inch (0.2540 mm) undersize. The bearings are in fact slightly more than the stated undersize as running clearances have been allowed for during their manufacture.

3   Very long engine life can be achieved by changing big end bearings at intervals of 30,000 miles (48,000 km) and main bearings at intervals of 50,000 miles (80,000 km), irrespective of bearing wear. Normally, crankshaft wear is infinitesimal and a change of bearings will ensure mileages of between 80,000 to 100,000 miles (128,000 to 161,000 km) before crankshaft regrinding becomes necessary. Crankshafts normally have to be reground because of scoring due to bearing failure.

Fig. 1.16. Crankcase fume emission tube (early 1100 models)

30   Cylinder bores - examination and renovation

1   The cylinder bores must be examined for taper, ovality, scoring and scratches. Start by carefully examining the top of the cylinder bores. If they are at all worn a very slight ridge will be found on the thrust side. This marks the top of the piston ring travel. The owner will have a good indication of the bore wear prior to dismantling the engine, or removing the cylinder head. Excessive oil consumption accompanied by blue smoke from the exhaust is a sure sign of worn cylinder bores and piston rings.

2   Measure the bore diameter just under the ridge with a micrometer and compare it with the diameter at the bottom of the bore which is not subject to wear. If the difference between the two measurements is more than 0.006 inch (0.1524 mm) it will be necessary to fit special pistons and rings or to have the cylinders rebored and fit oversize pistons. If a micrometer is not available, remove the rings from each piston in turn (do not mix the rings from piston to piston) and place each piston in its respective bore about ¾ inch (19.05 mm) below the top surface of the cylinder block. If an 0.010 inch (0.2540 mm) thick feeler gauge can be slid between the piston

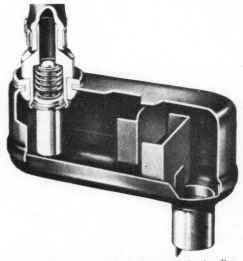

Fig. 1.17. Oil separator and emission control valve (later 1100 and all 1300 models)

and the cylinder wall on the thrust side of the bore, then the following action must be taken. Oversize pistons are available in the following sizes: +0.010 inch (0.2540 mm), +0.020 inch (0.508 mm), +0.030 inch (0.762 mm).

3 These are accurately machined to just below these measurements so as to provide correct running clearances in bores of the exact oversize dimensions.

4 If the bores are slightly worn but not so badly worn as to justify reboring them, then special oil control rings and pistons can be fitted which will restore compression and stop the engine burning oil. Several different types are available and the manufacturers' instructions concerning their fitting must be followed closely.

5 If new pistons are being fitted and the bores have not been reground, it is essential to slightly roughen the hard glaze on the sides of the bores with fine glass paper so the new piston rings will have a chance to bed in properly.

6 Newly fitted pistons should be tested for clearance using a feeler gauge and spring balance. Place the feeler gauge between the piston and cylinder wall and having attached the spring balance to it, check the pull required to remove it in accordance with the following data:

1100 cc engines

    7 to 11 lb (3.2 to 4.5 kg) pull using an 0.002 inch (0.05 mm) thick feeler 0.5 inch (12.7 mm) wide.

1300 cc engines

    7 to 11 lb (3.2 to 4.5 kg) pull using an 0.0025 inch (0.064 mm) thick feeler 0.5 inch (12.7 mm) wide.

31 Pistons and piston rings - examination and renovation

1 If the old pistons are to be refitted, carefully remove the piston rings and then thoroughly clean them. Take particular care to clean out the piston ring grooves. At the same time do not scratch the aluminium in any way. If new rings are to be fitted to the old pistons then the top ring should be stepped so as to clear the ridge left above the previous top ring. If a normal but oversize new ring is fitted, it will hit the ridge and break because the new ring will not have worn in the same way as the old. This will have worn in unison with the ridge.

2 Before fitting the rings on the pistons, each should be inserted approximately 2 inch (50.8 mm) down the cylinder bore and the gap measured with a feeler gauge. This should be between 0.009 inch (0.2286 mm) and 0.014 inch (0.3556 mm). It is essential that the gap should be measured at the bottom of the ring travel, as if it is measured at the top of a worn bore and gives a perfect fit, it could easily seize at the bottom. If the ring gap is too small rub down the ends of the ring with a very fine file until the gap, when fitted, is correct. To keep the rings square in the bore for measurement, line each up in turn by inserting an old piston in the bore upside down, and use the piston to push the ring down about 2 inches (50.8 mm). Remove the piston and measure the piston ring gap.

3 When fitting new pistons and rings to a rebored engine, the piston ring gap can be measured at the top of the bore as the bore will not now taper (photo). It is not necessary to measure the side clearance in the piston ring grooves with the rings fitted as the groove dimensions are accurately machined during manufacture. When fitting new oil control rings to old pistons, it may be necessary to have the grooves widened by machining to accept the new wider rings. In this instance the manufacturer's fitting instructions will indicate the procedure.

32 Camshaft and camshaft bearings - examination and renovation

1 Carefully examine the camshaft bearings for wear. If the bearings are obviously worn or pitted, then they must be renewed. This is an operation for your local Ford dealer or the local engineering works as it demands the use of specialised equipment. The bearings are removed with a special drift after

which new bearings are pressed in, care being taken to ensure the oil holes in the bearing line up with those in the block.

2 The camshaft itself should show no signs of wear. If scoring on the cams is noticed, the only permanently satisfactory cure is to fit a new camshaft.

3 Examine the skew gear for wear, chipped teeth or other damage.

4 Carefully examine the camshaft thrust plate. Excessive wear will be visually self-evident and will require the fitting of a new plate.

5 Note the recess on the front face of the camshaft fitted to GT/Sport models.

33 Valves and valve seats - examination and renovation

1 Examine the heads of the valves for pitting and burning, especially the heads of the exhaust valves. The valve seatings should be examined at the same time. If the pitting on valve and seat is very slight, the marks can be removed by grinding the exhaust seats and valves together with coarse, and then fine, valve grinding paste. **The inlet valves are aluminised and must not be ground in.** If the inlet valve seats are pitted, use a spare valve for grinding the seat. If the inlet valve itself is pitted or burned then it must be renewed.

2 Where bad pitting has occurred to the valve seats, it will be necessary to recut them and fit new valves. If the valve seats are so worn that they cannot be recut, then it will be necessary to fit new valve seat inserts. These latter two jobs should be entrusted to the local Ford agent or engineering works. In practice it is very seldom that the seats are so badly worn that they require renewal. Normally, it is the valve that is too badly worn for replacement, and the owner can easily purchase a new set of valves and match them to the seats by valve grinding.

31.3 Measuring piston ring end gap

3 Valve grinding is carried out as follows: Smear a trace of coarse carborundum paste on the seat face and apply a suction grinder tool to the valve head. With a semi-rotary motion, grind the valve head to its seat, lifting the valve occasionally to redistribute the grinding paste. When a dull matt even surface finish is produced on both the valve seat and the valve, then wipe off the paste and repeat the process with fine carborundum paste, lifting and turning the valve to redistribute the paste as before. A light spring placed under the valve head will greatly ease this operation. When a smooth, unbroken ring of light grey matt finish is produced, on both valve and valve seat faces, the grinding operation is completed.

4 Scrape away all carbon from the valve head and the valve stem. Carefully clean away every trace of grinding compound, taking great care to leave none in the ports or in the valve guides. Clean the valves and valve seats with a paraffin soaked rag then with a clean rag, and finally, if an air line is available, blow the valves, valve guides and valve ports clean.

34 Timing gears and chain - examination and renovation

1 Examine the teeth on both the crankshaft gear wheel and the camshaft gear wheel for wear. Each tooth forms an inverted V with the gearwheel periphery, and if worn the side of each tooth under tension will be slightly concave in shape when compared with the other side of the tooth, ie one side of the inverted V will be concave when compared with the other. If any sign of wear is present the gearwheels must be renewed.

2 Examine the links of the chain for side slackness and renew the chain if any slackness is noticeable when compared with a new chain. It is a sensible precaution to renew the chain at about 30,000 miles (48,000 km) and at a less mileage if the engine is stripped down for a major overhaul. The rollers on a very badly worn chain may be slightly grooved.

35 Rockers and rocker shaft - examination and renovation

1 Thoroughly clean the rocker shaft and then check it for distortion by rolling it on a piece of plate glass. If it is out of true, renew it. The surface of the shaft should be free from wear ridges and score marks.

2 Check the rocker arms for wear of the rocker bushes, for wear at the rocker arm face which bears on the valve stem, and for wear of the adjusting ball ended screws. Wear in the rocker arm bush can be checked by gripping the rocker arm tip and holding the rocker arm in place on the shaft, noting if there is any lateral rocker arm shake. If shake is present, and the arm is very loose on the shaft, a new bush or rocker arm must be fitted.

3 Check the tip of the rocker arm where it bears on the valve head for cracking or serious wear on the case hardening. If none is present re-use the rocker arm. Check the lower half of the ball on the end of the rocker arm adjusting screw. Check the pushrods for straightness by rolling them on a piece of plate glass. Renew any that are bent.

36 Tappets - examination and renovation

Examine the bearing surface of the mushroom tappets which lie on the camshaft. Any indentation in this surface or any cracks indicate serious wear and the tappets should be renewed. Thoroughly clean them out, removing all traces of sludge. It is most unlikely that the sides of the tappets will prove worn, but if they are a very loose fit in their bores and can readily be rocked, they should be exchanged for new units. It is very unusual to find any wear in the tappets, and any wear is likely to occur only at very high mileages.

37 Connecting rods - examination and renovation

1 Examine the mating faces of the big end caps to see if they have ever been filed in a mistaken attempt to take up wear. If so, the offending rods must be renewed.

2 Insert the gudgeon pin into the little end of the connecting rod. It should go in fairly easily, but if any slackness is present then take the rod to your local Ford dealer and exchange it for a rod of identical weight. Note the difference in length between the 1100 cc and 1300 cc connecting rods (Fig 1.20).

38 Flywheel - examination and renovation

1 The flywheel fitted to 1100 cc models weighs 16.75 lb and has Ford part No 2733E-6375-D. Of identical weight the flywheel fitted to 1300 GT Sport/1300E models makes use of a 7½ inch (190.5 mm) diameter clutch, instead of the normal 6½ inch (165.1 mm) unit and therefore carries the Part No 2733E-6375-C. Other 1300 engines have flywheels which weigh 18.5 lb (8.3 kg) or 26 lb (11.8 kg) and these can be identified by the Part No. 2731E-6380-D and 2731E-6380-C respectively. These numbers are stamped on the flywheels.

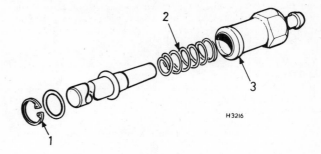

H3216

Fig. 1.18. Crankcase emission control valve - component parts

| 1 Circlip | 2 Return spring | 3 Body |

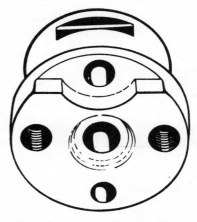

Fig. 1.18A Front face of G.T. type camshaft

Fig. 1.19. Engine front mountings

Starter ring gear

2 To remove a starter ring either split it with a cold chisel after making a cut with a hacksaw blade between two teeth, or heat the ring, and use a soft headed hammer (not steel) to knock the ring off, striking it evenly and alternately, at equally spaced points. Take great care not to damage the flywheel during this process.

3 Clean and polish with emery cloth four evenly spaced areas on the outside face of the new starter ring.

                                                    1100

                                                    1300

Fig. 1.20. Connecting rod identification and installation marking

4   Heat the ring evenly with an oxyacetylene flame until the polished portions turn dark blue (600°F/316°C). Hold the ring at this temperature for five minutes and then quickly fit it to the flywheel so the chamfered portion of the teeth faces the gearbox side of the flywheel (110 teeth for inertia engaged starters).

5   The ring should be tapped gently down onto its register and left to cool naturally when the contraction of the metal on cooling will ensure that it is a secure and permanent fit. Great care must be taken not to overheat the ring, indicated by it turning light metallic blue, as if this happens the temper of the ring will be lost.

6   It does not matter which way round the 132 toothed ring (for pre-engaged starters) is fitted as it has no chamfers on its teeth. This also makes for quick identification between the two rings.

7   If the teeth on the converter (automatic transmission) are worn then the converter must be renewed as an assembly.

Clutch pilot bearing

8   Whenever any repair work is being carried out on the clutch or flywheel, check that the clutch pilot bearing in the centre of the flywheel is serviceable. This bearing should fit snugly into the flywheel, and the gearbox input shaft should fit snugly into the bearing. If a replacement bearing is called for, prise out the old one, taking care not to damage the flywheel mating bore and press in a new one. If the replacement bearing has an integral grease seal, this should be facing towards the clutch side.

---

39 Cylinder head - decarbonising

---

1   This can be carried out with the engine either in or out of the car. With the cylinder head off, carefully remove with a wire brush mounted in an electric drill (photo) and blunt scraper, all traces of carbon deposits from the combustion spaces and the ports. The valve head stems and valve guides should also be freed from any carbon deposits. Wash the combustion spaces and ports down with petrol and scrape the cylinder head surface free of any foreign matter with the side of a steel rule, or a similar article.

2   Clean the pistons and top of the cylinder bores. If the pistons are still in the block then it is essential that great care is taken to ensure that no carbon gets into the cylinder bores as this could scratch the cylinder walls or cause damage to the piston and rings. To ensure that this does not happen, first turn the crankshaft so that two of the pistons are at the top of their bores. Stuff rag into the other two bores or seal them off with paper and masking tape. The waterways should also be covered with small pieces of

Fig. 1.21. Installing an oil seal to a circular crankshaft rear retainer

masking tape to prevent particles of carbon entering the cooling system and damaging the water pump.

3   There are two schools of thought as to how much carbon should be removed from the piston crown. One school recommends that a ring of carbon should be left round the edge of the piston and on the cylinder bore wall as an aid to low oil consumption. Although this is probably true for early engines with worn bores, on modern engines it is preferable to remove all traces of carbon deposits.

4   If all traces of carbon are to be removed, press a little grease into the gap between the cylinder walls and the two pistons which are to be worked on. With a blunt scraper carefully scrape away the carbon from the piston crown, taking great care not to scratch the aluminium. Also scrape away the carbon from the surrounding lip of the cylinder wall. When all carbon has been removed, scrape away the grease which will now be contaminated with carbon particles, taking care not to press any into the bores. To assist prevention of carbon build-up the piston crown can be polished with a metal polish. Remove the rags or masking tape from the other two cylinders and turn the crankshaft so that the two pistons which were at the bottom are now at the top. Place rag or masking tape in the cylinders which have been decarbonised and proceed as already described.

5   Thoroughly clean out the cylinder head bolt holes in the top face of the block. If these are filled with carbon, oil or

water it is possible for the block to crack when the bolts are screwed in due to the hydraulic pressure created by the trapped fluid.

40 Valve guides - examination and renovation

1   Examine the valve guides internally for scoring and other signs of wear. If a new valve is a very loose fit in a guide and there is a trace of lateral rocking then new guides will have to be fitted.
2   The fitting of new guides is a job which should be done by your local Ford dealer.

41 Engine reassembly - general

1   To ensure maximum life with minimum trouble from a rebuilt engine, not only must everything be correctly assembled, but everything must be spotlessly clean, all the oilways must be clear, locking washers and spring washers must always be fitted where indicated and all bearing and other working surfaces must be thoroughly lubricated during assembly.
2   Before assembly begins renew any bolts or studs if the threads of which are in any way damaged, and whenever possible use new spring washers.
3   Apart from your normal tools, a supply of clean rag, an oil can filled with engine oil, a new supply of assorted spring washers, a set of new gaskets, and a torque wrench, should be collected together.

42 Assembling the engine

1   Thoroughly clean the block and ensure that all traces of old gaskets etc are removed.
2   Fit a new rear main oil seal bearing retainer gasket to the rear of the cylinder block.
3   Then fit the rear main oil seal bearing retainer housing Note that on some engines the housing is not split as the semi-circular one shown here. Where a fully circular retainer housing is fitted, the oil seal is also circular and is simply prised out when removed, a new one being pressed in (Fig 1.21).
4   Lightly tighten the four retaining bolts with spring washers under their heads noting that two of the bolts arrowed in the photo are dowelled to ensure correct alignment and should be tightened first. Do not fully tighten the bolts until the crankshaft is in place and securely torqued down to ensure proper centralisation of the housing on the flywheel mounting flange.
5   On models with the split oil seal turn the block upside down and fit the crankshaft rear bearing oil seal.
6   Position the upper halves of the shell bearings in their correct positions so that the tabs of the shells engage in the machined keyways in the sides of the bearing locations.
7   Oil the main bearing shells after they have been fitted in position.
8   Thoroughly clean out the oilways in the crankshaft with the aid of a thin wire.
9   To check for the possibility of an error in the grinding of the crankshaft journal (presuming the crankshaft has been reground) smear engineers blue evenly over each big end journal in turn with the crankshaft end flange held firmly in position in a vice.
10 With new shell bearings fitted to the connecting rods fit the correct rod to each journal in turn, fully tightening down the securing bolts.
11 Spin the rod on the crankshaft a few times and then remove the big end cap. A fine unbroken layer of engineers blue should cover the whole of the journal. If the blue is much darker on one side than the other or if the blue has disappeared from a certain area (ignore the very edges of the journal) then something is wrong and the journal will have to be checked with a micrometer.
12 The main journals should also be checked in similar fashion

39.1 Removing carbon from cylinder head

42.14 Fitting a crankshaft thrust washer

42.17 Compression ring marking

42.19 Inserting a gudgeon pin

with the crankshaft in the crankcase. On completion of these tests remove all traces of the engineers blue.

13 The crankshaft can now be lowered carefully into place.

14 Fit new end float thrust washers. These locate in recesses on each side of the centre main bearing in the cylinder block and must be fitted with the oil grooves facing the crankshaft flange. With the crankshaft in position check for end float which should be between 0.003 and 0.011 inch (0.76 to 0.279 mm). If the end float is incorrect, remove the thrust washers and select suitable washers to give the correct end float (photo).

15 Place the lower halves of the main bearing shells in their caps, making sure that the locking tabs fit into the machined grooves. Refit the main bearing caps ensuring that they are the correct way round and that the correct cap is on the correct journal. The two front caps are marked 'F', the centre cap 'CENTRE' and the two rear caps 'R'. Tighten the cap bolts to a torque of 65 to 70 lb ft (9.0 kg m). Spin the crankshaft to make certain it is turning freely.

16 Check that the piston ring grooves and oilways are thoroughly clean and unblocked. Piston rings must always be fitted over the head of the piston and never from the bottom. Fit the rings by the same method used for removing them (Section 17).

17 When assembling the rings note that the compression rings are marked 'top', (photo) and that the upper ring is chromium plated. The ring gaps should be spaced at 120° angles round the piston.

18 If the same pistons are being used, then they must be mated to the same connecting rod with the same gudgeon pin. If new pistons are being fitted it does not matter which connecting rod they are used with. Note that the word FRONT is stamped on one side of each of the rods. On reassembly the side marked 'FRONT' must be towards the front of the engine.

19 Fit a gudgeon pin circlip in position at one end of the gudgeon pin hole in the piston and fit the piston to the connecting rod by sliding in the gudgeon pin (photo). The arrow on the crown of each piston must be on the same side as the word 'FRONT' on the connecting rod.

20 Fit the second circlip in position (photo). Repeat this procedure for the remaining three pistons and connecting rods.

21 Fit the connecting rod in position and check that the oil hole (arrowed), (photo) in the upper half of each bearing aligns with the oil squirt hole in the connecting rod.

22 With a wad of clean rag wipe the cylinder bores clean, and then oil them generously. The pistons complete with connecting rods, are fitted to their bores from above (photo). As each piston is inserted into its bore, ensure that it is the correct piston/connecting rod assembly for that particular bore and that the connecting rod is the right way round, and that the front of the piston is towards the front of the bore, ie towards the front of the engine.

23 The piston will only slide into the bore as far as the oil control ring. It is then necessary to compress the piston rings in a clamp (photo).

24 Gently tap the piston into the cylinder bore with a wooden or plastic hammer (photo). If a proper piston ring clamp is not available then a suitable jubilee clip does the job very well.

25 Note the directional arrow on the piston crown (Fig 1.22).

26 Fit the shell bearings to the big end caps so the tongue on the back of each bearing lies in the machined recess (photo).

27 Generously oil the crankshaft connecting rod journals and then replace each big end cap on the same connecting rod from which it was removed. Fit the locking plates under the head of the big end bolts, tap the caps right home on the dowels and then tighten the bolts to a torque of 30 to 35 lb ft (4.15 to 4.84 kg m). Lock the bolts in position by knocking up the tabs on the locking washers (photo).

28 The semi rebuilt engine will now look like this and is ready for the cam followers and cam to be fitted.

29 Fit the eight cam followers into the same holes in the block from which each was removed (photo). The cam followers can only be fitted with the block upside down.

30 Fit the Woodruff key in its slot on the front of the crankshaft and then press the timing sprocket into place so the timing mark

42.20 Fitting a gudgeon pin circlip

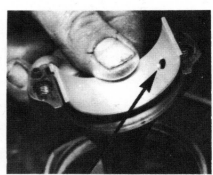

42.21 Big-end bearing oil hole

42.22 Installing piston/connecting rod assembly

42.23 Compressing piston rings

42.24 Tapping piston assembly into cylinder bore

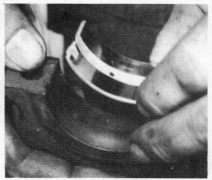
42.26 Fitting shell bearings to big-end caps

42.27 Locking big-end bolts

42.29 Installing cam followers (tappets)

42.30 Installing camshaft

42.31 Fitting camshaft thrust plate

42.32 Tightening camshaft flange bolts

42.33 Locking camshaft flange bolts

42.35 Camshaft sprocket correctly located on dowel

42.36 Locking camshaft sprocket bolts

42.37 Fitting crankshaft oil slinger

42.38 Fitting timing chain tensioner

42.39 Fitting timing chain tensioner cam

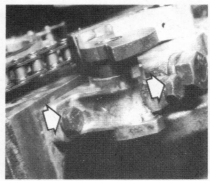
42.40 Bolting timing chain tensioner assembly to engine block

42.41 Pressing new timing cover oil seal into position

42.42 Sticking new timing cover gasket into position

42.43 Locating the timing cover

42.44 Fitting crankcase oil fume extraction tube

42.45 Fitting new sump gaskets

42.47 Re-fitting the sump

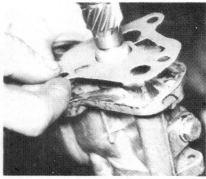
42.49 Positioning a new oil pump gasket

42.50 Fitting oil pump to crankcase

42.51 Tightening oil pump bolts

42.52 Fitting crankshaft pulley

42.53 Screwing in the crankshaft pulley bolt

42.55 Inserting valve into guide

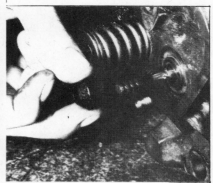
42.56 Fitting valve stem oil seal

42.57 Fitting valve spring

42.58 Fitting valve spring retainer

42.59 Compressing a valve spring

42.60 Fitting valve split collets

42.61 Locating cylinder head onto block

42.62 Inserting cylinder head bolts

42.64 Installing push-rods

42.65 Installing rocker shaft

42.69 Checking a valve clearance

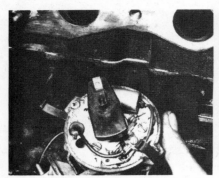

42.74 Position of rotor arm before installing distributor

42.75 Position of rotor arm after installing distributor

42.77 Fitting water pump to block

42.78 Location of generator adjustment strap

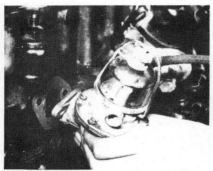

42.79 Fitting fuel pump

42.80 Fitting rocker box cover

faces forward. Oil the camshaft shell bearings and insert the camshaft into the block (which should still be upside down) (photo).

31 Make sure the camshaft turns freely and then fit the thrust plate behind the camshaft flange as shown (photo). Measure the end float with a feeler gauge - it should be between 0.0025 and 0.0075 inch (0.0635 and 0.1905 mm). If this is not so, then renew the plate.

32 Fit the two camshaft flange bolts into their joint washer and screw down the bolts securely (photo).

33 Turn up the tab (arrowed in photo) under the head of each bolt to lock it in place.

34 When refitting the timing chain round the gearwheels and to the engine, the two timing lines (arrowed) must be adjacent to each other on an imaginary line passing through each gearwheel centre (Fig 1.23).

35 With the timing marks correctly aligned turn the camshaft until the protruding dowel locates in the hole (arrowed) in the camshaft sprocket wheel.

36 Tighten the two retaining bolts and bend up the tabs on the lockwasher (photo).

37 Fit the oil slinger to the nose of the crankshaft, concave side facing outwards. The cut-out (arrowed in photo) locates over the Woodruff key.

38 Then slide the timing chain tensioner arm over its hinge pin on the front of the block (photo).

39 Turn the tensioner back from its free position so that it will apply pressure to the tensioner arm and replace the tensioner on the block sump flange (photo).

40 Bolt the tensioner to the block using spring washers under the heads of the two bolts (arrowed in photo).

41 Remove the front oil seal from the timing chain cover and with the aid of a vice, carefully press a new seal into position (photo). Lightly lubricate the face of the seal which will bear against the crankshaft.

42 Using jointing compound, fit a new timing cover gasket in place (photo).

42.81 Adjusting generator drive belt

43 Fit the timing chain cover, replacing and tightening the two dowel bolts first. These fit in the holes nearest the sump flange and serve to align the timing cover correctly. Ensure spring washers are used and then tighten the bolts evenly (photo).

44 Refit the tube or crankcase emission device to its recess adjacent to the top of the petrol pump, tapping it gently into place (photo). Replace the oil pump suction pipe using a new tab washer and position the gauze head so that it clears the crankshaft throw and the oil return pipe (where fitted). Tighten the nut and bend back the tab of the lockwasher.

45 Clean the flanges of the sump and fit new gaskets in place. Fit a new oil seal to the flange at the rear of the crankcase and at the front (photo).

46 Locate the flywheel or drive plate (automatic transmission) onto the crankshaft flange and tighten the securing bolts to a torque of between 45 and 50 lb ft (6.2 and 6.9 kg m).

47 Locate the sump in position on the crankcase and tighten the securing bolts evenly in diagonal sequence (photo). Where the

sump is being refitted with the engine in position in the vehicle, stick the gaskets in position on the face of the crankcase with jointing compound. Reconnect the dismantled steering and tighten the crossmember bolts to a torque of between 30 and 35 lb ft (4.1 to 4.8 kg m).

48 The engine can now be turned over so that it is the right way up. Coat the oil pump flanges with jointing compound.

49 Fit a new gasket in place on the oil pump (photo).

50 Position the oil pump against the block ensuring that the skew gear teeth on the drive shaft mate with those on the camshaft (photo).

51 Replace the three securing bolts and spring washers and tighten them down evenly (photo).

52 Moving to the front of the engine align the slot in the crankshaft pulley wheel with the key on the crankshaft and gently tap the pulley wheel home (photo).

53 Secure the pulley wheel by fitting the large flat washer, the spring washer and then the bolt which should be tightened securely (photo).

54 The next step is to thoroughly clean the faces of the block and cylinder head. Then fit a new cylinder head gasket. In order to correctly position the gasket it is a good idea to temporarily screw in two lengths of studding (one in each extreme diagonal hole) to act as locating dowels. These should be removed once two of the cylinder head bolts have been screwed into position.

55 With the cylinder head on its side lubricate the valve stems and refit the valves to their correct guides (photo). The valves should previously have been ground in (see Section 33).

56 Then fit the valve stem umbrella oil seals open ends down (photo).

57 Next slide the valve spring into place (photo). Use new ones if the old set has covered 20,000 miles (32,000 km).

58 Slide the valve spring retainer over the valve stem (photo).

59 Compress the valve spring with a compressor as shown in the photograph.

60 Then refit the split collets (photo). A trace of grease will help to hold them to the valve stem recess until the spring compressor is slackened off and the collets are wedged in place by the spring.

61 Carefully lower the cylinder head onto the block (photo).

62 Replace the cylinder head bolts and screw them down finger tight. Note that two of the bolts are of a different length and should be fitted to the holes indicated in the photograph.

63 With a torque wrench tighten the bolts to 65 to 70 lb ft (9.0 to 9.7 kg m) in the order shown in Fig. 1.4.

64 Fit the pushrods into the same holes in the block from which they were removed. Make sure the pushrods seat properly in the cam followers (photo).

65 Reassemble the rocker gear into the rocker shaft and fit the shaft to the cylinder head (photo). Ensure that the oil holes are clear and that the cut-outs for the securing bolts lie facing the holes in the brackets.

66 Tighten down the four rocker bracket washers and bolts to a torque of 17 to 22 lb ft (2.4 kg m).

67 The valve adjustments should be made initially with the engine cold. The importance of correct rocker arm/valve stem clearances cannot be overstressed as they vitally affect the performance of the engine. If the clearances are set too open, the efficiency of the engine is reduced as the valves open late and close earlier than was intended. If, on the other hand, the clearances are set too close there is a danger that the stems will expand upon heating and not allow the valves to close properly which will cause burning of the valve head and seat and possible warping. If the engine is in the car access to the rockers is by removing the four holding down screws from the rocker cover, and then lifting the rocker cover and gasket away.

68 It is important that the clearance is set when the tappet of the

valve being adjusted is on the heel of the cam (ie opposite the peak). This can be ensured by carrying out the adjustments in the following order (which also avoids turning the crankshaft more than necessary):

Valves open		Valves to adjust	
1 ex	6 in	3 in	8 ex
3 in	8 ex	1 ex	6 in
2 in	4 ex	5 ex	7 in
5 ex	7 in	2 in	4 ex

The valve positions are numbered from the front of the engine. The valve clearences for the different models are given in the Specifications.

69 Working from the front of the engine (no 1 valve) the correct clearance is obtained by slackening the hexagon locknut with a spanner while holding the ball pin against rotation with the screwdriver. Then, still pressing down with the screwdriver, insert a feeler gauge in the gap between the valve stem head and the rocker arm and adjust the ball pin until the feeler gauge will just move in and out without nipping (photo). Then, still holding the ball pin in the correct position, tighten the locknut.

70 Do not refit the rocker cover before replacing the distributor and setting the ignition timing. It is important to set the distributor drive correctly as otherwise the ignition timing will be totally incorrect. It is possible to set the distributor drive in apparently the right position, but, in fact, 180° out by omitting to select the correct cylinder which must not only be at TDC but must also be on its firing stroke with both valves closed. The distributor drive should therefore not be fitted until the cylinder head is in position and the valves can be observed. Alternatively, if the timing cover has not been replaced, the distributor drive can be replaced when the lines on the timing wheels are adjacent to each other.

71 Rotate the crankshaft so that No 1 piston is at TDC and on its firing stroke (the lines in the timing gears will be adjacent to each other). When No 1 piston is at TDC both valves will be closed and both rocker arms will 'rock' slightly because of the stem to arm pad clearance.

72 Note the two timing marks on the timing case and the notch on the crankshaft wheel periphery. When the cut-out is in line with the timing mark on the left this indicates 10° BTDC and when in line with the one on the right 6° BTDC. Set the crankshaft so the cut-out is in the right position of initial advance which varies, depending on the model and is detailed below:

1100 cc High compression	6° BTDC
1100 cc Low compression	10° BTDC
1300 cc High compression	10° BTDC
1300 cc Low compression	10° BTDC
1300 Sport/GT/1300E	10° BTDC

73 Hold the distributor in place so that the vacuum unit is towards the rear of the engine and at an angle of about 30° to the block. Do not yet engage the distributor drive gear with the skew gear on the camshaft.

74 Turn the rotor arm so that it points toward No 2 inlet port (photo).

75 Push the distributor shaft into its bore and note, as the distributor drive gear and skew gear on the camshaft mate, that the rotor arm turns so that it assumes a position of approximately 90° to the engine (photo). Fit the bolt and washer which holds the distributor clamp plate to the block.

76 Loosen the clamp on the base of the distributor and slightly turn the distributor body until the points just start to open while holding the rotor arm against the direction of rotation so no lost motion is present. Tighten the clamp. For a full description of how to do this accurately see Chapter 4.

77 Fit a new gasket to the water pump and attach the pump to the front of the cylinder block (photo).
78 Note that the generator adjustment strap fits under the head of the lower bolt on the water pump as shown (photo).
79 Replace the fuel pump using a new gasket and tighten up the two securing bolts (photo).
80 Fit the thermostat and thermostat gasket to the cylinder head and then replace the thermostat outlet pipe. Replace the spark plugs and refit the rocker cover using a new gasket (photo).
81 Refit the generator and adjust it so there is ½ inch (12.7 mm) play in the fan belt between the water pump and generator pulleys (photo). Refit the vacuum advance pipe to the distributor and refit the sender units.

43 Final assembly

1   Reconnect the ancillary components to the engine in the reverse order to which they were removed.
2   It should be noted that in all cases it is best to reassemble the engine as far as possible before refitting it to the car. This means that the inlet and exhaust manifolds, carburettor, generator, water thermostat, oil filter, distributor and engine mounting brackets, should all be in position.

44 Engine installation - general

1   Although the engine can be installed with one man and a suitable winch, it is easier if two are present. One to lower the engine into the engine compartment and the other to guide the engine into position and to ensure that it does not foul anything.
2   At this stage one or two tips may come in useful. Ensure all the loose leads, cables, etc are tucked out of the way. If not, it is easy to trap one and so cause much additional work after the engine is replaced. Smear grease on the tip of the gearbox input shaft before fitting the gearbox.
3   Always fit a new fan belt and new cooling hoses and jubilee clips as this will help eliminate the possibility of failure while on the road.

45 Engine installation without gearbox or automatic transmission

1   Position a sling round the engine and secure it to the hoist.
2   Lower the engine into the engine compartment, ensuring that nothing is fouling. Align the height of the engine with the gearbox or automatic transmission unit, which will still be supported on the jack which was located prior to removal of the engine.

On vehicles equipped with manual gearbox
3   Move the engine rearward until the splines of the gearbox first motion shaft enter the splined hub of the clutch driven plate (friction disc). The clutch driven plate will have already been aligned as described in Chapter 5. The engine may need turning fractionally to obtain engagement. If so, turn the crankshaft pulley using a spanner applied to its centre bolt.
4   Move the engine fully to the rear to mate the faces of the clutch bellhousing and the engine crankcase. Insert and tighten the securing bolts; fit the starter.

On vehicles equipped with automatic transmission
5   Check that the front pump drive tangs are fully engaged with the slots on the inner gear and that the torque converter is pushed fully rearwards (see Chapter 6, part 2).
6   Move the engine fully to the rear to mate the faces of the torque converter housing and the engine crankcase. Insert and tighten the lower two engine to converter housing bolts.
7   Rotate the crankshaft or torque converter until the holes in the drive plate are in alignment with those in the torque converter. It will only be possible to screw in and tighten one drive plate to converter bolt at a time through the converter

45.9 Engine front mounting bolt

46.2 Installing the engine in the vehicle

housing lower aperture, the crankshaft will then have to be turned through 90º to obtain access to the next bolt hole. When all four bolts are screwed in, tighten them finally to a torque of between 25 and 30 lb ft (3.6 to 4.14 kg m).
8   Reconnect the oil filler tube bracket, fill the unit with specified transmission fluid, fit the starter motor, then insert the remaining engine to torque converter housing bolts and tighten to a torque of 30 lb ft (4.14 kg m). Refit the semicircular dust cover to the torque converter housing.

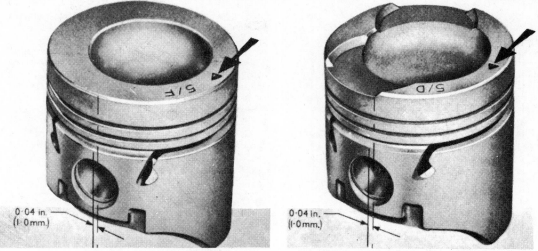

Fig. 1.22. Piston identification, gudgeon pin offset and front facing directional arrow

A   1100 and 1300 models   B   GT/Sport/1300E

Fig. 1.23. Timing marks on camshaft and crankshaft sprockets

Fig. 1.24. Upward facing side of cylinder head gasket

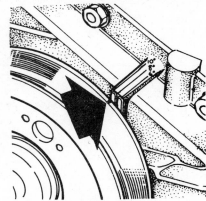

Fig. 1.25. Static ignition timing marks on timing cover and crankshaft pulley

On all vehicles

9   Reconnect the engine front mountings and bolt them to the body side frame members (it will be easier if the weight of the engine is still taken by the hoist so that it can be moved slightly to align the mounting bolt holes) (photo).
10 Connect the starter motor cable and the engine earth strap.
11 Fit the engine breather fume extraction pipe to the clutch housing.
12 Unplug the fuel line and connect it to the fuel pump.
13 Reconnect coil, distributor and spark plug leads.
14 Connect the exhaust downpipe and connect the accelerator and choke controls.
15 Connect the oil pressure switch and temperature gauge transmitter unit leads.
16 Fit the radiator together with radiator and heater hoses, followed by the engine shield and the air cleaner (do not over-tighten the air cleaner bolts or the carburettor may fracture).
17 Connect the leads to the rear of the dynamo or alternator and then connect the battery negative terminal.
18 Refill the cooling system (Chapter 2).
19 Refill the engine with the correct grade and quantity of oil (an extra pint will be required for absorption by the new filter element).

20 Refit the bonnet and check its alignment before tightening the hinge bolts fully. This operation will be easier to perform if the help of an assistant is obtained.

46 Engine installation with gearbox or automatic transmission unit attached

1   Position a sling round the engine/gearbox unit and support its weight on suitable lifting tackle. If using a fixed hoist raise the power unit and roll the car under it so the power unit will easily drop into the engine compartment.
2   Lower the power unit into position (photo) moving the car forward at the same time. When the engine is ¾ in it will be found helpful to place a trolley jack under the gearbox.
3   Connect the engine front mountings and the rear one with its supporting crossmember.
4   Fit the propeller shaft, aligning the drive flange mating marks made before removal. Connect the speedometer cable.

On vehicles equipped with manual gearbox

5 Connect the clutch operating cable and adjust the clutch as described in Chapter 5.

6 Refit the gear lever and gaiter.

On vehicles equipped with automatic transmission

7 Reconnect the speed selector linkage and test for correct operation (Chapter 6, Section 2).

8 Reconnect the leads to the combined starter-inhibitor/reversing light switch.

9 Refill the unit with the correct grade and quantity of transmission fluid.

On all vehicles

10 Carry out operations 9 to 20 as described in the preceding Section.

47 Engine - initial start up after major overhaul

1 There is no reason why the reassembled engine should not fire at the first operation of the starter switch.

2 If it fails to do so, make two or three more attempts as it may be that the carburettor bowl is empty and requires filling by a few revolutions of the camshaft operated fuel pump.

3 If the engine still does not fire, check the following points:

a) There is fuel in the tank

b) Ignition and battery leads are correctly and securely connected. (Check particularly the spark plug HT lead sequence - Chapter 4.)

c) The choke is correctly connected

d) The distributor has been correctly installed and not fitted 180° out (paragraphs 70 to 76, Section 42)

e) Work systematically through the fault finding chart at the end of this Chapter.

4 Run the engine until normal operating temperature is reached and check the torque setting of all nuts and bolts, particularly the cylinder head bolts. This is done by slackening the bolts slightly and retightening to the correct torque.

5 With the engine still hot, check and adjust the valve clearances.

6 Adjust the slow-running and carburettor mixture control screws (Chapter 3).

7 Check for any oil or water leaks and when the engine has cooled, check the levels of the radiator and sump and top up as necessary.

48 Overhaul differences - GT/Sport/1300E models

1 The overhaul and servicing procedure for these models is similar to that described for standard L or XL models, but reference should be made to the Specifications Section at the beginning of this Chapter for differences in mechanical and performance data.

2 The following modifications must also be noted when dismantling GT/Sport/1300E engines:

a) The air cleaner has two cover nuts and bolts and four nuts to secure its body to the carburettor

b) Prior to engine removal, detach the brake servo unit and bracket as described in Chapter 9

c) An oil pressure adaptor is installed in the engine block instead of the standard oil pressure switch unit.

49 Fault finding chart

Symptom	Reason/s	Remedy
ENGINE FAILS TO TURN OVER WHEN STARTER BUTTON OPERATED		
No current at starter motor	Flat or defective battery	Charge or replace battery. Push-start car.
	Loose battery leads	Tighten both terminals and earth ends of earth lead.
	Defective starter solenoid or switch or broken wiring	Run a wire direct from the battery to the starter motor or by-pass the solenoid.
	Engine earth strap disconnected	Check and retighten strap.
Current at starter motor	Jammed starter motor drive pinion	Place car in gear and rock from side to side. Alternatively, free exposed square end of shaft with spanner.
	Defective starter motor	Remove and recondition.
ENGINE TURNS OVER BUT WILL NOT START		
No spark at spark plug	Ignition damp or wet	Wipe dry the distributor cap and ignition leads.
	Ignition leads to spark plugs loose	Check and tighten at both spark plug and distributor cap ends.
	Shorted or disconnected low tension leads	Check the wiring on the CB and SW terminals of the coil and to the distributor.
	Dirty, incorrectly set, or pitted contact breaker points	Clean, file smooth, and adjust.
	Faulty condenser	Check contact breaker points for arcing, remove and fit new.
	Defective ignition switch	By-pass switch with wire.
	Ignition leads connected wrong way round	Remove and replace leads to spark plugs in correct order.
	Faulty coil	Remove and fit new coil.
	Contact breaker point spring earthed or broken	Check spring is not touching metal part of distributor. Check insulator washers are correctly placed. Renew points if the spring is broken.

Symptom	Reason/s	Remedy
Excess of petrol in cylinder or carburettor flooding	Too much choke allowing too rich a mixture to wet plugs	Remove and dry spark plugs or with wide open throttle, push-start the car.
	Float damaged or leaking or needle not seating	Remove, examine, clean and replace float and needle valve as necessary.
	Float lever incorrectly adjusted	Remove and adjust correctly.

ENGINE STALLS AND WILL NOT START

Symptom	Reason/s	Remedy
No spark at spark plug	Ignition failure - sudden	Check over low and high tension circuits for breaks in wiring.
	Ignition failure - misfiring precludes total stoppage	Check contact breaker points, clean and adjust. Renew condenser if faulty.
	Ignition failure - in severe rain or after traversing water splash	Dry out ignition leads and distributor cap.
No fuel at jets	No petrol in petrol tank	Refill tank.
	Petrol tank breather choked	Remove petrol cap and clean out breather hole or pipe.
	Sudden obstruction in carburettor(s)	Check jets, filter, and needle valve in float chamber for blockage.
	Water in fuel system	Drain tank and blow out fuel lines.

ENGINE MISFIRES OR IDLES UNEVENLY

Symptom	Reason/s	Remedy
Intermittent spark at spark plug	Ignition leads loose	Check and tighten as necessary at spark plug and distributor cap ends.
	Battery leads loose on terminals	Check and tighten terminal leads.
	Battery earth strap loose on body attachment point	Check and tighten earth lead to body attachment point.
	Engine earth lead loose	Tighten lead.
	Low tension leads to SW and CB terminals on coil loose	Check and tighten leads if found loose.
	Low tension lead from CB terminal side to distributor loose	Check and tighten if found loose.
	Dirty, or incorrectly gapped plugs	Remove, clean, and regap.
	Dirty, incorrectly set, or pitted contact breaker points	Clean, file smooth, and adjust.
	Tracking across inside of distributor cover	Remove and fit new cover.
	Ignition too retarded	Check and adjust ignition timing.
	Faulty coil	Remove and fit new coil.
No fuel at carburettor float chamber or at jets	No petrol in petrol tank	Refill tank!
	Vapour lock in fuel line (In hot conditions or at high altitude)	Blow into petrol tank, allow engine to cool or apply a cold wet rag to the fuel line.
	Blocked float chamber needle valve	Remove, clean, and replace.
	Fuel pump filter blocked	Remove, clean, and replace.
	Choked or blocked carburettor jets	Dismantle and clean.
	Faulty fuel pump	Remove, overhaul, and replace.
Fuel shortage at engine	Mixture too weak	Check jets, float chamber needle valve, and filters for obstruction. Clean as necessary. Carburettor incorrectly adjusted.
	Air leak in carburettor	Remove and overhaul carburettor.
	Air leak at inlet manifold to cylinder head, or inlet manifold to carburettor	Test by pouring oil along joints. Bubbles indicate leak. Renew manifold gasket as appropriate.
Mechanical wear	Incorrect valve clearances	Adjust rocker arms to take up wear.
	Burnt out exhaust valves	Remove cylinder head and renew defective valves.
	Sticking or leaking valves	Remove cylinder head, clean, check and renew valves as necessary.
	Weak or broken valve springs	Check and renew as necessary.
	Worn valve guides or stems	Renew valve guides and valves.
	Worn pistons and piston rings	Dismantle engine, renew pistons and rings.

LACK OF POWER AND POOR COMPRESSION

Symptom	Reason/s	Remedy
Fuel/air mixture leaking from cylinder	Burnt out exhaust valves	Remove cylinder head, renew defective valves.
	Sticking or leaking valves	Remove cylinder head, clean, check, and renew valves as necessary.
	Worn valve guides and stems	Remove cylinder head and renew valves and valve guides.
	Weak or broken valve springs	Remove cylinder head, renew defective springs.

Symptom	Reason/s	Remedy
	Blown cylinder head gasket (Accompanied by increase in noise)	Remove cylinder head and fit new gasket.
	Worn pistons and piston rings	Dismantle engine, renew pistons and rings.
	Worn or scored cylinder bores	Dismantle engine, rebore, renew pistons and rings.
Incorrect adjustments	Ignition timing wrongly set. Too advanced or retarded	Check and reset ignition timing.
	Contact breaker points incorrectly gapped	Check and reset contact breaker points.
	Incorrect valve clearances	Check and reset rocker arm to valve stem gap.
	Incorrectly set spark plugs	Remove, clean and regap.
	Carburation too rich or too weak	Tune carburettor for optimum performance.
Carburation and ignition faults	Dirty contact breaker points	Remove, clean, and replace.
	Distributor automatic balance weights or vacuum advance and retard mechanisms not functioning correctly	Overhaul distributor.
	Faulty fuel pump giving top end fuel starvation	Remove, overhaul, or fit exchange reconditioned fuel pump.
EXCESSIVE OIL CONSUMPTION Oil being burnt by engine	Badly worn, perished or missing valve stem oil seals	Remove, fit new oil seals to valve stems.
	Excessively worn valve stems and valve guides	Remove cylinder head and fit new valves and valve guides.
	Worn piston rings	Fit oil control rings to existing pistons or purchase new pistons.
	Worn pistons and cylinder bores	Fit new pistons and rings, rebore cylinders.
	Excessive piston ring gap allowing blow-by	Fit new piston rings and set gap correctly.
	Piston oil return holes choked	Decarbonise engine and pistons.
Oil being lost due to leaks	Leaking oil filter gasket	Inspect and fit new gasket as necessary.
	Leaking timing case gasket	Inspect and fit new gasket as necessary.
	Leaking timing case gasket	Inspect and fit new gasket as necessary.
	Leaking sump gasket	Inspect and fit new gasket as necessary.
	Loose sump plug	Tighten, fit new gasket if necessary.
UNUSUAL NOISES FROM ENGINE Excessive clearances due to mechanical wear	Worn valve gear. (Noisy tapping from rocker box	Inspect and renew rocker shaft, rocker arms, and ball pins as necessary.
	Worn big end bearing (regular heavy knocking)	Drop sump, if bearings broken up clean out oil pump and oilways, fit new bearings. If bearings not broken but worn fit bearing shells.
	Worn timing chain and gears (rattling from front of engine)	Remove timing cover, fit new timing wheels and timing chain.
	Worn main bearings (rumbling and vibration)	Drop sump, remove crankshaft, if bearings worn but not broken up, renew. If broken up strip oil pump and clean out oilways.
	Worn crankshaft (knocking, rumbling and vibration	Regrind crankshaft, fit new main and big end bearings.

Chapter 2 Cooling system

Contents

Specifications

Type of system	Pressurised pump impeller and fan assisted
Thermostat - type	Wax
Thermostat - location	In cylinder head
Starts to open	85° to 89°C (185° to 192°F)
Fully open	99° to 102°C (210° to 216°F)
Radiator pressure cap opens	13 lb/sq in. (0.91 kg/cm^2)
Fan type - saloon	10 blade assymetric
- van and estate	7 blade
Width of fan belt	0.38 in. (9.7 mm)
Outside length of fan belt	29 in. (740 mm)
Tension of fan belt	½ in. (12.8 mm) free play between generator and water pump pulley wheel
Water pump drive	Belt from crankshaft pulley
Coolant capacity - with heater	9.00 pints (10.8 US pints, 5.12 litres)
- without heater	7.90 pints (9.48 US pints, 4.98 litres)
Radiator type	Corrugated high efficiency fin
Core height	10.75 in. (273 mm)
Width	17.26 in. (438.4 mm)
Fins per inch 1,100	9
1300 and GT	12
1,100 van and estate	11
1300 van and estate	13

Torque wrench settings

Water pump nuts	5 to 7 lb/ft (0.69 to 0.97 kg.m)
Thermostat housing	12 to 15 lb/ft (1.66 to 2.07 kg.m)
Fan blade	5 to 7 lb/ft (0.69 to 0.97 kg.m)

1 General description

The engine cooling water is circulated by a thermo-syphon, water pump assisted system, and the whole system is pressurised. This is both to prevent the loss of water down the overflow pipe with the radiator cap in position and to prevent premature boiling in adverse conditions. The radiator cap is pressurised to 13 lb in^2. This has the effect of considerably increasing the boiling point of the coolant. If the water temperature goes above this increased boiling point the extra pressure in the system forces the internal part of the cap off its seat, thus exposing the overflow pipe down which the steam from the boiling water escapes thereby relieving the pressure. It is therefore, important to check that the radiator cap is in good condition and that the spring behind the sealing washer has not weakened. Most garages have a special machine in which radiator caps can be tested. The cooling system comprises the radiator, top and bottom water hoses, heater hoses, the impeller water pump (mounted on the

front of the engine, it carries the fan blades, and is driven by the fan belt), the thermostat and the two drain taps. The inlet manifold is water heated, also the automatic choke (fitted to vehicles with automatic transmission).

The system functions in the following fashion. Cold water in the bottom of the radiator circulates up the lower radiator hose to the water pump where it is pushed round the water passages in the cylinder block, helping to keep the cylinder bores and pistons cool.

The water then travels up into the cylinder head and circulates round the combustion spaces and valve seats absorbing more heat, and then, when the engine is at its proper operating temperature, travels out of the cylinder head, past the open thermostat into the upper radiator hose and so into the radiator header tank.

The water travels down the radiator where it is rapidly cooled by the in-rush of cold air through the radiator core, which is created by both the fan and the motion of the car. The water, now cold, reaches the bottom of the radiator, when the cycle is repeated.

When the engine is cold the thermostat (which is a valve which opens and closes according to the temperature of the water) maintains the circulation of the same water in the engine.

Only when the correct minimum operating temperature has been reached, as shown in the Specifications, does the thermostat begin to open, allowing water to return to the radiator.

2 Cooling system - draining

1 With the car on level ground drain the system as follows:
2 If the engine is cold remove the filler cap from the radiator by turning the cap anticlockwise. If the engine is hot, having just been run, then turn the filler cap very slightly until the pressure in the system has had time to disperse. Use a rag over the cap to protect your hand from escaping steam. If, with the engine very hot, the cap is released suddenly, the drop in pressure can result in the water boiling. With the pressure released the cap can be removed.
3 If anti-freeze is in the radiator drain it into a clean bucket or bowl for re-use.
4 Remove the two drain plugs and ensure that the heater control is in the hot position. The radiator plug is removed by hand, by unscrewing the wing nut, but the cylinder block plug must be removed with the aid of a spanner. The drain plugs are located at the bottom of the radiator and at the rear on the left hand side of the block. If no drain plug is fitted to the radiator disconnect the bottom hose.
5 When the water has finished running, probe the drain tap orifices with a short piece of wire to dislodge any particles or rust or sediment which may be blocking the taps and preventing all the water draining out.

3 Cooling system - flushing

1 Provided the coolant is kept to its recommended concentration with anti-freeze and it is renewed at the recommended intervals, flushing will not usually be required. However, due to neglect or gas or oil entering the system because of a faulty gasket the radiator may become choked with rust scales, deposits from the water and other sediment. To clean the system out, remove the radiator cap and the drain plugs and leave a hose running in the radiator cap orifice for ten to fifteen minutes.
2 Then close the drain taps and refill with water and a proprietary cleansing compound. Run the engine for 10 to 15 minutes and then drain it and flush out thoroughly for a further 10 minutes. All sediment and sludge should now have been removed.
3 In very bad cases the radiator should be reverse flushed. This can be done with the radiator in position. The cylinder block plug is closed and a hose placed over the open radiator drain plug. Water, under pressure, is then forced up through the radiator and out of the header tank filler orifice.
4 The hose is then removed and placed in the filler orifice and the radiator washed out in the usual fashion.

4 Cooling system - filling

1 Close the two drain taps, or reconnect the bottom hose.
2 Fill the system slowly to ensure that no air locks develop. The best type of water to use in the cooling system is rain water, so use this whenever possible.
3 Do not fill the system higher than within ½ inch (12.7 mm) of the filler orifice. Overfilling will merely result in wastage, which is especially to be avoided when anti-freeze is in use.
4 Only use anti-freeze mixture with a glycol or ethylene base (Section 13).
5 Replace the filler cap and turn it firmly clockwise to lock it in position.

Fig. 2.1. Location of radiator and cylinder block drain plugs

5 Radiator - removal, inspection, cleaning and refitting

1 To remove the radiator first drain the cooling system as described in Section 2.
2 Undo the wire clips which hold the top and bottom radiator hoses on the radiator and then pull off the two hoses.
3 Undo and remove the two bolts and washers on either side of the radiator which hold it in place. It may be helpful to remove the battery to give better access to the top right hand bolt.
4 Having removed the bolts, lift the radiator out of the engine compartment.
5 With the radiator out of the car any leaks can be soldered or repaired. Clean out the inside of the radiator by flushing as detailed in the Section before last. When the radiator is out of the car, it is advantageous to turn it upside down for reverse flushing. Clean the exterior of the radiator by hosing down the radiator matrix with a strong jet of water to clear away road dirt, dead flies etc.
6 Inspect the radiator hoses for cracks, internal or external perishing, and damage caused by overtightening of the securing clips. Replace the hoses as necessary. Examine the radiator hose securing clips and renew them if they are rusted or distorted. The drain taps should be renewed if leaking, but ensure the leak is not because of a faulty washer behind the tap. If the tap is suspected, try a new washer to see if this clears the trouble first.
7 Replacement is a straightforward reversal of the removal procedure.

6 Thermostat - removal, testing and refitting

1 To remove the thermostat partially drain the cooling system (four pints is enough) then loosen the wire clip retaining the top radiator hose to the outlet elbow and pull the hose off the elbow.
2 Undo the two bolts holding the elbow to the cylinder head and remove the elbow and gasket (photo).
3 The thermostat can now be lifted out (photo). Should the thermostat be stuck in its seat, do not lever it upwards but cut through the corrosion all round the edge of the seat with a sharp pointed knife. This will usually release the thermostat without causing any damage.
4 Test the thermostat for correct functioning by suspending it by a length of string in a saucepan of cold water together with a thermometer.
5 Heat the water and note when the thermostat begins to open. This temperature is stamped on the flange of the thermostat, and is also given in the Specifications.
6 Discard the thermostat if it opens too early. Continue heating

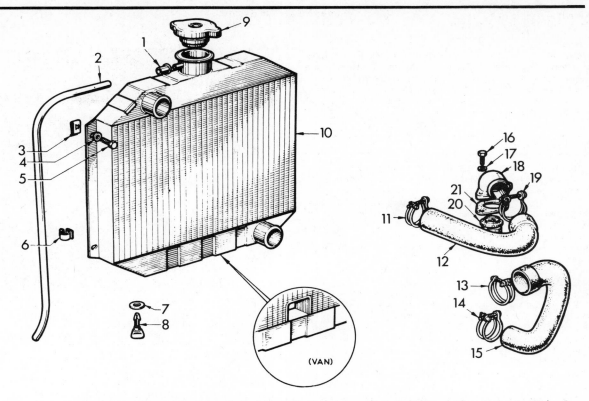

Fig. 2.2. Radiator and cooling system components (inset van radiator with cut-out for starting handle)

1	Overflow connection	7	Washer
2	Overflow pipe	8	Drain tap
3	Spire nut	9	Radiator cap
4	Washer	10	Radiator
5	Bolt	11	Clip
6	Clip		

12	Top hose	17	Washer
13	Clip	18	Outlet elbow
14	Clip	19	Clip
15	Bottom hose	20	Thermostat
16	Bolt	21	Gasket

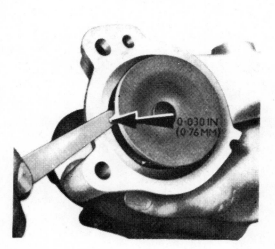

Fig. 2.3. Checking clearance between water pump impeller and body

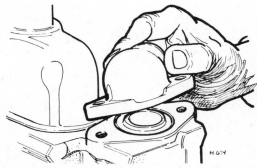

6.2 Removing thermostat housing cover

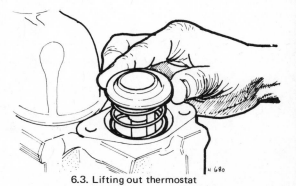

6.3. Lifting out thermostat

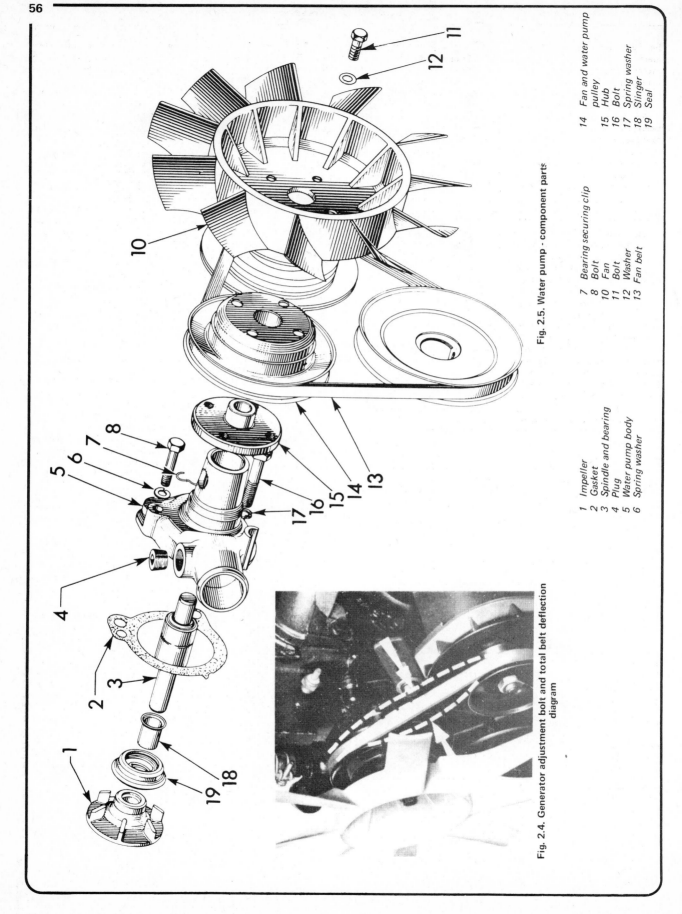

Fig. 2.5. Water pump - component parts

1 Impeller
2 Gasket
3 Spindle and bearing
4 Plug
5 Water pump body
6 Spring washer
7 Bearing securing clip
8 Bolt
10 Fan
11 Bolt
12 Washer
13 Fan belt
14 Fan and water pump pulley
15 Hub
16 Bolt
17 Spring washer
18 Slinger
19 Seal

Fig. 2.4. Generator adjustment bolt and total belt deflection diagram

the water until the thermostat is fully open. Then let it cool down naturally. If the thermostat will not open fully in boiling water, or does not close down as the water cools, then it must be renewed.

7 If the thermostat is stuck open when cold this will be apparent when removing it from the housing.

8 Replacing the thermostat is a reversal of the removal procedure. Remember to use a new gasket between the elbow and the cylinder head. If any pitting or corrosion is apparent, it is advisable to apply a layer of sealing compound such as Hermatite to the metal surfaces of the housing before reassembly. If the elbow is badly eaten away it must be replaced with a new component.

7 Water pump - removal and refitting

1 Drain the cooling system as described in Section 2, then loosen the spring clip on the bottom radiator hose at the pump inlet and pull off the hose. Also undo the clip on the small heater hose and pull off the hose.

2 All numbers used in this Section and Section 8 refer to Fig 2.5. Loosen the generator securing bolts and swing the generator in towards the cylinder block. This frees the generator fan belt (13) which can now be removed.

3 Undo the four bolts and washers (11, 12) which hold the fan (10) and the pulley wheel (14) in place.

4 Remove the fan (10) and the pulley wheel (14) and then undo the three bolts holding the water pump in place and withdraw the pump together with its gasket.

5 Replacement is a reversal of the above procedure but always remember to use a new gasket.

8 Water pump - dismantling and reassembly

1 Remove the hub (15) from the water pump shaft (3) by using a suitable hub puller.

2 Carefully pull out the bearing retainer wire (7) and then with the aid of two blocks (a small mandrel and a large vice, if the proper tools are not available) press out the shaft and bearing assembly (3) together with the impeller (1) and seal from the water pump body (5).

3 The impeller vane is removed from the spindle with an extractor.

4 Remove the seal (19) and the slinger (18) by splitting the latter with the aid of a sharp cold chisel.

5 The repair kit available comprises a new shaft and bearing assembly, a slinger, seal, bush, clip and gasket.

6 To reassemble the water pump, press the shaft and bearing assembly (3) into the housing with the short end of the shaft to the front, until the groove in the shaft is in line with the groove in the housing. The bearing retainer wire (7) can then be inserted.

7 Press the pulley hub (15) onto the front end of the shaft (3) until the end of the shaft is half an inch from the outer face of the hub.

8 Fit the new slinger bush (18) with the flanged end first onto the rear of the shaft (3) and refit the pump seal (19) with the thrust face towards the impeller (1).

9 Press the impeller (1) onto the shaft (3) until a clearance of 0.030 inch (0.76 mm) is obtained between the impeller blades and the housing face as shown in Fig 2.3.

10 It is important to check at this stage that the pump turns freely and smoothly before replacement onto the block. After replacement check carefully for leaks.

9 Fan belt - adjustment

1 The fan belt tension is correct when there is ½ inch (12.7 mm) of lateral movement at the midpoint position of the belt between the generator pulley wheel and the water pump pulley wheel.

2 To adjust the fan belt, slacken the generator securing bolts as indicated in Fig 2.4 and move the generator either in or out until the correct tension is obtained. It is easier if the generator

securing bolts are only slackened slightly so it requires some force to move the generator. In this way the tension of the belt can be arrived at more quickly than by making frequent adjustments.

3 If difficulty is experienced in moving the generator away from the engine, a long spanner or screwdriver placed behind the generator and resting against the cylinder block serves as a very good lever and can be held in this position while the generator securing bolts are tightened down.

10 Fan belt - removal and refitting

1 If the fan belt is worn or has stretched unduly it should be renewed. The most usual reason for renewal is that the belt has broken in service. It is therefore recommended that a spare belt is always carried. Replacement is a reversal of the removal sequence, but as renewal due to breakage is the most usual operation, it is described below.

2 To remove the belt loosen the generator securing bolts and push the generator in towards the engine.

3 Slip the old belt over the crankshaft, generator and water pump pulley wheels and lift it off over the fan blades.

4 Put on a new belt in the same way and adjust it as described in the previous Section. Note: after fitting a new belt it will require adjustment due to its initial stretch after about 250 miles (400 km).

11 Temperature gauge - fault finding

1 If the temperature gauge fails to work either the gauge, the sender unit, the wiring or the connections are at fault.

2 It is not possible to repair the gauge or the sender unit and they must be replaced by new units if at fault.

3 First check the wiring connections and if sound, check the wiring for breaks using an ohmmeter or continuity tester. The sender unit and gauge should be tested by substitution.

12 Temperature gauge and sender unit - removal and refitting

1 For details of how to remove and replace the temperature gauge see Chapter 10.

2 To remove the sender unit, drain half the coolant from the system, disconnect the wire leading into the unit as its connector and undo the unit with a spanner. The unit is located in the cylinder head just below the water outlet elbow on the left side. Replacement is a reversal of the above procedure.

13 Anti-freeze solution

1 Apart from the protection against freezing conditions which the use of anti-freeze provides, it is essential to minimise corrosion in the cooling system.

2 The cooling system is initially filled with a solution of 50% anti-freeze and it is recommended that this percentage is maintained.

3 With long-life types of anti-freeze mixtures, renew the coolant every two years. With other types, drain and refill the system every twelve months.

4 The following table gives a guide to protection against frost but a mixture of less than 30% concentration will not give protection against corrosion:

Amount of anti-freeze	Protection to
50%	−37°C (−34°F)
40%	−25°C (−13°F)
30%	−16°C (+ 3°F)
25%	−13°C (+ 9°F)
20%	−9°C (+ 15°F)
15%	−7°C (+ 20°F)

14 Fault diagnosis - Cooling system

Symptom	Cause	Remedy
Overheating	Insufficient water in cooling system	Top up radiator
	Fan belt slipping (accompanied by a shrieking noise on rapid engine acceleration)	Tighten fan belt to recommended tension or replace if worn
	Radiator core blocked or radiator grille restricted	Reverse flush radiator, remove obstructions.
	Bottom water hose collapsed, impeding flow	Remove and fit new hose
	Thermostat not opening properly	Remove and fit new thermostat.
	Ignition advance and retard incorrectly set (accompanied by loss of power, and perhaps, misfiring)	Check and reset ignition timing
	Carburettor incorrectly adjusted (mixture too weak)	Tune carburettor.
	Exhaust system partially blocked	Check exhaust pipe for constrictive dents and blockages
	Oil level in sump too low	Top up sump to full mark on dipstick
	Blown cylinder head gasket (water/steam being forced down the radiator overflow pipe under pressure)	Remove cylinder head, fit new gasket.
	Engine not yet run-in	Run-in slowly and carefully
	Brakes binding	Check and adjust brakes if necessary
Cool running	Thermostat jammed open	Remove and renew thermostat
	Incorrect thermostat fitted allowing premature opening of valve	Remove and replace with new thermostat which opens at a higher temperature
	Thermostat missing	Check and fit correct thermostat
Loss of cooling water	Loose clips on water hose	Check and tighten clips if necessary
	Top, bottom or by-pass water hoses perished and leaking	Check and replace any faulty hoses
	Radiator core leaking	Remove radiator and repair
	Thermostat gasket leaking	Inspect and renew gasket
	Radiator pressure cap spring worn or seal ineffective	Renew radiator pressure cap
	Blown cylinder head gasket (pressure in system forcing water/steam down overflow pipe	Remove cylinder head and fit new gasket
	Cylinder wall or head cracked	Dismantle engine, despatch to engineering works for repair

Chapter 3 Fuel system and carburation

Contents

Specifications

Fuel pump

Type	Mechanical driven from eccentric on camshaft
Delivery pressure - 1100, 1300	1 to 2 lb/in^2 (0.07 to 0.14 kg/cm^2)
- G.T.	3½ to 5 lb/in^2 (0.25 to 0.35 kg/cm^2)
Inlet vacuum	8.5 in. (21.60 mm) Hg

Diaphragm spring:
Test length 1100, 1300	0.468 in. (11.88 mm)
Test load	3¼ to 3½ lb (1.47 to 1.59 kg)
Test length G.T.	0.641 (16.27 mm)
Test load	10 to 12.75 lbs (4.54 to 5.78 kg)

Rocker arm spring:
Test length - all models	0.44 in. (11.18 mm)
Test load	5 to 5½ lb (2.27 to 2.5 kg)
Tank capacity	9.0 gallons (10.8 US gals, 40.9 litres)

Carburettor identification and application:
1100 cc - single venturi downdraught types
C7AH - A (Autolite)	Manually-operated choke
C7AH - E (Autolite)	Manually-operated choke - emission reduced
*C7AH - C (Autolite)	Automatic choke
*C7AH - G (Autolite)	Automatic choke - emission reduced

* Automatic choke carburettors not fitted to 1100 cc engines after September 1970.

1300 cc (up to September 1970) - single venturi type (not Sport/G.T.)
C7AH - B (Autolite)	Manually operated choke
C7AH - D (Autolite)	Automatic choke

1300 cc (after September 1970) - single venturi type (not Sport/G.T.)

711W 9510 BVB (Autolite)	Manually operated choke
711W 9510 CAB (Autolite)	Automatic choke

1300 cc Sport/G.T. up to September 1970 — twin barrel type

32 DFE (Weber)	Manually operated choke

1300 cc Sport/G.T. after September 1970 — twin barrel type

DGV - HA (Weber)	Manually operated choke

Types C7AH - A and C7AH - E

Idling speed	580 to 620 rev/min
Fast idle	900 to 1100 rev/min
(cold climates)	1100 to 1300 rev/min
Float setting up	1.12 to 1.16 in. (28.5 to 28.9 mm)
down	1.38 to 1.40 in. (35.1 to 35.5 mm)
Choke plate pull down	0.11 in. to 0.13 in. (3.6 to 4.1 mm)
Accelerator pump stroke	0.1 to 0.11 in. (2.7 to 2.9 mm)
Throttle barrel diameter	30 mm
Venturi diameter	21.5 mm *
* After September 1970	23 mm

	Up to September 1970	After September 1970
Main jet 0 to 3000 ft (920 m)	1.12 mm	1.17 mm
Emission reduced	1.17 mm	1.17 mm
3000 to 7000 ft (920 to 2130 m)	1.10 mm	1.12 mm
Emission reduced	1.15 mm	1.12 mm
over 7000 ft (2130 m)	1.07 mm	1.10 mm
Emission reduced	1.12 mm	1.10 mm
Air correction jet	1.40 mm	1.65 mm
Idling jet	0.55 mm	0.55 mm
Idling air bleed (first)	1.05 mm	0.85 mm
Emission reduced	1.10 mm	0.85 mm
(second)	0.60 mm	0.9 mm
Emission reduced	0.65 mm	0.9 mm
Idle channel restrictor	1.30 mm	1.15 mm
Emission reduced	1.40 mm	1.40 mm
Power jet	0.70 mm	0.75 mm
Pump jet	0.45 mm	0.45 mm
Pump lever (between centres)	0.3 in. (7.62 mm)	0.3 in. (7.62 mm)

Types C7AH - C and C7AH - G

Idling speed	580 to 620 rev/min
Fast idle	1400 to 1600 rev/min
(cold climates)	1700 to 1900 rev/min
Float setting up	1.12 to 1.16 in. (28.5 to 28.9 mm)
down	1.38 to 1.40 in. (35.1 to 35.5 mm)
Choke plate pull down	0.08 to 0.10 in. (2.1 to 2.5 mm)
Accelerator pump stroke	0.120 to 0.130 (3.1 to 3.3 mm)
Throttle barrel diameter	30 mm
Venturi diameter	21.5 mm
Main jet 0 to 3000 ft (920 m)	1.12 mm
3000 to 7000 ft (910 to 2130 m)	1.10 mm
over 7000 ft (2130 m)	1.07 mm
Air correction jet	1.50 mm
Idling jet	0.55 mm
Idling air bleed (first)	1.05 mm
(second)	0.60 mm
Idle channel restrictor	1.20 mm
Emission reduced	1.25 mm
Power jet	0.70 mm
De-choke	0.17 to 0.21 in. (4.32 to 5.33 mm)
Pump lever (between centres)	0.4 in. (10.16 mm)

Types C7AH - B and C7AH - D

Idling speed	580 to 620 rev/min
Fast idle - manual choke	1300 to 1500 rev/min
- automatic choke	1850 to 2050 rev/min
- automatic choke (cold climate)	2200 to 2400 rev/min
Float setting up	1.12 to 1.14 in. (28.5 to 28.9 mm)
down	1.38 to 1.40 in. (35.1 to 35.5 mm)
Choke plate pull-down	0.13 to 0.15 in. (3.3 to 3.8 mm)
Accelerator pump stroke	0.145 to 0.155 in. (3.7 to 3.9 mm)

Throttle barrel diameter	34 mm
Venturi diameter	25 mm
Main jet 0 to 3000 ft (920 m)	1.27 mm
3000 to 7000 ft (920 to 2130 m)	1.25 mm
over 7000 ft (2130 m)	1.20 mm
Air correction jet	1.50 mm
Idling jet	0.60 mm
Idling air bleed (first)	1.05 mm
(second)	0.65 mm
Idle channel restrictor	1.10 mm
Power jet	0.70 mm
De-choke	0.17 to 0.21 in. (4.32 to 5.33 mm)
Pump jet	0.45 mm
Pump lever (between centres)	0.4 in. (10.16 mm)

Type 711W 9510 BVB

Idling speed	580 to 620 rev/min
Fast idle	1300 to 1500 rev/min
Float setting up	1.12 to 1.16 in. (28.5 to 28.9 mm)
Float setting down	1.38 to 1.40 in. (35.1 to 35.5 mm)
Choke plate pull down	0.11 to 0.13 in. (3.6 to 4.1 mm)
Accelerator pump stroke	0.145 to 0.155 in. (3.7 to 3.9 mm)
Throttle barrel diameter	34 mm
Venturi diameter	25 mm
Main jet 0 to 3000 ft (920 m)	1.27 mm
3000 to 7000 ft (920 to 2130 m)	1.30 mm
over 7000 ft (2130 m)	1.25 mm
Air correction jet	1.50 mm
Idling jet	0.55 mm
Idling air bleed (first)	1.10 mm
(second)	0.95 mm
Idle channel restrictor	1.30 mm
Power jet	0.80 mm
Pump jet	0.45 mm

Type 711W 9510 CAB

Idling speed	580 to 620 rev/min
Fast idle	1850 to 2050 rev/min
(cold climate)	2200 to 2400 rev/min
Float setting up	1.12 to 1.16 in. (28.5 to 28.9 mm)
Float setting down	1.38 to 1.40 in. (35.1 to 35.5 mm)
Choke plate pull down	0.13 to 0.15 in. (3.3 to 3.8 mm)
Accelerator pump stroke	0.145 to 0.155 in. (3.7 to 3.9 mm)
Throttle barrel diameter	34 mm
Venturi diameter	25 mm
Main jet 0 to 3000 ft (920 m)	1.27 mm
300 to 7000 ft (920 to 2130 m)	1.25 mm
over 7000 ft (2130 m)	1.20 mm
Air correction jet	1.50 mm
Idling jet	0.55 mm
Idling air bleed (first)	1.10 mm
(second)	0.95 mm
Idle channel restrictor	1.30 mm
Power jet	0.80 mm
De-choke	0.29 to 0.31 in. (4.32 to 5.33 mm)
Pump jet	0.45 mm

Type 32 DFE

	Primary	Secondary
Venturi diameter	23	24
Auxiliary venturi	4.5	4.5
Main jet	125	115
Air correction jet	135	160
Emulsion tube type	F6	F6
Slow-running fuel jet	50	45
Slow-running air jet	185	100
Progression holes	1 x 110 - 1 x 70	2 x 120
Slow running volume control port	85	100
Full load enrichment jet	—	85
Full load air bleed	—	100
Full load mixture jet	—	100
Accelerator pump jet	60	
Accelerator pump back bleed	50	
Needle valve	2.0 mm	
Float level	7.0 to 7.5 mm	

Float stroke				8.0 mm
Fast idle setting				0.9 mm
Choke plate pull down				5.0 mm
Choke plate opening				7.5 to 8.5 mm with lever backed off 10 mm
Idling speed				680 to 720 rev/min
Fast idle				100 to 1300 rev/min
Air correction jet (sea level)	-	primary	... ...	135
	-	secondary	... ...	160
(3000 ft - 920 m)	-	primary	... ...	155
	-	secondary	... ...	180
(7000 ft - 2130 m)	-	primary	... ...	175
	-	secondary	... ...	200
(10000 ft - 3050 m)	-	primary	... ...	175
	-	secondary	... ...	200
Main jet (sea level)	-	primary	... ...	125
	-	secondary	... ...	115
(3000 ft - 920 m)	-	primary	... ...	125
	-	secondary	... ...	115
(7000 ft - 2130 m)	-	primary	... ...	125
	-	secondary	... ...	115
(10000 ft - 3050 m)	-	primary	... ...	120
	-	secondary	... ...	110

Type DGV - HA (Weber)

Venturi diameter	-	primary	... ...	23
	-	secondary	... ...	24
Auxiliary venturi	-	primary	... ...	4.5
	-	secondary	... ...	4.5
Main jet	-	primary	... ...	125
	-	secondary	... ...	140
Air correction jet	-	primary	... ...	180
	-	secondary	... ...	180
Emulsion tube	-	primary	... ...	F50
	-	secondary	... ...	F6
Slow-running (fuel) jet	-	primary	... ...	50
	-	secondary	... ...	45
Slow-running (air) jet	-	primary	... ...	185
	-	secondary	... ...	100
Progression holes	-	primary	... ...	1 x 110 - 1 x 70
	-	secondary	... ...	2 x 120
Slow-running volume control port	-	primary	... ...	85
	-	secondary	... ...	100
Full load enrichment jet	-	secondary	... ...	85
Full load air bleed	-	secondary	... ...	100
Full load mixture jet	-	secondary	... ...	100
Accelerator pump jet				55
Accelerator pump back bleed				40
Needle valve				2.0 mm
Float setting up				41 mm to bottom of float
Float setting down				50 mm to bottom of float
Fast idle setting				0.65 mm
Choke plate pull down				4.4 to 4.5 mm
Choke plate opening				7.5 to 8.5 mm with lever backed off 10 mm
Idling speed				730 to 770 rev/min
Fast idle				1000 to 1300 rev/min
Air correction jet (sea level)	-	primary	... ...	135
	-	secondary	... ...	160
(3000 ft - 920 m)	-	primary	... ...	155
	-	secondary	... ...	180
(7000 ft - 2130 m)	-	primary	... ...	175
	-	secondary	... ...	200
(10000 ft - 3050 m)	-	primary	... ...	175
	-	secondary	... ...	200
Main jet (sea level)	-	primary	... ...	125
	-	secondary	... ...	115
(3000 ft - 920 m)	-	primary	... ...	125
	-	secondary	... ...	115
(7000 ft - 2130 m)	-	primary	... ...	125
	-	secondary	... ...	115
(10000 ft - 3050 m)	-	primary	... ...	120
	-	secondary	... ...	110

Torque wrench settings

							lb ft	kg m
Fuel pump bolts	...	...	...	...	...	...	12 to 15	1.66 to 2.07
Manifold nuts	...	...	...	...	...	...	15 to 18	2.07 to 2.49
Manifold bolts	...	...	...	...	...	...	15 to 18	2.07 to 2.49
Air cleaner bolts (1100 and 1300 cc)			...	...	...	...	3 to 5	0.42 to 0.69
Air cleaner bolts (GT/Sport/1300E)			...	...	...	...	5 to 7	0.69 to 0.97

1 General description

The fuel system of all saloon models consists of a nine gallon fuel tank, a mechanically operated fuel pump, a single venturi downdraught Ford carburettor (GT/Sport/1300E models use a Weber twin barrel downdraught carburettor) and the necessary fuel lines between the tank and the pump and the pump and the carburettor.

Estate car models are fitted with a nine gallon fuel tank which is mounted under the rear floor pan. The remainder of the fuel system is identical in layout to saloon models.

2 Air cleaner - removal, servicing and refitting

1 On GT/Sport/1300E models a disposable paper element type air cleaner is fitted.
2 On other models a wire mesh or paper element type may be encountered.
3 With paper element types, remove the air cleaner cover bolt (GT/Sport 2 bolts), remove the cover and extract the element. Every 6000 miles (9600 km) tap the element on a hard surface or use compressed air from a tyre pump to remove surface dust. Never attempt to clean it in solvent or petrol.
4 Every 18,000 miles (29,000 km) renew the element. Always check the condition of the rubber sealing rings and renew them if they are perished or deformed.
5 With wire mesh types, wash the element in fuel and then sparingly re-oil it with engine oil and allow it to drain before refitting.
6 To remove the body of the air cleaner from the Weber carburettor, turn back the locking tabs and undo and remove the four nuts, tabs, plain and rubber washers from the bottom of the body. Then unclip the dipstick tube extension and the throttle cable (rhd vehicles only) and where fitted the support stay bolt. The air cleaner can then be lifted off complete with gasket and tubular inserts. On replacement fit the tubular inserts over the studs and then a new gasket. Offer up and correctly position the air cleaner body on the carburettor and fit the rubber and plain washers, lock tab and nuts. Tighten the nuts and turn up the tabs on the lockwashers. Reclip the dipstick tube extension and throttle cable and where fitted do up the support stay bolt. Centralise the element on its seat, and refit the top cover with the arrow towards the air cleaner spout and the front of the car.
7 To remove the air cleaner from other types of Ford (Autolite) carburettors, unscrew and remove the cover centre bolt securing the cover (early models) and body to a bracket across the mouth of the carburettor upper body. Unclip the throttle cable. Refitting is a reversal of removal but ensure that the air intake spout faces towards the radiator with the arrow marked on the cover in alignment with the spout. On later models, the cover is secured by four screws in addition to the centre bolt.
8 Instead of the straight type of air cleaner intake spout, later models have a variable position curved spout. The spout should be positioned 'S' (summer) or 'W' (winter) according to the season. In the winter position, the air is drawn from around the

exhaust pipe to prevent ice formation in the carburettor and to reduce condensation in the rocker box which is produced more readily with crankcase emission systems.

3 Fuel pumps - identification

1 One of three different types of fuel pump may be met within service. The AC type with two different designs of glass dome and one with a metal cover.
2 Servicing of the metal cover type should be limited to unscrewing the centre bolt and removing the cover and then cleaning the filter gauze and sediment chamber. In the event of failure, this type of pump should be regarded as disposable and a new one obtained.

4 AC fuel pump - description

1 The mechanically operated AC fuel pump is actuated through a spring loaded rocker arm. One arm of the rocker (20) bears against an eccentric on the camshaft and the other arm (21) operates a diaphragm pull rod (Fig 3.5).
2 As the engine camshaft rotates, the eccentric moves the pivoted rocker arm outward which in turn pulls the diaphragm pull rod and the diaphragm (15) down against the pressure of the diaphragm spring (5).
3 This creates sufficient vacuum in the pump chamber to draw in fuel from the tank through the fuel filter gauze (13) and non-return valve (4A).
4 The rocker arm is held in constant contact with the eccentric by an anti-rattle spring (16), and as the engine camshaft continues to rotate the eccentric allows the rocker arm to move inward. The diaphragm spring (5) is thus free to push the diaphragm (15) upward, forcing the fuel in the pump chamber out to the carburettor through the non-return outlet valve (4B). On some models different makes of fuel pump may be fitted. The system of operation and constructional features are virtually identical to the AC unit.
5 When the float chamber in the carburettor is full, the float chamber needle valve will close, so preventing further flow from the fuel pump.
6 The pressure in the delivery line will hold the diaphragm downward against the pressure of the diaphragm spring and it will remain in this position until the needle valve in the float chamber opens to admit more petrol.

5 Fuel pump - removal and refitting

1 Disconnect the fuel inlet and outlet pipes. The pipes may be held by unions or if of flexible fabric re-inforced type, they may be secured by spring clips or hose clips.
2 Unscrew and remove the two securing bolts from the pump flange and remove the pump with gasket from the crankcase.
3 Refitting is a reversal of removal but use a new gasket and make sure that the pump rocker arm is correctly positioned on top of the camshaft eccentric. Tighten the bolts to a torque of between 12 and 15 lb ft (1.66 to 1.07 kg m).

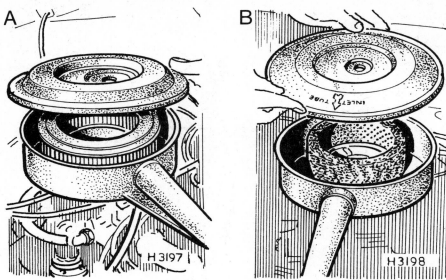

Fig. 3.1. 1100 cc and 1300 cc air cleaners

A Paper element   B Wire mesh

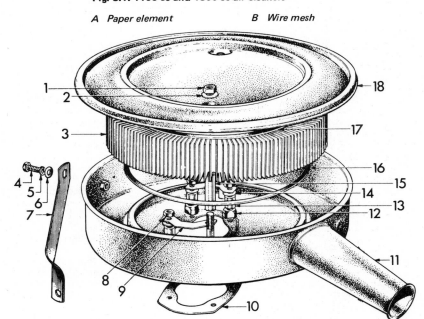

Fig. 3.2. GT/Sport air cleaner (early models) - later model has angular intake pipe - component parts

1	Nut	6	Washer	11	Air cleaner body	16	Sealing ring
2	Washer	7	Support bracket	12	Nut	17	Sealing ring
3	Paper element	8	Nut	13	Spacer	18	Cover
4	Bolt	9	Locking plate	14	Washer		
5	Locking washer	10	Gasket	15	Spacer		

6 Fuel pump - testing

1 To test the pump fitted in position on the crankcase, detach the fuel inlet pipe at the carburettor and disconnect the HT lead from the ignition coil.

2 Operate the starter switch when well defined spurts of petrol should be ejected from the disconnected end of the pipe.

3 If the pump is removed from the engine, place a finger over the inlet port and work the rocker arm several times. Remove the finger - a distinct suction noise should be heard.

4 Now place a finger over the outlet port, depress the rocker arm to its fullest extent and immerse the pump in paraffin. Watch for air bubbles which would indicate leakage at the pump flanges.

7 AC type fuel pump - dismantling, examination and reassembly

1 Unscrew the finger nut on top of the bowl and push the clamp aside. Lift off the glass cover.

2 Remove the sealing washer and the fine mesh filter gauze.

3 If the condition of the diaphragm is suspect or for any other reason it is wished to dismantle the pump fully, proceed as

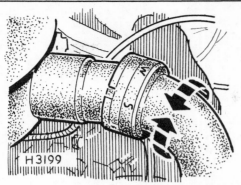

Fig. 3.3. Later type W (winter) S (summer) air cleaner intake pipe

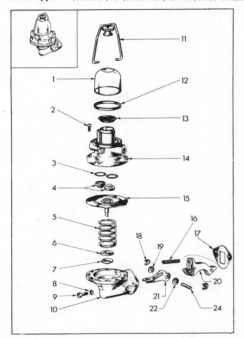

Fig. 3.5. AC fuel pump - component parts

1 Glass dome	13 Filter element
2 Screw	14 Upper pump body
3 Valve gasket	15 Diaphragm
4 Inlet and outlet valves	16 Actuating arm return spring
5 Diaphragm return spring	17 Gasket
6 Spring seat	18 Actuating arm swivel pin
7 Spring seat	retaining plates
8 Spring washer	19 Shim
9 Bolt	20 Primary actuating arm
10 Lower pump body	21 Secondary actuating arm
11 Dome retaining clamp	22 Shim
12 Dome to body sealing ring	24 Actuating arm swivel pin

follows. Mark the upper and lower flanges of the pump. Unscrew the five screws and spring washers which hold the two halves of the pump body together. Separate the two halves with great care, ensuring that the diaphragm does not stick to either of the two flanges.

4   Unscrew the screws which retain the valve plate and remove the plate and gasket together with the inlet and outlet valves. (Some later pumps have a simplified valve plate arrangement which is released by one screw. Still later models use staking to hold the valves in place.)

5   Press down and rotate the diaphragm a quarter of a turn (in either direction) to release the pull rod from the operating lever, and lift away the diaphragm and pull rod (which is securely fixed to the diaphragm and cannot be removed from it). Remove

Fig. 3.4. Metal cover fuel pump and filter screen

the diaphragm spring and the metal and fibre washer underneath it.

6   If it is necessary to dismantle the rocker arm assembly, remove the retaining circlips and washer from the rocker arm pivot rod and slide out the rod which will then free the rocker arm, operating rod, and anti-rattle spring.

7   Check the condition of the glass cover sealing washer. If it is perished or deformed, renew it. The diaphragm should be checked similarly and renewed if faulty. Clean the pump thoroughly and agitate the valves in paraffin to clean them out. This will also improve the contact between the valve seat and the valve. It is unlikely that the pump body will be damaged, but check for fractures and cracks.

8   To reassemble the pump, proceed as follows. Replace the rocker arm assembly comprising the operating link, rocker arm, anti-rattle spring and washer in their relative positions in the pump body. Align the holes in the operating link, rocker arm, and washers with the holes in the body and insert the pivot pin.

9   Refit the circlips to the grooves in each end of the pivot pin.

10 Earlier pumps used valves which had to be built up, while later versions used ready assembled valves which are merely dropped into place in the inlet and outlet ports. Ensure that the correct valve is dropped into each port. Stake the valves into place where this method of attachment is used.

11 Reassemble the earlier type of valve as follows. Position the delivery valve in place on its spring. Place the inlet valve in position in the pump body and then fit the spring. Place the small four legged inlet valve spring retainer over the spring with the legs positioned towards the spring.

12 Place the valve retaining gasket in position, replace the plate, and tighten down the three securing screws (or single screw in the case of some models). Check that the valves are working properly with a suitable piece of wire.

13 Position the fibre and steel washer in that order in the base of the pump and place the diaphragm spring over them.

14 Replace the diaphragm and pull rod assembly with the pull rod downward and the small tab on the diaphragm adjacent to the centre of the flange and rocker arm.

15 With the body of the pump held so that the rocker arm is facing away, press down the diaphragm, turning it a quarter of a turn to the left at the same time. This engages the slot on the pull rod with the operating lever. The small tab on the diaphragm should now be at an angle of 90° to the rocker arm and the diaphragm should be firmly located.

16 Move the rocker arm until the diaphragm is level with the body flanges and hold the arm in this position. Reassemble the two halves of the pump ensuring that the previously made marks on the flanges are in alignment.

17 Insert the five screws and lockwashers and tighten them down finger tight.

18 Move the rocker arm up and down several times to centralise the diaphragm, and then with the arm released, tighten the screws securely in a diagonal sequence.

19 Replace the gauze filter in position and fit a new glass dome

seal. Refit the glass dome to the pump body, pull over the clamp and tighten down the finger nut.

8 Fuel line filter - renewal

1   The filter is of disposable type and should be renewed at intervals of 18,000 miles (29,000 km) or earlier if symptoms of fuel starvation are experienced.
2   Removal is achieved by loosening the hose clips. When fitting the new filter, ensure that the flow directional arrow is correctly aligned.

9 Saloon fuel tank - removal and installation

1   The fuel tank is positioned in the right hand rear wing (Fig 3.10). Remove the filler cap and from under the car, disconnect the flexible fuel pipe from the metal pipe and allow the contents of the tank to drain into a suitable container.
2   Disconnect the battery and then open the boot lid. Pull off the wire from the fuel gauge sender unit; unclip and remove the vent pipe.
3   Undo the bolts which hold the fuel tank in place. Two inside the boot and two in the wing beneath the boot floor (Fig 3.11). Carefully note the positions of the spacers and washers.
4   Pull the filler neck of the tank out of the rubber grommet in the side of the car (or undo the filler pipe securing the clips, if fitted) and remove the tank from inside the boot of the car.
5   Replacement is quite straightforward and is a reversal of the removal sequence. Ensure that the grommet at the filler neck aperture in the body is in good condition and renew it if split or otherwise suspect. Make certain that the fuel pipe grommet is in place and ensure that the spacers and washers are correctly positioned. Finally check for leaks.

10 Estate car and van fuel tank - removal and installation

1   The fuel tank is located under the rear floor pan, and has to be removed from beneath the vehicle. Remove the filler cap and with a 4 ft (1.2 m) length of rubber tubing, syphon the petrol tank contents into a suitable container (no drain plug is fitted). Disconnect the battery.
2   Jack up the rear of the car and support securely on stands. Remove the spare wheel.
3   Loosen the clips from the filler connecting hose and slide the hose off the tank inlet pipe. Disconnect the fuel gauge sender unit wire, the fuel line, and the vent pipe from the fuel tank.
4   From under the car, undo and remove the ten bolts and washers which hold the tank in place. Lower the tank to the ground and remove it from under the car.
5   Replacement is a straightforward reversal of the removal sequence.

11 Fuel gauge sender unit - removal and refitting

1   On saloon models, the sender unit can be removed with the tank in position in the vehicle but with estate and van versions, the tank must first be removed as described in the preceding Section.
2   On saloons, disconnect the battery and place a container under the fuel tank. Disconnect the fuel pipe at the base of the tank and drain the fuel.
3   Disconnect the lead from the sender unit terminal.
4   From both types of fuel tank, unscrew the sender unit retaining ring using a suitably modified 'C' spanner or tapping the projections carefully with a hammer and cold chisel. Remove the sealing ring.
5   Refitting is a reversal of removal but always use a new sealing ring.

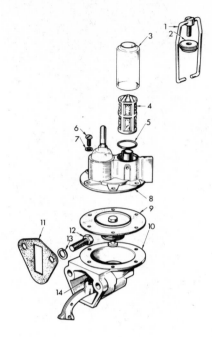

Fig. 3.6. Alternative glass dome fuel pump

1 Dome retaining clamp	8 Upper pump body
2 Finger nut	9 Diaphragm
3 Glass dome	10 Lower pump body
4 Filter element	11 Gasket
5 Dome to body retaining	12 Bolt
ring	13 Spring washer
6 Screw	14 Actuating arm return
7 Spring washer	spring

12 Fuel tank - cleaning and repair

1   With time it is likely that sediment will collect in the bottom of the fuel tank. Condensation, resulting in rust and other impurities, will usually be found in the fuel tank of any car more than three or four years old.
2   When the tank is removed, it should be swilled out using several changes of paraffin and finally rinsed out with clean petrol. Remember that the float mechanism is delicate and the tank should not be shaken violently or turned upside down quickly in case damage to the sender unit is incurred.
3   If the tank is leaking it should be renewed or taken to a specialist firm for repair. Do not attempt to solder, braze or weld it yourself, it can be lethal. A temporary repair may be made with fibreglass or similar material but a new tank should be fitted as quickly as possible.

13 Carburettors - general description

1   A single venturi downdraught carburettor is fitted to all vehicles except the Sport/GT/1300E versions which incorporate a Weber twin barrel carburettor.
2   The single venturi carburettor is basically the same unit whether fitted to an 1100 cc or 1300 cc engine and varies only in the sizes of internal jets and other components (refer to Specifications Section).
3   Vehicles fitted with automatic transmission use a carburettor which incorporates an automatic choke, heated by water from the cooling system.

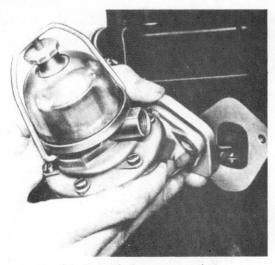

Fig. 3.7. Fitting fuel pump to crankcase

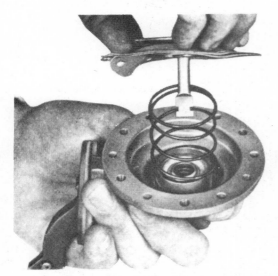

Fig. 3.8. Re-fitting fuel pump diaphragm

Fig. 3.9. Location of fuel line filter

14 Single venturi carburettor - removal and refitting

1   Remove the air cleaner and disconnect the vacuum and fuel inlet pipes from the carburettor.
2   Free the throttle shaft from the throttle lever by sliding back the securing clip and undo the screw which holds the end of the choke cable in place (Fig 3.13).
3   If an automatic choke is fitted drain about 5 pints from the cooling system and loosen the clips which hold the automatic choke water hoses to the carburettor. Pull off the hoses.
4   Undo the two nuts and spring washers which hold the carburettor in place and lift the carburettor off the inlet manifold.
5   Replacement is a straightforward reversal of the removal sequence but note the following points:

a)   Remove the old inlet manifold to carburettor gasket, clean the mating flanges and fit a new gasket in place.
b)   Ensure that the choke knob is in the off position before connecting the inner choke cable at the carburettor. After connection ensure that the choke opens and closes fully with a very slight amount of slack in the cable when the choke control is pushed right in.

15 Carburettors - dismantling and reassembly - general

1   After high mileages, the moving components of carburettors will wear and even jet calibrations will alter, solely due to the passage of fuel through them. When this occurs and is indicated by increased fuel consumption, poor idling and a general deterioration in performance, it is normally more economical to exchange the unit for a factory reconditioned one rather than attempt to rebuild it with new components.
2   Dismantling and reassembly of the carburettor should only be required to renew a faulty gasket or component or to clean out jets or the carburettor bowl. Never probe jets with wire to clear them, use air pressure from a tyre pump instead.
3   Before dismantling a carburettor obtain a repair kit which will contain all the necessary gaskets and washers for use on reassembly.

16 Single venturi carburettor - dismantling and reassembly

1   Undo the six screws and washers (33) which hold the carburettor top (35) to the main body (43) (Figs 3.14 and 3.15).
2   Lift off the top (35) from the main body (43) at the same time unlatching the choke control rod (12). Ensure that the gasket (39) comes off with the top cover (35). On cars fitted with an automatic choke, undo the screw which holds the fast idle cam and rod assembly to the lower body.
3   From the top cover pull out the float pivot pin (41) and remove the float (42). The needle valve and body (38) can then be unscrewed and the gasket (36) removed. Only on cars fitted with an automatic choke, undo the screw which holds the choke piston lever. Then take off the lever, the link, the choke control lever and finally the piston from the inner housing. Undo the two screws holding the inner housing to the carburettor, remove the housing and gasket, the choke housing lever, shaft assembly, choke control rod, an the Teflon bush.
4   On all models remove the accelerator pump discharge ball valve (14) and weight (13).
5   If it is wished to remove the choke plate (4) first cut the heads off the retaining pins (50) which hold the air cleaner retainer bracket in place (1). Next undo the grub screws (6) which hold the plate to the spindle (5) and pull out the plate.
6   Carefully smooth away the burrs from around the choke plate screw holes on the spindle and pull out the choke spindle at the same time sliding the choke control lever (2) and spring (3) off.
7   The main jet (40) can now be unscrewed from the top cover (35).
8   Undo the screw which holds the pump control lever (25) to

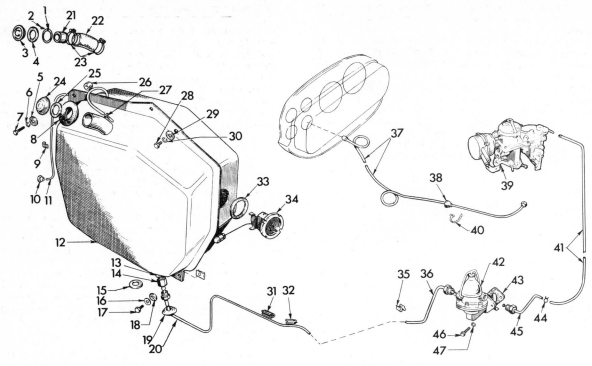

Fig. 3.10. Layout of car fuel system

1	Gasket	13	Washer	25	Gasket
2	Screw	14	'Female' unit	26	Spacer
3	Filler cap	15	Pad	27	Sealing plug
4	Gasket	16	Washer	28	Bolt
5	Washer	17	Bolt	29	Washer
6	Locking washer	18	Washer	30	Locking washer
7	Bolt	19	Grommet	31	Insulator
8	Grommet	20	Fuel pipe	32	Clip
9	Clip	21	Filler pipe	33	Gasket
10	Grommet	22	Filler hose	34	Fuel gauge sender unit
11	Breather tube	23	Clip	35	Clip
12	Tank body	24	Filler cap	36	Fuel pipe

37	Oil pressure tube
38	Grommet
39	Carburettor
40	Clip
41	Fuel piping
42	Fuel pump
43	Gasket
44	Clamp
45	Fuel piping
46	Bolt
47	Locking washer

the throttle spindle (20) and detach it from the pump actuating lever with spring and washer.

9 The four screws and split washers (31) which hold the accelerator pump cover (47) in place can now be undone and the cover, operating arm (49), diaphragm (46), and return spring (45) removed.

10 Undo the cheese head pivot screw (19) and remove the fast idle cam (17) and the return spring (16).

11 Undo the two grub screws (21) which hold the choke plate (22) in position on the spindle (20), and remove the plate.

12 Carefully file down any burrs round the grub screw holes on the spindle and slide the spindle out of the main body. Undo the idling mixture adjustment needle (27) and spring (26), and the throttle stop screw (24) and spring (23).

13 Reassembly commences by refitting the throttle stop screw (24) and spring (23), and the idling mixture adjustment needle (27) and spring (26). Screw in the latter so it just seats and then back off one turn.

14 Slide the choke spindle (5) into place on the top cover (35) after ensuring the spring (3) and choke control lever (2) are in position.

15 Refit the choke plate (4) so the small rectangular stamping on the plate faces upward and is adjacent to the spindle (5) when the plate is in the closed position. Tighten down the two grub screws (6) which hold the plate in place.

16 Refit the air cleaner retaining bracket (1) and tap in two new retaining pins.

17 Screw the main jet (40) into position and then replace the needle valve housing (38). Fit a new gasket on the top cover (35) and then refit the needle, conical end upward, to the valve housing.

18 Replace the float (42) securing it in position with the pin (41). Check the float and fuel level setting as described later in this Chapter.

19 Position the return spring (16) on the bearing abutment on the lower body (43), and refit the choke lever (17), retaining it in place by its pivot screw (19). **On automatic choke carburettors only** fit the piston, piston lever and link in the inner position to the inner housing. Refit the choke thermostat lever and then screw it into the inner housing. Next position the choke control rod in the choke lever and with the vacuum gasket in place, refit the inner housing with the two screws. Finally ensure that when the outer housing assembly is fitted to the inner housing the index marks align, the gasket is in place, and the three securing screws are tightened down evenly.

20 Carefully replace the accelerator pump discharge ball valve (14) and weight (13). Slide one end of the choke control lever into the pull down stop and the other end into the fast idle cam, and with a new gasket (39) positioned between the upper cover (35) and lower body (43) and with the choke plate closed fit the two halves together and retain with five of the six screws. Note that the sixth screw (A) holds the choke cable bracket in place.

21 Slide the throttle spindle (20) into the main body and refit

the throttle plate (22) so that the two recessed indentations in the plate are adjacent to the recesses of the screw heads when the throttle plate is closed. Ensure that the throttle plate is fully centralised.

22 Fit the accelerator pump diaphragm (46) to the pump cover (47), replace the return spring (45) larger diameter against the carburettor body and secure the assembly in place by means of the four screws and lockwashers (31).

23 The spring (30) and pushrod (28) are then connected to the accelerator pump lever (49) and the gooseneck end of the pushrod attached to the throttle arm. The arm is secured to the throttle spindle end with a screw and lockwasher.

24 This now completes the reassembly operations, but the fast idle setting, accelerator pump stroke, and choke plate pull down must be checked and adjusted as described in the following Sections.

17 Single venturi carburettor - float setting

1 Since the height of the float is important in the maintenance of a correct flow of fuel, the correct height is determined by measurement and by bending the tab which rests on the end of the needle valve. If the height of the float is incorrect there will either be fuel starvation symptoms or fuel will leak from the joint of the float chamber.

2 Remove the air cleaner as previously described.

3 Refer to Figs 3.14 and 3.15 and unscrew the choke cable clamp screw (7) and the six screws and washers (33) which hold the carburettor top cover (35) in position.

4 Remove the cover (35) taking care that the gasket (39) does not stick to the main carburettor body (43) and at the same time unlatch the choke link rod (12).

5 The float (42) can now be examined. Shake it to ensure that there is no fuel in it (metal type float only) and if it has been punctured discard immediately. Check too that the float arm is not bent or damaged.

6 To check the fuel level setting turn the cover (35) upside down so that the float closes the needle valve by its own weight. This corresponds to its true position in the float chamber when the needle valve is closed and no more fuel can enter the chamber.

7 Measure the distance from the normal base of the float to the mating surface of the gasket which should be between 1.12 and 1.14 inch (28.5 to 29.0 mm) as shown in Fig 3.23. If this measurement is not correct then bend the tab which rests on the fuel inlet needle valve until the correct measurement is obtained. Turn the cover the right way up and take the same measurement with the float in the fully open position. The measurement should now be between 1.38 and 1.40 inch (35.0 to 35.5 mm) as shown in Fig 3.24. Bend the other tab (the hinge tab) as required.

18 Single venturi carburettor - accelerator pump adjustment

1 Under normal conditions the accelerator pump requires no adjustment. If it is wished to check the accelerator pump action, first slacken the throttle stop screw so that the throttle plate is completely closed.

2 Press in the diaphragm plunger fully and check that there is then a 0.105 to 0.115 inch (2.67 to 2.92 mm) clearance on manual choke 1100 cc engines and 0.145 to 0.155 inch (3.68 to 3.93 mm) clearance on all 1300 cc engines between the operating lever and the plunger. The clearance is most easily checked by using a suitably sized drill (Fig 3.25).

3 To shorten the stroke open the gooseneck of the pump pushrod, and to length the stroke close the gooseneck.

4 If poor acceleration can be tolerated for maximum economy disconnect the operating lever to the accelerator pump entirely.

19 Single venturi carburettor - slow-running adjustment

1 Adjustment of the carburettor should only be carried out with the engine at normal operating temperature. Tuning by ear should be regarded as a temporary expedient only and one of two recommended methods (vacuum gauge or 'Colortune') used whenever possible.

2 To adjust the slow-running by ear, turn the throttle stop screw so that the engine is running at a fast idle. Turn the volume (mixture) control screw in or out until the engine runs evenly without 'hunting' or lumpiness. Reduce the idling speed and re-adjust the volume control screw.

3 To adjust the slow-running using a vacuum gauge, remove the blanking plug located just below the carburettor mounting flange on the inlet manifold. On vehicles fitted with a semi-closed crankcase ventilation system, remove the fume extraction hose from the manifold nozzle and substitute a tee-connector so that both the fume extraction hose and the vacuum pipe can be connected to the inlet manifold. On vehicles fitted with a semi-closed crankcase ventilation system and a brake vacuum servo unit, pull off the servo flexible hose from the inlet manifold tee-connector and substitute the vacuum gauge pipe. Set the throttle stop screw so that the engine is running at the recommended idling speed (see Specifications) and then turn the volume control screw so that the reading on the vacuum gauge is at maximum obtainable. Re-adjust both screws if necessary to reduce idling speed but maintain maximum vacuum reading.

4 To adjust the slow-running using 'Colortune', follow the manufacturer's instructions.

5 With any of these methods, satisfactory adjustment will not be obtained if there are any air leaks in the system. Check the security of the inlet manifold and carburettor flange gaskets, also the distributor vacuum pipe particularly the rubber or plastic connectors at each end for splits or looseness.

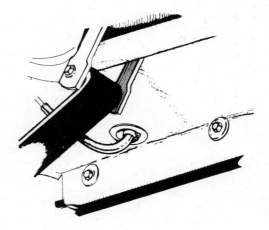

Fig. 3.11. Fuel tank support bolts

20 Single venturi carburettor - fast idling and choke adjustment

1 Remove the air cleaner and rotate the choke lever until it is against its stop.

2 Depress the choke plate and check the gap between the edge of the plate and the side of the carburettor air intake as shown in Fig 3.27. The gap is correct when it measures between 0.14 and 0.16 inch (3.6 to 4.1 mm) for the 1300 cc engine and 0.08 to 0.10 inch (2.0 to 2.5 mm) for the 1100 cc engine using the shank of a drill of the correct sixe as a measuring instrument.

3 If the gap is incorrect bend the tab on the choke spindle until the drill will just fit.

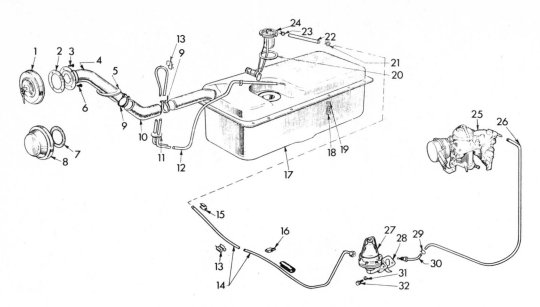

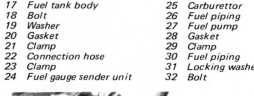

Fig. 3.12. Van and estate fuel system

1	Lockable filler cap	9	Clip	17	Fuel tank body	25	Carburettor
2	Gasket	10	Filler hose	18	Bolt	26	Fuel piping
3	Screw	11	Grommet	19	Washer	27	Fuel pump
4	Filler tube	12	Breather pipe	20	Gasket	28	Gasket
5	Grommet	13	Clip	21	Clamp	29	Clamp
6	Screw	14	Fuel piping	22	Connection hose	30	Fuel piping
7	Gasket	15	Clip	23	Clamp	31	Locking washer
8	Filler cap	16	Clip	24	Fuel gauge sender unit	32	Bolt

4 The fast idle check and any necessary adjustment should only be made after the choke has been checked and adjusted.
5 If the engine is cold, run it until it reaches its normal operating temperature and then allow it to idle naturally.
6 Hold the choke plate in the fully open vertical position and turn the choke lever until it is stopped by the choke linkage. With the choke lever in this position, the engine speed should rise to about 1100 rev/min as the fast idle cam will have opened the throttle very slightly.
7 Check how much radial movement is needed on the throttle lever to obtain this result and then stop the engine.
8 With a pair of mole grips clamp the throttle lever fully open on the stop portion of the casting boss and bend down the tab to decrease, or up to increase, the fast idle speed.
9 Remove the grips and check again if necessary repeating the operation until the fast idling is correct. It may also be necessary to adjust the slow idling speed and recheck the choke setting.

---

21 Single venturi carburettor - automatic choke adjustment

---

1 The water heated automatic choke fitted to models with automatic transmission is mounted on the side of the carburettor. The choke is actuated by a bi-metallic spring which rotates the choke spindle and causes the choke plate to open and close.
2 Refer to Fig 3.15 and remove the choke outer housing cover (14) and the bi-metallic spring (15).
3 Hold the vacuum piston (10) in its fully depressed position and manually close the choke plate (3) until its movement is stopped by the linkage. At the same time, partially open the throttle as necessary to permit the fast idle tab to clear the cam (29). The bottom of the choke plate should now be between 0.08 and 0.10 inch (2.0 to 2.5 mm) for the 1100 cc engine and 0.13 and 0.15 inch (3.3 to 3.8 mm) for the 1300 cc engine from

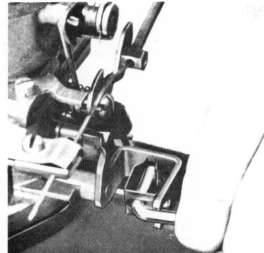

Fig. 3.13. Method of fitting throttle shaft to throttle lever

the carburettor body. Check the gap with a drill of appropriate size and if adjustment is required, bend the extension of the choke thermostat lever (the portion that abuts the vacuum piston lever).
4 Check the fast idle setting only after the choke has been checked and adjusted. Hold the choke plate in the fully closed position and observe if the fast idle tab on the throttle lever is in the first or high speed step of the fast idle cam. If necessary bend the fast idle rod at its cranked portion to achieve this.
5 Refit the bi-metallic spring so that it engages in the centre

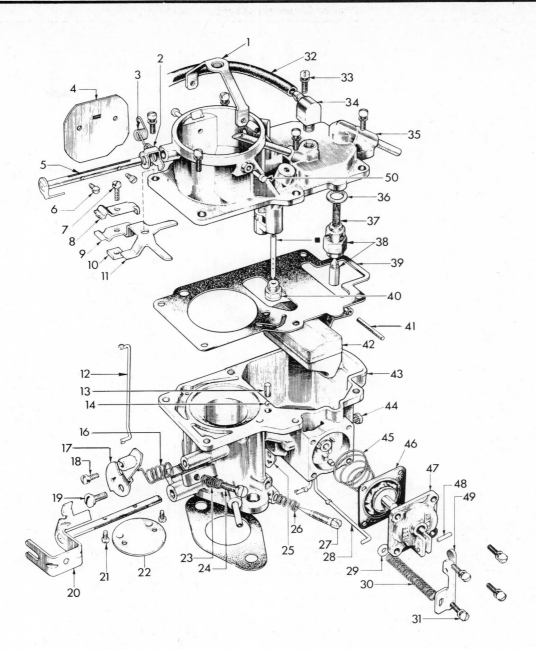

Fig. 3.14. Single venturi (manual choke) carburettor - component parts

1 Air cleaner retaining bracket
2 Choke control lever
3 Spring
4 Choke plate
5 Choke spindle
6 Plate to spindle retaining screws
7 Screw
8 Cable clamp - top
9 Cable clamp - bottom
10 Nut
11 Bracket
12 Choke control rod
13 Pump discharge ball weight

14 Discharge ball valve
16 Spring
17 Fast idle cam
18 Screw
19 Screw
20 Throttle lever & spindle assembly
21 Plate retaining screws
22 Throttle plate
23 Spring
24 Throttle stop screw
25 Pump control lever
26 Spring
27 Idling mixture adjustment needle

28 Accelerator pump link to lever rod
29 Washer
30 Spring
31 Screw
32 Overflow pipe
33 Screw
34 Adaptor
35 Carburettor top cover
36 Washer
37 Filter
38 Needle valve
39 Gasket

40 Main metering jet
41 Float pivot pin
42 Float
43 Carburettor body
44 Screw
45 Diaphragm return spring
46 Accelerator pump diaphragm
47 Accelerator pump cover
48 Actuating lever pivot pin
49 Actuating lever
50 Air cleaner bracket retaining pin

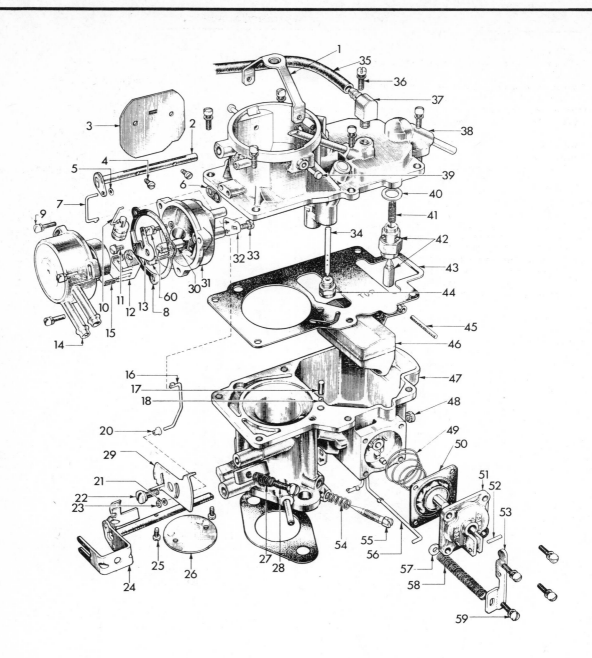

Fig. 3.15. Single venturi (automatic choke) carburettor - component parts

1 Air cleaner bracket	16 Fast idle rod	32 Bracket	47 Carburettor body
2 Choke spindle	17 Pump discharge ball weight	33 Screw	48 Screw
3 Choke plate	18 Pump discharge ball	34 Main metering jet tube	49 Diaphragm return spring
4 Screw	20 Bush	35 Overflow pipe	50 Diaphragm
5 Clip	21 Washer	36 Screw	51 Accelerator pump cover
6 Gasket	22 Screw	37 Adaptor	52 Lever pivot pin
7 Choke control rod	23 Shakeproof washer	38 Carburettor cover assembly	53 Accelerator pump actuating lever
8 Gasket	24 Throttle lever and spindle assembly	39 Air filter bracket retaining pin	54 Spring
9 Screw	25 Plate retaining screw	40 Washer	55 Idling mixture adjustment screw
10 Vacuum piston	26 Throttle plate	41 Filter	
11 Screw	27 Spring	42 Needle valve assembly	56 Pump to lever rod
12 Bi-metallic spring anchor	28 Throttle stop screw	43 Gasket	57 Spring retaining washer
13 Vacuum piston/spring link	29 Fast idle cam	44 Main metering jet	58 Spring
14 Automatic choke housing cover	30 Spindle	45 Float pivot spindle	59 Screw
15 Bi-metallic spring	31 Auto-choke housing	46 Float	60 Screw

slot of the retainer.

6 Refit the housing cover and align the marks before tightening the securing screws.

7 Connect a reliable tachometer to the engine and run the engine until normal operating temperature is reached.

8 Position the throttle lever fast idle tab on the first step of the cam and check the engine speed which should be:

1100 cc engines	1400 to 1600 rev/min
1300 cc engines	1850 to 2050 rev/min
1300 cc engines (cold climates)	2200 to 2400 rev/min

If necessary bend the fast idle tab to bring the engine speed within the range specified.

22 Weber twin barrel carburettor - removal and refitting

1 These operations are carried out in a similar manner to that described for single venturi carburettors (Section 14) but the following points must be observed.

2 The carburettor is secured to the inlet manifold by four nuts.

3 When refitting the air cleaner, first fit a rubber gasket to the top of the carburettor. Then fit the air cleaner body placing a rubber insulator round each mounting stud and a sleeve through each insulator. Place a flat washer and then double type tab washers over the studs and tighten down the securing nuts. Turn up the tab washers to lock the nuts in position.

23 Weber type 32-DFE carburettor - dismantling and reassembly

1 Refer to Fig 3.31 and unscrew the plug (4) and remove the fuel filter gauze (3). Free the choke actuating arm (22) at its lower end by removing the split pin (27) and nylon washer.

2 Undo the screws and spring washers (2) which hold the top cover (24) in place and lift off the cover and gasket (25).

3 Pull out the float pivot spindle (29) which retains the float (5) in place, lift out the needle valve (28) and unscrew the needle valve housing from the top cover. Remove the small washer (26).

4 On the side of the carburettor undo the four screws and washers (13) which hold the accelerator pump cover (14) in place. Remove the cover, diaphragm (15) and the diaphragm return spring (16).

5 If the accelerator pump lever is badly worn, drive out the pivot pin from the plain end. Note the setting (Fig 3.22).

6 Pull out the split pin (21) which holds the upper end of the choke actuating arm (22) to the choke spindle (20); undo the choke plate retaining grub screws (19); and pull out the choke plates (18). The choke spindle (20) can now be removed from the side of the carburettor.

7 Unscrew the primary (8) and secondary (6) main jets from the bottom of the float chamber.

8 With a screwdriver undo the accelerator pump discharge valve (31) from the middle of the carburettor and take off the pump discharge nozzle (33) and the gasket (34).

9 Directly behind the discharge nozzle orifice lie the two air correction jets (30) and their emulsion tubes (32). Unscrew the air correction jets (30), turn the carburettor upside down and shake out the emulsion tubes (32).

10 From either side of the carburettor (only one side is shown) unscrew the two idling jet holders (36) and the idling jets (39). From the bottom of the carburettor undo and remove the volume control screw (39) and the spring (40).

11 Take off the return spring from between the carburettor body and the secondary throttle lever.

12 Turn back the lock tab (65) on the primary throttle shaft (10) unscrew the nut (67) and pull off the throttle control lever (64), bush (63), secondary throttle control lever and the other components.

13 Then disconnect the fast idle connecting rod (47), and remove the bush, washers and fast idle lever.

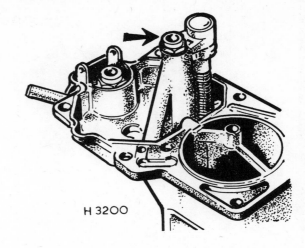

Fig. 3.16. Location of main jet (single venturi carburettor)

14 With all the levers, springs and bushes removed from the throttle spindles (9, 10) undo the grub screws (12) which hold the butterfly valves (11) to the spindles, remove the valves (11) and slide the spindles out of the carburettor.

15 Finally undo the retaining screw and take off the choke operating lever, spring and washer.

16 Reassembly commences with refitting the cleaned gauze filter (3) to the top cover (24) and securing the filter in place with the large brass plug (4).

17 Slide the choke spindle (20) into its bore in the top cover (24) so the lever on the spindle lies adjacent to the secondary choke. Replace the choke plates (18) ensuring that the smaller portion faces the rear and that when closed the plate chamfers are parallel to the sides of the air intake. Centralise and secure with grub screws (19). Peen over the ends of the screws to ensure no possibility of their working loose.

18 The dust seal (23) can now be fitted to the top cover flange and the choke rod (22) passed through the seal and the flange and connected by means of the split pin (21) to the choke spindle (20).

19 Fit the choke relay lever (53) and washer (54) to the spindle on the carburettor body and retain in place with the split pin (37).

20 Now assemble the fast idle rod (47) and the toggle spring to the choke control lever (42) and fit the return spring (41) around the carburettor body pivot boss, so the straight end rests in the location hole.

21 Place the choke control lever (42) on the pivot boss, and fix the toggle spring to the relay lever (53). Make sure that the relay lever toggle spring arm lies against the cam portion of the choke control lever (42) and that the fast idle rod lies between the two throttle spindle bosses. The screw (46) flat and spring washers which secure the lever (42) in place should now be refitted.

22 The end of the return spring should be hooked under the fast idle rod bracket.

23 Slide the primary (10) and secondary (9) throttle spindles into the carburettor, turning the spindles until the slots are parallel with the choke bore and the threaded holes face inward. Slide the butterfly valves into the slots so that the faces marked '780' are pointing outward with the numbers below the spindles. Ensure that the valves are centralised and then retain them in place with the grub screws (12). Peen over the threaded ends of the screws to ensure that they will not loosen.

24 Fit the throttle stop lever (44) to the secondary throttle spindle (9) so that the abutment rests against the stop. Replace the plain and spring washers (48, 49) and tighten the retaining nut (50).

Fig. 3.17. Fitting accelerator pump to a single venturi carburettor

Fig. 3.18. Fitting float to a single venturi type carburettor

Fig. 3.19. Removing spring retainer/lever from automatic choke of single venturi type carburettor

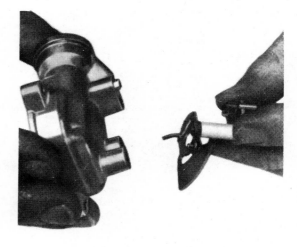

Fig. 3.20. Removing choke control lever from automatic choke of single venturi type carburettor

Fig. 3.21. Fitting automatic choke inner housing

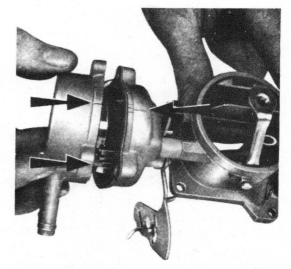

Fig. 3.22. Fitting automatic choke spring and water housing

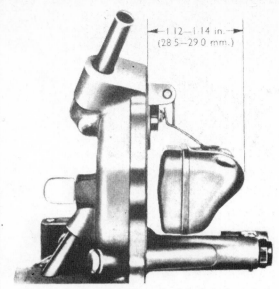

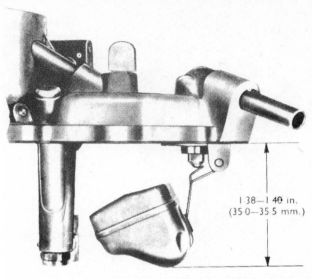

Fig. 3.23. Float setting (closed position) single venturi carburettor

Fig. 3.24. Float setting (open position) single venturi carburettor

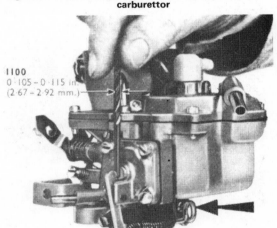

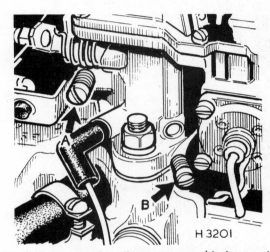

Fig. 3.25. Accelerator pump stroke adjustment (manual choke 1100 cc single venturi type carburettor)

Fig. 3.26. Slow-running adjustment screws (single venturi type carburettor)

A   Throttle speed   B   Volume (mixture) control

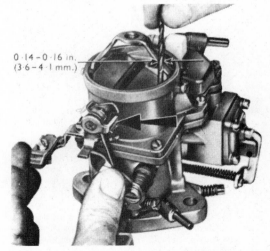

Fig. 3.27. Choke plate pull down adjustment (1300 cc single venturi type carburettor)

Fig. 3.28. Fast idling adjustment, single venturi type carburettor

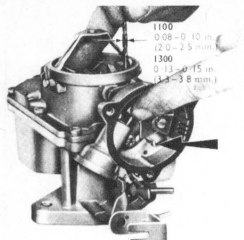

Fig. 3.29. Setting automatic choke (single venturi type carburettor)

1100
0·08 – 0·10 in.
(2·0 – 2·5 mm.)
1300
0·13 – 0·15 in.
(3·3 – 3·8 mm.)

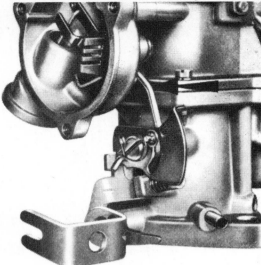

Fig. 3.30. Fast idle adjustment position (single venturi type carburettor)

25 Close the secondary throttle and then check with a feeler gauge the clearance between the carburettor barrel at its widest point and the butterfly valve. Adjust the stop to give a clearance of 0.0015 inch (0.038 mm).

26 Fit the slotted washer (55), return spring (56) and idling adjustment lever (58) to the primary throttle spindle (10), wrapping the hooked end of the spring around the lower arm of the idling adjustment lever, the other straight end resting on top of the flange between the two chokes.

27 Slide the spacer (60), fast idle lever (61), wave washer (62) and bush (63) onto the primary throttle spindle (10). Fit the fast idle rod (47) to the fast idle lever (61), securing the split pin (52).

28 The throttle relay lever (64) can now be fitted to the bush (63) so that the peg on the relay lever fits into the slot in the throttle stop lever (44).

29 Now fit the plain washer (66), throttle lever (68) and the tab washer (65) and tighten down the retaining nut (67). Turn up the tab on the lockwasher.

30 Fit the secondary idling jet (35) '45' to the secondary idling holder (36), and the primary idling jet '50' to its idling holder, and screw the holders one into each side of the float chamber.

31 The main primary (8) '125' and main secondary (6) '115' jets can now be screwed into their recesses in the float chamber.

32 Slide the emulsion tubes (32) into their wells and screw down the primary (30) '135' and secondary '160' air correction jets.

33 Fit a new accelerator pump discharge jet gasket (34) to the carburettor, position the nozzle (33) and secure with the discharge valve (31).

34 Slide the diaphragm return spring (16) into the recess in the carburettor and place the diaphragm (15) against the pump cover (14) so the plunger lies in the operating lever recess.

35 Fit the accelerator pump cover assembly (14) in place so that the operating lever engages the cam. Now insert and tighten down the four securing screws and washers (13) at the same time pulling the lever away from the cam to the limit of the diaphragm travel.

36 Fully screw in the volume control screw (39) and then unscrew it 1½ turns. Screw in a further half turn the throttle stop screw after it just contacts the throttle stop lever.

37 Fit a new gasket (26) to the threaded end of the needle valve housing (28) and screw the housing into the float chamber cover (24).

38 Place a new gasket (25) on the underside of the carburettor top cover, fit the needle valve to the housing, and then replace the float (5) and pivot spindle (29). Check the fuel level setting as described in the next Section.

38 Bring together the top cover and the main carburettor body at the same time connecting the relay lever (53) to the choke

plate operating rod (22). Evenly tighten down the securing screws with their spring washers. Reassembly is now complete.

24 Weber type 32-DFE carburettor - fuel level setting

1   The setting of the float is vitally important to the maintenance of a correct flow of fuel. Symptoms of mal-adjustment are fuel starvation or fuel leakage particularly from the area of the carburettor float chamber gasket.

2   First carefully remove the cover which contains the float and the fuel inlet needle valve. Hold the cover vertically so that the float hangs down, and it will be seen that a tab, hooked to the needle control valve is in light contact with the ball, and this should be perpendicular.

3   The distance between the float and the cover at this stage should be 7 mm as shown in Fig 3.33.

4   If this dimension is incorrect, bend the tabs carefully at the float end.

5   The operating stroke of the float is 8 mm so that when the needle valve is fully open, then the float to cover measurement should be 15 mm.

6   Always check the float setting whenever the fuel inlet needle valve has been removed or refitted or when a new inlet valve sealing gasket has been fitted.

25 Weber type 32-DFE carburettor - slow-running adjustment

1   The alternative methods of carrying out this adjustment are similar to those described in Section 19.

2   Refer to the Specifications Section for idling speeds and to Fig 3.35 for location of the throttle speed and volume control (mixture) screws.

26 Weber type 32-DFE carburettor - choke adjustment

1   If the choke is not working correctly, the choke plate pull down and the choke plate opening must be checked.

2   Close the choke and hold the choke lever against its stop. The choke plates should now be opened against the resistance of the toggle spring. The distance between the bottom edge of the plates and the side of the inside choke wall should be 5 mm checked with a correctly sized drill. If necessary bend the choke lever stop until the gap is correct.

3   To verify the choke plate opening from the fully closed position move the lever back 10 mm which can be most easily measured along the line of the choke cable. The distance between

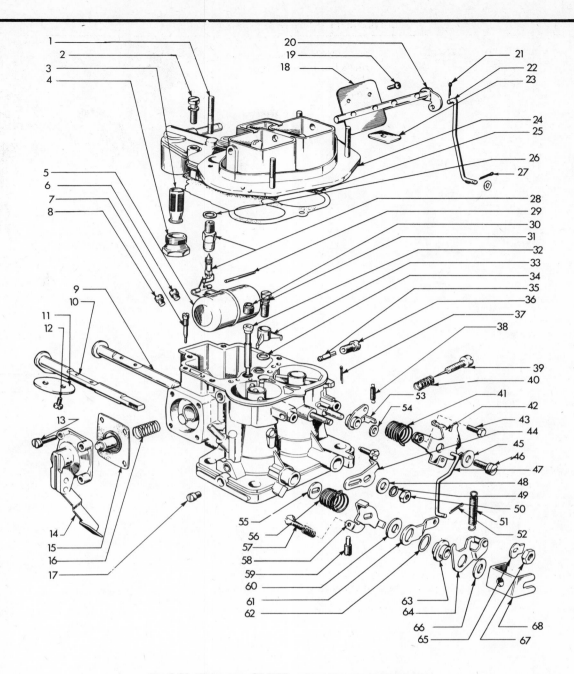

Fig. 3.31. Weber type 32 DFE carburettor - component parts

1 Stud	17 Plug	34 Gasket	52 Split pin
2 Screw	18 Choke spindle plate	35 Secondary idling jet	53 Choke relay lever
3 Gauze filter element	19 Retaining screw	36 Idling jet holder	54 Nylon washer
4 Plug	20 Choke spindle	37 Split pin	55 Slotted washer
5 Float	21 Split pin	38 Spring	56 Spring
6 Main secondary jet	22 Choke plate operating rod	39 Volume control screw	57 Idling adjustment lever screw
7 Accelerator pump blanking needle	23 Dust seal	40 Spring	58 Idling adjustment lever
8 Main primary jet	24 Carburettor top cover	41 Spring	59 Adjuster
9 Secondary throttle spindle	25 Gasket	42 Choke control lever	60 Spacer
10 Primary throttle spindle	26 Gasket	43 Bolt	61 Choke/throttle inter-connecting fast idle lever
11 Throttle plate butterfly valve	27 Split pin	44 Throttle stop lever	62 Washer (wave)
12 Grub screw	28 Needle valve	45 Washer	63 Bush
13 Screw	29 Float pivot spindle	46 Screw	64 Throttle relay lever
14 Accelerator pump lever	30 Starting air correction jet	47 Fast idle rod	65 Tab washer
15 Diaphragm	31 Accelerator pump discharge valve	48 Washer	66 Washer
16 Diaphragm return spring	32 Emulsion tubes	49 Spring washer	67 Nut
	33 Pump discharge nozzle	50 Nut	68 Throttle lever assembly
		51 Spring	

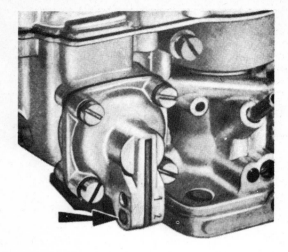

Fig. 3.32. Accelerator pump lever pivot pin (Weber carburettor) normal setting position 2

Fig. 3.33. Measuring float setting (closed) Weber 32DFE carburettor

Fig. 3.34. Measuring float stroke (fully extended) Weber 32DFE carburettor

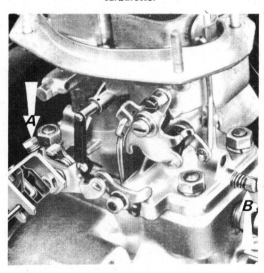

Fig. 3.35. Weber 32DFE carburettor adjustment screws

A Throttle stop   *B Volume (mixture) control*

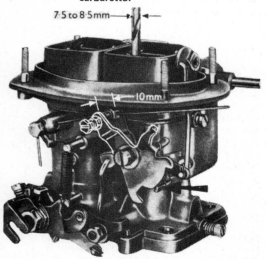

Fig. 3.36. Weber 32DFE carburettor choke plate adjustment

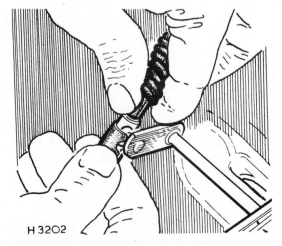

Fig. 3.37. Disconnecting accelerator inner cable from throttle shaft

the bottom edge of the plates and the inside choke wall should be 7.5 to 8.5 mm checked with a drill of this size.

4   If the gap is incorrect, bend the tag marked 'A' in Fig 3.36 in towards the cam to increase the opening and away from it to decrease it. Note: Bend the tag a very small amount at a time as a very small difference to the tag position will make a considerable difference to the position of the choke plates.

27   Weber type DGV-HA - servicing

This carburettor, fitted to GT/Sport/1300E models after September 1970, is serviced using the same operations as described for the type 32-DFE in this Chapter. Reference should be made to the Specifications Section for details of jet sizes and other internal components.

28   Accelerator cable - renewal

1   Disconnect the inner cable from the throttle shaft at the carburettor by sliding off the spring clip from the ball joint (Fig 3.37).
2   Unclip the outer cable retainer from the rocker cover bracket (LHD) or from the air cleaner cover (RHD).
3   Prise off the spring clip which retains the inner cable to the accelerator pedal rod.
4   Unclip the accelerator cable assembly from the point where it passes through the engine rear bulkhead and remove it.
5   Installation of the new cable is a reversal of removal but adjust the pedal and cable as described in the following Section.

29   Accelerator pedal and cable - adjustment

1   Peel back the floor covering and measure the distance between the metal surface of the floor pan and the upper surface of the pedal pad. This should be 4.5 inch (114.3 mm).
2   If necessary slacken the pedal rod return screw locknut and adjust the return stop so that with the accelerator pedal held in the specified position relative to the floor, there is a clearance of 0.015 inch (0.38 mm) between the return stop and the pedal rod, measured with a feeler gauge.
3   The accelerator cable should be detached from its rocker cover or air cleaner clip and allowed to take up its natural path. Re-clip the cable and then check the pedal to return stop clearance, adjusting if necessary.
4   Check the operation of the pedal at full throttle opening when the throttle plate(s) should be fully open, otherwise the adjustment must be re-checked.

30   Exhaust system and manifolds

1   The exhaust system may be of two or three section design, according to date of manufacture. 1100 cc models incorporate a single silencer box up to October 1973 whilst all other versions have a silencer plus an expansion box. Each system varies from model to model and it must be made quite plain when ordering a replacement exactly which model it is intended for.
2   Running down the left hand side of the car, early systems were suspended from brackets by means of O rings and clips, while later models use O rings only.
3   Before attempting to remove a badly rusted exhaust system, apply Plus-Gas or other fluid to all the joints, clamps and nuts and bolts. Raise the rear of the vehicle.
4   Disconnect the exhaust manifold to downpipe flange nuts and unhook the system support rings or straps.
5   Lower the complete system and withdraw it from under the vehicle.
6   Unscrew and remove the clamps at the pipe joints and pull them apart, using a twisting motion. If the joints are very tight, drive a blade up each of the slits in the outer socket joint connection to expand the socket and then pour some more freeing fluid into it.
7   Assembly and installation of the new system is a reversal of removal and dismantling but observe the following points:

locate the joint clamps finger tight only until the system is installed. Connect the support rings and the downpipe to the manifold and then check the alignment of the silencer and expansion boxes before finally tightening the clamp bolts.

31   Fuel system - fault finding

There are three main types of fault to which the fuel system is prone, and they may be summarised as follows:

a)   Lack of fuel at engine
b)   Weak mixture
c)   Rich mixture

32   Lack of fuel at engine

1   If it is not possible to start the engine, first positively check that there is fuel in the fuel tank, and then check the ignition system as detailed in Chapter 4. If the fault is not in the ignition system then disconnect the fuel inlet pipe from the carburettor and turn the engine over by the starter relay switch.
2   If petrol squirts from the end of the inlet pipe, reconnect the pipe and check that the fuel is getting to the float chamber. This is done by unscrewing the bolts from the top of the float chamber and lifting the cover just enough to see inside.
3   If fuel is there, then it is likely that there is a blockage in the starting jet, which should be removed and cleaned.
4   No fuel in the float chamber is caused either by a blockage in the pipe between the pump and float chamber or a sticking float chamber valve. Alternatively, on the twin choke GT carburettor the gauze filter at the top of the float chamber may be blocked. Remove the securing nut and check that the filter is clean. Washing in petrol will clean it.
5   If it is decided that it is the float chamber valve that is sticking, remove the fuel inlet pipe, and lift away the cover, complete with valve and floats.
6   Remove the valve spindle and valve and thoroughly wash them in petrol. Petrol gum may be present on the valve or valve spindle and this is usually the cause of a sticking valve. Replace the valve in the needle valve assembly, ensure that it is moving freely, and then reassemble the float chamber. It is important that the same washer is placed under the needle valve assembly as this determines the height of the floats and therefore the level of petrol in the chamber.
7   Reconnect the fuel pipe and refit the air cleaner.
8   If no petrol squirts from the end of the pipe leading to the carburettor, then disconnect the pipe leading to the inlet side of the fuel pump. If fuel runs out of the pipe, then there is a fault in the fuel pump and the pump should be checked as has already been detailed.
9   No fuel flowing from the tank when it is known that there is fuel in it indicates a blocked pipe line. The line to the tank should be blown out. It is unlikely that the fuel tank vent would become blocked, but this could be a reason for the reluctance of the fuel to flow. To test for this, blow into the tank down the filler orifice. There should be no build up of pressure in the fuel tank, as the excess pressure should be carried away down the vent pipe.

33   Weak mixture

1   If the fuel/air mixture is weak there are six main clues to this condition:

a)   The engine will be difficult to start and will need much use of the choke, stalling easily if the choke is pushed in.
b)   The engine will overheat easily.
c)   If the spark plugs are examined (as detailed in the Section on engine tuning), they will have a light grey/white deposit on the insulator nose.

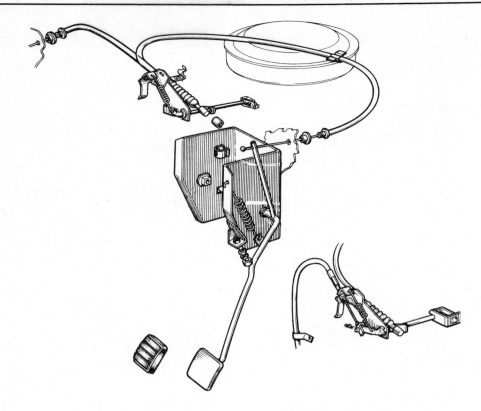

Fig. 3.38. Accelerator control components up to September 1970

d) The fuel consumption may be light.
e) There will be a noticeable lack of power.
f) During acceleration and on the over-run there will be a certain amount of spitting back through the carburettor.

2   As the carburettors are of the fixed jet type, these faults are invariably due to circumstances outside the carburettor. The only usual fault likely in the carburettor is that one or more of the jets may be partially blocked. If the car will not start easily but runs well at speed, then it is likely that the starting jet is blocked, whereas if the engine starts easily but will not rev then it is likely that the main jets are blocked.
3   If the level of petrol in the float chamber is low, this is usually due to a sticking valve or incorrectly set floats.
4   Air leaks either in the fuel lines, or in the induction system should also be checked for. Also check the distributor vacuum pipe connection as a leak in this is directly felt in the inlet manifold.
5   The fuel pump may be at fault as has already been detailed.

34 Rich mixture

1   If the fuel/air mixture is rich there are also six main clues to this condition:

a) If the spark plugs are examined they will be found to have a black sooty deposit on the insulator nose.
b) The fuel consumption will be heavy.
c) The exhaust will give off a heavy black smoke, especially when accelerating.
d) The interior deposits on the exhaust pipe will be dry, black and sooty (if they are wet, black and sooty, this indicates worn bores, and much oil being burnt).
e) There will be a noticeable lack of power.
f) There will be a certain amount of back-firing through the

exhaust system.

2   The faults in this case are usually in the carburettor and the most usual is that the level of petrol in the float chamber is too high. This is due either to dirt behind the needle valve, or a leaking float which will not close the valve properly, or a sticking needle.
3   With a very high mileage (or because someone has tried to clean the jets out with wire), it may be that the jets have become enlarged.
4   If the air correction jets are restricted in any way, the mixture will tend to become very rich.
5   Occasionally it is found that the choke control is sticking or has been maladjusted.
6   Again, on rare occasions, the fuel pump pressure may be excessive so forcing the needle valve open slightly until a higher level of petrol is reached in the float chamber.

35 Fuel gauge and sender unit - fault finding

1   If the fuel gauge fails to give a reading with the ignition on or reads 'Full' all the time, then a check must be made to see if the fault is in the gauge, sender unit, or wire in between.
2   Turn the ignition on and disconnect the wire from the fuel tank sender unit. Check that the fuel gauge needle is on the empty mark. To check if the fuel gauge is in order now earth the fuel tank sender unit wire. This should send the needle to the full mark.
3   If the fuel gauge is in order, check the wiring for leaks or loose connections. If none can be found, then the sender unit will be at fault and must be replaced.
4   Should both the fuel gauge and where fitted, the temperature gauge fail to work, or if they both give unusually high readings, then a check must be made of the instrument voltage regulator which is positioned behind the speedometer.

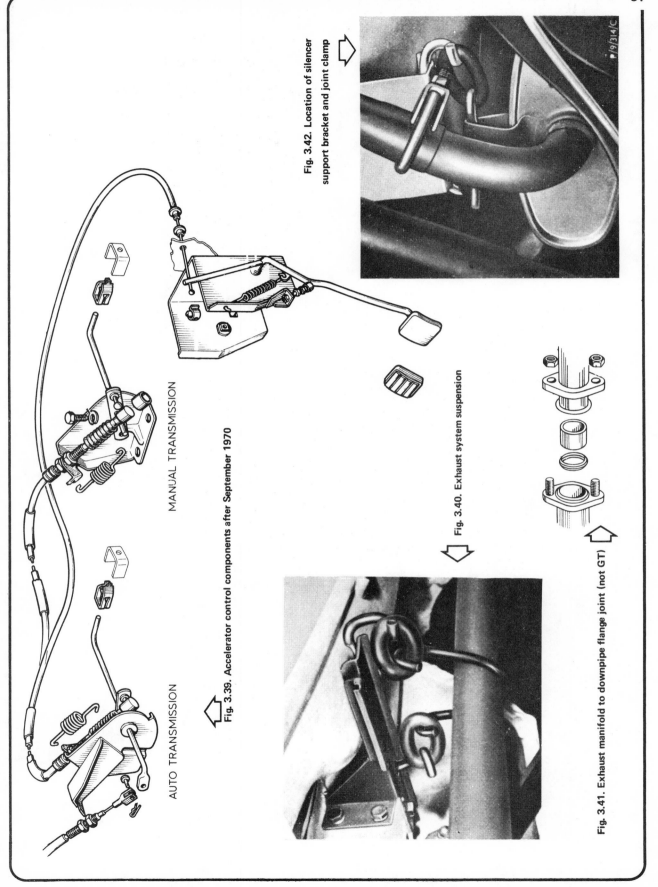

Fig. 3.42. Location of silencer support bracket and joint clamp

MANUAL TRANSMISSION

Fig. 3.39. Accelerator control components after September 1970

AUTO TRANSMISSION

Fig. 3.40. Exhaust system suspension

Fig. 3.41. Exhaust manifold to downpipe flange joint (not GT)

P/9/314/C

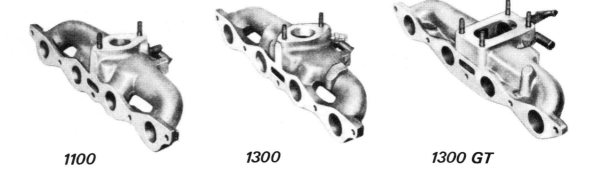

1100   *1300*   *1300 GT*

Fig. 3.43. Differing types of inlet manifold

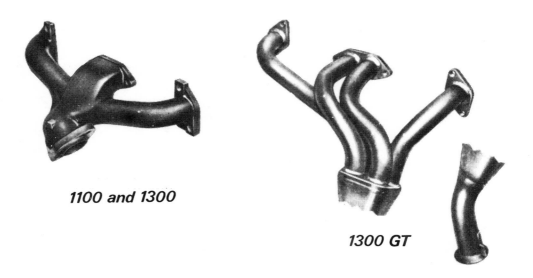

1100 and 1300

1300 GT

Fig. 3.44. Differing types of exhaust manifold

36 Fault finding chart

Symptom	Reason/s	Remedy
FUEL CONSUMPTION EXCESSIVE		
Carburation and ignition faults	Air cleaner choked and dirty giving rich mixture	Remove, clean and replace air cleaner.
	Fuel leaking from carburettor, fuel pumps, or fuel lines	Check for and eliminate all fuel leaks. Tighten fuel line union nuts.
	Float chamber flooding	Check and adjust float level.
	Generally worn carburettor	Remove, overhaul and replace.
	Distributor condenser faulty	Remove, and fit new unit.
	Balance weights or vacuum advance mechanism in distributor faulty	Remove, and overhaul distributor.
Incorrect adjustment	Carburettor incorrectly adjusted, mixture too rich	Tune and adjust carburettor.
	Idling speed too high	Adjust idling speed.
	Contact breaker gap incorrect	Check and reset gap.
	Valve clearances incorrect	Check rocker arm to valve stem clearances and adjust as necessary.
	Incorrectly set sparking plugs	Remove, clean, and regap.
	Tyres under-inflated	Check tyre pressures and inflate if necessary.
	Wrong sparking plugs fitted	Remove and replace with correct units.
	Brakes dragging	Check and adjust brakes.
INSUFFICIENT FUEL DELIVERY OR WEAK MIXTURE DUE TO AIR LEAKS		
Dirt in system	Petrol tank air vent restricted	Remove petrol tank and clean out air vent pipe.
	Partially clogged filters in pump and carburettor	Remove and clean filters.
	Dirt lodged in float chamber needle housing	Remove and clean out float chamber and needle valve assembly.
	Incorrectly seating valves in fuel pump	Remove, dismantle, and clean out fuel pump.
Fuel pump faults	Fuel pump diaphragm leaking or damaged	Remove, and overhaul fuel pump.
	Gasket in fuel pump damaged	Remove, and overhaul fuel pump.
	Fuel pump valves sticking due to petrol gumming	Remove, and thoroughly clean fuel pump.
Air leaks	Too little fuel in fuel tank. (Prevalent when climbing steep hills)	Refill fuel tank.
	Union joints on pipe connections loose	Tighten joints and check for air leaks.
	Split in fuel pipe on suction side of fuel pump	Examine, locate, and repair.
	Inlet manifold to block or inlet manifold to carburettor gasket leaking	Test by pouring oil along joints - bubbles indicate leak. Renew gasket as appropriate.

Chapter 4 Ignition system

Contents

Specifications

Spark plugs ... ...   Autolite A.G.22
   Size ... ...   14 mm
   Plug gap ... ...   0.023 in. (0.58 mm)

Coil
   Type ... ...   Oil filled low voltage
   Resistance at 20° C (68° F):
      Primary ... ...   1.25 to 1.5 ohms
      Secondary ... ...   5900 to 6990 ohms
   Output ... ...   30 k.v.

Distributor
   Contact points gap setting ... ...   0.025 in. (0.64 mm)
   Rotation of rotor ... ...   Anti-clockwise
   Automatic advance ... ...   Mechanical and vacuum
   Condenser capacity ... ...   0.21 to 0.25 microfarad
   Contact breaker spring tension ... ...   17 to 21 oz. (481.9 to 567.0 gms.)

Serial numbers:		Up to September 1970	September 1970 onward
1,100 and 1300 -	High C	C8AH-A	71-EB-12100-CA
1,100 and 1300 -	Low C	C8AH-B	71-EB-12100-FA
1300 G.T.		C8AH-C	71-EB-12100-JA

Identification colour:
   High C ... ...   Red
   Low C ... ...   Green
   G.T. ... ...   Blue

Initial advance timing:

Compression ratio	Fuel Octane No.	Star rating	1100 cc	Initial advance 1300 cc	GT
GT (cr - 9.2 : 1)	97	4	—	—	10°
HC (9 : 1)	97	4	6°	10°	—
	94	3	2°	6°	—
LC (8 : 1)	89	—	10°	10°	—
	86	—	10°	4°	—

Torque wrench setting
   Spark plugs ... ...   24 to 28 lb ft (3.32 to 3.87 kg m)

1 General description

In order that the engine can run correctly it is necessary for an electrical spark to ignite the fuel/air mixture in the combustion chamber at exactly the right moment in relation to engine speed and load. The ignition system is based on feeding low tension voltage from the battery to the coil where it is converted to high tension. voltage. The high tension voltage is powerful enough to jump the spark plug gap in the cylinders many times a second under high compression, providing that the system is in good condition and that all adjustments are correct.

The ignition system is divided into two circuits, the low tension circuit and the high tension circuit.

The low tension (sometimes known as the primary) circuit consists of the battery, lead to the control box, lead to the ignition switch, lead from the ignition switch to the low tension or primary coil windings (terminal SW), and the lead from the low tension coil windings (coil terminal CB) to the contact breaker points and condenser in the distributor.

The high tension circuit consists of the high tension or secondary coil windings, the heavy ignition lead from the centre of the coil to the centre of the distributor cap, the rotor arm, and the spark plug leads and spark plugs.

The system functions in the following manner. Low tension voltage is changed in the coil into high tension voltage by the opening and closing of the contact breaker points in the low tension circuit. High tension voltage is then fed via the carbon brush in the centre of the distributor cap to the rotor arm of the distributor cap, and each time it comes in line with one of the four metal segments in the cap, which are connected to the spark plug leads, the opening and closing of the contact breaker points causes the high tension voltage to build up, jump the gap from the rotor arm to the appropriate metal segment and so via the spark plug lead to the spark plug, where it finally jumps the spark plug gap before going to earth.

The ignition is advanced and retarded automatically, to ensure that the spark occurs at just the right instant for the particular load at the prevailing engine speed.

The ignition advance is controlled both mechanically and by a vacuum operated system. The mechanical governor mechanism comprises two weights, which move out from the distributor shaft as the engine speed rises due to centrifugal force. As they move outwards they rotate the cam relative to the distributor shaft, and so advance the spark. The weights are held in position by two light springs and it is the tension of the springs which is largely responsible for correct spark advancement.

The vacuum control consists of a diaphragm, one side of which is connected via a small bore tube to the carburettor, and the other side to the contact breaker plate. Depression in the inlet manifold and carburettor, which varies with engine speed and throttle opening, causes the diaphragm to move, so moving the contact breaker plate, and advancing or retarding the spark. A fine degree of control is achieved by a spring in the vacuum assembly.

2 Contact breaker - adjustment

1 To adjust the contact breaker points to the correct gap, first pull off the two clips securing the distributor cap to the distributor body, and lift away the cap. Clean the cap inside and out with a dry cloth. It is unlikely that the four segments will be badly burned or scored, but if they are the cap will have to be renewed.

2 Inspect the carbon brush contact located in the top of the cap - see that it is unbroken and stands proud of the plastic surface.

3 Check the contact spring on the top of the rotor arm. It must be clean and have adequate tension to ensure good contact.

4 Gently prise the contact breaker points open to examine the condition of their faces. If they are rough, pitted or dirty, it will be necessary to remove them for resurfacing, or for new points to be fitted.

2.5 Heel of contact breaker on highest point of cam

2.7 Loosening the contact breaker arm securing screw

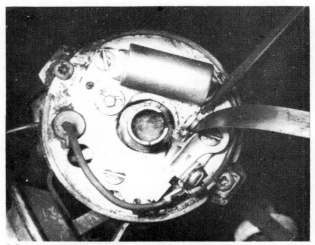

2.8 Adjusting the movable contact breaker arm

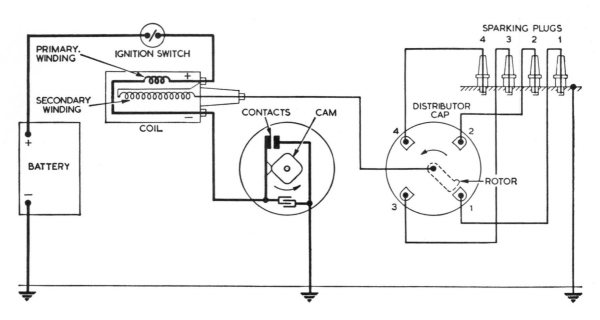

Fig. 4.1. Ignition circuit. Heavier line indicates LT (primary) circuit

5   Assuming the points are satisfactory, or that they have been cleaned and replaced, measure the gap between the points by turning the engine over until the heel of the breaker arm is on the highest point of the cam (photo).

6   An 0.025 inch (0.64 mm) feeler gauge should now just fit between the points (see Fig 4.2).

7   If the gap varies from this amount slacken the contact plate securing screw (photo).

8   Adjust the contact gap by inserting a screwdriver in the notched hole (photo) in the breaker plate. Turn clockwise to increase and anticlockwise to decrease the gap. When the gap is correct, tighten the securing screw and check the gap again.

9   Making sure the rotor is in position replace the distributor cap and clip the spring blade retainers into position.

3   Contact breaker points - removal and refitting

1   If, on inspection, the faces of the contacts are burned, pitted or worn, the contact breaker points must be removed for refacing or renewal.

2   Lift off the rotor arm by pulling it straight up from the spindle.

3   Slacken the self-tapping screw holding the condenser and low tension leads to the contact breaker and slide out the forked ends of the leads.

4   Remove the points by taking out the two retaining screws and lifting off the points assembly.

5   Dress the face of each contact squarely on an oilstone or a piece of fine emery cloth until all traces of 'pips' or 'craters' have been removed. After two or three times, regrinding of the points in this manner will reduce the thickness of the metal so much that a new contact set will have to be fitted. Before fitting the points, clean them with methylated spirit.

6   Refitting the points assembly is a reversal of removal but take care not to trap the wires between the points and the contact breaker plate.

7   Set the points gap as described in the preceding Section.

8   Refit the rotor arm and the distributor cap.

9   Whenever the contact breaker points are serviced or adjusted, the distributor should be lubricated. Smear the high points of the

Fig. 4.2. Adjusting the contact breaker points

cam with petroleum jelly and apply two or three drops of engine oil to the felt pad which is located at the top of the cam assembly. Squirt a few drops of engine oil through the distributor baseplate to lubricate the mechanical advance and retard assembly. Do not lubricate the distributor too liberally otherwise the points will become contaminated and misfiring will occur.

4   Condenser - removal, testing and refitting

1   The purpose of the condenser (capacitor) is to ensure that when the contact breaker points open, there is no sparking across them which would waste voltage and cause wear.

2   The condenser is fitted in parallel with the contact breaker points. If it develops a short circuit, it will cause ignition failure as the points will be prevented from interrupting the low tension circuit.

3 If the engine becomes very difficult to start or begins to miss after several miles running and the breaker points show signs of excessive burning, then the condition of the condenser must be suspect. A further test can be made by separating the points by hand with the ignition switched on. If this is accompanied by a flash it is indicative that the condenser has failed.

4 Without special test equipment the only sure way to diagnose condenser trouble is to replace a suspected unit with a new one and note if there is any improvement.

5 To remove the condenser from the distributor, take off the distributor cap and rotor arm. Slacken the self-tapping screw holding the condenser lead and low tension lead to the points, and slide out the fork on the condenser lead. Undo the condenser retaining screw and remove the condenser from the breaker plate.

6 To refit the condenser simply reverse the order of removal. Take care that the condenser lead is clear of the moving part of the points assembly.

5 Distributor - removal, dismantling and inspection

1 To remove the distributor from the engine, pull off the four leads from the spark plugs.

2 Disconnect the high tension and low tension leads from the distributor.

3 Pull off the rubber union holding the vacuum pipe to the distributor vacuum advance housing.

4 Remove the distributor body clamp bolt which holds the distributor clamp plate to the engine and lift out the distributor.

5 With the distributor on the bench, pull off the two spring clips retaining the cover and lift the cover off.

6 Pull the rotor arm off the distributor camshaft. Remove the points from the breaker plate as detailed in Section 3.

7 Undo the condenser retaining screw and take off the condenser.

8 Next prise off the small circlip from the vacuum unit pivot post.

9 Take out the two screws holding the breaker plate to the distributor body and lift away.

10 Take off the circlip flat washer and wave washer from the pivot post. Separate the two plates by bringing the holding down screw through the keyhole slot in the lower plate. Be careful not to lose the spring now left on the pivot post.

11 Pull the low tension wire and grommet from the lower plate.

12 Undo the two screws holding the vacuum unit to the body. Take off the unit.

13 To dismantle the vacuum unit unscrew the bolt on the end of the unit and withdraw the vacuum spring, stop and shims.

14 The mechanical advance is next removed but first make a careful note of the assembly, particularly which spring fits which post and the position of the advance springs. Then remove the advance springs.

15 Prise off the circlips from the governor weight pivot pins and take out the weights.

16 Dismantle the shaft by taking out the felt pad in the top of the spindle. Expand the exposed circlip and take it out.

17 Now mark which slot in the mechanical advance plate is occupied by the advance stop which stands up from the action plate, and lift off the cam spindle.

18 It is only necessary to remove the lower shaft and action plate if it is excessively worn. If this is the case, with a small punch, drive out the gear retaining pin and remove the gear with the two washers located above it.

19 Withdraw the shaft from the distributor body and take off the two washers from below the action plate. The distributor is now completely dismantled.

20 Check the points as described in Section 3. Check the distributor cap for signs of tracking, indicated by a thin black line between the segments. Renew the cap if any signs of tracking are found.

21 If the metal portion of the rotor arm is badly burned or loose, renew the arm. If only slightly burned, clean the end with

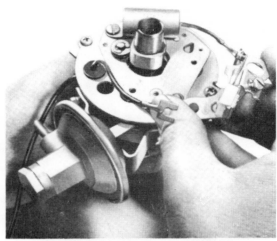

Fig. 4.3. Fitting contact breaker assembly

a fine file. Check that the contact spring has adequate pressure and the bearing surface is clean and in good condition.

22 Check that the carbon brush in the distributor cap is unbroken and stands proud of its holder.

23 Examine the fly weights and pivots for wear and the advance springs for slackness. They can best be checked by comparing with new parts. If they are slack they must be renewed.

24 Check the points assembly for fit on the breaker plate, and the cam follower for wear.

25 Examine the fit of the lower shaft in the distributor body. If this is excessively worn, it will be necessary to fit a new assembly.

6 Distributor - reassembly and installation

1 Reassembly is a reversal of dismantling but observe the following points:

2 Apply a film of engine oil to the shaft and mechanical advance assembly before fitting.

3 When fitting the lower shaft, first replace the thrust washers below the action plate before inserting into the distributor body. Next fit the wave washer and thrust washer at the lower end and replace the drive gear. Secure it with a new pin.

4 Assemble the upper and lower shaft with the advance stop in the correct slot (the one which was marked) in the mechanical advance plate.

5 After assembling the advance weights and springs check that they move freely without binding.

6 Before assembling the breaker plates, make sure that the three nylon bearing studs are properly located in their holes in the upper breaker plate, and that the small earth spring is fitted on the pivot post.

7 As you refit the upper breaker plate, pass the holding down spindle through the keyhole slot in the lower plate.

8 Hold the upper plate in position by refitting the wave washer, flat washer and large circlip.

9 When all is assembled, remember to set the contact breaker gap to 0.025 inch (0.64 mm).

10 If a new gear of shaft is being fitted, it is necessary to drill a new pin hole. Proceed this way.

11 Make a 0.015 inch (0.38 mm) thick forked shim to slide over the drive shaft (Fig 4.5).

12 Assemble the shaft, wave washer, thrust washer, shim and gear wheel in position in the distributor body.

13 Hold the assembly in a large clamp such as a vice or carpenter's clamp using only sufficient pressure to take up all end play.

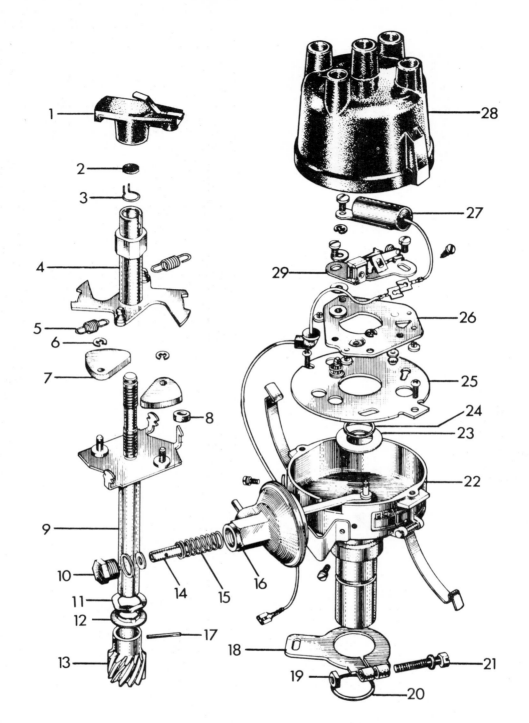

Fig. 4.4. The distributor - component parts

1	Rotor arm	8	Stop	15	Spring	23	Washer
2	Lubrication pad	9	Action plate/shaft	16	Vacuum capsule	24	Thrust washer
3	Circlip		assembly	17	Gear retaining pin	25	Baseplate
4	Cam assembly	10	Plug	18	Clamp plate	26	Moving plate
5	Counterweight spring	11	Wave washer	19	Nut	27	Condenser (capacitor)
6	Circlip	12	Thrust washer	20	'O' ring	28	Cap
7	Counterweight	13	Drive gear	21	Pinch bolt	29	Contact breaker assembly
		14	Stop	22	Distributor body		

14 There is a pilot hole in a new gear wheel for drilling the new hole. Set this pilot hole at 90° to the existing hole in an old shaft if the old shaft is being re-used. Drill an 1/8 inch (3.18 mm) hole through both gear and shaft.

15 Fit a new pin in the hole. Release the clamp and remove the shim. The shaft will now have the correct amount of clearance.

16 When fitting an existing gear wheel (still in good condition) to a new shaft, drill a new pin hole through the gear wheel at 90° to the existing hole. Secure with a new pin.

17 Refer to the Specifications Section and note the initial advance for the particular model being serviced.

18 By means of the crankshaft pulley centre bolt, turn the engine until No 1 piston is rising on the compression stroke. This can be checked by removing No 1 spark plug and feeling the compression with a finger placed over the plug hole. Alternatively, remove the rocker cover and observe when the inlet and exhaust valves for No 4 cylinder are in balance (inlet just opening, exhaust just closing when the engine is turned fractionally in either direction).

19 Continue turning the engine until the notch on the crankshaft pulley is opposite the appropriate mark on the timing cover.

20 Now hold the distributor above its crankcase opening so that the vacuum advance unit is pointing to the rear of the car and set the contact end of the rotor arm to align with No 2 inlet port. Insert the distributor; as its driveshaft meshes with the camshaft gear the rotor will rotate slightly and take up a position of approximately 90° to the centre line of the engine.

21 Fit the clamp plate retaining bolt to hold the assembly to the engine block and tighten it.

22 Slacken the distributor clamp pinch bolt.

23 Gently turn the distributor body until the contact breaker points are just opening when the rotor is pointing at the contact in the distributor cap which is connected to No 1 spark plug. A convenient way is to put a mark on the outside of the distributor body in line with the terminal cover, so that it shows when the cover is removed.

24 If this position cannot easily be reached, check that the drive gear has meshed on the correct tooth by lifting out the distributor once more. If necessary rotate the drive shaft one tooth and try again.

25 Tighten the distributor body clamp enough to hold the distributor, but do not overtighten.

7 Ignition timing

1 The basic procedure for timing the ignition is fully described in the preceding Section.

2 The precise point of opening of the contact breaker points can best be checked by connecting a test bulb between the distributor LT terminal and a good earth. Switch on the ignition and rotate the distributor until the lamp just lights; this indicates that the points are just opening.

3 If the ignition timing is to be checked by stroboscope, the manufacturer's instructions should be followed. Always remove the vacuum pipe from the distributor before testing by this method.

4 Since the ignition timing setting enables the firing point to be correctly related to the grade of fuel used, the fullest advantage of a change of grade from that recommended for the engine will only be attained by re-adjustment of the ignition setting.

8 Spark plugs and leads

1 The correct functioning of the spark plugs is vital for the correct running and efficiency of the engine.

2 At intervals of 6000 miles (9600 km) the plugs should be removed, examined, cleaned, and if worn excessively, renewed. The condition of the spark plugs will also tell much about the overall condition of the engine.

3 If the insulator nose of the spark plug is clean and white, with no deposits, this is indicative of a weak mixture, or too hot a

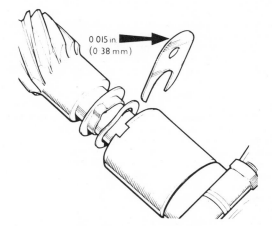

Fig. 4.5. Shaft end-float adjustment plate

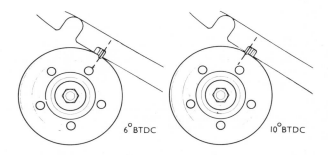

Fig. 4.6. Ignition timing marks showing static (initial) settings

plug. (A hot plug transfers heat away from the electrode slowly - a cold plug transfers it away quickly.)

4 The plugs fitted as standard are Autolite as listed in the Specifications at the head of this Chapter. If the tip and insulator nose is covered with hard black looking deposits, then this is indicative that the mixture is too rich. Should the plug be black and oily, then it is likely that the engine is fairly worn, as well as the mixture being too rich.

5 If the insulator nose is covered with light tan to greyish brown deposits, then the mixture is correct and it is likely that the engine is in good condition.

6 If there are any traces of long brown tapering stains on the outside of the white portion of the plug, then the plug will have to be renewed, as this shows that there is a faulty joint between the plug body and the insulator, and compression is being lost.

7 Plugs should be cleaned by a sand blasting machine, which will free them from carbon more thoroughly than cleaning by hand. The machine will also test the condition of the plugs under compression. Any plug that fails to spark at the recommended pressure should be renewed.

8 The spark plug gap is of considerable importance, as, if it is too large or too small, the size of the spark and its efficiency will be seriously impaired. The spark plug gap should be set to the figure given in the Specifications at the beginning of this Chapter.

9 To set it, measure the gap with a feeler gauge, and then bend open, or close, the **outer** plug electrode until the correct gap is achieved. The centre electrode should **never** be bent as this may crack the insulation and cause plug failure if nothing worse.

10 When replacing the plugs, remember to replace the leads from the distributor in the correct firing order, which is 1, 2, 4, 3 No 1 cylinder being the one nearest the radiator. No 1 lead from the distributor runs from the one o'clock position when looking down on the distributor cap. 2, 3 and 4 are anticlockwise from No 1 (Fig 4.1).

11 The plug leads require no routine attention other than being kept clean and wiped over regularly. At intervals of 6000 miles (9600 km), however, pull the leads off the plugs and distributor one at a time and make sure no water has found its way onto the connections. Remove any corrosion from the brass ends, wipe the collars on top of the distributor and refit the leads.

12 Every 10,000 to 12,000 miles (16,000 to 19,000 km) it is recommended that the spark plugs are renewed to maintain optimum engine performance.

13 Later vehicles are fitted with carbon cored HT leads. These should be removed from the spark plugs by gripping their crimped terminals. Provided the leads are not bent in a tight loop and compressed there is no reason why this type of lead should fail. A legend has arisen which blames this type of lead for all ignition faults and many owners replace them with the older copper cored type and install separate suppressors. In the majority of cases, it would be more profitable to establish the real cause of the trouble before going to the expense of new leads.

9 Ignition system - fault finding

By far the majority of breakdown and running troubles are caused by faults in the ignition system either in the low tension or high tension circuits.

10 Ignition system - fault symptoms

There are two main symptoms indicating ignition faults. Either the engine will not start or fire, or the engine is difficult to start and misfires. If it is a regular misfire, ie the engine is only running on two or three cylinders, the fault is almost sure to be in the secondary, or high tension, circuit. If the misfiring is intermittent, the fault could be in either the high or low tension circuits. If the car stops suddenly, or will not start at all, it is likely that the fault is in the low tension circuit. Loss of power and overheating, apart from faulty carburation settings, are normally due to faults in the distributor or incorrect ignition timing.

11 Fault diagnosis - engine fails to start

1 If the engine fails to start and the car was running normally when it was last used, first check there is fuel in the petrol tank. If the engine turns over normally on the starter motor and the battery is evidently well charged, then the fault may be in either the high or low tension circuits. First check the HT circuit. **Note**: If the battery is known to be fully charged; the ignition light comes on, and the starter motor fails to turn the engine, **check the tightness of the leads on the battery terminals** and the security of the earth lead to its **connection to the body**. It is quite common for the leads to have worked loose, even if they look and feel secure. If one of the battery terminal posts gets very hot when trying to work the starter motor, this is a sure indication of a faulty connection to that terminal.

2 One of the commonest reasons for bad starting is wet or damp spark plug leads and distributor. Remove the distributor cap. If condensation is visible internally dry the cap with a rag and wipe over the leads. Replace the cap.

3 If the engine still fails to start, check that current is reaching the plugs, by disconnecting each plug lead in turn at the spark plug end, and hold the end of the cable about 3/16 inch away from the cylinder block. Spin the engine on the starter motor.

4 Sparking between the end of the cable and the block should be fairly strong with a regular blue spark. (Hold the lead with rubber to avoid electric shocks.) If current is reaching the plugs, then remove them and clean and regap them to 0.025 inch. The engine should now start.

5 If there is no spark at the plug leads, take off the HT lead from the centre of the distributor cap and hold it to the block as before. Spin the engine on the starter once more. A rapid succession of blue sparks between the end of the lead and the block indicate that the coil is in order and that the distributor cap is cracked, the rotor arm faulty or the carbon brush in the top of the distributor cap is not making good contact with the spring on the rotor arm. Possibly the points are in bad condition. Clean and reset them.

6 If there are no sparks from the end of the lead from the coil, check the connections at the coil end of the lead. If it is in order, start checking the low tension circuit.

7 Use a 12 volt voltmeter on a 12 volt bulb and two lengths of wire. With the ignition switch on and the points open test between the low tension wire to the coil (it is marked SW or +) and earth. No reading indicates a break in the supply from the ignition switch. Check the connections at the switch to see if any are loose. Refit them and the engine should run. A reading shows a faulty coil or condenser or broken lead between the coil and the distributor.

8 Take the condenser wire off the points assembly and with the points open, test between the moving point and earth. If there now is a reading, then the fault is in the condenser. Fit a new one and the fault is cleared.

9 With no reading from the moving point to earth, take a reading between earth and the CB or (—) terminal of the coil. A reading here indicates a broken wire which must be renewed between the coil and distributor. No reading confirms that the coil has failed and must be renewed. Remember to connect the condenser wire to the points assembly. For these tests it is sufficient to separate the contact breaker points with a piece of paper.

12 Fault diagnosis - engine misfires

1 If the engine misfires regularly, run it at a fast idling speed. Pull off each of the plug caps in turn and listen to the note of the engine. Hold the plug cap in a dry cloth or with a rubber glove as additional protection against a shock from the HT supply.

2 No difference in engine running will be noticed when the lead from the defective circuit is removed. Removing the lead from one of the good cylinders will accentuate the misfire.

3 Remove the plug lead from the end of the defective plug and hold it about 3/16 inch away from the block. Restart the engine. If the sparking is fairly strong and regular, the fault must lie in the spark plug.

4 The plug may be loose, the insulation may be cracked, or the points may have burnt away, giving too wide a gap for the spark to jump. Worse still, one of the points may have broken off. Either renew the plug, or clean it, reset the gap, and then test it.

5 If there is no spark at the end of the plug lead, or if it is weak and intermittent, check the ignition lead from the distributor to the plug. If the insulation is cracked or perished, renew the lead. Check the connections at the distributor cap.

6 If there is still no spark, examine the distributor cap carefully for tracking. This can be recognised by a very thin black line running between two or more electrodes, or between an electrode and some other part of the distributor. These lines are paths which now conduct electricity across the cap, thus letting it run to earth. The only answer is a new distributor cap.

7 Apart from the ignition timing being incorrect, other causes of misfiring have already been dealt with under the section

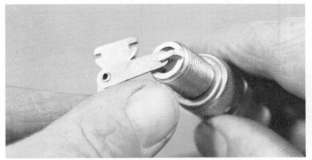

Measuring plug gap. A feeler gauge of the correct size (see ignition system specifications) should have a slight 'drag' when slid between the electrodes. Adjust gap if necessary

Adjusting plug gap. The plug gap is adjusted by bending the earth electrode inwards, or outwards, as necessary until the correct clearance is obtained. Note the use of the correct tool

Normal. Grey-brown deposits lightly coated core nose. Gap increasing by around 0.001 in (0.025 mm) per 1000 miles (1600 km). Plugs ideally suited to engine and engine in good condition

Carbon fouling. Dry, black, sooty deposits. Will cause weak spark and eventually misfire. Fault: over-rich fuel mixture. Check: carburettor mixture settings, float level and jet sizes; choke operation and cleanliness of air filter. Plugs can be re-used after cleaning

Oil fouling. Wet, oily deposits. Will cause weak spark and eventually misfire. Fault: worn bores/piston rings or valve guides; sometimes occurs (temporarily) during running-in period. Plugs can be re-used after thorough cleaning

Overheating. Electrodes have glazed appearance, core nose very white - few deposits. Fault: plug overheating. Check: plug value, ignition timing, fuel octane rating (too low) and fuel mixture (too weak). Discard plugs and cure fault immediately

Electrode damage. Electrodes burned away; core nose has burned, glazed appearance. Fault: initial pre-ignition. Check: as for 'Overheating' but may be more severe. Discard plugs and remedy fault before piston or valve damage occurs

Split core nose (may appear initially as a crack). Damage is self-evident, but cracks will only show after cleaning. Fault: pre-ignition or wrong gap-setting technique. Check: ignition timing, cooling system, fuel octane rating (too low) and fuel mixture (too weak). Discard plugs, rectify fault immediately

dealing with the failure of the engine to start. To recap, these are that:

a) The coil may be faulty giving an intermittent misfire
b) There may be a damaged wire or loose connection in the low tension circuit
c) The condenser may be short circuiting
d) There may be a mechanical fault in the distributor (broken driving spindle or contact breaker spring)

8   If the ignition timing is too far retarded, it should be noted that the engine will tend to overheat, and there will be a quite noticeable drop in power. If the engine is overheating and the power is down, and the ignition timing is correct, then the carburettor should be checked, as it is likely that this is where the fault lies.

Chapter 5 Clutch and actuating mechanism

Contents

Specifications

Type	Single dry plate, diaphragm spring	
Actuation	Cable	
Diameter - driven plate (friction disc):		
1100 cc	6.5 in. (165.1 mm)	
1300 cc and vans	7.5 in. (190.5 mm)	
Total friction lining area:		
1100 cc	34.57 in^2 (222.7 cm^2)	
1300 cc and G.T.	42.10 in.^{2} (271.3 cm^2)	
Release bearing		
Type	Sealed ball	
Release bearing identification:		
1100 cc (6½ in. driven plate)	Knurled outer edge	
1300 cc (7½ in. driven plate)	Plain outer edge	

Torque wrench setting	lb ft	kg m
Clutch pressure plate to flywheel bolts	12 to 15	1.66 to 2.07

1 General description

All 1100 cc saloons are fitted with a 6½ inch (165.1 mm) single dry plate diaphragm clutch. All Estate cars, vans and the 1300 cc saloons employ a 7½ inch (190.5 mm) clutch of identical design. The unit comprises a steel cover which is dowelled and bolted to the rear face of the flywheel and contains the pressure plate diaphragm spring and fulcrum rings.

The clutch disc is free to slide along the splined gearbox first motion shaft and is held in position between the flywheel and the pressure plate by the pressure of the pressure plate spring. Friction lining material is riveted to the clutch disc and it has a spring cushioned hub to absorb transmission shocks and to help ensure a smooth take-off.

The circular diaphragm spring is mounted on shouldered pins and held in place in the cover by two fulcrum rings. The spring is also held to the pressure plate by three spring steel clips which are riveted in position.

The clutch is actuated by a cable controlled by the clutch pedal. The clutch release mechanism consists of a release fork and bearing which are in permanent contact with the release fingers on the pressure plate. There should therefore never be any free play at the release fork. Wear of the friction material in the clutch is taken up by means of a cable adjuster on the rear engine bulkhead (early models) or on the clutch bellhousing (later models).

Depressing the clutch pedal actuates the clutch release arm by means of the cable.

The release arm pushes the release bearing forward to bear against the release fingers, so moving the centre of the diaphragm spring inward. The spring is sandwiched between two annular rings which act as fulcrum points. As the centre of the spring is pushed in the outside of the spring is pushed out, so moving the pressure plate backward and disengaging the pressure plate from the clutch disc.

When the clutch pedal is released, the diaphragm spring forces the pressure plate into contact with the high friction linings on the clutch disc and at the same time pushes the clutch disc a fraction of an inch forward on its splines so engaging the clutch disc with the flywheel. The clutch disc is now firmly sandwiched between the pressure plate and the flywheel so the drive is taken up.

2 Clutch - adjustment

1 Every 6000 miles (9600 km) the clutch pedal free movement must be checked and adjusted if necessary to compensate for wear in the friction linings.

2 Slacken the locknut on the threaded portion of the outer cable either at the engine bulkhead or the clutch bellhousing, according to type.

3 Have an assistant pull the clutch pedal fully back against its stop on the pedal bracket and then screw the outer cable adjusting nut in or out until there is a clearance of 9/64 inch (3.5 mm) between the face of the nut and its abutment. If this setting is correctly made there should be free movement at the

Fig. 5.1. Bulkhead located clutch cable locknut and adjusting nut — early vehicles

Fig. 5.2. Bellhousing located clutch cable adjusting nuts - later vehicles

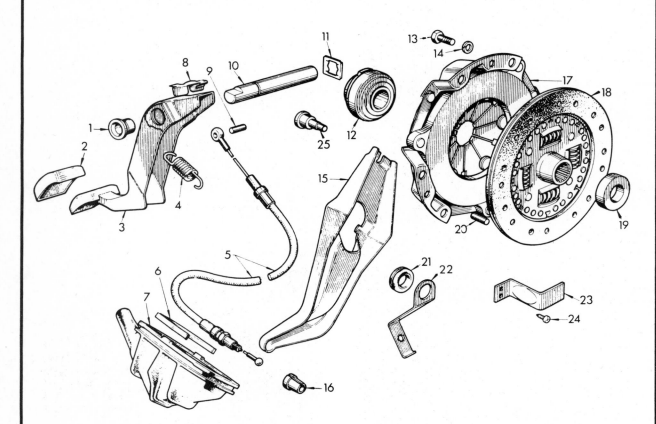

Fig. 5.3. Clutch mechanism - component parts

1	Bush	7	Dirt excluding gaiter	13	Bolt	19	Bearing
2	Pedal pad	8	Pedal shaft retaining clip	14	Locking washer	20	Dowel
3	Pedal	9	Pin	15	Clutch actuating arm	21	Grommet
4	Spring	10	Pedal pivot shaft	16	Cable socket	22	Bracket
5	Clutch actuating cable	11	Clip	17	Pressure plate	23	Bracket
6	Gaiter retaining clip	12	Clutch release bearing	18	Friction disc	24	Screw
						25	Release arm pivot post

clutch pedal of between ½ and ¾ inch (12.7 to 19.05 mm).

3 Clutch - removal

1 Remove the gearbox as described in the next Chapter.
2 Scribe a mating line from the clutch cover to the flywheel to ensure identical positioning on replacement and then remove the clutch assembly by unscrewing the six bolts holding the cover to the rear face of the flywheel. Unscrew the bolts diagonally half a turn at a time to prevent distortion of the cover flange.
3 With all the bolts and spring washers removed, lift the clutch assembly off the locating dowels. The driven plate may fall out at this stage as it is not attached to either the clutch cover assembly or the flywheel (photo).

4 Clutch - installation

1 It is important that no oil or grease gets onto the clutch disc friction linings, or the pressure plate and flywheel faces. It is advisable to replace the clutch with clean hands and to wipe down the pressure plate and flywheel faces with a clean, dry rag before assembly begins.
2 Place the clutch disc against the flywheel with the longer end of the splined hub facing toward the flywheel.
3 Locate the clutch cover/pressure plate assembly on the dowels with the mating marks in alignment.
4 Insert the six bolts and their spring washers finger tight so that the driven plate is just gripped but can be slid sideways.
5 The clutch driven plate must now be centralised so that when the gearbox is mated to the engine, the gearbox first motion shaft will pass smoothly through the splined hub of the driven plate.
6 Centralising is best carried out using an old first motion shaft but a rod of equivalent diameter with a stepped end to engage in the spigot bush located in the centre of the flywheel will serve as a good substitute.
7 Insert the centralising tool and move it in all directions to centralise the driven plate. The tool should be easy to withdraw without any side pressure.
8 Tighten the clutch cover to flywheel bolts evenly in diagonal sequence and finally tighten to a torque of between 12 and 15 lb ft (1.66 to 2.07 kg m).
9 Refit the gearbox as described in the next Chapter.

5 Clutch assembly - servicing

1 It is recommended that the driven plate is exchanged for a factory reconditioned unit. Do not attempt to fit new friction linings yourself. This is seldom satisfactory and the small saving in cost is not worthwhile.
2 The pressure plate assembly should also be renewed on an exchange basis as if dismantled, it requires the use of jigs and considerable skill to set up.
3 If the driven plate is being renewed, always renew the release bearing at the same time to avoid later dismantling (see Section 7).
4 The driven plate should be renewed if the friction linings have worn down to, or almost down to, the rivets. If the linings are oil stained, renew the friction plate and establish and rectify the cause which will almost certainly be the gearbox front oil seal or the crankshaft rear oil seal having failed.
5 Also check that the clutch pilot bearing in the centre of the flywheel is serviceable. Further information on this will be found under 'Flywheel - examination and renovation' in Chapter 1, Section 38.

6 Clutch cable - renewal

1 Slacken the locknut on the threaded portion of the outer cable. This is located either at the engine rear bulkhead or the

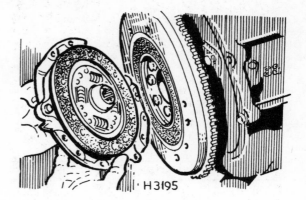

3.3 Removing clutch pressure plate assembly and driven plate (friction disc)

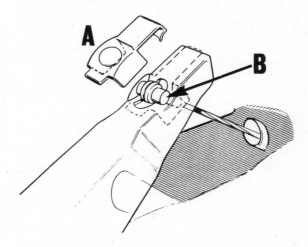

Fig. 5.4. Attachment of clutch cable to operating pedal

A Clip   *B Pivot*

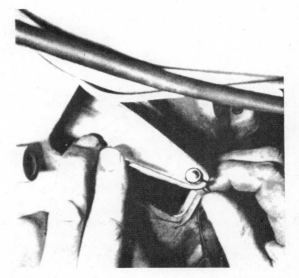

Fig. 5.5. Detaching clutch inner cable from release arm

clutch bellhousing according to date of manufacture.

2   Unscrew the adjusting nut so that the clutch inner cable becomes quite slack.

3   Detach the clip (A), push out the pivot pin (B) and withdraw the cable into the engine compartment (Fig 5.4).

4   Peel back the dust excluding gaiter from the bellhousing aperture through which the release arm emerges and then detach the clutch cable from the release arm by passing the inner cable through the slot in the arm.

5   Fitting the new cable is a reversal of removal but grease the pivot pin before fitting and adjust the free movement as described in Section 2.

7   Release bearing - removal and refitting

1   Whenever the gearbox is withdrawn for servicing of the clutch to be carried out, the clutch release bearing, which is located within the bellhousing on the clutch release arm, should be renewed.

2   Detach the release arm dust excluding gaiter and withdraw the release arm and bearing assembly. Unhook the release bearing from the release arm.

3   Using a suitable piece of tube as a distance piece, press the bearing from its retaining hub.

4   To install the bearing, first locate the release arm within the clutch bellhousing and then fit the bearing to it. Make sure that the projecting tags of the release arm engage securely with the hooked ends of the release bearing and apply a smear of high melting point grease to the clutch release arm pivot post.

8   Clutch - faults

There are four main faults to which the clutch and release mechanism are prone. They may occur by themselves or in conjunction with any of the other faults. They are clutch squeal, slip, spin and judder.

9   Clutch squeal - diagnosis and cure

1   If, on taking up the drive or when changing gear, the clutch squeals, this is a sure indication of a badly worn clutch release bearing.

2   As well as regular wear due to normal use, wear of the clutch release bearing is much accentuated if the clutch is ridden, or held down for long periods in gear, with the engine running. To minimise wear of this component, the car should always be taken out of gear at traffic lights and for similar hold-ups.

3   The clutch release bearing is not an expensive item, but difficult to get at.

10   Clutch slip - diagnosis and cure

1   Clutch slip is a self-evident condition which occurs when the clutch friction plate is badly worn, oil or grease have got onto the flywheel or pressure plate faces, or the pressure plate itself is faulty.

2   The reason for clutch slip is that, due to one of the faults listed above, there is either insufficient pressure from the pressure plate, or insufficient friction from the friction plate to ensure solid drive.

3   If small amounts of oil get onto the clutch, they will be burnt off under the heat of clutch engagement and in the process, gradually darkening the linings. Excessive oil on the clutch will burn off leaving a carbon deposit which can cause quite bad slip, or fierceness, spin and judder.

4   If clutch slip is suspected, and confirmation of this condition is required, there are several tests which can be made.

5   With the engine in second or third gear and pulling lightly up a moderate incline, sudden depression of the accelerator pedal may cause the engine to increase its speed without any increase in road speed. Easing off on the accelerator will then give a

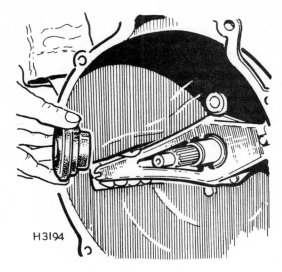

Fig. 5.6. Installing clutch release arm and bearing

definite drop in engine speed without the car slowing.

6   In extreme cases of clutch slip the engine will race under normal acceleration conditions.

11   Clutch spin - diagnosis and cure

1   Clutch spin is a condition which occurs when the release arm travel is excessive, there is an obstruction in the clutch, either on the primary gear splines, or in the operating lever itself, or the oil may have partially burnt off the clutch linings and have left a resinous deposit which is causing the clutch disc to stick to the pressure plate or flywheel.

2   The reason for clutch spin is that due to any, or a combination, of the faults just listed, the clutch pressure plate is not completely freeing from the centre plate even with the clutch pedal fully depressed.

3   If clutch spin is suspected, the condition can be confirmed by extreme difficulty in engaging first gear from rest, difficulty in changing gear, and very sudden take-up of the clutch drive at the fully depressed end of the clutch pedal travel as the clutch is released.

4   Check that the clutch cable is correctly adjusted and if in order, then the fault lies internally in the clutch. It will then be necessary to remove the clutch for examination and to check the gearbox input shaft.

12   Clutch judder - diagnosis and cure

1   Clutch judder is a self-evident condition which occurs when the gearbox or engine mountings are loose or too flexible, when there is oil on the faces of the clutch friction plate, or when the clutch pressure plate has been incorrectly adjusted during assembly.

2   The reason for clutch judder is that due to one of the faults just listed, the clutch pressure plate is not freeing smoothly from the friction disc, and is snatching.

3   Clutch judder normally occurs when the clutch pedal is released in first or reverse gears, and the whole car shudders as it moves backward or forward.

Chapter 6
Manual gearbox and automatic transmission

Contents

Specifications

Manual Gearbox

Number of gears	4 forward, 1 reverse
Type of gears	Helical constant mesh
Synchromesh	All forward gears

Gearbox ratios 1100 and 1300 cc

First	3.656 to 1
Second	2.185 to 1
Third	1.425 to 1
Top	1.000 to 1
Reverse	4.235 to 1

Overall ratios with 3.777 to 1 axle ratio:

First	13.809 to 1
Second	8.260 to 1
Third	5.382 to 1
Top	3.777 to 1
Reverse	15.995 to 1

Overall ratios with 3.900 to 1 axle ratio:

First	13.258 to 1
Second	8.522 to 1
Third	5.558 to 1
Top	3.900 to 1
Reverse	16.517 to 1

Overall ratios with 4.125 to 1 axle ratios:

First	15.081 to 1
Second	9.013 to 1
Third	5.878 to 1
Top	4.125 to 1
Reverse	17.469 to 1

Overall ratios with 4.444 to 1 axle ratio:

First	16.247 to 1
Second	9.710 to 1
Third	6.333 to 1
Top	4.444 to 1
Reverse	18.820 to 1

Gearbox ratios 1300 G.T.
First	3.337 to 1
Second	1.995 to 1
Third	1.418 to 1
Top	1.000 to 1
Reverse	3.869 to 1

Overall ratios with 3.777 to 1 axle ratio:
First	12.604 to 1
Second	7.535 to 1
Third	5.356 to 1
Top	3.777 to 1
Reverse	14.606 to 1

Overall ratios with 4.125 to 1 axle ratio:
First	13.765 to 1
Second	8.229 to 1
Third	5.849 to 1
Top	4.125 to 1
Reverse	15.951 to 1

Oil capacity ... ...   1½ pints (0.90 litres)

Selective circlips (availability for gearbox re-building)

Mainshaft bearing to extension housing:	Colour Code
0.0679 to 0.0689 in. (1.725 to 1.750 mm)	Magenta
0.0691 to 0.0701 in. (1.755 to 1.781 mm)	Violet
0.0703 to 0.0713 in. (1.786 to 1.811 mm)	Blue
0.0715 to 0.0724 in. (1.826 to 1.839 mm)	Plain
0.0725 to 0.0736 in. (1.842 to 1.869 mm)	Orange
0.0738 to 0.0748 in. (1.875 to 1.900 mm)	Red
0.0750 to 0.0760 in. (1.905 to 1.930 mm)	Green

1st/2nd gear synchroniser to mainshaft:	Colour Code
0.0602 to 0.0612 in. (1.529 to 1.554 mm)	Brown
0.0614 to 0.0624 in. (1.560 to 1.585 mm)	Black
0.0626 to 0.0636 in. (1.590 to 1.615 mm)	Blue
0.0638 to 0.0648 in. (1.621 to 1.646 mm)	Plain
0.0650 to 0.0659 in. (1.651 to 1.674 mm)	Copper

Front bearing to input shaft (small circlip)	Colour Code
0.0504 to 0.0524 in. (1.280 to 1.331 mm)	Plain
0.0528 to 0.0548 in. (1.341 to 1.392 mm)	Blue
0.0552 to 0.0571 in. (1.402 to 1.450 mm)	Orange
0.0575 to 0.0591 in. (1.461 to 1.501 mm)	Magenta

Mainshaft bearing to mainshaft:	Colour Code
0.059 to 0.061 in. (1.499 to 1.549 mm)	Plain
0.061 to 0.062 in. (1.549 to 1.575 mm)	Blue
0.062 to 0.064 in. (1.575 to 1.626 mm)	Violet
0.064 to 0.065 in. (1.626 to 1.651 mm)	Magenta
0.065 to 0.067 in. (1.651 to 1.702 mm)	Orange

The foregoing circlip selection tables should be read in conjunction with Fig. 6.1.

Automatic transmission
Type	3 speed epicyclic with 3 element hydro-kinetic torque converter (Borg-Warner type 35)
Gear ratios: - 1st	2.393 : 1
2nd	1.450 : 1
3rd	1.000 : 1
Reverse	2.094 : 1
Stall speed (1100 cc)	1700 to 1900 rev/min
(1300 cc)	1900 to 2000 rev/min
Operating temperature of fluid	212 to 236° F (100 to 115° C)
Fluid capacity	11¼ pints (6.39 litres)

Shift speeds with 4.444 : 1 axle ratio:	1 to 2	2 to 3	3 to 2	2 to 1
Light throttle	6 to 10 mph (10 to 16 km/hr)	8 to 12 mph (13 to 19 km/hr)	—	—
Full throttle	21 to 28 mph (33 to 45 km/hr)	33 to 43 mph (53 to 69 km/hr)	—	—

	1 to 2	2 to 3	3 to 2	2 to 1
Kickdown	26 to 34 mph (42 to 54 km/hr)	46 to 53 mph (74 to 85 km/hr)	39 to 50 mph (62 to 80 km/hr)	18 to 29 mph (29 to 45 km/hr)
Zero throttle	—	—	9 to 11 mph (14 to 17 km/hr)	5 to 8 mph (8 to 13 km/hr)
Shift speeds with 4.125 : 1 axle ratio:	**1 to 2**	**2 to 3**	**3 to 2**	**2 to 1**
Light throttle	6 to 11 mph (10 to 18 km/hr)	9 to 13 mph (14 to 21 km/hr)	—	—
Full throttle	22 to 30 mph (35 to 48 km/hr)	35 to 46 mph (56 to 74 km/hr)	—	—
Kickdown	28 to 36 mph (45 to 58 km/hr)	49 to 57 mph (78 to 91 km/hr)	42 to 53 mph (67 to 85 km/hr)	19 to 32 mph (30 to 51 km/hr)
Zero throttle	—	—	10 to 12 mph (16 to 19 km/hr)	6 to 8 mph (9 to 14 km/hr)

Torque wrench settings:	lb ft	kg m
Manual gearbox		
Extension housing to bearbox bolts	32 to 36	4.5 to 5.0
Top cover bolts	5 to 8	0.6 to 1.2
Clutch bellhousing to engine bolts	22 to 26	3.0 to 3.7
Automatic transmission		
Transmission case to converter housing bolts	8 to 13	1.11 to 1.80
Extension housing to transmission casing	30 to 55	4.15 to 7.60
Oil pan bolts	8 to 13	1.11 to 1.80
Starter inhibitor switch locknut	4 to 6	0.55 to 0.83
Drive plate to torque converter bolts	25 to 30	3.45 to 4.14

1 General description

The gearbox fitted to all models contains four constant mesh helically cut forward gears and one straight cut reverse gear. Synchromesh is fitted between 1st and 2nd, 2nd and 3rd, and 3rd and 4th. The iron bellhousing and gearbox casing are a combined casting. Attached to the rear of the gearbox casing is an aluminium alloy extension which supports the rear of the mainshaft and the gearchange shaft cum selector rod arm.

The gearbox is of a simple but clever design, using the minimum of components to facilitate speed of assembly; and the minimum of matched items to simplify fitting. Where close tolerances and limits are required, manufacturing tolerances are compensated for and excessive endfloat or backlash eliminated by fitting selective circlips. These are fitted in position 1, 4, 5 and 6 as shown in Fig 6.1. When overhauling the gearbox, always use new circlips, never replace circlips that have already been used.

The availability of circlips is shown in the Specifications at the beginning of this Chapter.

The gear selector mechanism is unusual in that the selector forks are free to slide on the one selector rod which also serves as the gearchange shaft. At the gearbox end of this rod lies the selector arm, which, depending on the position of the gearlever, places the appropriate selector fork in the position necessary for the synchroniser sleeve to engage with the dog teeth on the gear selected. Another unusual feature is that some of the bolts are metric sizes. In particular this applies to the top cover bolts and some of the bellhousing bolts. The reverse idler shaft thread is also metric (a bolt is only inserted here when it is wished to remove the shaft).

It is impossible to select two gears at once because of an interlock guard plate which pivots on the right hand side of the gearbox casing. The selector forks, when not in use, are positively held by the guard plate in their disengaged positions.

The GT Escort makes use of a 'close ratio' gearbox. Identical in design and layout to the ordinary gearbox, differences in the number of teeth on the main drive gear, third gear, and the corresponding gears on the laygear, means that these components are not interchangeable with those from an ordinary gearbox.

2 Gearbox - removal and installation

1 The gearbox can be removed in unit with the engine through the engine compartment as described in Chapter 1. Alternatively, the gearbox can be separated from the rear of the engine at the bellhousing and the gearbox lowered from under the car.

2 If a hoist or an inspection pit are not available, then run the back of the car up a pair of ramps or jack it up and fit stands. Jack up the front of the car and fit stands.

3 From inside the car, lift up the gearlever gaiter, and then remove the circlip from its groove in the gearlever to release the tension in the spring. The circlip is fitted adjacent to the smaller diameter of the spring (arrowed in photo).

4 Bend back the lock tab and with a pair of mole grips or similar across the flats undo the plastic dome nut and lift out the gearlever from the car.

5 With the bonnet opened, undo the clamp securing the exhaust manifold to the exhaust downpipe, and disconnect the battery by removing the earth (negative) lead.

6 When underneath the car, it will be necessary to disconnect the clutch cable from the clutch release arm. So that this can be done later, while still working in the engine compartment, loosen the clutch cable at the adjuster on the rear bulkhead or clutch

2.2 Location of gear lever spring circlip (arrowed)

bellhousing to make the cable as slack as possible.

7 At the engine undo the four bellhousing bolts accessible from inside the engine compartment and then move under the car.

8 Support the rear of the engine on a jack. Undo the nut which holds the starter motor lead to the starter motor and then undo the three bolts (two bolts on models fitted with a pre-engaged starter) which hold the starter motor in place. Take off the starter motor.

10 Free the speedometer cable from the gearbox extension housing by extracting the circlip which holds the cable in place.

11 Push away the rubber gaiter on the clutch release arm, push the clutch cable forward, and then slide it out of the slot in the end of the release arm.

12 Scratch a mating line across the propeller shaft and rear axle flanges, and then undo the four nuts and bolts which hold the flanges together. Drop the rear of the propeller shaft and pull the front off the gearbox mainshaft splines. Place a bowl under the rear of the extension housing to catch the oil which will now leak.

13 Undo the bolts which hold the flywheel dust cover in place and remove the cover. Undo the four bolts, two at each end, which hold the gearbox crossmember to the bodyshell.

14 Undo the two remaining bellhousing to engine bolts, lower the jack slightly and pull the gearbox off the rear of the engine. Take great care that the gearbox does not hang on the input shaft. It is preferable to have an assistant available to help with the removal of the gearbox as it is a heavy unit. Alternatively, if a trolley jack is available, this can be placed under the gearbox to take much of the weight, the jack and gearbox being rolled back together.

15 To separate the gearbox from the crossmember simply remove the central bolt.

16 Replacement commences by fitting the crossmember to the rubber mounting and securing them to the gearbox by the large central bolt and washer which should be tightened to 40 to 45 lb ft (4.5 to 5.2 kg m).

17 Check that the adaptor plate is in place on the rear of the engine and then fit the gearbox. A certain amount of movement and positioning may be necessary to get the input shaft splines fully into the splined hub in the middle of the clutch. When the gearbox is fully home, replace the two lower bellhousing bolts.

18 Then refit the four crossmember bolts and spring washers, refit the flywheel dust cover, and replace and reconnect the starter motor.

19 Reconnect the propeller shaft, gearbox end first, and ensure that the mating marks across the rear axle and rear propeller shaft flanges align.

20 Refit the speedometer cable to the extension housing and the clutch cable to the release arm. Remove the jack from the rear of the engine.

21 From inside the engine compartment refit the remaining bellhousing to engine backplate bolts, noting that the top two are 9/16 inch AF, while the others are 17 mm.

22 Adjust the clutch pedal free movement as described in the preceding Chapter.

23 Connect the exhaust downpipe to the exhaust manifold.

24 Reconnect the battery.

25 Refit the gearlever. On early models without a tab locking plate, smear Loctite over the threads on the plastic dome and over the threads in the extension housing, and allow to partly dry before screwing the dome nut down.

26 Fill the gearbox with a recommended lubricant.

3 Gearbox - dismantling

1 Undo and remove the eight bolts and spring washers which hold the gearbox cover in place (photo).

2 Lift the cover off and place on one side.

3 Undo the plug from the left hand side of the gearbox (photo) and remove the spring and plunger from the drilling. It may be necessary to shake the plunger out.

4 Carefully tap out the spring pin (photo) which holds the gear

3.1 Removing gearbox cover bolt

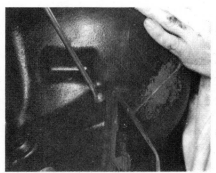
3.3 Removing selector plunger plug

3.4 Drifting out selector arm pin

3.5 Removing extension housing bolt

3.6 Prising out speedo. drive pinion cap

3.7 Withdrawing speedo. drive gear

3.8 Removing extension housing blanking plate

3.9 Removing gearchange/shaft selector rod

3.10 Removing selector forks and lever

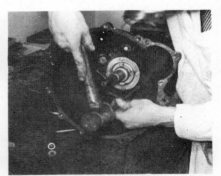

3.11 Tapping layshaft from gearbox

selector arm in place on the gearchange shaft.
5 Then undo the four bolts and spring washer holding the rear extension to the back of the gearbox casing (photo).
6 With the aid of a sharp screwdriver, carefully prise out the speedometer drive pinion cap (photo), taking great care not to distort the rim of the cap or damage the housing orifice.
7 Remove the speedometer drive pinion and its shaft from the extension (photo).
8 Knock out the large plug using a soft drift and a hammer at the rear of the remote control extension tube casing (photo).
9 The gearchange shaft/selector rod can now be removed rearwards. It may be necessary to tap it gently with a soft drift hammer (photo) to get it started.
10 The selector forks and the selector lever can then be lifted out from the gearbox (photo).
11 Tap the extension housing slightly rearward and then rotate it until the end of the layshaft fits into the cutaway in the extension housing flange. Drive the layshaft rearward from inside the bellhousing with a metal drift (photo).
12 The layshaft can then be pulled out from the rear of the gearbox casing (photo).
13 The extension complete with mainshaft can now be pulled away and out from the back of the gearbox (photo).
14 Inside the bellhousing unscrew the four bolts and spring washers (photo) which hold the input shaft bearing retainer in place and remove the retainer.
15 The input shaft complete with bearing can then be withdrawn from the front of the gearbox casing through the bellhousing (photo).
16 With the aid of a thin metal drift, tap out the pivot pin from the lug on the right hand side of the gearbox (photo) and remove the interlock plate.
17 Remove the laygear through the mainshaft bearing hole in the rear of the gearbox (photo).
18 Screw a suitably sized bolt into the metric thread cut in the centre of the reverse gear idler shaft and then with one of the

jaws of a large spanner resting under the head of the bolt (photo) lever the idler shaft out of the gearbox. Lift out the reverse idler gear.

4 Gearbox - examination and renovation

1 Clean all dismantled components in paraffin and examine them for wear, distortion, cracks or chipped teeth.
2 Examine the gearwheels for excessive wear and chipping of the teeth. Renew them as necessary. If the laygear endfloat is above the permitted tolerance of 0.020 inch (0.5080 mm) the thrust washers must be renewed. New thrust washers will almost certainly be required on any car that has completed more than 30,000 miles (48,000 km).
3 Examine the layshaft for signs of wear, where the laygear needle roller bearings bear. If a small ridge can be felt at either end of the shaft, it will be necessary to renew it.
4 The four synchroniser rings (4, 25, 28, 38) (Fig 6.5) are bound to be badly worn and it is a false economy not to renew them. New rings will improve the smoothness and speed of the gearchange considerably.
5 The needle roller bearing and cage (24) located between the nose of the mainshaft and the annulus in the rear of the input shaft is also liable to wear and should be renewed as a matter of course. Check that the nose of the mainshaft has not worn too.
6 Examine the condition of the two ball bearing assemblies, one on the input shaft (22) and one on the mainshaft (41). Check them for noisy operation, looseness between the inner and outer races, and for general wear. Normally they should be renewed on a gearbox that is being rebuilt.
7 If either of the synchroniser units (6 and 7, 31 and 32) are worn, it will be necessary to buy a complete assembly as the parts are not sold individually.
8 Examine the ends of the selector forks where they rub against the channels in the periphery of the synchroniser units. If possible

3.12 Extracting layshaft from rear of gearbox

3.13 Extracting mainshaft with extension housing

3.14 Removing input shaft bearing retainer

3.15 Withdrawing input shaft and bearing

3.16 Drifting out interlock plate pivot pin

3.17 Withdrawing laygear

compare the selector forks with new units to help determine the wear that has occurred. Renew them if worn.

9   If the bush bearing in the extension is badly worn it is best to take the extension to your local Ford garage to have the bearing pulled out and a new one fitted.

10   The rear oil seal should be renewed as a matter of course. Drive out the old seal with the aid of a drift or broad screwdriver.

11   The seal is surrounded by a metal ring and comes out fairly easily.

12   With a piece of wood to spread the load evenly, carefully tap a new seal into place, ensuring that it enters its bore in the extension squarely.

13   It is unlikely that any of the mainshaft bearing surfaces will be worn, but if there is any sign of scoring, picking up, or flats on the shaft, then it must be renewed.

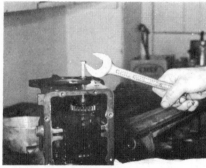

3.18 Levering idler shaft from gearbox

5 Input shaft - dismantling and reassembly

1   The only reasons for dismantling the input shaft are to fit a new ball bearing assembly or, if the input shaft is being renewed and the old bearing is in excellent condition, then the fitting of a new shaft to an old bearing.

2   With a pair of expanding circlip pliers, remove the circlip from the input shaft (photo).

3   With a soft headed hammer, gently tap the bearing forward and then remove it from the shaft (photo).

4   When fitting the new bearing, ensure that the groove cut in the outer periphery faces away from the gear. If the bearing is fitted the wrong way round, it will not be possible to fit the large circlip which retains the bearing against the gearbox casing.

5   Using the jaws of a vice as a support behind the bearing, tap the bearing squarely into place by hitting the rear of the input shaft with a plastic or hide faced hammer (photo).

6   Fit the widest circlip that will fit in the groove in the input shaft. (See circlip selection table - Section 1.)

6 Mainshaft - dismantling and reassembly

1   Before the mainshaft can be fully dismantled, it has to be removed from the extension housing. Mount the extension housing between two flat pieces of wood in the jaws of a vice.

2   With a pair of circlip pliers, remove the circlip (3) (Fig 6.5) (photo) which holds the 3rd and 4th gear synchroniser hub assembly in place.

3   Slide the synchroniser assembly (6, 7) complete with its sleeve forwards off the nose of the mainshaft and follow it with the 4rd gear (26) (photo). To get the gear started may call for a little prising between the gear and the raised shoulder on the mainshaft because of the raised shoulder round the periphery of the mainshaft.

4   With a pair of thin nosed pliers, squeeze together the ends of the circlip (40) in the extension housing (photo) and remove the

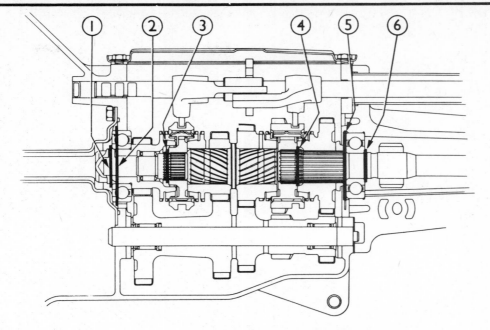

Fig. 6.1. Circlip locations in manual gearbox

1	Bearing to input shaft (small circlip)
2	Bearing to input shaft (outer circlip)
3	3rd/4th synchroniser circlip

4	1st/2nd synchroniser to mainshaft
5	Mainshaft bearing to extension housing
6	Mainshaft bearing to mainshaft

Numbers 1, 4, 5 and 6 are selective (see specifications)

Fig. 6.2. Location of speedometer drive circlip and crossmember (manual gearbox)

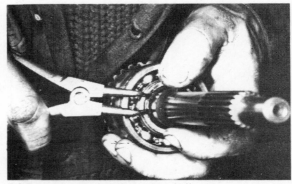

5.2 Extracting input shaft bearing circlip

5.3 Tapping bearing from input shaft

5.5 Re-fitting input shaft bearing

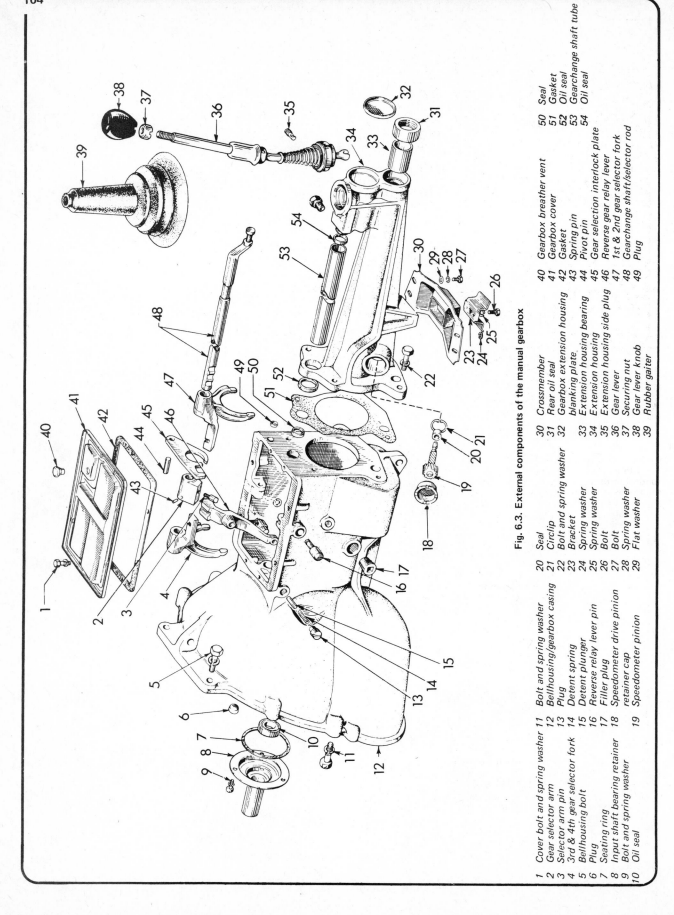

Fig. 6.3. External components of the manual gearbox

1	Cover bolt and spring washer
2	Gear selector arm
3	Selector arm pin
4	3rd & 4th gear selector fork
5	Bellhousing bolt
6	Plug
7	Seating ring
8	Input shaft bearing retainer
9	Bolt and spring washer
10	Oil seal
11	Bolt and spring washer
12	Bellhousing/gearbox casing
13	Plug
14	Detent spring
15	Detent plunger
16	Reverse relay lever pin
17	Filler plug
18	Speedometer drive pinion retainer cap
19	Speedometer pinion
20	Seal
21	Circlip
22	Bolt and spring washer
23	Bracket
24	Spring washer
25	Spring washer
26	Bolt
27	Bolt
28	Spring washer
29	Flat washer
30	Crossmember
31	Rear oil seal
32	Gearbox extension housing blanking plate
33	Extension housing bearing
34	Extension housing
35	Extension housing side plug
36	Gear lever
37	Securing nut
38	Gear lever knob
39	Rubber gaiter
40	Gearbox breather vent
41	Gearbox cover
42	Gasket
43	Spring pin
44	Pivot pin
45	Gear selection interlock plate
46	Reverse gear relay lever
47	1st & 2nd gear selector fork
48	Gearchange shaft/selector rod
49	Plug
50	Seal
51	Gasket
52	Oil seal
53	Gearchange shaft tube
54	Oil seal

6.2 Extracting 3rd/4th synchro. hub circlip

6.3 Removing 3rd/4th synchro. assembly and 3rd gear

6.4 Extracting mainshaft bearing to extension housing circlip

6.5 Tapping mainshaft from extension housing

6.7 Levering speedo. drive gear and bearing from mainshaft

6.9 Extracting mainshaft bearing circlip

circlip from its groove in the housing.

5 With a soft faced hammer, tap the rear end of the mainshaft (photo) until the large bearing (41) is clear of the housing.

6 The mainshaft can now be completely removed from the extension housing.

7 To remove the speedometer drive gear (43) and the bearing (41) can be very difficult as they are both a very tight interference fit on the mainshaft. Ideally they should be removed in a hydraulic press. They can be removed with the aid of long tyre levers (photo) or similar, but only if the bearing is going to be renewed as the levers have to rest against the side face of the bearing and this is almost sure to damage it.

8 The speedometer drive may be obstinate to remove right up to the last 1/16 inch of its shoulder. To enable the levers to continue leverage when the gap between the drive and the bearing becomes very large, fit a spanner adjacent to the bearing over the mainshaft to take up some of the gap.

9 With a pair of circlip pliers, remove the circlip (42) which holds the main bearing in place on the mainshaft (photo).

10 The bearing must then be removed from the shaft in exactly the same way as the speedometer drive (photo). Take the greatest care if using tyre levers or similar tools not to chip any of the teeth on 1st gear.

11 The spacer washer or oil slinger (37), 1st gear (36), and the synchroniser ring (38) can now be slid from the mainshaft (photo).

12 Remove the circlip (29) which holds the 1st and 2nd gear synchroniser assembly (31, 32) in place (photo).

13 Once again with the aid of screwdrivers or tyre levers, carefully lever the synchroniser assembly and second gear (27) off the mainshaft (photo). The mainshaft is now completely dismantled.

14 If a new synchroniser assembly is being fitted it is necessary to take it to pieces first to clean off all the preservative. These instructions are also applicable in instances where the outer sleeve has come off the hub accidentally during dismantling.

15 To dismantle an assembly for cleaning slide the synchroniser

sleeve off the splined hub and clean all the preservative from the blocker bars, spring rings, the hub itself and the sleeve.

16 Oil the components lightly and then fit the sleeve to the hub. Note the three slots in the hub and fit a blocker bar in each.

17 Fit the two spring rings one on the front and one on the rear face of the inside of the synchroniser sleeve under the blocker bars with the tagged end of each spring locating the U section of the same bar. One spring must be put on anticlockwise and one clockwise (Fig 6.6). When either side of the assembly is then viewed, the directional pattern of the two springs will appear to coincide.

18 Reassembly of the mainshaft commences by replacing 2nd gear (27) and a new synchroniser ring (28) on the longer portion of the mainshaft (photo). Ensure that the gearwheel teeth lie adjacent to the shoulder on the mainshaft.

19 Then slide the 1st and 2nd gear synchroniser sleeve and hub (31, 32) into place, with the straight cut gear teeth adjacent to 2nd gear. Follow on with the synchroniser ring (38) (photo).

20 Make certain that the cut-outs in the synchroniser rings (28, 38) (arrowed in photo) fit over the blocker bars in the synchroniser hub and that any marks on the mainshaft and hub are in line.

21 Then replace the circlip which holds the synchroniser hub in place on the mainshaft (photo). Circlips are available in a variety of thicknesses (see Specifications). It is essential that the thickest circlip that will fit the groove is used so that all endfloat is eliminated.

22 Refit 1st gear (36), cone side facing towards the 1st and 2nd gear synchroniser hub and follow with the spacer washer (oil slinger (37) so that the larger diameter on the spacer lies adjacent to the gearwheel (photo).

23 To drive on the mainshaft bearing (41) use a length of suitable diameter tubing so that the end of the tube just fits over the mainshaft and bears against the INNER race of the bearing (photo). Several heavy blows to the top end of the tube will drive the bearing fully home.

24 Select the thickest circlip (42) which will fit in the groove adjacent to the bearing and with the aid of a pair of circlip pliers, fit the circlip in place (photo).

6.10 Levering bearing from mainshaft

6.11 Sliding spacer/oil slinger, first gear and synchro. ring from mainshaft

6.12 Extracting 1st/2nd synchro. circlip

6.13 Levering 1st/2nd synchro. unit and 2nd gear from mainshaft

6.18 Fitting 2nd gear and synchro. ring to mainshaft

6.19 Fitting 1st/2nd synchro. baulk ring

6.20 Synchro. ring alignment (arrowed)

6.21 Fitting synchro hub circlip

6.22 Fitting 1st gear and spacer/oil slinger

25 Then place the large circlip (40) loosely behind the bearing. This large circlip holds the bearing in place in the extension housing. This is a selective circlip and once again it is essential that the largest circlip that will fit the groove in the housing is used. Circlips are available in a variety of thicknesses (see Specifications) and can be fitted to, or removed from, the mainshaft while it is in position in the extension housing.

26 Next fit the speedometer drive to the mainshaft using the same method described in paragraph 23 (photo).

27 Ensure that a new oil seal has been fitted to the rear of the extension. See Section 4.

28 Heat the front end of the extension in boiling water and then fit the mainshaft, tapping the front end of the shaft with a soft headed hammer (photo) until the bearing is fully home in its housing in the extension.

29 With a pair of thin nosed pliers, fit the large circlip into the groove in the extension (photo) so securing the mainshaft ball bearing.

30 Fit a new rubber seal in the groove round the gearchange shaft tube in the front of the extension (photo).

31 Then fit a new gasket in place on the extension front face (photo).

32 Slide 3rd gear (26) into place on the mainshaft so the helically cut teeth face 2nd gear and then fit a new synchroniser ring (photo).

33 Then fit the 3rd and 4th gear synchroniser assembly (6, 7) in place, ensuring that the cut-outs on the outside periphery of the synchroniser ring line up with the blocker bars in the synchroniser hub and sleeve (photo).

34 Fit the thickest circlip (3) that will fit the groove in front of the synchroniser assembly (photo).

35 Then slide the caged roller bearing (24) into place on the nose of the mainshaft (photo). The mainshaft is now fully assembled.

6.23 Driving mainshaft bearing into position

6.24 Installing mainshaft bearing circlip

6.26 Driving speedo drive gear onto mainshaft

6.28 Tapping mainshaft into extension housing

6.29 Fitting mainshaft bearing outer circlip to extension housing

6.30 Fitting gearchange shaft tube oil seal

6.31 Locating extension housing gasket

6.32 Fitting 3rd gear and synchroniser ring

6.33 Fitting 3rd/4th synchro. assembly

6.34 Fitting synchro. assembly circlip

6.35 Fitting needle roller bearing to mainshaft

7.2 Inserting thrust washer to laygear

7.5 Inserting laygear into gearbox

7.8 Correct location of input shaft bearing retainer oil hole

7.9 Tightening input shaft bearing retainer bolts

7.10 Inserting mainshaft assembly into gearbox

7.11 Aligning laygear and thrust washer

7.12 Installing layshaft

7.13 Tapping layshaft fully home

7.14 Tightening extension housing to gearbox bolts

7.15 Fitting interlock plate

7.16 Driving in interlock pivot pin

7.17 Fitting 1st/2nd selector fork

7.18 Fitting 3rd/4th selector fork

7 Gearbox - reassembly

1 Fit the reverse gear relay lever, the reverse idler gear and the shaft to the gearbox casing so that the bottom end of the lever seats in the groove on the forward end of the gearwheel.

2 Slide a thrust washer into either end of the laygear so that they abut the internal machined shoulders. Smear thick grease in the laygear orifice and fit the needle rollers one at a time until all are in place at each end. Note that some models are fitted with caged roller bearings which are simply slid into place as one unit at each end. Then fit a thrust washer (photo) to each end of the laygear orifice.

3 Smear the front end of the laygear with grease and fit the thrust washer.

4 Then fit a thrust washer to the other end of the laygear in similar fashion.

5 Insert the laygear (large gearwheel first) into the gearbox through the large hole in the rear of the gearbox casing (photo).

6 Carefully position the laygear so it lies in the bottom of the gearbox with the tabs on the thrust washers engaged in the cutaways.

7 Then fit the input shaft with the circlip already in place round the outside periphery of the bearing. Tap the bearing in until it is fully home and the circlip is up tight against the front face of the casing.

8 Then fit the input shaft bearing retainer and ensure that the oil hole in the nose of the retainer faces downward to the bottom of the bellhousing (photo).

9 Securely tighten up the four nuts and bolts which hold the input shaft bearing retainer in place (photo).

10 Ensure that the remaining synchroniser ring is in place over the nose of the input shaft gearwheel and the cut-outs align with the blocker bars and then carefully slide the mainshaft into the rear of the gearbox (photo).

11 Turn the extension so that the cut-out in the extension flange lines up with the hole for the layshaft. Bring the laygear into mesh with the mainshaft by carefully turning the gearbox upside down so that the laygear is at the top. Line up the laygear and thrust washer at the rear of the gearbox using a rod or screwdriver (photo). Take the greatest care not to displace any of the rollers. Repeat at the front of the gearbox.

12 Then fit the layshaft (flat end first) into the gearbox casing from the rear (photo).

13 Ensure that the lug on the rear of the layshaft is horizontal and then with the aid of a soft drift or hammer tap the layshaft fully home (photo). Ensure that the lug protrudes so that it can locate in the recess in the extension housing.

14 Pull back the extension housing half an inch, rotate it until the bolt holes are in the correct position and then push the extension housing fully home. Replace and tighten down to a torque of 34 lb ft (4.7 kg m) the bolts and spring washers which hold the extension housing to the end of the gearbox (photo).

15 Turn the gearbox the right way up and fit the interlock plate in position between the two lugs on the inside of the gearbox (photo).

16 Tap the pivot pin which holds the interlock plate into place (photo).

17 Fit the 1st and 2nd gear selector fork to the gearbox so that the prongs of the fork locate in the groove in the 1st and 2nd gear synchroniser sleeve (photo).

18 Then fit the 3rd and 4th gear selector fork so that the prongs of the fork locate in the groove of the 3rd and 4th gear synchroniser sleeve (photo).

19 The arm of the 3rd and 4th gear sleector fork (arrowed) should lie on top of the 1st and 2nd gear arm (photo).

20 Fit the gear selector arm in the hole in the interlock plate so that the selector arm pin (arrowed) rests in the V shaped cutaway of the interlock plate (photo).

21 Slide the gearchange shaft arm selector rod into the gearbox from the rear of the extension (photo).

22 First slide the shaft through the hole in the 1st and 2nd gear selector fork (photo).

23 Drop the interlock plate and selector arm into place and then slide the shaft through the holes in the gear selector arm and the 3rd and 4th gear selector fork. Ensure that the cut-outs on the forward end of the shaft face toward the left hand side of the gearbox.

24 When the hole in the gearchange shaft lines up with the small hole in the gear selector arm, drive in the spring pin which holds the arm to the shaft (photo).

25 Replace the detent plunger and spring in the drilling in the side of the gearbox (photo).

26 Then replace the plug (photo) and screw it in tightly.

27 Refit the gearlever to the extension housing. The slot in the base of the lever goes over the gearchange shaft (photo).

28 Screw down the domed nut (photo) and lock in place by turning down some of the tabs on the tab washer on the base of the dome.

29 Compress the conical spring and slide the circlip down the

8 Fault finding chart

Symptom	Reason/s	Remedy
WEAK OR INEFFECTIVE SYNCHROMESH		
General wear	Baulk ring synchromesh dogs worn, or damaged	Dismantle and overhaul gearbox. Fit new baulk ring synchromesh.
JUMPS OUT OF GEAR		
General wear or damage	Broken gearchange fork rod spring	Dismantle and renew spring..
	Gearbox coupling dogs badly worn	Dismantle gearbox. Fit new coupling dogs.
	Selector fork rod groove badly worn	Fit new selector fork rod.
	Selector fork rod securing screw and locknut loose	Remove side cover, tighten securing screw and locknut.
EXCESSIVE NOISE		
Lack of maintenance	Incorrect grade of oil in gearbox or oil level too low	Drain, refill, or top up gearbox with correct grade of oil.
	Bush or needle roller bearings worn or damaged	Dismantle and overhaul gearbox. Renew bearings.
	Gearteeth excessively worn or damaged	Dismantle, overhaul gearbox. Renew gear wheels.
	Laygear thrust washers worn allowing excessive end play	Dismantle and overhaul gearbox. Renew thrust washers.
EXCESSIVE DIFFICULTY IN ENGAGING GEAR		
Clutch not fully disengaging	Clutch pedal adjustment incorrect	Adjust clutch pedal correctly.

gearlever (photo) until it rests in its groove and locates the spring securely. Check that all the gears are working correctly by turning the input shaft with the gearlever, engaging each gear in turn.

30 Fit a new gasket to the gearbox cover, replace the cover and tighten down the eight bolts and spring washers which hold it in place (photo).

31 Replace the speedometer drive pinion and the retainer cup (photo). Smear the edges of the cup with jointing compound to ensure that no oil leaks develop.

32 Smear the edges of the extension plug with jointing compound and fit the blanking plate to the rear of the extension (photo). Reassembly of the gearbox is now complete.

7.19 Correct location of 3rd/4th selector fork arm

7.20 Correct location of gear selector arm pin

7.21 Inserting gearchange shaft arm selector rod

7.22 Selector rod passing through 1st/2nd selector fork

7.24 Driving in gearchange arm to shaft pin

7.25 Fitting detent plunger and spring

7.26 Screwing in detent plunger plug

7.27 Installing gearchange lever in extension housing

7.28 Tightening the gear lever domed nut

7.29 Fitting the gear lever spring circlip

7.30 Tightening top cover bolts

7.31 Fitting extension housing plug

7.32 Fitting extension housing rear blanking plate

H3217

Fig. 6.4. Gear selector plunger, spring and retaining plug

Automatic transmission

9 General description

Automatic transmission could be optionally specified on 1100 cc and 1300 cc cars. After September 1970 however, automatic transmission could only be specified on 1300 cc cars.

This form of transmission can also be specified on vans and estate vehicles but not on GT/Sport versions.

Normally, carburettors with automatic chokes are fitted with automatic transmission.

The unit comprises a three element hydrokinetic torque converter coupling, capable of torque multiplication at an infinitely variable ratio between 2 : 1 and 1 : 1. A torque/speed responsive and hydraulically operated epicyclic gearbox comprising a planetary gearset providing three forward ratios and one reverse ratio.

Due to the complexity of the automatic transmission unit, if performance is not up to standard, or overhaul is necessary, it is imperative that this be left to a main agent who will have the special equipment and knowledge for fault diagnosis and rectification.

The contents of the following Sections are therefore confined to supplying general information and any service information and instruction that can be used by the owner.

10 Maintenance

1 It is important that transmission fluid manufactured only to the correct specification such as Castrol TQF, is used. The capacity of the complete unit is 11.25 pints (6.4 litres). Drain and refill capacity will be less as the torque converter cannot be completely drained but this operation should not be necessary except for repairs to the internal mechanism.

2 Ensure that the exterior of the converter housing and gearbox is always kept free from dust or mud, otherwise overheating will occur.

3 Every 6000 miles (9600 km) check the fluid level as described in the Routine Maintenance Section of this manual.

4 If the unit has been drained, it is recommended that only new fluid is used. Fill up to the correct 'HIGH' level gradually refilling the unit, the exact amount will depend on how much was left in the converter after draining.

11 Removal and installation

1 Disconnect the lead from the battery negative terminal.

2 Detach the downshift cable from the rocker box cover and from the throttle linkage.

3 Unscrew and remove the upper four engine to converter housing bolts, noting that one bolt secures the combined dipstick/filler tube.

4 Either jack up the car and support securely on stands, or position it over a pit or on ramps.

5 Disconnect the speedometer cable from the transmission extension housing by removing the bolt and clip.

6 Remove the starter motor. Remove the dipstick/filler tube.

7 Unscrew each of the drive plate to converter bolts. These are accessible one at a time through the starter motor aperture - the engine will have to be rotated to bring each bolt into view.

8 Detach the engine to transmission stiffener bracket.

9 Remove the cover plate from the lower half of the converter housing.

10 Drain the transmission fluid into a suitably large container by removing the slotted drain plug from the oil pan.

11 Disconnect the speed selector cable from the operating lever on the side of the transmission casing, also from the support bracket.

12 Mark the edges of the propeller shaft rear flange and the rear

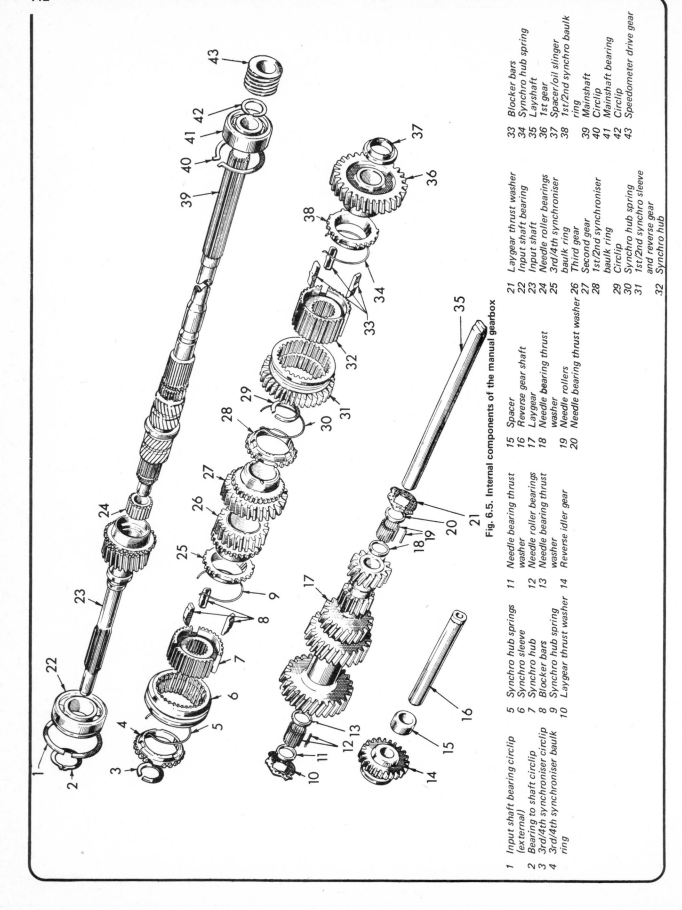

Fig. 6.5. Internal components of the manual gearbox

1 Input shaft bearing circlip (external)
2 Bearing to shaft circlip
3 3rd/4th synchroniser circlip
4 3rd/4th synchroniser baulk ring
5 Synchro hub springs
6 Synchro sleeve
7 Synchro hub
8 Blocker bars
9 Synchro hub spring
10 Laygear thrust washer
11 Needle bearing thrust washer
12 Needle roller bearings
13 Needle bearing thrust washer
14 Reverse idler gear
15 Spacer
16 Reverse gear shaft
17 Laygear
18 Needle bearing thrust washer
19 Needle rollers
20 Needle bearing thrust washer
21 Laygear thrust washer
22 Input shaft bearing
23 Input shaft
24 Needle roller bearings
25 3rd/4th synchroniser baulk ring
26 Third gear
27 Second gear
28 1st/2nd synchroniser baulk ring
29 Circlip
30 Synchro hub spring
31 1st/2nd synchro sleeve and reverse gear
32 Synchro hub
33 Blocker bars
34 Synchro hub spring
35 Layshaft
36 1st gear
37 Spacer/oil slinger
38 1st/2nd synchro baulk ring
39 Mainshaft
40 Circlip
41 Mainshaft bearing
42 Circlip
43 Speedometer drive gear

axle pinion flange and remove the four connecting bolts. Push the propeller shaft slightly forward to separate the two flanges and then withdraw the shaft. If the propeller shaft is a centre bearing type, the removal procedure is the same except that the two centre bearing bolts must first be removed.

13 Support the weight of the transmission unit with a trolley jack and remove the rear supporting crossmember.

14 Disconnect the leads from the inhibitor switch which is secured into the side of the transmission unit. The larger terminals are for the reversing lights.

15 Disconnect the exhaust downpipe from the manifold.

16 Lower the trolley jack slightly and then support the rear of the engine sump with a second jack.

17 Remove the remaining two engine to converter housing bolts.

18 Lower both jacks together until the transmission unit can be removed toward the rear and drawn out from underneath the vehicle.

19 Installation is a reversal of removal but the following points must be observed.

20 If the torque converter has been removed, before refitting the transmission unit, it will be necessary to align the front drive tangs with the slots in the inner gear and then carefully replace the torque converter. Take extreme precautions not to damage the oil seal.

21 Adjust the selector cable and inhibitor switch as described later in this Chapter.

22 Refill the transmission unit with Castrol TQF and check the oil level before starting the engine.

12 Downshift cable - adjustment

1 The downshift cable is accurately set and the crimped collar positioned on the inner cable when the vehicle is manufactured. Any adjustment should be limited to ensuring that the crimped collar just contacts the end face of the outer cable threaded adjuster.

2 Where this is not the case, loosen the locknut on the adjuster and turn the adjuster to correct the setting. This adjustment should be carried out under the following conditions:

a) The engine and transmission are at normal operating temperature
b) The throttle linkage is correctly adjusted and no wear is evident
c) The engine idling speed is correctly set (see Specifications).

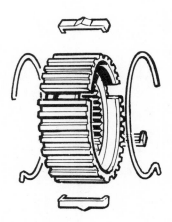

Fig. 6.6. Synchroniser hub, spring rings and blocker bars

13 Downshift cable - renewal or resetting

1 In the event of the downshift cable breaking or in the rare event of the crimped collar becoming loose and moving, then the following method should be employed to set it. All new downshift cables are supplied with the crimped collar loose for crimping after installation.

2 Set the engine idling speed to the specified rpm and then switch off.

3 Drain the transmission fluid.

4 Unscrew and remove the sump retaining bolts and their washers.

5 If the cable has broken, detach it from both the carburettor end and the downshift valve within the transmission housing.

6 Attach the new cable and with the accelerator pedal released, the relative position of cam and downshift valve should be as shown in Fig 6.10.

7 Depress the accelerator pedal fully (through 'kickdown') when the relative position of the cam and downshift valve should be as shown in Fig 6.11.

8 To obtain the correct cable adjustment in both these positions, rotate the threaded outer cable adjuster.

9 When adjustment is correct, tighten the adjuster locknut.

10 With the accelerator pedal released (idling position), crimp the inner cable sleeve so that it is just in contact with the end face of the outer cable adjuster.

11 Refit the oil pan using a new gasket, tighten the oil pan bolts and refill the transmission.

14 Speed selector linkage - adjustment

1 Disconnect the operating cable from the speed selector arm on the side of the transmission casing by removing the split pin and clevis pin.

2 Place the speed selector lever in position 1.

3 Pull the selector arm fully to the rear.

4 Adjust the operating cable by means of the nut and locknut at the support bracket so that when the eye of the cable is offered to the selector arm, the holes will be in perfect alignment and the clevis pin will pass through as a sliding fit.

5 Temporarily insert the clevis pin and have an assistant move the selector lever to each position. A distinct click should be heard from the selector arm as each position is selected and the arm should not be subjected to any tension from the linkage in any one position.

6 When adjustment is completed, fit a new split pin to the clevis and oil the clevis pin.

15 Starter inhibitor/reversing light switch - adjustment

1 Detach the leads from the switch (small terminals for starter, large terminals for reversing lights).

2 Slacken the switch locknut.

3 Place the speed selector in 'D', '1' or '2' position.

4 Connect a lamp and battery across the two smaller (starter) terminals of the switch and another set across the two larger (reversing light) terminals.

5 Unscrew the switch about two turns and then screw it slowly in until the test lamp across the reversing light terminals extinguishes. With a pencil or piece of chalk, mark the relative position of the switch by making one line on the switch body and another on the transmission housing.

6 Continue to screw the switch in until the test lamp across the starter inhibitor terminals lights. Mark the relative position of the switch in a similar manner to that already described, by putting a second mark on the switch body in alignment with the mark previously made on the transmission housing.

7 Unscrew the switch until the mark on the transmission housing is midway between the two marks on the switch body and holding the switch in this position, tighten the locknut.

8 Reconnect the switch leads and check for correct operation of the starter inhibitor and reversing light circuits of the switch.

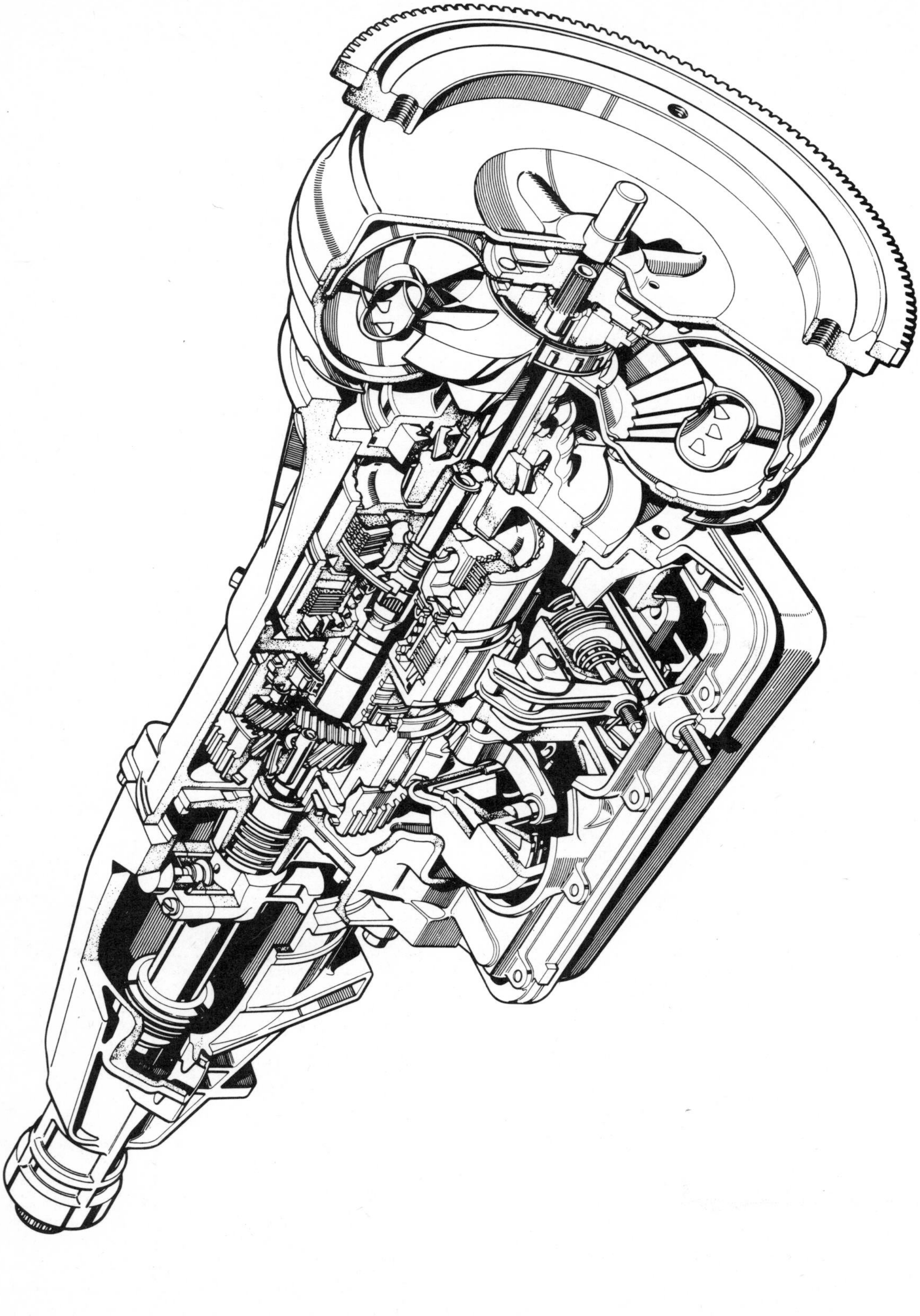

Fig. 6.7. Cut-away of the automatic transmission unit

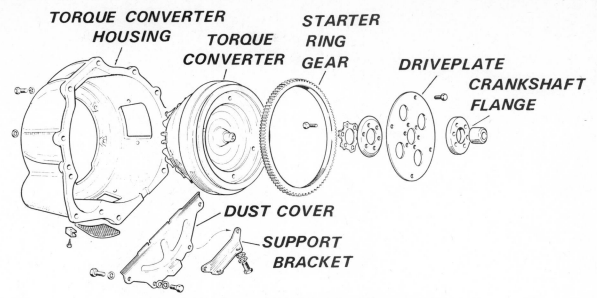

TORQUE CONVERTER HOUSING

TORQUE CONVERTER

STARTER RING GEAR

DRIVEPLATE

CRANKSHAFT FLANGE

DUST COVER

SUPPORT BRACKET

Fig. 6.8. Torque converter and drive plate - main components

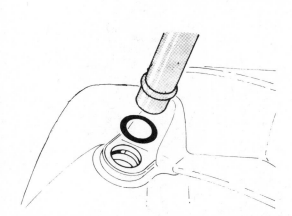

Fig. 6.9. Late type oil filler tube connection to transmission (early types have union nut)

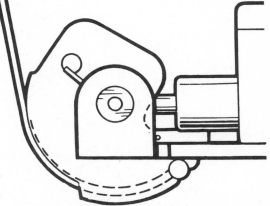

Fig. 6.10. Downshift valve cam position (idling)

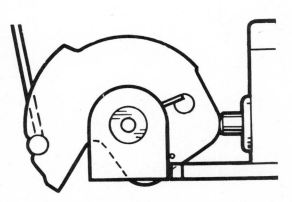

Fig. 6.11. Downshift valve cam position (kick-down)

Fig. 6.12. Starter inhibitor/reversing light switch locknut wrench

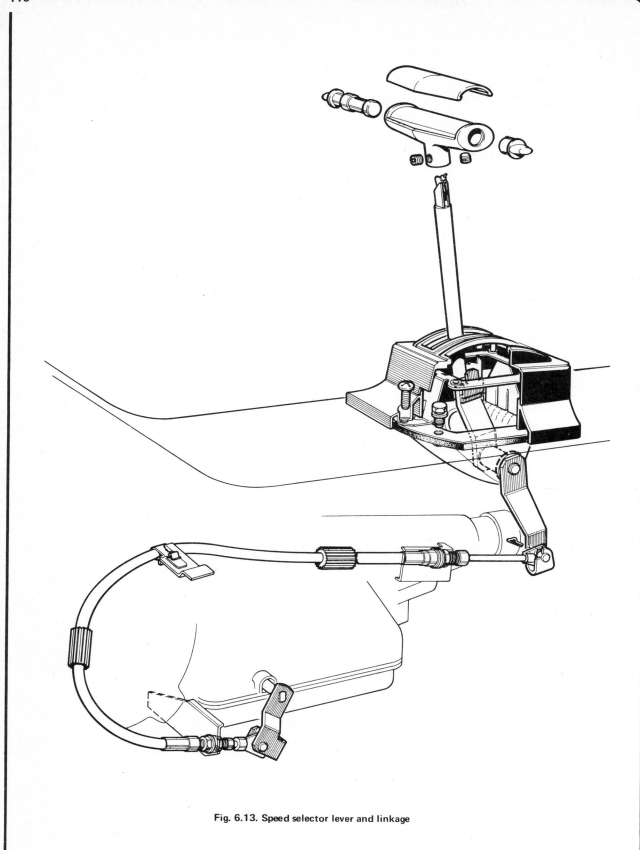

Fig. 6.13. Speed selector lever and linkage

Provided that the adjustment has been correctly carried out, then any malfunction is due to a faulty switch which must be renewed.

16 Fault finding - stall test procedure

The function of a stall test is to determine that the torque converter and gearbox are operating satisfactorily.

1 Check the condition of the engine. An engine which is not developing full power will affect the stall test readings.

2 Allow the engine and transmission to reach correct working temperatures.

3 Connect a tachometer to the vehicle.

4 Chock the wheels and apply the handbrake and footbrake.

5 Select '1' or 'R' and depress the throttle to the kickdown position. Note the reading on the tachometer which should be 1800 rev/min. If the reading is below 1000 rev/min suspect the converter for stator slip. If the reading is down to 1200 rev/min the engine is not developing full power. If the reading is in excess of 2000 rev/min suspect the gearbox for brake bind or clutch slip. Note: Do not carry out a stall test for a longer period than 10 seconds, otherwise the transmission will become overheated.

6 Inability to start on steep gradients, combined with poor acceleration from rest and low stall speed (100 rev/min) indicate that the converter stator uni-directional clutch is slipping. This condition permits the stator to rotate in an opposite direction to the impeller and turbine, and torque multiplication cannot occur.

7 Poor acceleration in 3rd gear above 30 mph and reduced maximum speed indicates that the stator uni-directional clutch has seized. The stator will not rotate with the turbine and impeller and the 'fluid flywheel' phase cannot occur. This condition will also be indicated by excessive overheating of the transmission although the stall speed will be correct.

17 Road testing for fault diagnosis

1 Check that the engine will only start with the selector lever in 'P' or 'N' and that the reverse light operates only in 'R'.

2 Apply the handbrake and with the engine idling select 'N' — 'D', 'N' — 'R' and 'N' — '1'. Engagement should be positive.

3 With the transmission at normal running temperature, select 'D', release the brakes and accelerate with minimum throttle. Check 1 — 2 and 2 — 3 shift speeds and quality of change (see Specifications).

4 Stop the vehicle, select 'D and re-start, using 'full throttle'. Check 1 — 2 and 2 — 3 shift speeds and quality of change.

5 At 25 mph apply 'full throttle'. The vehicle should accelerate in 3rd gear and should not downshift to 2nd.

6 At a maximum of 45 mph, 'kickdown' fully, the transmission should downshift to 2nd.

7 At a maximum of 31 mph in 2nd gear 'kickdown' fully. The transmission should downshift to 1st gear.

8 Stop the vehicle, select 'D' and re-start using 'kickdown'. Check the 1 — 2 and 2 — 3 shift speeds.

9 At 40 mph in 3rd gear, select '1' and release the throttle. Check 2 — 3 downshift and engine braking.

10 With '1' still engaged, stop the vehicle and accelerate to over 25 mph using 'kickdown'. Check for slip, "squawk' and absence of upshifts.

11 Stop the vehicle and select 'R'. Reverse using 'full throttle' if possible. Check for slip and clutch 'squawk'.

12 Stop the vehicle on a gradient. Apply the handbrake and select 'P'. Check the parking pawl hold when the handbrake is released. Turn the vehicle around and repeat the procedure. Check that the selector lever is held firmly in the gate in 'P'.

13 In the event of a discharged battery or faulty starter motor, a vehicle with automatic transmission can be started by running down a gradient or by towing. With the gear selector in 'N', a speed of 25 to 28 mph must be attained before pulling the selector into 'D'. It will be realised that these are high speeds for a car to be moving without engine control. It is most important that the ignition is switched on **before** moving the vehicle as otherwise the steering will remain locked.

Chapter 7 Propeller shaft and universal joints

Contents

Specifications

Type (1100 cc)	...	...	...	...	...	...	...	Single section open shaft with two universal joints
(1300 cc)	...	...	...	...	...	...	...	Two section open shaft with three universal joints and centre support bearing

	lb ft	kg m
Torque wrench setting		
Universal joint flange to rear axle pinion flange bolts	15 to 18	2.1 to 2.4

1 General description

On 1100 cc models drive is transmitted from the gearbox to the rear axle by a single finely balanced tubular propeller shaft. Fitted at each end of the shaft is a universal joint which allows vertical movement of the rear axle. Each universal joint comprises a four legged centre spider, four needle roller bearings and two yokes.

This type of universal joint can be dismantled and a repair kit is available to rebuild a worn unit. On 1300 cc models, the drive is transmitted by a two section tubular shaft supported at its centre by a rubber insulated bearing which is bolted to the underbody. The universal joints on this type of propeller shaft are not repairable and in the event of wear occurring, the complete shaft assembly must be renewed.

All universal joints are of lubricant-sealed type and require no maintenance.

On all models the movement of the rear axle is absorbed by a sliding spline in the front of the propeller shaft which slides over a mating spline on the rear of the gearbox mainshaft. A supply of oil through very small oil holes from the gearbox lubricates the splines.

2 Single section propeller shaft - removal and installation

1 Jack up the rear of the car, or position the rear of the car over a pit or on a ramp.

2 If the rear of the car is jacked up, supplement the jack with support blocks so that danger is minimised, should the jack collapse.

3 If the rear wheels are off the ground, place the car in gear or put the handbrake on to ensure that the propeller shaft does not turn when an attempt is made to loosen the four nuts securing the propeller shaft to the rear axle.

4 Unscrew and remove the four self-locking nuts, bolts and securing washers which hold the flange on the rear axle.

5 The propeller shaft is carefully balanced to fine limits and it is important that it is replaced in exactly the same position it was in prior to its removal. Scratch a mark on the propeller shaft and rear axle flange edges to ensure accurate mating when the time comes for reassembly.

6 Slightly push the shaft forward to separate the two flanges and then lower the end of the shaft and pull it rearward to disengage the gearbox mainshaft splines.

7 Place a large can or tray under the rear of the gearbox extension to catch any oil which is likely to leak through the spline lubricating holes, when the propeller shaft is removed.

8 Replacement of the propeller shaft is a reversal of the above procedure. Ensure that the mating marks scratched on the propeller shaft and rear axle flanges line up.

9 Finally tighten the flange bolts to a torque of between 15 and 18 lb ft (2.1 to 2.4 kg m).

3 Single section propeller shaft joints - examination

1 Wear in the needle roller bearings is characterised by vibration in the transmission, 'clonks' on taking up the drive, and in extreme cases of lack of lubrication, metallic squeaking, and ultimately grating and shrieking sounds as the bearings break up.

2 It is easy to check if the needle roller bearings are worn with the propeller shaft in position, by trying to turn the shaft with one hand, the other hand holding the rear axle flange when the rear universal is being checked, and the front half coupling when the front universal is being checked. Any movement between the propeller shaft and the front and the rear half couplings is indicative of considerable wear. If worn, the old bearings and spiders will have to be discarded and a repair kit, comprising new universal joint spiders, bearings, oil seals and retainers purchased. Check by trying to lift the shaft and noticing any movement in the joints.

3 Examine the propeller shaft splines for wear. If worn it will be necessary to purchase a new front half coupling, or if the yokes are badly worn, an exchange propeller shaft. It is not

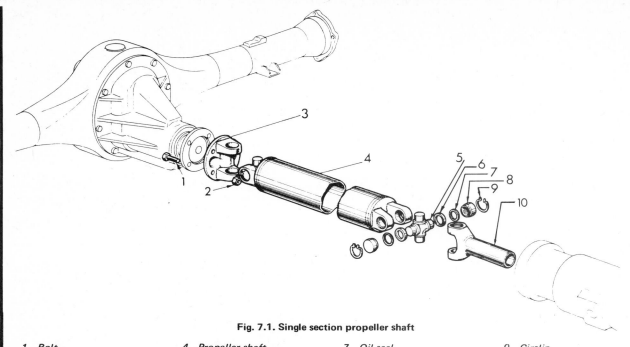

Fig. 7.1. Single section propeller shaft

1 Bolt	4 Propeller shaft	7 Oil seal	9 Circlip
2 Nut	5 Spider (trunnion)	8 Needle roller bearings	10 Yoke/sliding sleeve
3 Flange	6 Oil seal retainer	and cup	assembly

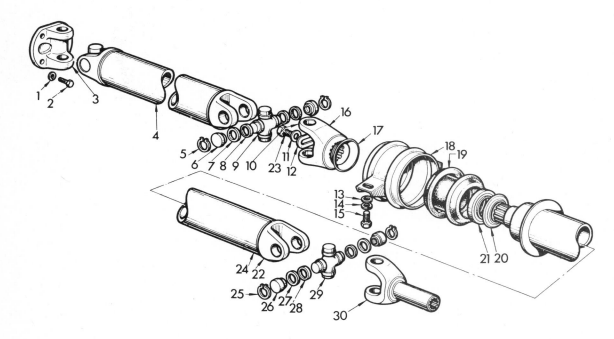

Fig. 7.2. Two section propeller shaft

1 Lockwasher	9 Spider (trunnion)	18 Bearing housing	25 Circlip
2 Bolt	10 Splined centre yoke	19 Rubber insulator	26 Needle roller bearing
3 Drive shaft flange yoke	11 Washer	20 Bearing cup	and cap
4 Rear section propeller shaft	12 'U' washer	21 Bearing	27 Oil seal
5 Circlip	13 Washer	22 Front section yoke	28 Oil seal retainer
6 Needle roller bearing and	14 Lockwasher	23 Bolt	29 Spider (trunnion)
cap	15 Bolt	24 Front section propeller	30 Yoke/sliding sleeve
7 Oil seal	16 Yoke	shaft	assembly
8 Oil seal retainer	17 Bearing cup		

possible to fit oversize bearings and journals to the trunnion bearing holes.

4 Single section propeller shaft joints - servicing

1   Clean away all dirt from the ends of the bearings on the yokes so that the circlips may be removed using a pair of contracting circlip pliers. If they are very tight, tap the end of the bearing race (inside the circlip) with a drift and hammer to relieve the pressure (photo).
2   Once the circlips are removed, tap the universal joints at the yoke with a soft hammer and the bearings and races will come out of the housing and can be removed easily (photo).
3   If they are obstinate they can be gripped in a self-locking wrench for final removal provided they are to be renewed.
4   Once the bearings are removed from each opposite journal the trunnion can be easily disengaged.
5   Fitting the new trunnions and needle rollers and races is a reversal of the removal procedure.
6   Keep the grease seals on the inner ends of each trunnion as dry as possible.
7   Place the needles in each race and fill the race 1/3 full with grease prior to placing it over the trunnion and press into position using a vice. Any grease exuding from the fourth bearing journal after three have been fitted should be removed before fitting the fourth race.
8   Replace the circlips ensuring that they seat neatly in the retaining grooves.
9   The use of a suitably sized socket spanner as a distance piece will ensure that the bearing cups are pressed fully home into the yokes.

5 Two section propeller shaft - removal and installation

1   The method of removal of this type of shaft is identical to that described in Section 2 except that the two bolts which secure the centre bearing to the bodyframe must also be unscrewed and removed.
2   Installation is a reversal of removal.

6 Two section propeller shaft - centre bearing removal and refitting

1   Mark the relative positions of the front and rear sections of the propeller shaft so that they will be in their original alignment when refitted.
2   Refer to Fig 7.2 and knock back the tab washer and slacken the bolt (23) and then remove the U ring (12) from underneath it.
3   With the U ring removed the rear yoke can now be drawn off the splines of the front section. The centre bolt and its washer remain attached to the splined front section.
4   Slide the bearing housing with its rubber insulator from the shaft. Bend back the six metal tabs on the housing and remove the rubber insulator.
5   The bearing and its protective caps should now be withdrawn from the splined section of the propeller shaft by careful levering with two large screwdrivers or tyre levers. If a suitable

4.1 Removing universal joint circlip

4.2 Screwing bearing cup from universal joint yoke

puller tool is available this should always be used in preference to any other method as it is less likely to cause damage to the bearing.
6   To replace the bearing, select a piece of piping or tubing for use as a tubular drift. Place the splined part of the drive shaft upright in a vice, position the bearing on the shaft and using a soft hammer on the end of the piece of tubing, drive the bearing firmly and squarely onto the shaft.
7   Replace the rubber insulator in the bearing housing, ensuring that the boss on the insulator is at the top of the housing and will be adjacent to the underframe when the propeller shafts are replaced.
8   When the insulator is correctly positioned bend back the six metal tabs and slide the housing and insulator assembly over the bearing.
9   Slide the splined end of the shaft into the rear yoke, ensuring that the previously scribed mating marks are correctly aligned.
10 Replace the U ring under the centre bolt with its smooth surface facing the front section of the propeller shaft. Tighten down the centre bolt to a torque of 28 lb ft (3.9 kg m) and bend up its tab washer to secure it.

Chapter 8 Rear axle

Contents

Specifications

Type ... ...   Semi-floating - hypoid

Ratios:

		Up to September 1970		After September 1970	
		Standard	Optional	Standard	Optional
Saloons	1100 cc manual	3.900 to 1	3.777 to 1	3.900 to 1	4.125 to 1
	1300 cc and G.T. manual	3.777 to 1	4.125 to 1	3.900 to 1	4.125 to 1
	* 1100 cc automatic	4.125 to 1	None	None	None
	1300 cc automatic	4.125 to 1	3.777 to 1	3.900 to 1	4.125 to 1
Estates	1100 cc manual and automatic *	4.444 to 1	4.125 to 1	4.125 to 1	None
	1300 cc manual and automatic	4.125 to 1	3.777 to 1	3.90 to 1	4.125 to 1 (std. auto.)
Van	1100 cc manual	4.444 to 1	4.125 to 1	4.444 to 1	4.125 to 1
	1300 cc manual and automatic	4.125 to 1	3.777 to 1	4.125 to 1	3.777 to 1

* Not available after September 1970.

Pinion/crownwheel number of teeth:

3.900 to 1 ratio	10/39
4.125 to 1 ratio	8/33
3.777 to 1 ratio	9/34
4.444 to 1 ratio	9/40

Pinion/crownwheel backlash ... ...   0.005 to 0.007 in. (0.13 to 0.17 mm)
Pinion bearing pre-load ... ...   20 to 26 lb (9 to 11.7 kg) with new bearings
           12 to 18 lb (5 to 8 kg) with original bearings
Oil capacity ... ...   2.0 pints (1.1 litres)

Torque wrench settings

	lb ft	kg m
Crownwheel to differential case bolts	50 to 55	7.0 to 7.6
Differential carrier to axle housing nuts	25 to 30	3.45 to 4.41
Differential bearing locking plate bolts	12 to 15	1.7 to 2.0
Differential bearing cap bolts	45 to 50	6.3 to 6.9
Axle shaft bearing retainer bolts	15 to 18	2.1 to 2.4
Universal joint flange to pinion flange	15 to 18	2.1 to 2.4

1 General description

The rear axle is of the semi-floating type, retained and supported by semi-elliptic leaf type road springs.

The axle casing of banjo design carries the differential assembly. This comprises a crownwheel and pinion mounted in the differential carrier which is bolted to the front of the axle casing.

The pinion is mounted on two taper roller bearings which are pre-loaded to partially collapse the tubular spacer which is located between them. The crownwheel is bolted to the differential case which is also supported on two taper roller bearings.

The axle shafts (half shafts) are splined to the differential side gears and run in ball races in the axle casing at their outer ends. The ball races have integral oil seals.

Overhaul of the differential assembly is beyond the scope of the home mechanic due to the need for special tools and guages but the design of the rear axle makes the renewal of the differential assembly on an exchange basis a simple matter after withdrawal of the half shafts.

The owner is not recommended to proceed beyond the operations described in this Chapter.

No provision is made for draining the rear axle but the oil level should be checked regularly as described in the Routine Maintenance Section.

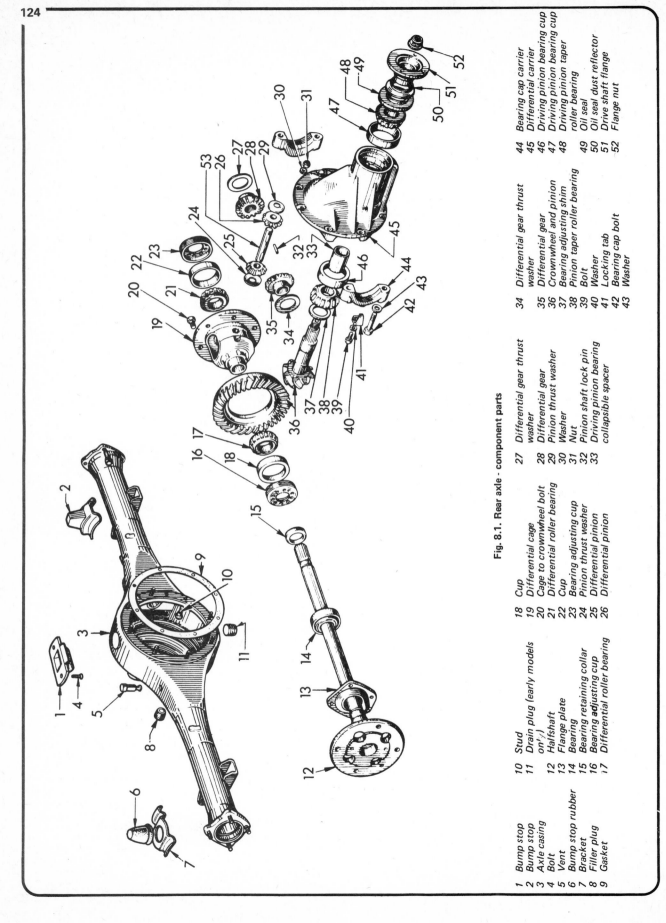

Fig. 8.1. Rear axle - component parts

1	Bump stop	10	Stud	
2	Bump stop	11	Drain plug (early models	
3	Axle casing		on'½)	
4	Bolt	12	Halfshaft	
5	Vent	13	Flange plate	
6	Bump stop rubber	14	Bearing	
7	Bracket	15	Bearing retaining collar	
8	Filler plug	16	Bearing adjusting cup	
9	Gasket	17	Differential roller bearing	

18	Cup	27	Differential gear thrust	
19	Differential cage		washer	
20	Cage to crownwheel bolt	28	Differential gear	
21	Differential roller bearing	29	Pinion thrust washer	
22	Cup	30	Washer	
23	Bearing adjusting cup	31	Nut	
24	Pinion thrust washer	32	Pinion shaft lock pin	
25	Differential pinion	33	Driving pinion bearing	
26	Differential pinion		collapsible spacer	

34	Differential gear thrust	44	Bearing cap carrier	
	washer	45	Differential carrier	
35	Differential gear	46	Driving pinion bearing cup	
36	Crownwheel and pinion	47	Driving pinion bearing cup	
37	Bearing adjusting shim	48	Driving pinion taper	
38	Pinion taper roller bearing		roller bearing	
39	Bolt	49	Oil seal	
40	Washer	50	Oil seal dust reflector	
41	Locking tab	51	Drive shaft flange	
42	Bearing cap bolt	52	Flange nut	
43	Washer			

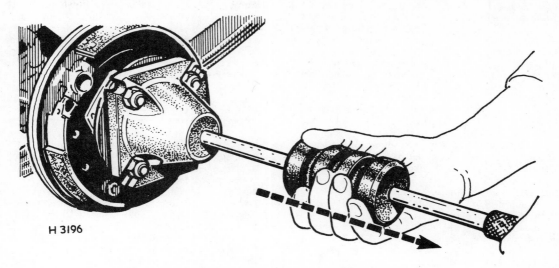

H 3196

Fig. 8.2. Withdrawing an axle shaft using a slide hammer

2 Rear axle - removal and installation

1   Remove the rear wheel hub caps and loosen the wheel nuts.
2   Raise and support the rear of the body and the differential casing with chocks or jacks so that the rear wheels are clear of the ground. This is most easily done by placing a jack under the centre of the differential, jacking up the axle and then fitting chocks under the mounting points at the front of the rear springs to support the body.
3   Remove both rear wheels and place the wheel nuts in the hub caps for safe keeping.
4   Mark the propeller shaft and differential drive flanges to ensure replacement in the same relative positions. Undo and remove the nuts and bolts holding the two flanges together.
5   Release the handbrake inside the car, then detach the handbrake transverse rod from the right rear brake by removing the spring clip and clevis pin.
6   Detach the rear end of the handbrake primary cable from the left hand rear brake by removing the spring clip and clevis pin. Slacken the cable adjusting nuts on the bracket on the left rear of the axle casing and slide out the cable.
7   Unscrew the union on the brake pipe at the junction on the rear axle and have handy either a jar to catch the hydraulic fluid or a plug to block the end of the pipe.
8   Undo the self-locking nuts holding the shock absorbers to spring plates thus freeing their lower ends. It may be necessary to slightly raise the jack under the axle casing to successfully free the shock absorbers.
9   Unscrew the nuts from under the spring retaining plates. These nuts screw onto the ends of the inverted U bolts which retain the axle to the spring. Remove the U bolts, bump stops and spring retaining plates.
10 The axle assembly will now be resting free on the centre jack and can now be removed by lifting it through the space between the road spring and the bodyframe side member.
11 As from October 1973 a rear anti-roll bar was fitted to all Escort vehicles and this will have to be disconnected before the rear alxe can be withdrawn.
12 Reassembly is a direct reversal of the removal procedure, but the U bolt nuts must be tightened down to a torque of 20 to 25 lb ft (2.8 to 3.4 kg m) and the brakes must be bled as described in Chapter 9.

3 Axle shafts (halfshafts) - removal and refitting

1   Jack up the car, remove the road wheel and then unscrew the

brake drum retaining screw and withdraw the brake drum. If the drum is tight, slacken the shoe adjuster right off and then tap the drum from its location using a block of wood and a wooden or plastic mallet.
2   Unscrew and remove the four self-locking nuts which secure the flange plate (13) to the axle casing end flanges (Fig 8.1).
3   A slide hammer should now be attached to the hub studs and the axle shaft withdrawn. A slide hammer can be made up quite easily, but an alternative method of removing the shaft is to bolt on the road wheel and strike it simultaneously on both inside edges of the rim at opposite points. It must be emphasised that it is quite useless to attempt to try and pull the halfshaft from the axle casing as you will only succeed in pulling the vehicle off the jacks or stands.
4   Refitting is a reversal of removal. Pass the halfshaft into the axle casing holding the shaft horizontally until the splines at its inner end engage with the splines in the differential gears. Tap the hub/bearing assembly fully home with a hammer and wooden block.

4 Hub bearing/oil seal - renewal

1   The combined bearing and oil seal, also the bearing retaining collar, are an interference fit on the halfshaft. The removal and refitting of these components must be carried out using a press and correct bearing support tools.
2   It is therefore recommended that the halfshaft is removed as described in the preceding Section and taken to a Ford dealer for the work to be carried out.

5 Pinion bearing oil seal - renewal

1   The rear axle pinion bearing oil seal may be renewed with the axle in position in the vehicle provided the following operations are adhered to.
2   Disconnect and remove the propeller shaft from the rear axle as described (according to type) in the preceding Chapter.
3   The rear axle pinion must now be held quite still during removal of the pinion flange nut. To do this, either fit two old bolts into the flange holes and position a rod between them to act as a lever or alternatively, drill two holes in a length of flat steel

bar and bolt it to the flange.

4   Carefully mark the relative position of the pinion flange nut to the flange so that the nut can be tightened to exactly the same position on refitment. An alternative method of establishing the pinion pre-load is to jack up the rear axle, remove the road wheels and brake drums and then using a spring balance with a length of cord attached to it and wound round the pinion flange, rotate the flange by pulling on the spring balance. Read off the force required to rotate the pinion, this is the bearing pre-load.

5   Holding the pinion flange quite still with the tool previously described, unscrew the pinion flange nut.

6   Remove the flange, dust deflector and prise out the defective oil seal. This can usually be done by carefully drifting in one side of the seal which will have the effect of ejecting the opposite side, it can then be gripped and pulled out of the differential housing.

7   Tap the new seal into position using a suitable tubular drift to bear upon its outside edge. Make sure that the face of the seal is flush with the differential housing.

8   Fit the dust deflector and the pinion flange but grease the lips of the seal before inserting the flange.

9   Examine the pinion flange nut. This is of self-locking type and may be removed and refitted on up to six occasions. If it did not provide much resistance when unscrewing however, always renew it.

10   Hold the pinion flange quite still and screw on the securing nut until either (i) the positioning mark made before removal is in alignment or (ii) by using the spring balance and cord method, the pre-load matches that existing before dismantling. This should be between 12 and 18 lb (5 to 8 kg). **Tighten the flange nut only a fraction of a turn at a time before re-checking, whichever method is used**. If the nut is tightened beyond its original setting, it cannot be backed off to correct the situation as the collapsible spacer will have over-compressed and the pinion bearing will have to be removed to fit a new spacer.

6   Differential carrier - removal and installation

1   Jack up the rear of the vehicle, remove both road wheels and withdraw the halfshafts as described in Section 3.

2   If a drain plug is fitted (early models) drain the oil.

3   Disconnect and remove the propeller shaft from the rear axle as described (according to type) in Chapter 7.

4   Undo the eight self-locking nuts holding the differential carrier assembly to the axle casing. If an oil drain plug has not been fitted, pull the assembly slightly forward and allow the oil to drain in a suitable tray or bowl. The carrier complete with the crownwheel can now be lifted clear with the gasket.

5   Before replacement, carefully clean the mating surfaces of the carrier and the axle casing and always fit a new gasket. Replacement is then a direct reversal of the above instructions. The eight nuts retaining the differential carrier assembly to the axle casing should be tightened to a torque of 25 to 39 lb ft (3.45 to 4.41 kg m).

Chapter 9 Braking system

Contents

Specifications

Type	Disc or drum at front, drum at rear
Footbrake	Hydraulic on all 4 wheels
Handbrake	Mechanical to rear wheels only

Front brakes

1100 cc saloon	8 x 1½ in. drum
1300 cc saloon	8 x 1¾ in. drum
1300 cc G.T.	8.6 in. disc. Servo assisted
1100 cc estate	8 x 1¾ in. drum
1300 cc estate	8.6 in. disc. Servo assisted
6 cwt van (manual)	8 x 1¾ in. drum
6 cwt van (automatic) all 8 cwt vans	8.6 in. disc

Rear brakes

All models	8 x 1½ in. drum (G.T. and 1300 estate are servo assisted)

	8 x 1½ in.	8 x 1¾ in.
Drum brake details		
Drum diameter	8 in. (203.2 mm)	8 in. (203.2 mm)
Lining width	1.5 in. (38.1 mm)	1.75 in. (44.5 mm)
Lining thickness	0.188 in. (4.8 mm)	0.188 in. (4.8 mm)
Lining area (per shoe)	9.43 sq in. (60.8 cm^2)	11.00 sq in. (71.0 cm^2)
Total swept area	75.5 sq in. (489.0 cm^2)	88.0 sq in. (570.0 cm^2)
Brake cylinder diameter	0.75 in. (19.1 mm)	0.070 in. (17.78 mm)

Disc brake details	
Disc diameter	8.6 in. (218.4 mm)
Disc thickness	0.375 in. (9.5 mm)
Disc run out	0.002 in. (0.05 mm)
Pad lining area	15.64 sq in. (100.1 cm^2)
Swept area	153.8 sq in. (991 cm^2)
Brake cylinder diameter	1.892 in. (48.06 mm)

Master cylinder:	
Bore diameter 1,100 x 1,300 (single line)	.625 in. (15.9 mm)
Disc brake (single line)	.75 in. (19.1 mm)
1100 cc (dual line)	.75 in. (19.1 mm)
1300 and disc brake (dual line)	.81 in. (10.6 mm)

Dual circuit braking systems are fitted to all export models as an essential safety feature and may be optionally specified on all models in the range supplied within the U.K.

Front disc brakes and vacuum servo assistance may also be optionally specified on all models.

Torque wrench settings

	lb ft	kg m
Brake caliper to front suspension	45 to 50	6.22 to 6.91
Rear backplate to axle housing	15 to 18	2.07 to 2.49
Hydraulic unions	7 to 8	.97 to 1.11
Bleed valves	5 to 7	.69 to .97
Front brake disc to hub	30 to 34	4.15 to 4.70

1 General description

According to model, either disc or drum brakes are fitted to the front wheels while all models have single leading shoe drum brakes at the rear. The mechanically operated handbrake operates on the rear wheels only.

Where front drum brakes are fitted, these are of the two leading shoe type with a separate cylinder for each shoe. Two adjusters are provided on each front wheel so that wear can be taken up on the brake linings. One adjuster is provided on each rear wheel for the same purpose. It is unusual to have to adjust the handbrake system as the efficiency of this system is largely dependent on the condition of the rear brake linings and the adjustment of the brake shoes. The handbrake can however be adjusted separately to the footbrake operated hydraulic system (Section 21).

The hydraulic brake system on drum brakes operates in the following manner: On application of the brake pedal, hydraulic fluid under pressure is pushed from the master cylinder to the brake operating cylinders in each wheel by a union, steel pipelines and flexible hoses.

The hydraulic fluid moves the pistons out of the wheel cylinders so pushing the brake shoes into contact with the brake drums. This provides an equal degree of retardation on all four wheels in direct proportion to the brake pedal pressure. Return springs draw the shoes together again when the brake pedal is released.

The front disc brakes fitted to certain models (Specifications) are rotating disc and static caliper type, with one caliper per disc. The caliper is positioned to act on the trailing edge of the disc. Each caliper contains two piston operated friction pads, which on application of the footbrake, pinch the disc between them.

Application of the footbrake creates hydraulic pressure in the master cylinder and fluid from the cylinder travels via steel and flexible pipes to the cylinders in each half of the calipers, thus pushing the pistons, to which are attached the friction pads, into contact with either side of the disc.

Two seals are fitted to the operating cylinders, the outer seal prevents moisture and dirt entering the cylinder, while the inner seal which is retained in a groove inside the cylinder, prevents fluid leakage.

As the friction pads wear so the pistons move further out of the cylinders and the level of the fluid in the hydraulic reservoir drops. Disc pad wear is therefore taken up automatically, and eliminates the need for periodic adjustment by the owner.

The handbrake lever on all models is located between the front seats. A single cable runs from the lever to an equaliser bracket on the left of the rear axle. The cable runs through the equaliser and operates the left hand rear brake. At the same time the bracket is deflected and a solid rod attached to it running across the rear of the axle casing, operates the right hand rear brake.

A mechanical servo, suspended vacuum type, is fitted as standard on all GT models and 8 cwt vans. A dual circuit braking system is fitted to export vehicles and may be optionally specified on all models.

Should one circuit fail, the other circuit is unaffected and the car can still be stopped. A warning light is fitted on the facia which illuminates should either circuit fail. The bulb in the light can also be tested by means of the switch provided.

Either front disc brakes or servo assisted braking can be fitted as an optional extra on any model of the Escort range.

2 Braking system - maintenance and inspection

1 Check the fluid level in the reservoir as described in the Routine Maintenance Section at the beginning of this manual. Always use the specified fluid - Castrol Universal Brake and Clutch Fluid or Ford's own product for topping up or refilling the system. The use of other fluid could result in brake failure caused by perishing or swelling of the seals within the master and operating cylinders.

2 If topping up becomes frequent, then check the metal piping and flexible hoses for leaks, and check for woen brake or master cylinders which will also cause loss of fluid.

3 At intervals of 3000 miles (4800 km) or more frequently if pedal travel becomes excessive, adjust the brake shoes to compensate for wear of the brake linings. On models with disc brakes on the front it will only be necessary to adjust the rear brakes.

4 Every 6000 miles (9600 km) in the case of drum brakes, remove the drums, inspect the linings for wear and renew them as necessary. At the same time, thoroughly clean out all dust from the drum using a dry cloth. With disc brakes, remove the pads and examine them for wear. If they are worn down to 1/8 inch or less (the distance being measured between the contact face of the pad and the face of the brake pad support plate) then they should be renewed.

5 Every 36,000 miles (58,000 km) or three years, whichever comes sooner, it is advisable to change the fluid in the braking system and at the same time renew all hydraulic seals and flexible hoses. At the same mileage, it is recommended that the vacuum servo unit (where fitted) is renewed on an exchange basis.

3 Drum brakes - adjustment

1 Jack up one side of the car to attend to the brakes on that side.

2 The brakes on all models are taken up by turning square headed adjusters on the rear of each backplate. The edges of the adjuster are easily burred if an ordinary spanner is used. Use a square headed brake adjusting spanner if possible. **When adjusting the rear brakes make sure the handbrake is off.**

3 Two adjusters are fitted to each of the front wheels (Fig 9.4) and one adjuster on the rear wheel backplate (Fig 9.5).

4 Turn the adjuster a quarter of a turn at a time until the wheel is locked. Then turn back the adjuster one notch so that the wheel will rotate without binding.

5 Spin the wheel and apply the brakes hard to centralise the shoes. Recheck that it is not possible to turn the adjusting screw further without locking the shoe. A rubbing noise when the wheel is spun is usually due to dust in the brake drum. If there is no obvious slowing of the wheel due to brake binding there is no need to slacken off the adjusters. Better to remove the,

4.3 Withdrawing split pin from axle nut retainer

4.4 Removing front hub outer bearing and thrust washer

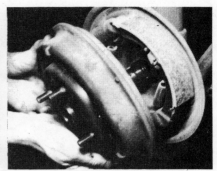

4.5 Withdrawing a front brake drum

4.7 Removing shoe steady post retaining spring

4.8 Detaching lower shoe of front wheel brake

4.9 Shoe return spring hole marked for identification

drum and blow out the dust.

6   Repeat this process to the other three brake drums.

4 Front drum brake shoes - inspection and renewal

1   Every 6000 miles (9600 km) the brake drums should be removed and the linings and drums brushed free from dust and inspected.

2   Remove the hub cap, slacken off the wheel nuts, securely jack up the car and remove the road wheel.

3   Slacken off the brake adjusters two or three turns, then referring to Fig 9.6, carefully prise off the dust cover (2) and remove the split pin (1) (photo) from the castellated nut retainer (3).

4   Remove the castellated nut retainer (3) and undo the hub adjusting nut (4). Then pull off the thrust washer (5) and the conical outer bearing (6) (photo).

5   Remove the brake drum (photo). If it proves obstinate, tap the rim gently with a soft headed hammer to free it. The shoes are now exposed for inspection.

6   The brake linings should be renewed if they are so worn that the rivet heads are flush with the surface of the lining. If bonded linings are fitted, they must be removed when the material has worn down to 1/32 inch (0.7938 mm) at its thinnest point. If the shoes are being removed to give access to the wheel cylinders, then cover the linings with masking tape to prevent any possibility of their becoming contaminated with grease or oil.

7   Depress the retaining clips which hold the brake steady pins in place, remove the clips (photo), by turning the steady pin through 90º and withdraw the pins through the brake backplate.

8   Detach the bottom of the rear brake shoe from its slot in the lower wheel cylinder (photo), lift it up to allow the spring to fully compress, then detach the spring from the brake shoe, but leave the other end in the brake backplate.

9   Scribe a mark on the hole from which the spring was removed

in the shoe to ensure correct reassembly (photo). Now repeat the same procedure on the other brake shoe.

10 Place rubber bands over the wheel cylinders to prevent any possibility of the pistons dropping out.

11 Thoroughly clean all traces of dust from the shoes, backplates, and brake drums with a dry paintbrush and compressed air, if available. Brake dust can cause squeal and judder and it is therefore important to clean out the brakes thoroughly.

12 Check that the pistons are free in their cylinders and that the rubber dust covers are undamaged and in position and that there are no hydraulic fluid leaks.

13 Prior to reassembly, smear a trace of brake grease on all sliding surfaces. The shoes should be quite free to slide on the closed end of the cylinder and the piston anchorage point. It is vital that no grease or oil comes in contact with the brake drums or the brake linings.

14 Replacement is a straightforward reversal of the removal procedure, but note the following points:

a) Fully slacken off the two brake adjusters so as to make it easier to replace the drum.

b) The hub adjusting nut should be tightened down to a torque of 27 lb ft (3.73 kg m) whilst the hub is being rotated, to ensure correct bedding in of the bearings. When fully tightened down, the nut must be slackened back 90º, the retainer fitted and a new split pin used to secure the retainer.

c) Finally adjust the brakes (Section 3).

5 Rear drum brake shoes - inspection and renewal

1   Remove the hub cap, loosen off the wheel nuts, then securely jack up the car, and remove the road wheel. Chock the front wheels and fully release the handbrake.

2   Undo the single screw retaining the brake drum, where fitted, and then pull off the drum.

3   Remove the small holding down springs from each shoe by

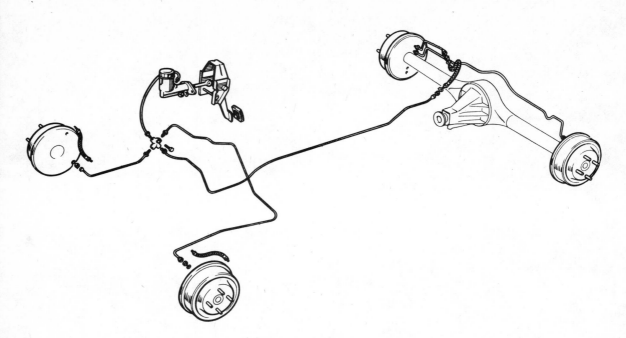

Fig. 9.1 Layout of single circuit hydraulic braking system

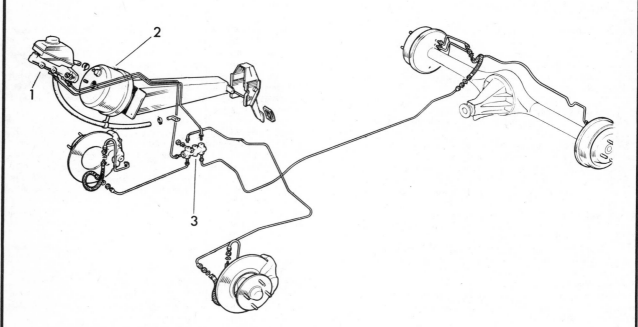

Fig. 9.2 Layout of dual circuit hydraulic braking system

1   Master cylinder
2   Vacuum servo unit

3   Pressure differential actuating valve

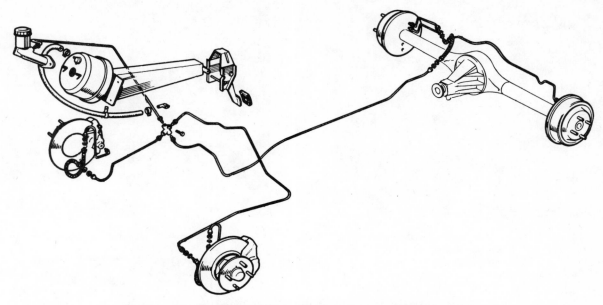

Fig. 9.3 Layout of single circuit hydraulic braking system with vacuum servo unit

turning the two small top washers through 90º.

4   Pull out the ends of each shoe from their locating slots in the fixed pivot on one side of the drum and the wheel cylinder on the other side. When removing the shoes from their slots in the wheel cylinder, great care should be taken not to allow the piston to fall out of the wheel cylinder. This can be kept in place by an elastic band.

5   Remove the shoes with the return springs still attached; then take off the return springs noting that they are of different lengths and the positions in which they are fitted.

6   Fully slacken off the single adjuster to ensure easy replacement of the drum during reassembly.

7   The brake linings should be examined and must be renewed if they are so worn that the rivet heads are flush with the surface of the lining. If bonded linings are fitted, these must be renewed when the material has worn down to 1/32 inch (0.7938 mm) at its thinnest point.

8   Replacement of the shoes is a direct reversal of the removal procedure but great care must be taken to ensure that the return springs are correctly fitted. If the replacement shoes do not have a support plate and retaining spring (Fig.9.8), transfer these items from the original shoes.

9   Finally adjust the brakes (Section 3).

---

6 Drum brake wheel operating cylinders - removal and refitting

1   Remove the brake drum and shoes (Sections 4 or 5).

Front brakes

2   Disconnect the flexible hose at its junction with the top wheel cylinder, remembering to plug the pipe to prevent loss of fluid.

3   Remove the small hydraulic pipe connecting the two wheel cylinders.

4   Undo and remove the two bolts and shakeproof washers securing the wheel cylinders to the brake backplate, noting that there is a small rubber sealing ring located between the wheel cylinder and the backplate.

5   This sealing ring must be renewed if it is not in perfect condition.

6   Replacement of the wheel cylinder is a direct reversal of the above procedure. Remember to bleed the brakes when the shoes and drum have been reassembled.

Rear brakes

7   Free the hydraulic pipe from the wheel cylinder at the union on the brake backplate (there are two unions on the right hand backplate).

8   Working on the inside of the brake backplate, remove the spring clip and clevis pin from the handbrake link.

9   From the back of the brake backplate, prise off and remove the rubber boot on the back of the wheel cylinder.

10 Pull off the two U shaped retainers holding the wheel cylinder to the backplate, noting the curved spring retainer is fitted from the handbrake link end of the cylinder, and the flat retainer from the other end, the flat retainer being located between the spring retainer and the wheel cylinder.

11 Now the wheel cylinder together with the handbrake link can be removed from the brake backplate.

12 Before commencing replacement, smear the area where the wheel cylinder slides on the backplate and the brake shoe support pads with Girling brake grease or other approved brake grease.

13 Replacement is a straightforward reversal of the removal sequence but the following points should be noted:

14 After fitting the rubber boot on the brake backplate, check that the wheel cylinder is free to slide in the carrier plate. Finally, bleed the brakes.

---

7 Wheel operating cylinders - servicing

1   Clean the exterior of the unit by brushing off all dust and wiping with a piece of rag soaked in methylated spirit.

2   Pull off the rubber dust covers. In the case of rear wheel brake cylinders, the cover is retained by a small clip (14) (Fig 9.8).

3   Eject the piston/seal assembly from its cylinder either by tapping or applying air pressure from a tyre pump at the fluid inlet union.

4   Examine the surfaces of the piston and cylinder bore for scoring or 'bright' wear areas. If these are evident, renew the complete cylinder assembly.

5   Discard the old seals and purchase a repair kit which will contain all the necessary seals and renewable components.

Fig. 9.4 Location of front drum brake shoe adjusters

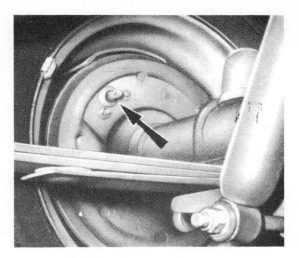

Fig. 9.5 Location of rear drum brake adjuster

6 Dip the new seal in clean hydraulic fluid and fit it to the piston, using only the fingers to manipulate it. Ensure that the flat face of the seal is against the piston rear shoulder. Insert the piston into the cylinder body, taking care not to trap the lips of the seal.

7 Fit a new dust cover.

8 Disc brake pads - inspection and renewal

1 Remove the front wheels and inspect the amount of friction material left on the friction pads. The pads must be renewed when the thickness of the material has worn down to 1/8 inch (3.2 mm).

2 With a pair of pliers, pull out the two small wire clips (12) which hold the main retaining pins in place (Fig 9.10).

3 Remove the main retaining pins which run through the caliper, the metal backing of the pads and the shims.

4 The friction pads and shims can now be removed from the caliper. If they prove difficult to move by hand, a pair of long nosed pliers can be used (photo).

5 Carefully clean the recesses in the caliper in which the friction pads and shims lie, and the exposed faces of each piston from all trace of dirt and rust.

6 Release the bleed nipple one half turn on the caliper unit and press each piston squarely into its cylinder bore. The fluid displaced by this operation will be ejected from the bleed nipple.

7 Fit new friction pads and their shims, the main retaining pins and their clips.

8 Tighten the bleed nipple and then depress the brake pedal hard two or three times.

9 Repeat the operation on the opposite caliper and then check the level in the fluid reservoir and top up as necessary.

9 Disc calipers - removal, servicing and refitting

1 Jack up the front of the vehicle, remove the road wheel, friction pads and shims as previously described.

2 Disconnect the hydraulic fluid line either at the rear of the caliper body or at the suspension leg.

3 Bend back the locking tabs on the caliper mounting bolts and unscrew and remove the bolts. The caliper unit can now be withdrawn from the disc.

4 Remove the retaining rings (4) and detach the dust excluding covers (1) from each of the cylinders.

5 Apply air pressure from a tyre pump at the fluid inlet port of the caliper and eject the pistons. Do not allow the pistons to fall to the ground during this operation. Mark them with their respective locations using a piece of masking tape.

8.4 Withdrawing a disc pad

6 Pick out the rubber seals from the cylinder bores, taking great care not to scratch the surface of the bore.

7 Clean all components in brake fluid or methylated spirit and discard the old seals. Examine the surfaces of the pistons and cylinder bores for scoring or 'bright' wear areas. If these are evident, renew the complete caliper unit.

8 Obtain a repair kit and assemble the seals into the cylinder grooves using only the fingers to manipulate them.

9 Dip the pistons in clean hydraulic fluid and insert them into the cylinder bores. Press each piston as far as it will go into the cylinder, making sure that the piston crown (solid end) enters first.

10 Engage the dust excluders into the piston recessed ends and then attach them to the caliper body; then fit the retaining rings.

11 Refitting is a reversal of removal but tighten the securing bolts to a torque of between 45 and 50 lb ft (6.2 to 6.9 kg m). Bleed the system (Section 17).

10 Brake disc - removal and refitting

1 The brake disc is not normally removed from the hub unless it is to be renewed.

2 Remove the hub and disc assembly complete (Chapter 11, Section 4).

3 Separate the hub from the disc by knocking back the locking tabs and undoing the four bolts. Discard the disc, bolts and locking tabs.

4 Before fitting a new disc to the hub, thoroughly clean the mating surfaces of both components. If this is not done properly, and dirt is allowed to get between the hub and the

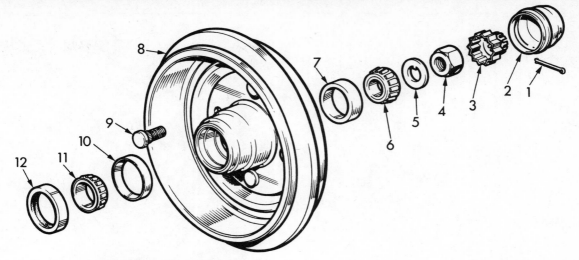

Fig. 9.6 Front hub/drum assembly

1 Split pin
2 Dust cover
3 Nut retainer
4 Nut
5 Thrust washer
6 Outer bearing

7 Bearing cap
8 Drum
9 Wheel stud
10 Bearing cap
11 Inner bearing
12 Grease seal

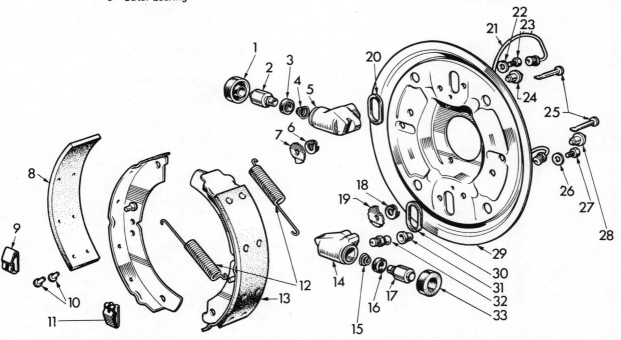

Fig. 9.7 Right hand front drum brake (note position of leading edge of shoe this is reversed on left hand brake)

1 Dust excluding boot
2 Piston
3 Seal
4 Spring
5 Operating cylinder
6 Spring
7 Cam (snail) adjuster
8 Friction lining
9 Shoe steady post clip
10 Rivets
11 Shoe steady post clip
12 Shoe return springs
13 Shoe
14 Operating cylinder
15 Spring
16 Seal
17 Piston

18 Spring
19 Cam (snail) adjuster
20 Rubber gasket
21 Hydraulic interconnecting pipe
22 Washer
23 Bolt
24 Adjuster stud
25 Shoe steady posts
26 Washer
27 Bolt
28 Adjuster stud
29 Backplate
30 Rubber gasket
31 Bleed nipple dust cap
32 Bleed nipple
33 Rubber dust excluding boot

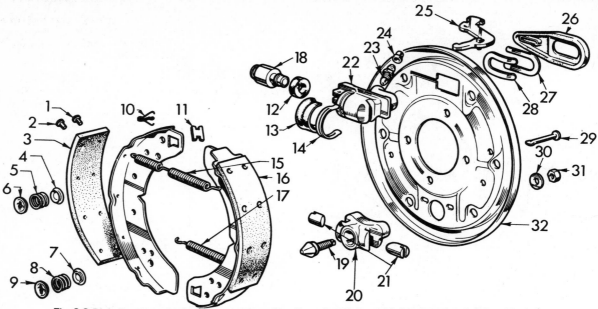

Fig. 9.8 Right hand rear brake (note position of leading edge of shoe, this is reversed on left hand brake)

1 Rivet	17 Shoe return spring
2 Rivet	18 Piston
3 Friction lining	19 Adjuster wedge
4 Spring seats	20 Adjuster body
5 Steady post spring	21 Adjuster tappets
6 Steady post cap	22 Operating cylinder
7 Spring seat	23 Bleed nipple
8 Steady post spring	24 Bleed nipple dust cap
9 Steady post cap	25 Handbrake operating lever
10 Support plate retaining spring	26 Rubber dust excluder
11 Shoe support plate	27 Operating cylinder retaining clip
12 Seal	28 Operating cylinder retaining clip
13 Dust excluder	29 Shoe steady post
14 Dust excluder clip	30 Washer
15 Shoe return spring	31 Nut
16 Brake shoe	32 Backplate

disc, this will seriously affect disc brake run-out when it is checked after reassembly.

5   Fit the hub and disc together using new locking tabs and nuts. Tighten the nuts down to a torque of 30 to 34 lb ft (4.15 to 4.70 kg m) and bend up the locking tabs.

6   Refit the disc and hub assembly and check the disc brake run-out (Chapter 11, Section 4).

---

11   Brake master cylinder - removal and installation

1   Working inside the vehicle, disconnect the pushrod from the brake pedal by removing the spring clip, the clevis pin and bushes.

2   On single circuit type master cylinders, disconnect the single fluid pipe at the union on the master cylinder body. On tandem (dual circuit) type master cylinders, disconnect the two fluid pipes from the master cylinder body.

3   Plug the fluid lines to prevent the ingress of dirt.

4   Unscrew and remove the two nuts and spring washers which secure the master cylinder to the engine rear bulkhead and remove it.

5   Installation is a reversal of removal but bleed the brakes as described later in this Chapter when the refitment is completed.

---

12   Master cylinder (single type) - dismantling and reassembly

1   To dismantle the master cylinder, pull off the rubber dust cover where the pushrod enters the master cylinder then with a pair of long nosed pliers, remove the circlip holding the pushrod in place in the cylinder and remove the pushrod.

2   Now withdraw the piston and valve assembly complete from

the master cylinder. The piston is held in the spring retainer by a tab which engages under a shoulder on the front of the piston. Gently lift this tab and remove the piston.

3   Carefully compress the spring and move the spring retainer to one side. This will release the end of the valve stem from the retainer.

4   Slide the valve spacer and shim off the valve stem. Remove the rubber seal from the piston and the valve seal off the other end of the valve stem.

5   Examine the bore of the cylinder carefully for any scores or ridges, and if none are found, new seals can be fitted. If there is any doubt as to the condition of the bore, then a new cylinder must be fitted.

6   Before reassembly, wash all parts in methylated spirit, commerical alcohol, or approved brake fluid. Do not use any other type of oil or cleaning liquid or the seals will be damaged.

7   To reassemble the master cylinder, start by fitting the piston seal to the piston with the sealing lips toward the narrow end and fit the valve seal to the valve stem with the lip toward the front of the valve. Fig 9.12 clearly shows the correct fitting of the seals.

8   Place the shim wahser on the valve stem, ensuring that the convex face abuts the shoulder flange on the valve stem. Fit the seal spacer onto the valve stem so that the legs of the spacer are facing the valve seal.

9   Refit the spring to the valve stem, then insert the spring retainer into the open end of the spring. Compress the spring and engage the small boss on the end of the valve stem into its recess in the spring retainer.

10 Place the narrow end of the piston in its slot in the spring retainer and secure it there by pressing down the tab.

Fig. 9.9 Fitting rear wheel cylinder retainers

11 Dip the complete assembly in clean approved hydraulic fluid and with the valve leading slide it into the cylinder.

12 Replace the pushrod in the master cylinder and secure it with the circlip. Finally replace the rubber dust cap.

13 Master cylinder (tandem type) - dismantling and reassembly

1 This type of master cylinder is used in conjunction with dual circuit hydraulic systems. Also incorporated is a pressure differential warning actuator, its purpose and servicing being described in Sections 14 and 15.

2 The tandem master cylinder comprises two piston assemblies, one behind the other operating in a common bore. There are two outlets from the master cylinder, one to the front brakes and one to the rear brakes, both going via the pressure differential warning actuator.

3 To dismantle the unit, pull off the rubber dust cover and remove the circlip and washer under the dust cover which holds the pushrod in place. Remove the pushrod.

4 Take the hydraulic fluid reservoir off the cylinder assembly by undoing the screw on each side of the cylinder.

5 From the top of the cylinder, remove the circlip and spring from the primary recuperating valve and with a suitable hexagon headed key, take out the plug which holds this valve in place, then remove the valve assembly.

6 Fit plugs to the two outlet holes and to the primary recuperating valve aperture, then using a suitable air line, blow gently into the other hole on the top of the cylinder. This will

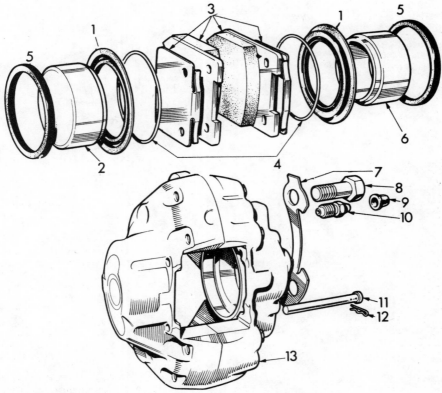

Fig. 9.10 Front caliper unit

1   Dust excluders
2   Piston
3   Friction pads and shims
4   Dust excluder retaining rings
5   Piston seals
6   Piston
7   Locking plate

8   Bolt
9   Dust cap
10 Bleed valve
11 Pad retaining pin
12 Pin retaining clip
13 Caliper body

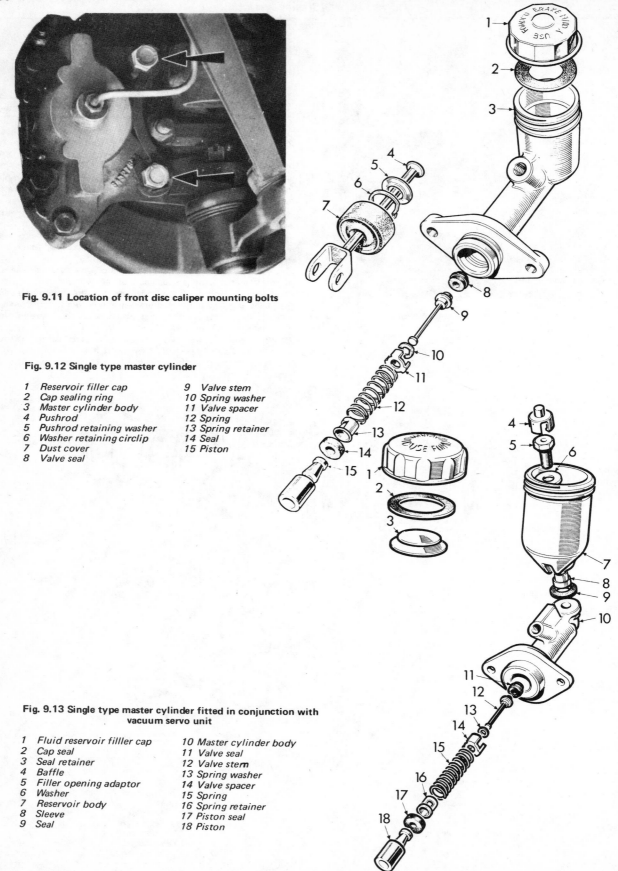

Fig. 9.11 Location of front disc caliper mounting bolts

Fig. 9.12 Single type master cylinder

1	Reservoir filler cap	9	Valve stem
2	Cap sealing ring	10	Spring washer
3	Master cylinder body	11	Valve spacer
4	Pushrod	12	Spring
5	Pushrod retaining washer	13	Spring retainer
6	Washer retaining circlip	14	Seal
7	Dust cover	15	Piston
8	Valve seal		

Fig. 9.13 Single type master cylinder fitted in conjunction with
vacuum servo unit

1	Fluid reservoir filler cap	10	Master cylinder body
2	Cap seal	11	Valve seal
3	Seal retainer	12	Valve stem
4	Baffle	13	Spring washer
5	Filler opening adaptor	14	Valve spacer
6	Washer	15	Spring
7	Reservoir body	16	Spring retainer
8	Sleeve	17	Piston seal
9	Seal	18	Piston

remove from the cylinder bore the primary piston and spring, the secondary piston and the secondary recuperating valve assemblies.

7 Remove the piston seal from the primary piston. Lift the tab on the secondary piston spring retainer and remove the piston. Compress the secondary piston spring, move the retainer to one side and remove the secondary recuperating valve stem from the retainer. Then slide the valve spacer and shim from the valve stem, noting the way in which the shim is fitted.

8 Remove the small rubber valve seal and the secondary piston seal. Examine the state of the cylinder bore for signs of scoring or corrosion. If this is damaged in any way, a new master cylinder must be fitted. It is also advisable to renew all rubber seals as a matter of course, whether they are damaged or not.

9 Clean all parts with approved hydraulic fluid prior to reassembly in the cylinder bore.

10 Fit a new seal onto the secondary piston and a new seal to the valve stem. Use the fingers only to manipulate them. Replace the shim on the valve stem, making sure that the convex side faces toward the seal spacer which is fitted next, with its legs toward the valve seal.

11 Refit the secondary piston spring over the valve stem, insert the spring retainer, compress the spring and fit the boss in the valve stem into its location in the spring retainer.

12 Place the narrow end of the secondary piston into the spring retainer and secure it by pressing down the tab. Dip the now complete secondary assembly in approved hydraulic fluid and carefully slide it into the cylinder bore with the secondary recuperating valve leading.

13 Place the primary piston spring into the cylinder, fit a new rubber seal to the primary piston, dip it in clean brake fluid and carefully slide it into the cylinder, drilled end first.

14 Fit the pushrod into the end of the primary piston and retain it with the washer and circlip.

15 Place the primary recuperating valve into its location in the top of the cylinder and check that it is properly located by moving the pushrod up and down a small amount. Screw the retaining plug into position and refit the spring and circlip to the valve plunger.

16 Move the pushrod in and out of the cylinder and check that the recuperating valve opens when the rod is fully withdrawn and closes again when it is pushed in.

17 Check the condition of the front and rear reservoir gaskets and if there is any doubt as to their condition, new ones must be fitted. Refit the reservoir to the cylinder with its two retaining screws.

14 Pressure differential warning actuator - description and centralising

1 The actuator is essentially a shuttle valve to the opposing sides of which are connected the front and rear hydraulic brake circuits (dual system). Whilst equal pressure is maintained in both circuits, the valve remains centralised (in balance) but should the pressure drop in either circuit due to a leaking pipe or cylinder seal, then the valve is displaced - blocking the affected circuit and closing an electrical contact to illuminate a warning light on the facia panel.

2 In the event of a pressure drop (i) in one of the circuits, (ii) air in the hydraulic system or (iii) during bleeding of the braking system, the valve will have to be centralised.

3 This can be done by getting hold of an old screwdriver and cutting it down or grinding it into a tool of the dimensions shown in Fig 9.15.

4 The rubber cover should be removed from the bottom of the pressure differential warning actuator and the tool inserted through the hole where it will engage in a slot in the larger piston, thus drawing it into a central position.

5 During bleeding of the brakes, the piston must be held in this position throughout the operation or it will prove very difficult to get the waring light to stay extinguished.

15 Pressure differential warning actuator - servicing

1 Disconnect the five hydraulic pipes at their unions on the pressure differential warning actuator and to prevent too much loss of hydraulic fluid, either place a piece of polythene under the cap of the master cylinder and screw it down tightly, or plug the ends of the two pipes leading from the master cylinder.

2 Referring to Fig 9.16, disconnect the wiring from the switch assembly (2).

3 Undo the single bolt holding the assembly to the rear of the engine compartment and remove it from the car.

4 To dismantle the assembly, start by undoing the end plug (4) and discarding the copper gasket (5). Then undo the adaptor (8) and discard its copper gasket as they must be renewed.

5 Unscrew the switch assembly (2) from the top of the unit, then push the small and large pistons (7) out of their bores, taking extreme care not to damage the bores during this operation.

6 Take the small seals (1, 3) from their pistons, making a careful note that the seals are slightly tapered and that the large diameter on each seal is fitted to the slotted end of the pistons. Discard the seals.

7 Pull the dust cover (6) off the bottom of the unit and discard this component for the same reasons as above.

8 Carefully examine the pistons (7) and the bore of the actuator for score marks, scratches or damage; if any are found, the complete unit must be exchanged.

9 To test if the switch assembly (2) is working correctly, reconnect the wiring and press the plunger against any part of the bare metal of the engine or the bodywork when the warning lamp should light. If it does not, check the switch by substitution and check the warning lamp.

10 To reassemble the unit, start by fitting new seals (1, 3) to the pistons (7) making sure that they are correctly fitted as detailed in paragraph 6.

11 With the slotted end outward, gently push the larger piston into the bore until the groove in the other end of the piston is opposite the hole in which the switch assembly (2) is fitted.

12 Screw the switch assembly (2) into position and tighten it down to a torque of 2 to 2.5 lb ft (0.28 to 0.34 kg m). Then gently push the shorter piston, with the slotted end outward, into the other end of the actuator.

14 Fit new copper washers (5) to the adaptor (8) and the end plug (4) and replace them in the assembly, tightening them down to a torque of 16 to 20 lb ft (2.22 to 2.80 kg m). Fit a new dust cover (6) over the bottom aperture.

15 Replacement of the pressure differential warning actuator on the car is a direct reversal of the removal sequence. The brakes must be bled after refitting.

16 Flexible brake hoses - inspection, removal and refitting

1 Inspect the condition of the flexible hydraulic hoses leading from under the front wings to the brackets on the front suspension units, and the single hose on the rear axle casing. If they are swollen, damaged or chafed, they must be renewed.

2 Undo the locknuts at both ends of the flexible hoses and then, holding the hexagon nut on the flexible hose steady, undo the other union nut and remove the flexible hose and washer.

3 Replacement is a reversal of the removal procedure, but carefully check that all the securing brackets are in a sound condition and that the locknuts are tight. Check the path taken by the hose when installed to ensure that it does not foul the tyres or steering in any position of lock. If this does occur, loosen the union with the rigid pipe and twist the flexible hose not more than one quarter turn in either direction to correct matters. Retighten the union whilst holding the flexible hose perfectly still.

17 Bleeding the hydraulic system

1 Removal of all air from the hydraulic system is essential

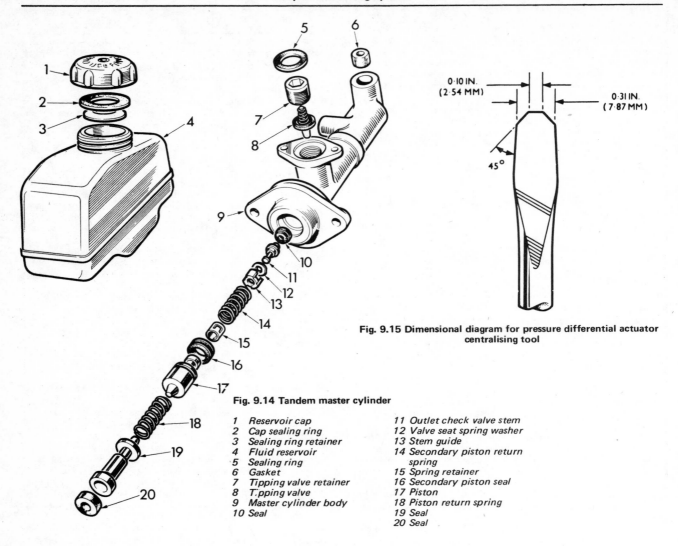

Fig. 9.15 Dimensional diagram for pressure differential actuator
centralising tool

Fig. 9.14 Tandem master cylinder

1 Reservoir cap	11 Outlet check valve stem
2 Cap sealing ring	12 Valve seat spring washer
3 Sealing ring retainer	13 Stem guide
4 Fluid reservoir	14 Secondary piston return
5 Sealing ring	spring
6 Gasket	15 Spring retainer
7 Tipping valve retainer	16 Secondary piston seal
8 Tipping valve	17 Piston
9 Master cylinder body	18 Piston return spring
10 Seal	19 Seal
	20 Seal

to the correct working of the braking system, and before
undertaking this, examine the fluid reservoir cap to ensure that
both vent holes, one on top and the second underneath but not
in line, are clear; check the level of fluid and top up if required.
2 Check all brake line unions and connections for possible
seepage, and at the same time, check the condition of the rubber
hoses which may be perished.
3 If the condition of the wheel cylinders is in doubt, check for
possible signs of fluid leakage.
4 If there is any possibility of incorrect fluid having been put
into the system, drain all the fluid out and flush through with
methylated spirits. Renew all piston seals and cups since these
will be affected and could possibly fail under pressure.
5 Gather together a clean jam jar, a 9 inch (228.6 mm) length
of rubber tubing which fits tightly over the bleed nipples, and
the correct brake fluid, which has remained unshaken for
24 hours and has been stored in an airtight container.
6 To bleed the system, clean the areas around the bleed valves
and start on the front brakes first by removing the rubber cup
over the bleed valve, if fitted, and fitting a rubber tube in
position.
7 Place the end of the tube in a clean glass jar containing
sufficient fluid to keep the end of the tube submerged during
the operation.
8 Open the bleed valve with a spanner and have an assistant
quickly press down the brake pedal. After slowly releasing the
pedal, pause for a moment to allow the fluid to recoup in the

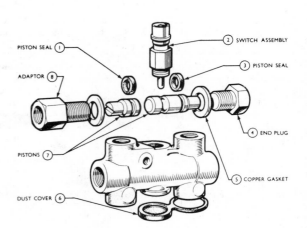

Fig. 9.16 Pressure differential actuator

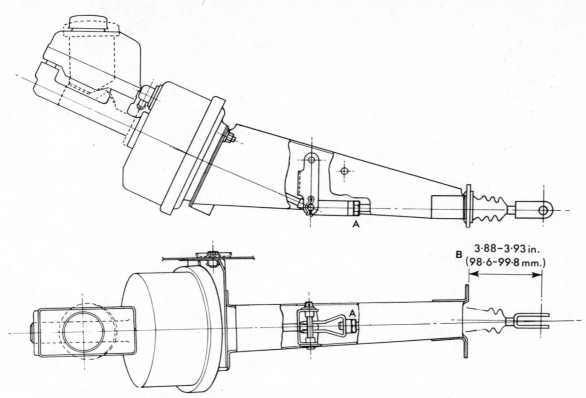

Fig. 9.17 Push-rod adjustment for vacuum servo unit

A   adjuster nut   B   pedal to mounting flange dimension

B   3·88–3·93 in.
(98·6–99·8 mm.)

Fig. 9.18 Separating front and rear shells of servo

Fig. 9.19 Fitting stop key to vacuum servo

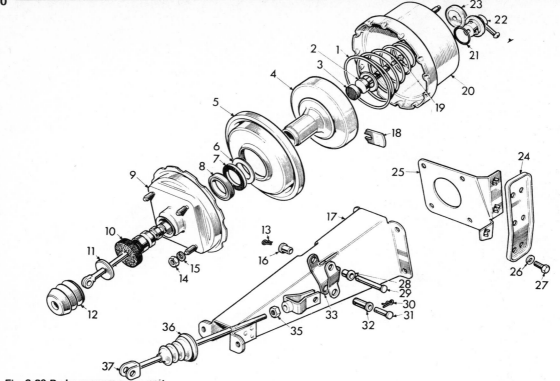

Fig. 9.20 Brake vacuum servo unit

1 Spring	11 Filter retainer	21 Sealing ring	30 Retaining clip
2 Pushrod	12 Dust cover	22 Check valve assembly	31 Clevis pin
3 Reaction disc	13 Retaining clip	23 Plate seat	32 Bush
4 Diaphragm plate	14 Nut	24 Apron mounting reinforce-	33 Pushrod relay link
5 Diaphragm	15 Locking washer	ment	35 Nut
6 Washer	16 Pushrod bush	25 Support bracket	36 Dust cover
7 Piston guide	17 Mounting bracket	26 Locking washer	37 Relay link pushrod
8 Piston seal	18 Valve plunger stop key	27 Bolt	
9 Rear housing assembly	19 Pushrod adjustment bolt	28 Bush	
10 Air filter	20 Housing	29 Pin	

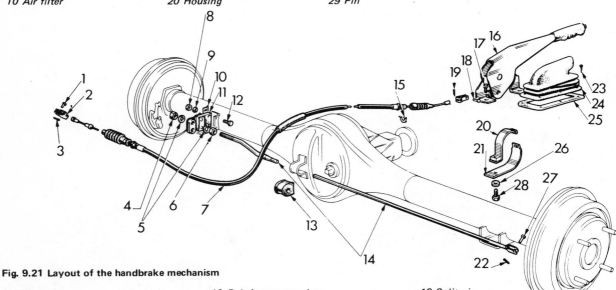

Fig. 9.21 Layout of the handbrake mechanism

1 Clevis pin	10 Reinforcement plate	19 Split pin
2 Clevis	11 Flexible equaliser bracket	20 Stoneguard retainers
3 Split pin	12 Bolt	21 Stoneguard retainers
4 Nut	13 Rubber bush	22 Split pin
5 Lock washers	14 Transverse rod	23 Self-tapping screw
6 Nut	15 Cable guide	24 Rubber gaiter
7 Operating cable	16 Handbrake lever	25 Retaining plate
8 Nut	17 Bolt	26 Washer
9 Washer	18 Clevis pin	27 Clevis pin
		28 Bolt

master cylinder and then depress again. This will force air from the system. Continue until no more air bubbles can be seen coming from the tube.

9 Press the pedal fully to the floor and holding it in this position, tighten the bleed nipple. At intervals, make certain that the reservoir is kept topped up, otherwise air will enter at this point.

10 Repeat this operation on the other front brake and the left hand rear brake, there being no bleed valve on the right hand rear brake. When completed, check the level of the fluid in the reservoir and then check the feel of the brake pedal, which should be firm and free from any 'spongy' action, which is normally associated with air in the system.

11 On vehicles fitted with tandem master cylinders, the bleeding operation is similar but the pressure differential actuator valve must be held in a central position (Section 14). Both sections of the fluid reservoir must be kept topped up throughout the operation.

18 Vacuum servo unit - removal and refitting

1 Remove the vacuum supply pipe from the servo unit and then undo the brake fluid pipes from the master cylinder. Block the ends of the pipes to prevent the entry of dirt.

2 Take the master cylinder off the front of the servo unit by undoing the two retaining nuts and washers.

3 Detach the servo pushrod from the brake pedal by removing the spring clip, clevis pin and clevis pin bushes.

4 Working underneath the right hand wing, undo and remove the two nuts and one bolt which hold the servo unit mounting bracket to the side of the car.

5 From under the bonnet, undo and remove the two nuts which hold the rear of the servo mounting bracket to the bulkhead. Remove the servo unit complete with its mounting bracket from the car.

6 From halfway along the mounting bracket, separate the servo pushrod and the pedal pushrod from the pivoted relay lever by removing the spring clip, the clevis pin and clevis bush.

7 Then undo the four nuts and spring washers holding the servo unit to its mounting bracket and detach the servo.

8 Replacement of the servo unit and its mounting bracket are a direct reversal of the above procedure but note the following points.

9 When fitted correctly the pushrod which is attached to the brake pedal must have the yellow paint mark round the hole facing toward the centre of the car.

10 Measure the distance between the centre of the brake pushrod hole and the rear face of the servo mounting bracket (Fig 9.17). This dimension should be between 3.88 to 3.93 inch (98.6 to 99.8 mm). If found to be incorrect, adjust the length of the pedal pushrod by undoing the locknut at 'A' and adjusting the pushrod to the correct length before tightening down the locknut.

19 Vacuum servo unit - servicing

1 Before starting to dismantle the servo unit, it will be necessary to make up two pieces of angle iron or similar metal flat rod about three feet (1 m) long each with holes drilled in them to fit over the four studs on the pushrod side of the servo unit. You will also require another piece of angle iron about 12 inches (305 mm) long with holes drilled to coincide with the master cylinder attachment bolts.

2 Scribe marks on both halves of the servo unit so that the shells can be refitted in exactly the same position on reassembly.

3 Fit the three pieces of angle iron to the servo unit (Fig 9.18) and clamp the shorter piece in a vice so that the servo non-return valve is accessible and pointing downward. Ensure that the nuts on the angle irons are tight.

4 As it is not possible to separate the two shells with the spring pressure still on the diaphragm, it is necessary to create a vacuum behind the diaphragm. This is done by connecting a suitable

length of hose to the servo non-return valve and the engine manifold and starting up the engine.

5 It will probably be necessary to get two assistants to help with the next operation, one to steady the servo unit in the vice and one on the end of one of the longer angle irons. Using the top angle irons as leverage, turn the servo top shell in an anti-clockwise direction until a mark on the top shell aligns with a cutaway on the bottom shell. At this point the shells should separate, but if they fail to do so, they can be gently tapped with a soft headed hammer. It is important to maintain the vacuum all the time or, under the action of the diaphragm spring, the two shells will fly apart possibly causing injury and damage.

6 Once the two shells have been separated the vacuum can be destroyed and the diaphragm and diaphragm plate assembly, which includes the control rod and valve assembly, can be withdrawn.

7 The control rod and valve assembly should now be removed from the plate and the diaphragm taken from its plate by carefully pulling its centre from the locating groove in the plate.

8 Take off and discard the air filter which is found in the extension flange on the rear edge of the diaphragm plate.

9 Withdraw the seal from the larger front shell and the internal pushrod and remove the slotted disc from the diaphragm plate.

10 With a screwdriver, prise off the seal retainer from the smaller rear whell and take out the seal.

11 With a suitable spanner, unscrew the non-return valve and its seal from the larger front shell.

12 Carefully examine and clean all parts of the servo before reassembly and as a matter of course renew all rubber parts, including the diaphragm. The control and valve assembly are replaced as a unit and sould not be broken down.

13 Commence reassembly by fitting a new seal to the non-return valve and replacing the valve in the front shell.

14 Place a new seal into its recess in the rear shell and fit the seal retainer which can be forced into place with a socket just smaller than the retainer.

15 Fit a new air filter to the rear of the diaphragm plate, then insert the control rod and valve assembly into the centre of the diaphragm plate and apply an approved lubricant to the bearing surfaces of the control rod and valve assembly. Secure the complete assembly in the plate with the stop key (Fig 9.19).

16 Assemble the new diaphragm to its plate, making sure that its centre is correctly located in the groove on the plate. It is advisable to lightly grease the areas of the diaphragm which contact the shells with an approved lubricant. This will help during reassembly and also during later dismantling operations. This grease must not be allowed to come into contact with any of the hydraulic brake system seals or damage will result.

17 Refit the lengths of angle iron as in paragraph 3 and replace the unit in the vice. Reconnect the vacuum pipe, check that the two shells are correctly lined up and start the engine.

18 With the help of the vacuum created and by applying further pressure to the rear shell completely engage the two shells together and with the aid of the angle irons turn the rear shell in a clockwise direction until the scribe marks made prior to dismantling are in line.

19 With the vacuum still being applied, check how far the pushrod extends beyond the front shell. This must be from 0.011 to 0.016 inch (0.28 to 0.40 mm). Adjust if necessary by the domed nut (19) (Fig 9.20) and then lock it in position using two or three drops of Loctite B.

20 Brake pedal - removal and refitting

1 Disconnect the brake master cylinder pushrod from the brake pedal as described in Section 11.

2 Take off the spring clip holding the clutch cable to the top of its pedal and withdraw the short pivot pin.

3 Remove the circlip from the groove on the pedal pivot pin between the brake pedal and the right hand side of the pedal mounting bracket.

4   Withdraw the pedal pivot pin from the clutch pedal end, then remove the two pedals from the car carefully noting the position of the bushes at either end and the single spacer washer.

5   Replacement is a direct reversal of the removal procedure detailed above.

21 Handbrake - adjustment

1   The handbrake is normally adjusted automatically when the adjusters on the brake backplates are rotated to take up wear in the brake shoe linings. However, if the operating cable has stretched or in the event of a new cable having been fitted (Section 22), carry out the following procedure.

2   Chock the front wheels; release the handbrake fully and then jack up the rear road wheels.

3   Rotate the adjuster on each brake backplate until the shoes just start to bind on the drums.

4   Check the position of the equaliser bracket on the left hand side of the rear axle casing. It should be set centrally or be offset toward the centre of the vehicle by not more than 1/8 inch (3.175 mm). If its position is not correct, adjust the effective length of the transverse rod (14) (Fig 9.21) by moving the locknut and adjusting nut at the equaliser bracket.

5   Do not adjust excessively however, as it will actuate the operating lever at the wheel cylinder.

6   Check that the drums still drag by the same amount and then remove any slack from the handbrake cable by altering the position of the outer cable nuts on the equaliser bracket.

7   Slacken both rear brake adjusters by two or three clicks and then rotate the roadwheels to check that no drag exists. If drag is evident, back off the adjuster one more click.

8   Lower the jack and apply the handbrake. If the adjustment has been correctly carried out, then the rear wheels should be fully locked when the handbrake lever moves through three or four notches of its quadrant.

22 Handbrake cable - renewal

1   Chock the front road wheels, jack up the rear of the vehicle and release the handbrake fully.

2   Disconnect the handbrake cable from the brake operating lever by removing the clip (or split pin) and the clevis pin.

3   Slacken the nuts which secure the outer cable to the equaliser bracket.

4   Disconnect the front end of the cable from the handbrake lever which projects below the floor of the bodyshell, by removing the clip (or split pin) and clevis pin.

5   Withdraw the cable towards the rear of the vehicle by pulling it through its guides which are attached to the underbody.

6   Fitting the new cable is a reversal of removal but grease the guides and when installed, adjust it as described in Section 21.

23 Fault finding chart

Symptom	Reason/s	Remedy
PEDAL TRAVELS ALMOST TO FLOORBOARDS BEFORE BRAKES OPERATE		
Leaks and air bubbles in hydraulic system	Brake fluid level too low	Top up master cylinder reservoir. Check for leaks.
	Wheel cylinder leaking	Dismantle wheel cylinder, clean, fit new rubbers and bleed brakes.
	Master cylinder leaking (Bubbles in master cylinder fluid)	Dismantle master cylinder, clean, and fit new rubbers. Bleed brakes.
	Brake flexible hose leaking	Examine and fit new hose if old hose leaking. Bleed brakes.
	Brake line fractured	Replace with new brake pipe. Bleed brakes.
	Brake system unions loose	Check all unions in brake system and tighten as necessary. Bleed brakes.
Normal wear	Linings over 75% worn	Fit replacement shoes and brake linings.
Incorrect adjustment	Brakes badly out of adjustment	Jack up car and adjust brakes.
	Master cylinder push rod out of adjustment causing too much pedal free movement (servo. system)	Reset to specification.
BRAKE PEDAL FEELS SPRINGY		
Brake lining renewal	New linings not yet bedded-in	Use brakes gently until springy pedal feeling leaves.
Excessive wear or damage	Brake drums badly worn and weak or cracked	Fit new brake drums.
Lack of maintenance	Master cylinder securing nuts loose	Tighten master cylinder securing nuts. Ensure spring washers are fitted.
BRAKE PEDAL FEELS SPONGY AND SOGGY		
Leaks or bubbles in hydraulic system	Wheel cylinder leaking	Dismantle wheel cylinder, clean, fit new rubbers, and bleed brakes.
	Master cylinder leaking (Bubbles in master cylinder reservoir)	Dismantle master cylinder, clean, and fit new rubbers and bleed brakes. Replace cylinder if internal walls scored.
	Brake pipe line or flexible hose leaking	Fit new pipe line or hose.
	Unions in brake system loose	Examine for leaks, tighten as necessary.

Symptom	Reason/s	Remedy
EXCESSIVE EFFORT REQUIRED TO BRAKE CAR		
Lining type or condition	Linings or pads badly worn	Fit replacement brake shoes, linings and pads.
	New linings recently fitted - not yet bedded-in	Use brakes gently until braking effort normal
	Harder linings or pads fitted than standard causing increase in pedal pressure	Remove linings or pads and replace with normal units.
Oil or grease leaks	Linings, brake drums or discs contaminated with oil, grease, or hydraulic fluid	Rectify source of leak, clean brake drums, or discs, fit new linings
BRAKES UNEVEN AND PULLING TO ONE SIDE		
Oil or grease leaks	Linings, pads and brake drums or discs contaminated with oil, grease, or hydraulic fluid	Ascertain and rectify source of leak, clean brake drums, discs or pads and fit new linings.
	Tyre pressures unequal	Check and inflate as necessary.
	Radial ply tyres fitted at one end of car only	Fit radial ply tyres of the same make to all four wheels
	Brake backplate loose	Tighten backplate securing nuts and bolts.
	Brake shoes or pads fitted incorrectly	Remove and fit shoes correct way round.
	Different type of linings fitted at each wheel	Fit the linings specified by the manufacturers all round
	Anchorages for front suspension or rear axle loose	Tighten front and rear suspension pick-up points including spring anchorage.
	Brake drums or discs badly worn, cracked or distorted	Fit new brake drums or discs.
BRAKES TEND TO BIND, DRAG, OR LOCK-ON		
Incorrect adjustment	Brake shoes adjusted too tightly	Slacken off brake shoe adjusters two clicks.
	Handbrake cable over-tightened	Slacken off handbrake cable adjustment.
Wear or dirt in hydraulic system or incorrect fluid	Reservoir vent hole in cap blocked with dirt.	Clean and blow through hole.
	Master cylinder by-pass port restricted - brakes seize in 'on' position	Dismantle, clean, and overhaul master cylinder. Bleed brakes.
	Wheel cylinder seizes in 'on' position	Dismantle, clean, and overhaul wheel cylinder. Bleed brakes.
Mechanical wear	Brake shoe pull off springs broken, stretched or loose	Examine springs and renew if worn or loose.
Incorrect brake assembly	Brake shoe pull off springs fitted wrong way round, omitted, or wrong type used	Examine, and rectify as appropriate.
Neglect	Handbrake system rusted or seized in the 'on' position	Apply 'Plus Gas' to free, clean and lubricate.

Chapter 10 Electrical system

Contents

Specifications

Battery

Type	Lead acid, 12 volt
Earth	Negative
Capacity at 20 hour rate:	
1100 cc (U.K.)	32 amp/hr.
1100 cc (export)	38 amp/hr.
1300 cc (all)	38 amp/hr.
Cold climate	53 amp/hr.
Plates per cell - Standard	9
- Cold climate	13
Specific gravity charged	1.275 to 1.290
Electrolyte capacity - Standard	4.5 pints (5.4 US pints, 2.5 litres)
- Cold climate	6.4 pints (7.7 US pints, 3.6 litres)

Dynamo ... ...

	Lucas C40 (C40/L on cold start models)
Maximum charge	22 amps (C40) 25 amps (C40L)
Number of brushes	2
Brush length new	0.718 in. (18.23 mm)
Brush spring tension	18 to 24 ozs
Field resistance	6.0 ohms

Alternator ... ... Lucas 16 ACR
    Nominal rated output at 14 volts and 6000 rev/min ... ... 34 amps
    Maximum continuous speed ... ... 12500 rev/min
    Length of slip ring brushes ... ... ½ in. (12.7 mm)
    Brush spring tension ... ... 9 to 13 oz (255 to 368 g)
    Regulating voltage ... ... 14 to 14.4 volts
    Regulator/control box (with dynamo only) ... ... Lucas RB.340
    Cut-in voltage ... ... 12.6 to 13.4 volts
    Drop-off voltage ... ... 9.25 to 11.25 volts
    Armature to core air gap ... ... 0.035 to 0.045 in. (0.89 to 1.14 mm)
    Current regulator, on-load setting ... ... Max. generator output + or − 1½ amps
    Armature to core air gap ... ... 0.052 to 0.056 in. (1.32 to 1.42 mm)
    Voltage regulator, open circuit setting ... ... 13.8 to 14.2 volts at 20º C (68º F)
    Armature to core air gap ... ... 0.052 to 0.056 in. (1.32 to 1.42 mm)
    Reverse current ... ... 3.0 to 5.0 amps
    Voltage setting at 2,000 ... ... 10º C (50º F) 14.9 to 15.5 volts
    20º C (68º F) 14.7 to 15.3 volts
    30º C (86º F) 14.5 to 15.1 volts
    40º C (104º F) 14.3 to 14.9 volts

Starter motor (inertia type)
    Number of brushes 4
    Minimum brush length ... ... .3 in. (7.5 mm)
    Brush spring tension ... ... 34 ozs (.96 kg)
    Gear ratio ... ... 11 to 1
    Teeth on pinion 10
    Teeth on ring gear 110

Starter motor (pre-engaged type)
    Specification similar to (inertia type) but with the following differences:
    Gear ratio ... ... 12 to 1
    Teeth on pinion 11
    Teeth on ring gear 132

Fuse unit

	Up to September 1969	After September 1969
Number of fuses	6	7
Number of spare fuses in holder	1	2

Bulbs
    Headlamp (sealed beam) circular ... ... 60/45 watts
    Headlamp (semi-sealed beam) rectangular ... ... 45/40 watts
    Sidelamps ... ... 6 watts
    Stop/tail lamps ... ... 32/4 candle power
    Flasher lamps ... ... 32 candle power
    Number plate lamp ... ... 6 watts
    Interior lamp ... ... 6 watts
    Instrument panel illumination ... ... 3.6 watts
    Warning lights ... ... 2.2 watts

Torque wrench settings

	lb ft	kg m
Starter motor retaining bolts	20 to 25	2.76 to 3.46
Dynamo or alternator pulley	14 to 17	1.93 to 2.35
Dynamo or alternator mounting bolts	15 to 18	2.07 to 2.49
Dynamo or alternator mounting bracket	20 to 25	2.76 to 3.46

1 General description

The electrical system is 12 volt negative earth and the major components include a battery and a generator which may be a dynamo or alternator up to October 1973, thereafter an alternator was fitted as standard.

A separate voltage regulator is fitted in conjunction with a dynamo but the alternator has integral voltage control.

The starter motor may be of inertia or pre-engaged type, the latter being a factory fitted option.

All electrical circuits are protected by fuses and later models have spare fused terminals for the connection of accessories.

2 Battery - removal and refitting

1 The battery is positioned on a tray in the front of the engine compartment forward of the nearside suspension.
2 Disconnect the earthed negative lead and then the positive lead by slackening the retaining nuts and bolts or by unscrewing the retaining screws if these are fitted.
3 Remove the battery clamp and carefully lift the battery off its tray. Hold the battery vertically to ensure that no electrolyte is spilled.
4 Replacement is a direct reversal of this procedure. **Note:** Replace the positive lead and the earth (negative) lead, smearing

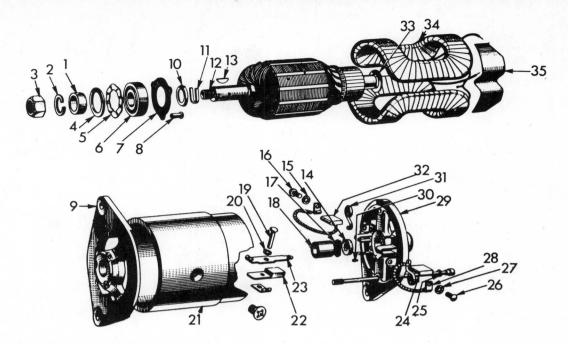

Fig. 10.1 Dynamo - component parts

1 End bearing collar	10 Locating ring retainer	19 Rivet	28 Terminal
2 Locking washer	11 Locating ring	20 Washer	29 Endplate
3 Nut	12 Armature assembly	21 Dynamo body	30 Endplate dowel
4 Felt ring	13 Woodruff key	22 Insulating block	31 Brush spring
5 Spring washer	14 Felt ring	23 Lucar terminal	32 Brush assembly
6 Bearing	15 Shakeproof washer	24 Brush assembly	33 Washer
7 Bearing retaining plate	16 Screw	25 Tie bolt	34 Field coils
8 Rivet	17 Felt ring retainer	26 Screw	35 Insulator
9 Endplate	18 Bush	27 Shakeproof washer	

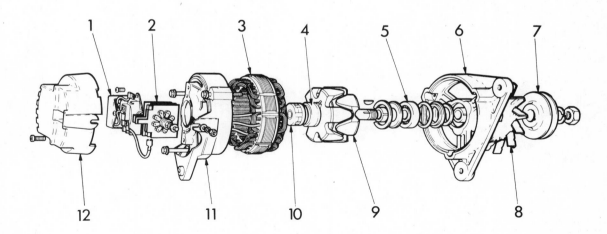

Fig. 10.2 Alternator - component parts

1 Brushgear and regulator assembly	7 Pulley
2 Rectifier pack	8 Fan
3 Stator	9 12 pole rotor
4 Ball race bearing	10 Slip ring
5 Ball race bearing	11 Slip ring end bracket
6 Drive end bracket	12 Cover

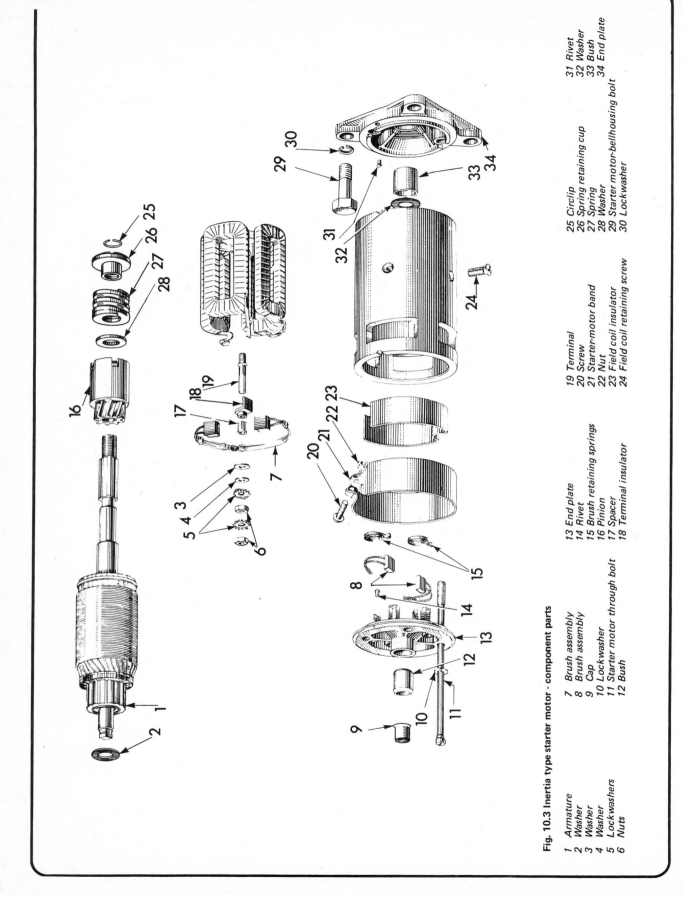

Fig. 10.3 Inertia type starter motor - component parts

1 Armature	7 Brush assembly	13 End plate	19 Terminal	25 Circlip	31 Rivet
2 Washer	8 Brush assembly	14 Rivet	20 Screw	26 Spring retaining cup	32 Washer
3 Washer	9 Cap	15 Brush retaining springs	21 Starter-motor band	27 Spring	33 Bush
4 Washer	10 Lockwasher	16 Pinion	22 Nut	28 Washer	34 End plate
5 Lockwashers	11 Starter motor through bolt	17 Spacer	23 Field coil insulator	29 Starter motor-bellhousing bolt	
6 Nuts	12 Bush	18 Terminal insulator	24 Field coil retaining screw	30 Lockwasher	

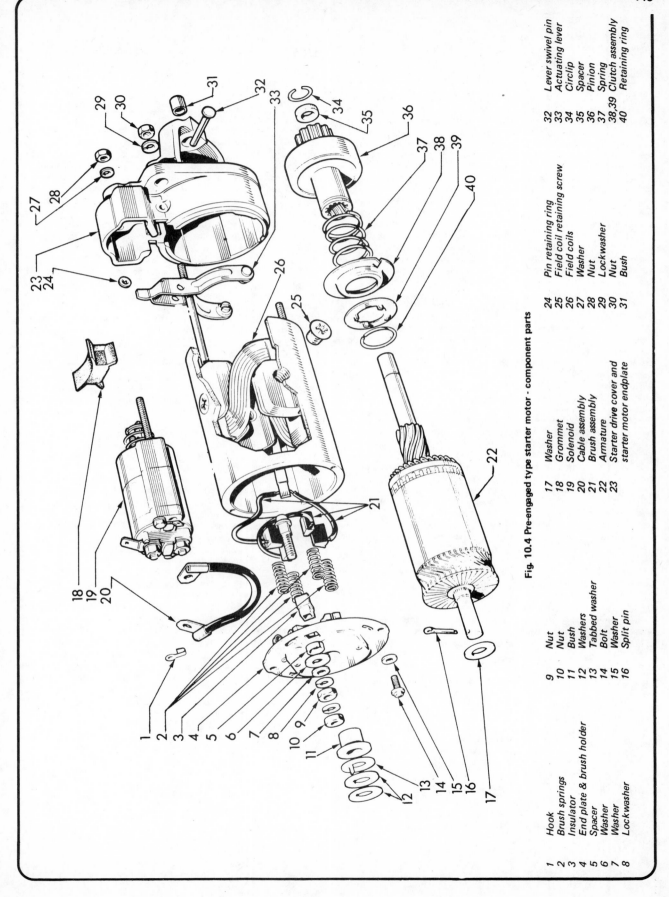

Fig. 10.4 Pre-engaged type starter motor - component parts

1 Hook
2 Brush springs
3 Insulator
4 End plate & brush holder
5 Spacer
6 Washer
7 Washer
8 Lockwasher
9 Nut
10 Nut
11 Bush
12 Washers
13 Tabbed washer
14 Bolt
15 Washer
16 Split pin
17 Washer
18 Grommet
19 Solenoid
20 Cable assembly
21 Brush assembly
22 Armature
23 Starter drive cover and
    starter motor endplate
24 Pin retaining ring
25 Field coil retaining screw
26 Field coils
27 Washer
28 Nut
29 Lockwasher
30 Nut
31 Bush
32 Lever swivel pin
33 Actuating lever
34 Circlip
35 Spacer
36 Pinion
37 Spring
38,39 Clutch assembly
40 Retaining ring

the terminals with petroleum jelly to prevent corrosion. Never use an ordinary grease as applied to other parts of the car.

---

3 Battery - maintenance and inspection

1   Normal weekly battery maintenance consists of checking the electrolyte level of each cell to ensure that the separators are covered by ¼ inch (6.35 mm) of electrolyte. If the level has fallen top up the battery using distilled water only. Do not overfill. If a battery is overfilled or any electrolyte spilled, immediately wipe away the excess as electrolyte attacks and corrodes any metal it comes into contact with very rapidly.

2   As well as keeping the terminals clean and covered with petroleum jelly, the top of the battery, and especially the top of the cells, should be kept clean and dry. This helps prevent corrosion and ensures that the battery does not become partially discharged by leakage through dampness and dirt.

3   Once every three months remove the battery and inspect the battery securing bolts, the battery clamp plate, tray, and battery leads for corrosion (white fluffy deposits on the metal which are brittle to touch). If any corrosion is found, clean off the deposits with ammonia and paint over the clean metal with an anti-rust/anti-acid paint.

4   At the same time inspect the battery case for cracks. If a crack is found, clean and plug it with one of the proprietary compounds marketed by firms such as Holts for this purpose. If leakage through the crack has been excessive then it will be necessary to refill the appropriate cell with fresh electrolyte as detailed later. Cracks are frequently caused to the top of the battery cases by pouring in distilled water in the middle of winter **after** instead of **before** a run. This gives the water no chance to mix with the electrolyte and so the former freezes and splits the battery case.

5   If topping up the batteries becomes excessive and the cases have been inspected for cracks that could cause leakage, but none are found, the batteries are being overcharged and the voltage regulator will have to be checked and reset.

6   Every three months check, measure the specific gravity with a hydrometer to determine the state of charge and condition of the electrolyte. There should be very little variation between the different cells and if a variation in excess of 0.025 is present, it will be due to either:

a) Loss of electrolyte from the battery caused by spillage or a leak resulting in a drop in the specific gravity of the electrolyte. The deficiency was probably made up with distilled water instead of fresh electrolyte.

b) An internal short circuit caused by buckling of the plates or a similar malady pointing to the likelihood of total battery failure in the near future.

7   The specific gravity of the electrolyte for fully charged conditions at the electrolyte temperature indicated is listed in Table A. The specific gravity of a fully discharged battery at different temperatures of the electrolyte is given at Table B.

Table A

Specific gravity - battery fully charged

1.268 at 100°F or   38°C electrolyte temperature
1.272 at   90°F or   32°C electrolyte temperature
1.276 at   80°F or   27°C electrolyte temperature
1.280 at   70°F or   21°C electrolyte temperature
1.284 at   60°F or   16°C electrolyte temperature
1.288 at   50°F or   10°C electrolyte temperature
1.292 at   40°F or   4°C electrolyte temperature
1.296 at   30°F or -1.5°C electrolyte temperature

Table B

Specific gravity - battery fully discharged

1.098 at 100°F or   38°C electrolyte temperature
1.102 at   90°F or   27°C electrolyte temperature
1.106 at   80°F or   27°C electrolyte temperature

1.110 at   70°F or   21°C electrolyte temperature
1.114 at   60°F or   16°C electrolyte temperature
1.118 at   50°F or   10°C electrolyte temperature
1.122 at   40°F or   4°C electrolyte temperature
1.126 at   30°F or -1.5°C electrolyte temperature

---

4 Electrolyte replenishment

1   If the battery is in a fully charged state and one of the cells maintains a specific gravity reading which is 0.025 or more lower than the others, and a check of each cell has been made with a voltmeter to check for short circuits (a four to seven second test should give a steady reading of between 1.2 to 1.8 volts), then it is likely that electrolyte has been lost from the cell which shows the low reading.

2   Top up the cell with a solution of 1 part sulphuric acid to 2.5 parts of water. If the cell is already fully topped up, draw some electrolyte out of it with a pipette. The total capacity of each cell is ¾ pint.

3   When mixing the sulphuric acid and water **never add water to sulphuric acid** - always pour the acid slowly into the water in a glass container. **If water is added to sulphuric acid it will explode.**

4   Continue to top up the cell with the freshly made electrolyte and then recharge the battery and check the hydrometer readings.

---

5 Battery - charging

1   In winter time when heavy demand is placed upon the battery, such as when starting from cold, and much electrical equipment is continually in use, it is a good idea to occasionally have the battery fully charged from an external source at the rate of 3.5 to 4 amps.

2   Continue to charge the battery at this rate until no further rise in specific gravity is noted over a four hour period.

3   Alternatively, a trickle charger charging at the rate of 1.5 amps can be safely used overnight.

4   Specially rapid boost charges which are claimed to restore the power of the battery in 1 to 2 hours are most dangerous as they can cause serious damage to the battery plates through over-heating.

5   While charging the battery, note that the temperature of the electrolyte should never exceed 100°F.

---

6 Dynamo - general description

The dynamo has two brushes and works in conjunction with the voltage regulator and cut-out. The dynamo is cooled by a multi-bladed fan mounted behind the dynamo pulley and blows air through cooling holes in the dynamo end brackets. The output from the dynamo is controlled by the voltage regulator which ensures a high output if the battery is in a low state of charge or the demands from the electrical equipment high, and a low output if the battery is fully charged and there is little demand from the electrical equipment.

---

7 Dynamo - lubrication

1   Every 6000 miles (9600 km) apply two or three drops of engine oil to the dynamo rear bearing.

2   The front bearing is grease sealed and requires no attention.

---

8 Dynamo drive belt (fan belt) - adjustment

1   The fan belt should be tight enough to ensure no slip between the belt and the dynamo pulley. If a shrieking noise comes from the engine when the unit is accelerated rapidly, it is likely that it is the fan belt slipping. On the other hand, the belt must not be too taut or the bearings will wear rapidly and cause dynamo failure or bearing seizure. Ideally ½ inch (12.7 mm)

total free movement should be available at the fan belt midway between the fan and the dynamo pulley.

2   To adjust the fan belt tension slightly slacken the three dynamo retaining bolts, and swing the dynamo on the upper two bolts outward to increase the tension, and inward to lower it.

3   It is best to leave the bolts fairly tight so that considerable effort has to be used to move the dynamo otherwise it is difficult to get the correct setting. If the dynamo is being moved to increase the tension and the bolts have only been slackened a little, a long spanner acting as a lever placed behind the dynamo with the lower end resting against the block, works very well in moving the dynamo outward. Retighten the dynamo bolts and check that the dynamo pulley is correctly aligned with the fan belt.

9   Dynamo - testing in position

1   If, with the engine running, no charge comes from the dynamo, or the charge is very low, first check that the fan belt is in place and is not slipping. Then check that the leads from the control box to the dynamo are firmly attached and that one has not come loose from its terminal.

2   The lead from the D terminal on the dynamo should be connected to the D terminal on the control box, and similarly the F terminals on the dynamo and control box should also be connected together. Check that this is so and that the leads have not been incorrectly fitted.

3   Make sure none of the electrical equipment (such as the lights or radio) is on and then pull the leads off the dynamo terminals marked D and F, join the terminals together with a short length of wire.

4   Attach to the centre of this length of wire the positive clip of a 0—20 volts voltmeter and run the other clip to earth on the dynamo yoke. Start the engine and allow it to idle at approximately 750 rev/min. At this speed the dynamo should give a reading of about 15 volts on the voltmeter. There is no point in raising the engine speed above a fast idle as the reading will then be inaccurate.

5   If no reading is recorded then check the brushes and brush connections. If a very low reading of approximately 1 volt is observed, then the field winding may be suspect.

6   If a reading of between 4 to 6 volts is recorded, it is likely that the armature winding is at fault.

7   On early dynamos it was possible to remove the dynamo cover band and check the dynamo and brushes in position. With the Lucas C40-1 windowless yoke dynamo it must be removed and dismantled before the brushes and commutator can be serviced.

8   If the voltmeter shows a good reading then, with the temporary link still in position, connect both leads from the control box to D and F on the dynamo (D to D and F to F). Release the lead from the D terminal at the control box end and clip one lead from the voltmeter to the end of the cable, and the other lead to a good earth. With the engine running at the same speed as previously, an identical voltage to that recorded at the dynamo should be noted on the voltmeter. If no voltage is recorded then there is a break in the wire. If the voltage is the same as recorded at the dynamo, then check the F lead in similar fashion. If both readings are the same as at the dynamo, then it will be necessary to test the control box.

10   Dynamo - removal and refitting

1   Slacken the two dynamo retaining bolts and the nut on the sliding link and move the dynamo in toward the engine so that the fan belt can be removed.

2   Disconnect the two leads from the dynamo terminals.

3   Remove the nut from the sliding link bolt and remove the two upper bolts. The dynamo is then free to be lifted away from the engine.

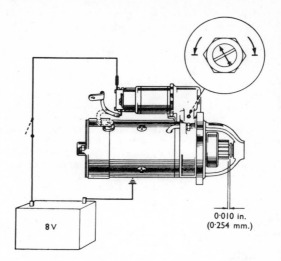

Fig. 10.5 Pre-engaged type starter end-float (solenoid actuated)

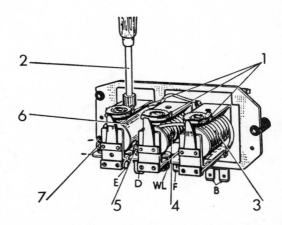

Fig. 10.6 Details of control box (cover removed) fitted in conjunction with dynamo only

1   Adjustment cams
2   Setting tool
3   Cut-out relay
4   Current regulator
5   Current regulator contacts
6   Voltage regulator
7   Voltage regulator contacts

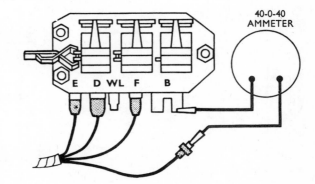

Fig. 10.7 On-load test diagram for current regulator

4 Replacement is a reversal of the above procedure. Do not finally tighten the retaining bolts and the nut on the sliding link until the fan belt has been tensioned correctly.

11 Dynamo - dismantling and servicing

1 Mount the dynamo in a vice and unscrew and remove the two tie bolts from the commutator end bracket (photo).
2 Mark the commutator end bracket and the dynamo casing so that the end bracket can be replaced in its original position. Pull the end bracket off the armature shaft. **Note:** Some versions of the dynamo may have a raised pip on the end bracket which locates in a recess on the edge of the casing. If so, marking the end bracket and casing is not necessary. A pip may also be found on the drive end bracket at the opposite end of the casing (photo).
3 Lift the two brush springs and draw the brushes out of the brush holders.
4 Measure the brushes and, if worn down to 9/32 inch (7.14 mm) or less, unscrew the screws holding the brush leads to the end bracket. Take off the brushes complete with leads. Old and new brushes are compared in the photograph.
5 If no locating pip can be found, mark the drive end bracket and the dynamo casing so that the drive end bracket can be replaced in its original position. Then pull the drive end bracket, complete with armature, out of the casing (photo).
6 Check the condition of the ball bearing in the drive end plate by firmly holding the plate and noting if there is visible side movement of the armature shaft in relation to the end plate. If play is present the armature assembly must be separated from the end plate. If the bearing is sound there is no need to carry out the work described in the following two paragraphs.
7 Hold the armature in one hand (mount it carefully in a vice if preferred) and undo the nut holding the pulley wheel and fan in place. Pull off the pulley wheel and fan.
8 Next remove the Woodruff key from its slot in the armature shaft and the bearing locating ring.
9 Place the drive end bracket across the open jaws of a vice with the armature downward and gently tap the armature shaft from the bearing (photo) in the end plate with the aid of a suitable drift.
10 Carefully inspect the armature and check it for open or short circuit windings. It is a good indication of an open circuit armature when the commutator segments are burnt. If the armature has a short circuit, the commutator segments will be very badly burnt, and the overheated armature windings badly discoloured. If open or short circuits are suspected, then test by substituting the suspect armature for a new one.
11 Check the resistance of the field coils. To do this, connect an ohmmeter between the field terminal and the yoke and note the reading on the ohmmeter which should be about 6 ohms. If the ohmmeter reading is infinity this indicates an open circuit in the field winding; if the ohmmeter reading is below 5 ohms, this indicates that one of the field coils is faulty and must be renewed.
12 Field coil replacement involves the use of a wheel operated screwdriver, a soldering iron, caulking and riveting and this operation is considered to be beyond the scope of most owners. Therefore, if the field coils are at fault, either purchase a rebuilt dynamo, or take the casing to a Ford dealer or electrical engineering works for new field coils to be fitted.
13 Next check the condition of the commutator. If it is dirty and blackened as shown, clean it with a petrol dampened rag. If the commutator is in good condition the surface will be smooth and quite free from pits or burnt areas, and the insulated segments clearly defined.
14 If, after the commutator has been cleaned, pits and burnt spots are still present, wrap a strip of fine glass paper round the commutator taking great care to move the commutator ¼ of a turn every ten rubs till it is thoroughly clean (photo).
15 In extreme cases of wear the commutator can be mounted in a lathe and with the lathe turning at high speed, a very fine cut may be taken off the commutator. Then polish the commutator with fine glass paper. If the commutator has worn so

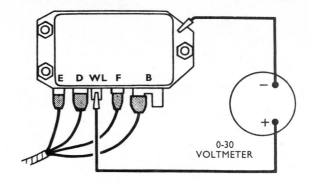

Fig. 10.8 Cut-in voltage test diagram

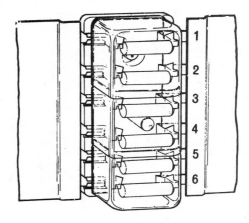

Fig. 10.9 Early type six-position fuse block

1　R.H. Main beam
2　L.H. Main beam
3　R.H. Dipped beam
4　L.H. Dipped beam
5　R.H. Side and tail lamps
6　L.H. Side and tail lamps

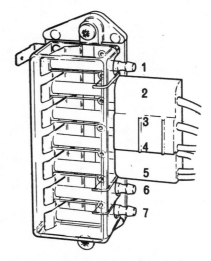

Fig. 10.10 Later type seven-position fuse block

1　Interior lamp, cigar lighter
2　L.H. Side and tail lamp, licence plate lamp
3　R.H. Side and tail lamp, Instrument illumination
4　Main beam
5　Dipped beam
6　Direction indicators, Stop lamps, Heater motor, Reversing lamps
7　Wiper motor

11.1 Removing dynamo tie-bolts

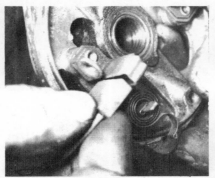

11.3 Dynamo brush holders

11.4 Comparing worn dynamo brushes with new

11.5 Withdrawing dynamo drive end bracket

11.8 Removing Woodruff key from dynamo armature shaft

11.9 Drifting out dynamo armature shaft from bearing

11.13 Dynamo commutator supported for cleaning

11.14 Cleaning dynamo commutator with glass paper

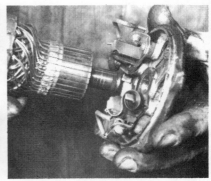

11.16 Location of dynamo commutator end bracket bearing

11.23 Fitting felt washer and wave washer to dynamo end bracket

11.24 Fitting bearing to dynamo end bracket

11.25 Driving bearing in to end bracket using a drift

11.26 Locating dynamo end bracket bearing plate

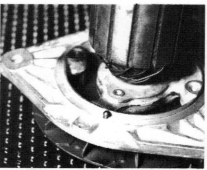

11.27 Riveting dynamo end bracket bearing plate

12.1 Fitting dynamo drive end bracket to armature shaft

12.2 Fitting spacer to dynamo armature shaft

12.3 Fully assembled state of dynamo drive end bracket

12.5 Connecting dynamo brush leads

that the insulators between the segments are level with the top of the segments, then undercut the insulators to a depth of 1/32 inch (0.8 mm). The best tool to use for this purpose is half a hacksaw blade ground to the thickness of the insulator, and with the handle end of the blade covered in insulating tape to make it comfortable to hold.

16 Check the brush bearing in the commutator end bracket for wear by noting if the armature spindle rocks when placed in it. If worn, it must be renewed.

17 The bush bearing can be removed by a suitable extractor or by screwing a 5/8 inch (15.9 mm) tap four or five times into the bush. The tap complete with bush is then pulled out of the end bracket.

18 **Note:** Before fitting the new bush bearing which is of the porous bronze type, it is essential that it is allowed to stand in SAE 30 engine oil for at least 24 hours before fitment. In an emergency the bush can be immersed in hot oil (100°C) for two hours.

19 Carefully fit the new bush into the endplate, pressing it in until the end of the bearing is flush with the inner side of the end plate. If available, press the bush in with a smooth shouldered mandrel of the same diameter as the armature shaft.

20 To renew the ball bearing fitted to the drive end bracket, drill out the rivets which hold the bearing retainer plate to the end bracket and lift off the plate.

21 Press out the bearing from the end bracket and remove the corrugated and felt washers from the bearing housing.

22 Thoroughly clean the bearing housing and the new bearing and pack with high melting point grease.

23 Place the felt washer and wave washer in that order in the end bracket bearing housing (photo).

24 Then fit the new bearing as shown.

25 Gently tap the bearing into place with the aid of a suitable drift.

26 Replace the bearing plate and fit three new rivets (photo).

27 Open up the rivets with the aid of a suitable cold chisel (photo).

28 Finally peen over the open end of the rivets with the aid of a ball hammer.

12 Dynamo - reassembly

1 Refit the drive end bracket to the armature shaft. Do not try and force the bracket on but with the aid of a suitable socket abutting the bearing, tap the bearing on gently, so pulling the end bracket down with it (photo).

2 Slide the spacer up the shaft and refit the Woodruff key (photo).

3 Replace the fan and pulley wheel and then fit the spring washer and nut and tighten the latter. The drive bracket end of the dynamo is now fully assembled as shown.

4 If the brushes are little worn and are to be used again, then ensure that they are placed in the same holders from which they

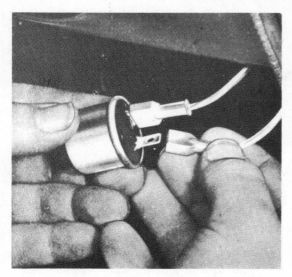

Fig. 10.11 Direction indicator flasher unit and leads

were removed. When refitting brushes, either new or old, check that they move freely in their holders. If either bush sticks, clean with a petrol moistened rag and, if still stiff, lightly polish the sides of the brush with a very fine file until the brush moves quite freely in its holders.

5 Tighten the two retaining screws and washers which hold the leads to the brushes in place (photo).

6 It is far easier to slip the end piece with brushes over the commutator if the brushes are raised in their holders using two hooked pieces of wire.

7 Refit the armature to the casing and then the commutator end plate and screw up the two tie bolts.

8 Finally, hook the ends of the two springs off the flanks of the brushes and onto their heads so the brushes are forced down into contact with the armature as shown and held in this position by the pressure of the springs resting against their flanks.

13 Alternator - general description

1 The main advantage of the Lucas alternator lies in its ability to provide a high charge at low revolutions. Driving slowly in heavy traffic with a dynamo invariably means no charge is reaching the battery. In similar conditions, even with the wiper, heater, lights and perhaps radio switched on, the alternator will ensure a charge reaches the battery.

2 An important feature of the alternator is a built-in output control regulator, based on 'thick film' hybrid integrated microcircuit technique, which results in the alternator being a self-contained generating and control unit.

3 The system provides for direct connection of a charge indicator light, and eliminates the need for a field switching relay or warning light control unit, necessary with former systems.

4 The alternator is of rotating field, ventilated design. It comprises, principally, a laminated stator on which is wound a star connected three-phase output winding; a twelve pole rotor carrying the field windings - each end of the rotor shaft runs in ball race bearings which are lubricated for life; natural finish aluminium die cast end brackets, incorporating the mounting lugs; a rectifier pack of converting the AC output of the machine to DC for battery charging; and an output control regulator.

5 The rotor is belt driven from the engine through a pulley keyed to the rotor shaft. A pressed steel fan adjacent to the pulley draws cooling air through the alternator. This fan forms an integral part of the alternator specification. It has been designed to provide adequate air flow with minimum noise, and to withstand the high stresses associated with maximum

speed. Rotation is clockwise viewed on the drive end. Maximum continuous rotor speed is 12500 rev/min.

6 Rectification of the alternator output is achieved by six silicone diodes housed in a rectifier pack and connected as a three-phase full wave bridge. The rectifier pack is attached to the outer face of the slip ring end bracket and contains also three 'field' diodes; at normal operating speeds, rectified current from the stator output windings flows through these diodes to provide the self-excitation of the rotor field, via brushes bearing on face type slip rings.

7 The slip rings are carried on a small diameter moulded drum attached to the rotor shaft outboard of the slip ring end bearing. The inner ring is centred on the rotor shaft axle, while the outer ring has a mean diameter of ¾ inch (19.05 mm) approximately. By keeping the mean diameter of the slip rings to a minimum, relative speeds between brushes and rings, and hence wear, are also minimal. The slip rings are connected to the rotor field winding by leads carried in grooves in the rotor shaft.

8 The brush gear is housed in a moulding screwed to the outside of the slip ring and bracket. This moulding thus encloses the slip ring and brush gear assembly, and together with the shielded bearing, protects the assembly against the entry of dust and moisture.

9 The regulator is set during manufacture and requires no further attention. Briefly, the 'thick film' regulator comprises resistors and conductors screen printed onto an alumina substrate. Mounted on the substrate are Lucas semi-conductor dice consisting of three transistors, a voltage reference diode and a field recirculation diode, together with two capacitors. The internal connections between these components and the substrate are made by special Lucas patented connectors. The whole assembly is 0.0625 inch (1.588 mm) thick, and is housed in a recess in an aluminium heat sink, which is attached to the slip ring and bracket. Complete hermetic sealing is achieved by a silicone diode rubber, encapsulant to provide environmental protection.

10 Electrical connections to external circuits are brought out to Lucar connector blades, these being grouped to accept a moulded connector socket which ensures correct connection.

14 Alternator - maintenance

1 The equipment has been designed for minimum maintenance in service, the only items subject to wear being the brushes and bearings.

2 Brushes should be examined after about 75,000 miles (120,000 km) and renewed if necessary. The bearings are pre-packed with grease for life, and should not require further attention.

3 Check the fan belt every 6000 miles (9600 km) for correct adjustment which should be 0.5 inch (13 mm) total movement at the centre of the run between the alternator and water pump pulleys.

15 Alternator - special procedures

Whenever the electrical system of the car is being attended to, or external means of starting the engine are used, there are certain precautions that must be taken otherwise serious and expensive damage can result.

1 Always make sure that the negative terminal of the battery is earthed. If the terminal connections are accidentally reversed or if the battery has been reverse charged the alternator diodes will burn out.

2 The output terminal on the alternator marked 'BAT' or B+ must never be earthed but should always be connected directly to the positive terminal of the battery.

3 Whenever the alternator is to be removed or when disconnecting the terminals of the alternator circuit always disconnect the battery earth terminal first.

4 The alternator must never be operated without the battery to alternator cable connected.

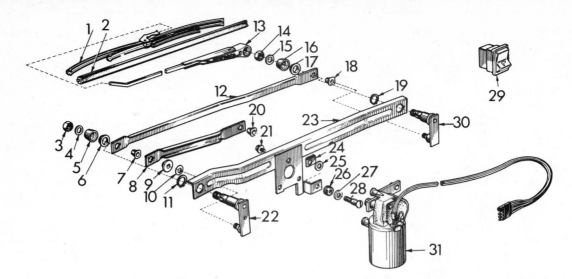

Fig. 10.12 Components of the windscreen wiper mechanism

1	Blade holder	9	Pivot shaft bushing	17	Seal	25 Washer
2	Wiper blade	10	Washer	18	Bushing	26 Grommet
3	Nut	11	Circlip	19	Circlip	27 Washer
4	Washer	12	Long link arm	20	Bushing	28 Screw
5	Outer spacer	13	Wiper arm	21	Screw	29 Switch
6	Seal	14	Nut	22	Arm and pivot shaft assembly	30 Arm and pivot shaft assembly
7	Bushing	15	Washer	23	Mounting bracket	31 Wiper motor
8	Short link arm	16	Spacer	24	Screw clip	

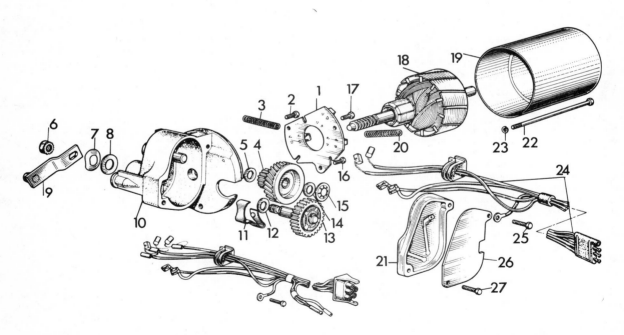

Fig. 10.13 Single speed wiper motor. Inset-two speed brush gear and harness

1	Brush holder plate	9	Output arm	16	Screw	23 Locking washers
2	Screw	10	Housing	17	Screw	24 Wiring loom and brush assembly
3	Spring	11	Stop assembly	18	Armature	25 Screw
4	Wiper gear and pinion	12	Washer	19	Casing and magnet	26 Switch wiring cover
5	Washer	13	Shaft and circuit assembly	20	Spring	27 Screw
6	Nut	14	Washer	21	Switch and cover assembly	
7,8	Washers	15	Clip	22	Tie bolt	

5 If the battery is to be charged by external means, always disconnect both battery cables before the external charge is connected.

6 Should it be necessary to use a booster charger or booster battery to start the engine, always double check that the negative cable is connected to negative terminal and the positive cable to positive terminal.

16 Alternator - removal and refitting

1 Disconnect the battery leads.

2 Note the terminal connections at the rear of the alternator and disconnect the plug or multi-pin connector.

3 Undo and remove the alternator adjustment arm bolt, slacken the alternator mounting bolts and push the alternator inward towards the engine. Lift away the fan belt from the pulley.

4 Remove the remaining two mounting bolts and carefully lift the alternator away from the car.

5 Take care not to knock or drop the alternator otherwise this can cause irreparable damage.

6 Refitting the alternator is the reverse sequence to removal. Adjust the fan belt so that it has 0.5 inch (13 mm) total movement at the centre of the run between the alternator and water pump pulleys.

17 Alternator brushes - inspection, removal and refitting

1 Undo and remove the two screws which hold on the end cover. Lift away the end cover (Fig 10.2).

2 To inspect the brushes correctly, the brush holder moulding should be removed by undoing the two securing bolts and disconnecting the Lucar connector to the diode plates.

3 With the brush holder moulding removed and the brush assemblies still in position, check that they protrude from the face of the moulding by at least 0.2 inch (5.0 mm). Also check that when depressed, the spring pressure is 7–10 oz (198–283 gms) when the end of the brush is flush with the face of the brush moulding. To be done with any accuracy, this requires a push type spring scale.

4 Should either of the foregoing requirements not be fulfilled, the spring assemblies must be renewed. This can be done by simply removing the holding screws of each assembly and fitting the new components in position.

5 With the brush holder moulding removed the slip rings on the face end of the rotor are exposed. These can be cleaned with a petrol soaked cloth and any signs of burning may be removed very carefully with fine glass paper. On no account should any other abrasive be used or any attempt at machining be made.

6 When the brushes are refitted they should slide smoothly in their holders. Any sticking tendency may first be rectified by wiping with a fuel soaked cloth, or if this fails, by carefully polishing with a very fine file where any binding marks may appear.

7 Reassemble in the reverse order of dismantling.

18 Alternator - fault finding and repair

Due to the specialist knowledge and equipment required to test or service an alternator, it is recommended that if the performance is suspect, the car be taken to an automobile electrician who will have the facilities for such work. Because of this recommendation, information is limited to the inspection and renewal of the brushes. Should the alternator not charge or the system be suspect, the following points may be checked before seeking further assistance:

1 Check the fan belt tension as described in Section 14.

2 Check the battery as described in Section 3.

3 Check all electrical cable connections for cleanliness and security.

19 Starter motor (inertia type) - general description

1 The starter motor is held in position by three bolts which also clamp the bellhousing flange.

2 The motor has four field coils, four pole pieces and four spring-loaded commutator brushes. Two of these brushes are earthed, and the other two are insulated and attached to the field coil ends.

3 The starter drive is a conventional pinion and spring engaging with a ring gear on either the flywheel or torque converter (automatic transmission).

20 Starter motor (inertia type) - testing on engine

1 If the starter motor fails to operate then check the condition of the battery by turning on the headlamps. If they glow brightly for several seconds and then gradually dim, the battery is in discharged condition.

2 If the headlamps glow brightly and it is obvious that the battery is in good condition, then check the tightness of the battery wiring connections (and in particular the earth lead from the battery terminal to its connection on the bodyframe). If the positive terminal on the battery becomes hot when an attempt is made to work the starter, this is a sure sign of a poor connection on the battery terminal. To rectify, remove the terminal, clean the inside of the cap and the terminal post thoroughly and reconnect. Check the tightness of the connections at the relay switch and at the starter motor. Check the wiring for breaks or shorts with a suitable meter.

3 If the wiring is in order then check that the starter motor is operating. To do this, press the rubber covered button in the centre of the solenoid under the bonnet. If it is working, the starter motor will be heard to click as it tries to rotate. Alternatively, check it with a voltmeter.

4 If the battery is fully charged, the wiring in order, and the switch working and the starter motor fails to operate, then it will have to be removed from the car for examination. Before this is done, however, ensure that the starter pinion has not jammed in mesh with the flywheel. Check by turning the square end of the armature shaft with a spanner. This will free the pinion if it is stuck in engagement with the flywheel teeth. On some models the square on the end of the shaft will be covered by a metal cap; this can be prised off.

21 Starter motor (inertia type) - removal and refitting

1 Disconnect the battery earth lead from the negative terminal.

2 Disconnect the starter motor cable from the terminal on the starter motor end plate.

3 Remove the upper starter motor securing bolt.

4 Working under the car, loosen and remove the two lower starter motor securing bolts, taking care to support the motor so as to prevent damage to the drive components.

5 Lift the starter motor out of engagement with the flywheel ring gear and lower it out of the car.

6 Replacement is a straightforward reversal of the removal procedure.

22 Starter motor (inertia type) - dismantling and reassembly

1 With the starter motor on the bench, loosen the screw on the cover band and slip the cover band off. With a piece of wire bent into the shape of a hook, lift back each of the brush springs in turn and check the movement of the brushes in their holders by pulling on the flexible connectors. If the brushes are so worn that their faces do not rest against the commutator, or if the ends of the brush leads are exposed on their working face, they must be renewed.

2 If any of the brushes tend to stick in their holders, then wash them with a fuel moistened cloth and, if necessary, lightly polish the sides of the brush with a very fine file, until the brushes move

Fig. 10.14 Withdrawing windscreen wiper assembly

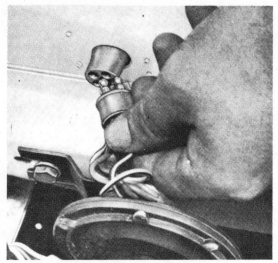

Fig. 10.15 Detaching horn connecting plug

quite freely in their holders.

3   If the surface of the commutator is dirty or blackened, clean it with a fuel dampened rag. Secure the starter motor in a vice and check it by connecting a heavy gauge cable between the starter motor terminal and a 12 volt battery.

4   Connect the cable from the other battery terminal to earth on the starter motor body. If the motor turns at high speed it is in good order.

5   If the starter motor still fails to function, or if it is wished to renew the brushes, it is necessary to further dismantle the motor.

6   Lift the brush springs with the wire hook and lift all four brushes out of their holders one at a time.

7   Remove the terminal nuts and washers from the terminal post on the commutator end bracket.

8   Unscrew the two tie bolts which hold the end plates together and pull off the commutator end bracket. Remove the driving end bracket which will come away complete with the armature.

9   At this stage, if the brushes are to be renewed, their flexible connectors must be unsoldered and the connectors of new brushes soldered in their place. Check that the new brushes move freely in their holders as detailed above. If cleaning the commutator with fuel fails to remove all the burnt areas and spots, then wrap a piece of fine glass paper round the commutator and rotate the armature. If the commutator is very badly worn, remove the drive gear as detailed in the following Section. Then mount the armature in a lathe and with the lathe turning at high speed, take a very fine cut out of the commutator and finish the surface by polishing with fine glass paper. **Do not undercut the mica insulators between the commutator segments.**

10   With the starter motor dismantled, test the four field coils for an open circuit. Connect a 12 volt battery with a 12 volt bulb in one of the leads between the field terminal post and the tapping point of the field coils to which the brushes are connected. An open circuit is proved by the bulb not lighting.

11   If the bulb lights, it does not necessarily mean that the field coils are in order, as there is a possibility that one of the coils will be earthing to the starter yoke or pole shoes. To check this, remove the lead from the brush connector and place it against a clean portion of the starter yoke. If the bulb lights, the field coils are earthing. Replacement of the field coils calls for the use of a wheel operated screwdriver, a soldering iron, caulking and riveting operations and is beyond the scope of the majority of owners. The starter yoke should be taken to a reputable electrical engineering works for new field coils to be fitted. Alternatively, purchase an exchange starter motor.

12   If the armature is damaged, this will be evident after visual inspection. Look for signs of burning, discolouration, and for conductors that have lifted away from the commutator. Re-

assembly is a straightforward reversal of the dismantling procedure.

---

23 Starter motor (inertia type) - servicing the drive

1   The starter motor drive is of the outboard type. When the starter motor is operated the pinion moves into engagement with the flywheel gear ring by moving in toward the starter motor.

2   If the engine kicks back, or the pinion fails to engage with the flywheel gear ring when the starter motor is actuated, no undue strain is placed on the armature shaft, as the pinion sleeve disengages from the pinion and turns independently.

3   Whenever the starter motor is removed the drive should be thoroughly washed in paraffin, shaken and a little thin oil applied.

4   This operation should be undertaken at least every three or four months on vehicles fitted with automatic transmission. The air intakes located at the base of the torque converter housing cause dampness from the road surface to be drawn in and slight rusting of the starter drive occurs which in turn causes the drive to stick.

---

24 Starter motor (inertia type) - drive removal and refitting

1   On early type starter motors, the drive spring is retained and partially compressed by a nut and split pin. Dismantling consists of simply withdrawing the split pin and unscrewing the nut until the spring tension is released.

2   On later type starter motors, the spring is retained by a cup and circlip. The spring must be compressed by using a proprietary compressor (available from most accessory stores) so that the circlip can be extracted from the armature shaft.

3   Once removed, examine the pinion and barrel assembly and renew them if they are worn or chipped.

4   Refitting is a reversal of removal but ensure that the pinion teeth are toward the armature windings and then lubricate the sliding surfaces with a little thin oil.

---

25 Starter motor (pre-engaged type) - general description

1   This type of starter motor is normally only fitted as original equipment to cars with 'cold start' specifications, but it can be fitted as an optional extra on all other models. The motor is wave wound and uses an end face commutator instead of the normal drum type.

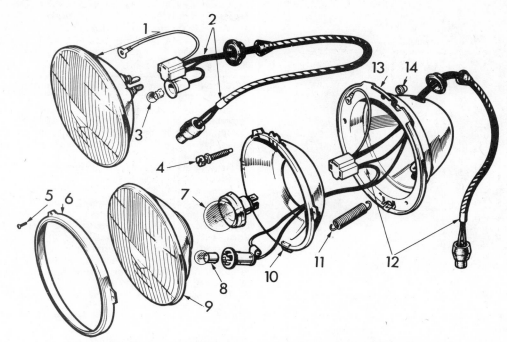

Fig. 10.16 Circular headlamp with either sealed beam or bulb-type light unit

1	Sealed beam headlight unit	5 Screw	9 Headlamp lens and reflector assembly	12 Headlamp wiring loom
2	Headlamp wiring loom	6 Rim	10 Seating rim	13 Headlamp body assembly
3	Sidelamp bulb	7 Headlamp bulb	11 Seating rim retaining spring	14 Nut
4	Adjusting screw	8 Sidelamp bulb		

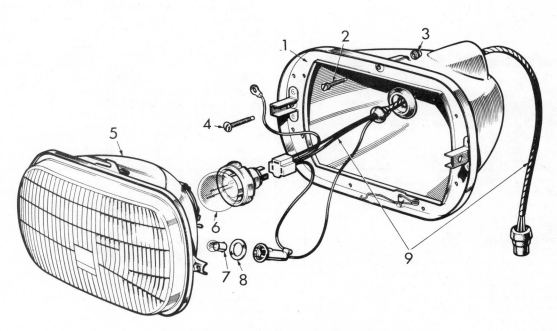

Fig. 10.17 Rectangular lens headlamp

1 Headlamp body assembly	4 Adjusting screw	6 Headlamp bulb	9 Headlamp wiring loom
2 Adjusting screw	5 Headlamp lens and reflector assembly	7 Sidelamp bulb	
3 Nut		8 Washer	

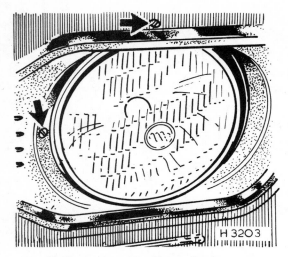

Fig. 10.18 Location of headlamp adjusting screws

2   The method of engagement on the pre-engaged starter is that the drive pinion is brought into mesh with the starter ring gear before the main starter current is applied.

3   When the ignition is switched on, current flows from the battery to the solenoid which is mounted on the top of the starter motor body. The plunger in the solenoid moves inward so causing a centrally pivoted lever to move in such a manner that the forked end pushes the drive pinion into mesh with the starter ring gear. When the solenoid plunger reaches the end of its travel, it closes an internal contact and full starting current flows to the stator field coils. The armature is then able to rotate the crankshaft so starting the engine.

4   A special one way clutch is fitted to the starter drive pinion so that when the engine just fires and starts to operate on its own, it does not drive the starter motor.

26 Starter motor (pre-engaged type) - removal and refitting

1   Disconnect the battery by removing the earth lead from the negative terminal.

2   Disconnect the starter motor cable from the terminal on the starter motor end plate.

3   Remove the two solenoid retaining nuts and the connecting strap and lift off the solenoid.

4   Remove the upper starter motor retaining bolt.

5   Working under the car, remove the lower retaining bolt,

taking care to support the motor so as to prevent damage to the drive components.

6   Withdraw the starter motor from the bellhousing and lower it from the car.

7   Replacement is a straightforward reversal of the removal procedure.

27 Starter motor (pre-engaged type) - dismantling and reassembly

Due to the fact that this type of starter motor uses a face commutator, on which the brushes make contact end on, a certain amount of thrust is created along the armature shaft. A thrust bearing is therefore incorporated in the motor at the commutator end.

1   Remove the split pin from the end of the shaft and slide off the shim(s), washer and thrust plate.

2   Remove the two screws which retain the end plate and pull off the end plate complete with the brush holders and brushes.

3   If the brushes are badly worn, cut off the brush flexible connectors as near to their terminals as possible. Solder the new brush leads to the terminal posts.

4   Cut off the other two brush flexible connectors at a distance of 1/8 inch (3.2 mm) from their connection with the field windings. Solder the new brush leads into position, localise the heat applied.

5   To remove the armature, unscrew the nuts on the holding studs at the drive end bracket.

6   Withdraw the armature complete with the drive and the one-way clutch operating lever.

7   If necessary, clean the end face of the commutator with a petrol soaked cloth. It may be carefully polished with very fine glass paper - **never use emery cloth and never undercut the mica insulation.**

8   Reassembly is a direct reversal of the above procedure, but the armature end float should be measured as indicated in Fig 10.5. The correct end float should be 0.010 inch (.254 mm) with an 8 volt current activating the solenoid. If the end float is found to be incorrect, it can be adjusted by fitting shims between the thrust plate and the split pin. After dismantling, always use a new split pin.

28 Voltage control unit (dynamo only) - general description

1   The control box is positioned on the left hand wing valance and comprises three units; two separate vibrating armature type single contact regulators and a cut-out relay. One of the regulators is sensitive to changes in current and the other to changes in voltage.

2   Adjustment can only be made with a special tool which resembles a screwdriver with a multi-toothed blade. This can be obtained through Lucas agents.

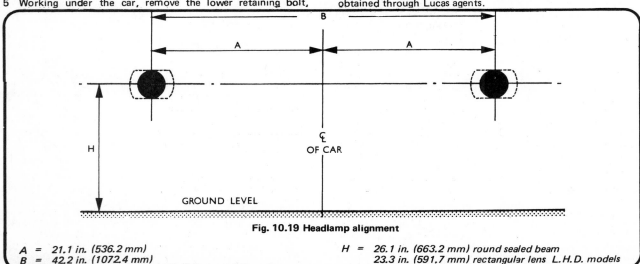

Fig. 10.19 Headlamp alignment

A = 21.1 in. (536.2 mm)
B = 42.2 in. (1072.4 mm)

H = 26.1 in. (663.2 mm) round sealed beam
      23.3 in. (591.7 mm) rectangular lens L.H.D. models

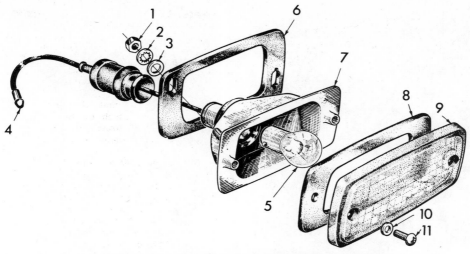

Fig. 10.20 Front direction indicator (flasher) lamp assembly

1 Nut
2 Shakeproof washer
3 Washer

4 'Bullet' connector
5 Bulb
6 Gasket

7 Lamp body
8 Gasket
9 Lens

10 Washer
11 Screw

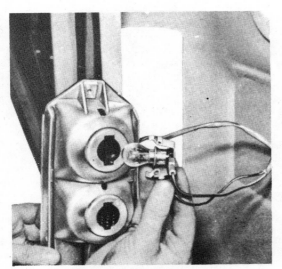

Fig. 10.21 Removing a rear lamp bulb

Fig. 10.22 Rear lamp securing screws (van)

3 The regulators control the output from the dynamo, depending on the state of the battery and the demands of the electrical equipment, and ensures that the battery is not overcharged. The cut-out is really an automatic switch and connects the dynamo to the battery when the dynamo is turning fast enough to produce a charge. Similarly, it disconnects the battery from the dynamo when the engine is idling or stationary so that the battery does not discharge through the dynamo.

29 Cut-out and regulator contacts - maintenance

1 Every 12,000 miles (19,000 km) check the cut-out and regulator contacts. If they are dirty or rough or burnt, place a piece of fine glass paper (**do not use emery paper or carborundum paper**) between the cut-out contacts, close them manually, and draw the glass paper through several times.

2 Clean the regulator contacts in exactly the same way, but use emery or carborundum paper and not glass paper. Carefully clean both sets of contacts from all traces of dust with a rag moistened in methylated spirit.

30 Voltage regulator - adjustment

1 The regulator requires very little attention during its service life, and should there be any reason to suspect its correct functioning, tests of all circuits should be made to ensure that they are not the reason for the trouble.
2 These checks include the tension of the fan belt to make sure that it is not slipping and so providing only a very low charge rate. The battery should be carefully checked for possible low charge rate due to a faulty cell, or corroded battery connections.
2 The leads from the generator may have been crossed during

Fig. 10.23 Rear lamp assembly (estate car)

replacement, and if this is the case, then the regulator points will have stuck together as soon as the generator starts to charge. Check for loose or broken leads from the generator to the regulator.

4   If, after a thorough check, it is considered advisable to test the regulator, this should only be carried out by an electrician who is well acquainted with the correct method, using test bench equipment.

5   Pull off the Lucar connections from the two adjacent control box terminals 'B'. To start the engine it will now be necessary to join together the ignition and battery leads with a suitable wire.

6   Connect a 0-30 volt voltmeter between terminal D on the control box and terminal WL. Start the engine and run it at 2000 rev/min. The reading on the voltmeter should be steady and lie between the limits detailed in the Specifications.

7   If the reading is unsteady, this may be due to dirty contacts. If the reading is outside the specified limits, stop the engine and adjust the voltage regulator in the following manner.

8   Take off the control box cover and start and run the engine at 2000 rev/min. Using the correct tool, turn the voltage adjustment cam anticlockwise to raise the setting and clockwise to lower it. To check that the setting is correct, stop the engine, and then start it and run it at 2000 rev/min, noting the reading. Refit the cover and the connections to the WL and D terminals.

31 Current regulator - adjustment

1   The output from the current regulator should equal the maximum output from the dynamo which is 22 amps. To test this, it is necessary to bypass the cut-out by holding the contacts together.

2   Remove the cover from the control box and with a bulldog clip, hold the cut-out contacts together (Fig 10.7).

3   Pull off the wires from the adjacent terminals B and connect a 0-40 moving coil ammeter to one of the terminals and to the leads.

4   All the other load connections including the ignition must be made to the battery.

5   Turn on all the lights and other electrical accessories and run the engine at 2000 rev/min. The ammeter should give a steady reading between 19 and 22 amps. If the needle flickers it is likely that the points are dirty. If the reading is too low, turn the special Lucas tool clockwise to raise the setting and anticlockwise to lower it.

32 Cut-out - adjustment

1   Check the voltage required to operate the cut-out by connecting a voltmeter between the control box terminals D and WL. Remove the control box cover, start the engine and gradually increase its speed until the cut-outs close. This should occur when the reading is between 12.6 to 13.4 volts (Fig 10.8).

2   If the reading is outside these limits, turn the cut-out adjusting cam by means of the adjusting tool, a fraction at a time clockwise to raise the voltage, and anticlockwise to lower it.

3   To adjust the drop off voltage bend the fixed contact blade carefully. The adjustment to the cut-out should be completed within 30 seconds of starting the engine as otherwise heat build-up from the shunt coil will affect the readings.

4   If the cut-out fails to work, clean the contacts, and, if there is still no response, renew the cut-out and regulator unit.

33 Fuses

1   Prior to September 1969 a six position fuse box was fitted to the rear bulkhead. These six fuses provided protection for all the external lighting circuits with the exception of the direction indicator lights.

2   From September 1969 on, a seven position fuse box was fitted which gives protection to all lighting circuits, the heater, wiper motor and cigar lighter.

3   The later fuse box (Fig 10.10) provides spare positions for accessories at Nos 1, 6 and 7. No 1 is live at all times while 6 and 7 are only live when the ignition is switched on. All fuses are of 8 amp rating.

34 Direction indicator (flasher) circuit - fault tracing and rectification

1   The flasher unit is in a small cylindrical metal container located in a spring clip under the dashboard on the cowl side panel. The unit is actuated by the direction indicator switch.

2   If the flasher unit fails to operate, or works very slowly or rapidly, check out the flasher indicator circuit, as detailed below, before assuming there is a fault in the unit itself.

a) Examine the direction indicator bulbs, front and rear for broken filaments.

b) If the external flashers are working, but the internal flasher warning light has ceased to function, check the filament, in the warning light bulb and replace with a new bulb if necessary.

c) If a flasher bulb is sound but does not work, check all the flasher circuit connections with the aid of the wiring diagram.

d) In the event of total indicator failure, check fuse No 6 on the seven fuse box (if fitted). It will be fairly obvious if this fuse has blown as it also protects the stop lamps, heater motor and reversing lights (if fitted).

e) With the ignition switched on, check that the current is reaching the flasher unit by connecting a voltmeter between the positive (3) terminal and earth. If it is found that current is reaching the unit, connect the two flasher unit terminals together and operate the flasher switch. If the flasher warning light comes on, this proves that the flasher unit itself is at fault and must be renewed as it is not possible to dismantle and repair it.

35 Windscreen wiper blades - removal and refitting

1   The wiper blades should be renewed every year or whenever they fail to wipe the screen cleanly.

2   Lift the wiper arm away from the windscreen and remove the old blade by turning it in toward the arm and then disengage the arm from the slot in the blade.

3   To fit a new blade, slide the end of the wiper arm into the slotted spring fastening in the centre of the blade. Push the blade firmly onto the arm until the raised portion of the arm is fully home in the hole in the blade.

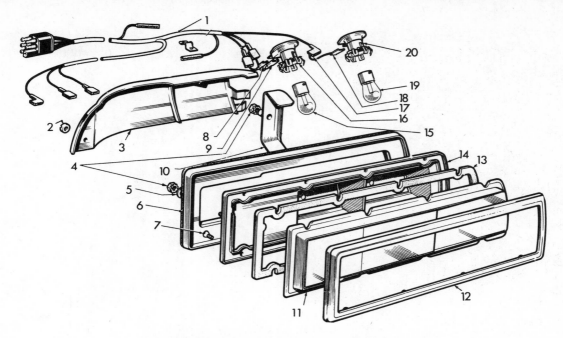

Fig. 10.24 Rear flasher and tail lamp assembly (saloon)

1 Wiring loom	6 Gasket	11 Lens	16 Bulb holder
2 Nut	7 Screw	12 Outer rim	17 Insulator
3 Moulding	8 Lucar connector	13 Gasket	18 Lucar connector
4 Nuts	9 Lucar connector	14 Lamp body	19 Bulb
5 Washer	10 'U' Clamp	15 Bulb	20 Bulb holder

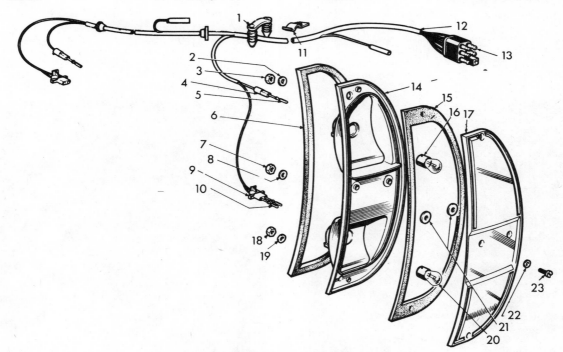

Fig. 10.25 Rear flasher and tail lamp assembly (estate)

1 Cable clip	7 Nut	13 Multi-pin connector	19 Washer
2 Washer	8 Washer	14 Lamp body	20 Bulb
3 Nut	9 Plug body	15 Gasket	21 Washers
4 Plug body	10 Plug terminal	16 Bulb	22 Washer
5 Plug terminal	11 Clip	17 Lens	23 Screw
6 Gasket	12 Wiring loom	18 Nut	

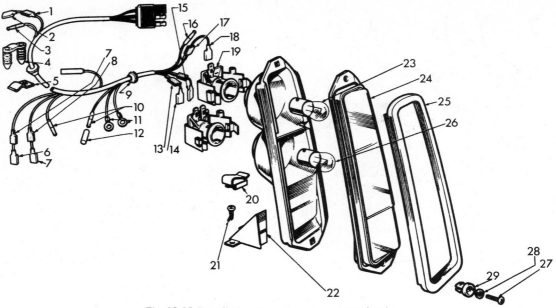

Fig. 10.26 Rear flasher and tail lamp assembly (van)

1 Insulator	9 Grommet	17 Insulator	25 Outer rim
2 Lucar connector	10 'Bullet' connectors	18 Lucar connector	26 Bulb
3 'Bullet' connector	11 Terminals	19 Bulb holder	27 Screw
4 Cable clip	12 Insulator	20 Clip	28 Washer
5 Clip	13 Insulator	21 Screw	29 Expanding plug
6 Lucar connector	14 Lucar connector	22 Bracket	
7 Lucar insulator and connector	15 Lucar connector	23 Bulb	
8 Insulator	16 Bullet connector	24 Lens	

Fig. 10.27 Courtesy light switch removed from door pillar

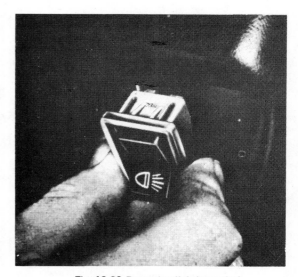

Fig. 10.28 Removing lighting switch

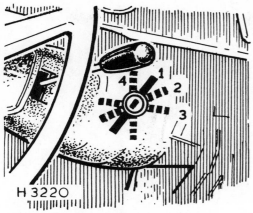

Fig. 10.29 Early type ignition switch

1 Ignition off   3 Start
2 Ignition and auxiliary circuits 4 Accessories

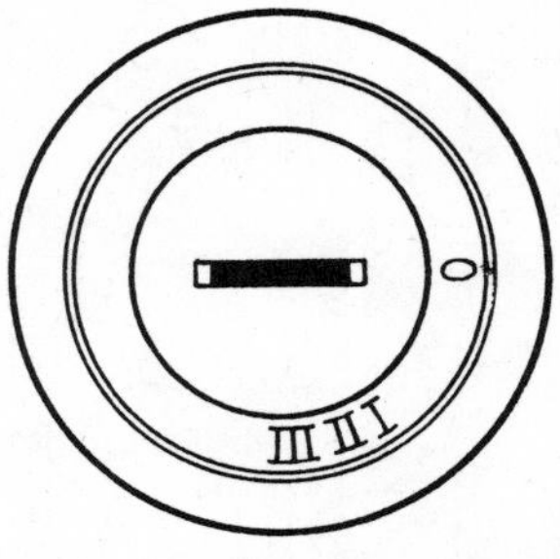

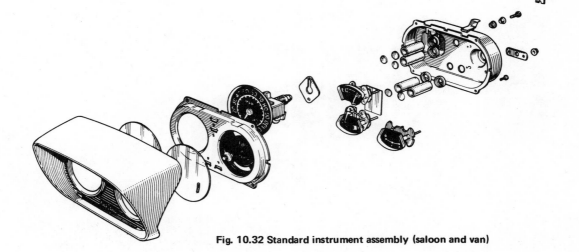

Fig. 10.30 Later type combined ignition switch and steering lock

1 Lock   3 Ignition
2 Accessory 4 Start

Fig. 10.32 Standard instrument assembly (saloon and van)

36 Windscreen wiper arms - removal and refitting

1 Before removing a wiper arm, turn the windscreen wiper switch on and off to ensure the arms are in their normal parked position parallel with the bottom of the windscreen.
2 To remove an arm, pivot the arm back and pull the wiper arm head off the splined drive. If the arm proves difficult to remove, a screwdriver with a large blade can be used to lever the wiper arm head off the splines. Care must be taken not to damage the splines.
3 When replacing an arm, position it so it is in the correct relative parked position and then press the arm head onto the splined drive until it is fully home on the splines.

37 Windscreen wiper mechanism - fault diagnosis and rectification

1 Should the windscreen wipers fail, or work very slowly, then check the terminals on the motor for loose connections, and make sure that the insulation of the wiring is not cracked or broken possibly causing a short circuit. If this is in order, then check the current the motor is taking by connecting an ammeter in the circuit and turning on the wiper switch. Consumption should be between 2.3 to 3.1 amps.
2 If no current is passing through the motor, check that the

Fig. 10.31 Location of brake stop lamp switch

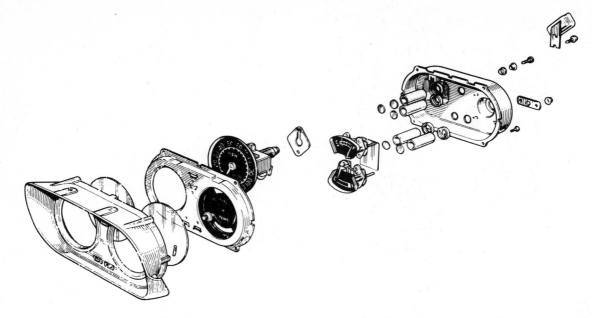

Fig. 10.33 Instrument assembly (L or LX models)

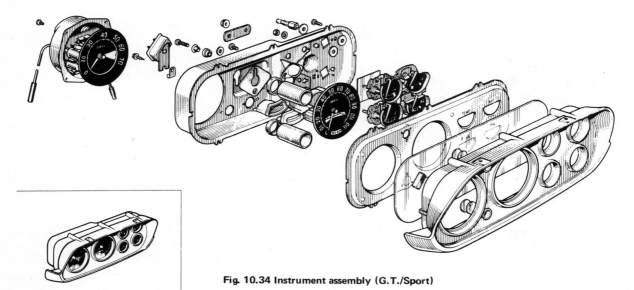

Fig. 10.34 Instrument assembly (G.T./Sport)

switch is operating correctly.

3   If the wiper motor takes a very high current, check the wiper blades for freedom of movement. If this is satisfactory, check the gearbox cover and gear assembly for damage.

4   If the motor takes a very low current ensure that the battery is fully charged. Check the brush gear and ensure the brushes are bearing on the commutator. If not, check the brushes for freedom of movement and, if necessary, renew the tension springs. If the brushes are very worn, they should be replaced with new ones. Check the armature by substitution if this unit is suspect.

38   Windscreen wiper motor, gearbox and linkage - removal and refitting

1   Disconnect the battery by removing the negative earth lead, and remove the wiper arms and blades.

2   Remove the spindle nuts, washers, spacers and sealing washers

from outside the car.

3   Working inside the car, remove the three screws securing the bottom edge of the heater trim panel and then gently pull down the upper edge of the panel to release the four locating pegs. Move the trim panel to one side.

4   Disconnect the lower ends of the heater flexible pipes from the heater and move them to one side so as to give enough space to work on the windscreen wiper motor.

5   Pull out the multi-pin plug from the windscreen wiper motor wiring.

6   From under the dashboard unscrew the single screw which holds the windscreen wiper motor to the scuttle panel.

7   Lower the motor and linkage complete and pass it in front of the heater and out from under the dashboard on the left hand side.

8   Replacement is a straightforward reversal of the above procedure, but care must be taken to ensure that the spindles are properly located in their holes in the scuttle panel before tightening down the screw which holds the motor in place.

Fig. 10.35 Removing speedometer head

Fig. 10.36 Removing the fuel gauge

39 Windscreen wiper motor - dismantling and reassembly

1 Start by removing the linkage mechanism from the motor. Carefully prise the short wiper link off the motor operating arm and remove the plastic pivot bush.

2 Undo the three screws which hold the linkage to the wiper motor and separate the two.

3 Unscrew the two bolts which hold the motor case to the gearbox housing and withdraw the motor case complete with the armature.

4 Take the brushes out of their holders and remove the brush springs.

5 Undo the three screws which hold the brush mounting plate to the wiper gearbox and withdraw the brush mounting plate.

6 Remove the earth wire on the gearbox cover plate by undoing the screw nearest the motor case. Undo the other screw on the gearbox cover plate and remove the cover plate and switch assembly.

7 Pull the spring steel armature stop out of the gearbox casing. Then remove the spring clip and washer which retain the wiper pinion gear in place and withdraw the gear and washer.

8 Undo the nut securing the wiper motor operating arm and remove the lockwasher, arm, wave washer and flat washer in that order.

9 Having removed the operating arm, withdraw the output gear,

park switch assembly and washer from the gearbox casing.

10 Carefully examine all parts for signs of wear or damage and renew as necessary.

11 Reassembly is a direct reversal of the above procedure.

40 Combined wiper/washer switch - description and servicing

1 Later models are fitted with a floor mounted 'one wipe' combined washer/wiper switch. This switch is supplementary to the facia mounted one and operates only when the ignition is switched on, irrespective of the operating mode of the facia mounted switch.

2 Access to the floor mounted switch is gained by peeling back the floor covering. In the event of failure of either the electrical or washer sections of the control, remove the switch retaining screws, disconnect the electrical leads and the washer water tubes and remove the control switch.

3 Renew the washer pump rubber diaphragm or if there is an electrical fault, renew the control as an assembly as it is not repairable.

41 Horn - fault diagnosis and rectification

1 If the horn operates weakly or fails to sound at all, check the wiring leading to the horn plug which is located on the body panel next to the horn itself. Also check that the plug is properly pushed home and is in a clean condition, free from corrosion etc.

2 Check that the horn is secure on its mounting and that there is nothing lying on the horn body.

3 If the fault is not an external one, remove the horn cover and check the leads inside the horn. If these are sound, check the contact breaker contacts. If these are burnt or dirty, clean them with a fine file and wipe all traces of dirt and dust away with a fuel moistened rag.

42 Headlamp (sealed beam type) - removal and refitting

1 Disconnect the battery by removing the negative earth lead.

2 Remove the radiator grille by removing the nine retaining screws.

3 Unscrew the three Phillips headed screws which retain the lamp inner ring in place and remove the inner ring.

4 Lift out the unit and disconnect the three pin wiring plug from the rear of the unit. Remove the sidelamp bulb which is located just below the three pin plug.

5 Replacement is a straightforward reversal of the above procedure. After reassembly, check that the headlamps are correctly aligned, before refitting the radiator grille.

43 Headlamp (rectangular lens type) - removal and refitting

1 Disconnect the battery by removing the negative earth lead.

2 Remove the radiator grille by removing the nine retaining screws.

3 Unscrew the three screws holding the reflector unit in place and draw it forward together with the headlamp and sidelamp bulbs.

4 Release the headlamp bulb retaining clip, withdraw the bulb and unplug it from its three pin plug. Remove the sidelamp bulb which is located just below the headlamp bulb.

5 Replacement is a straightforward reversal of the above procedure. After reassembly check that the headlamps are correctly aligned before refitting the radiator grille.

44 Headlamp (round lens type) - removal and refitting

The procedure is identical to that described for sealed beam units in Section 40.

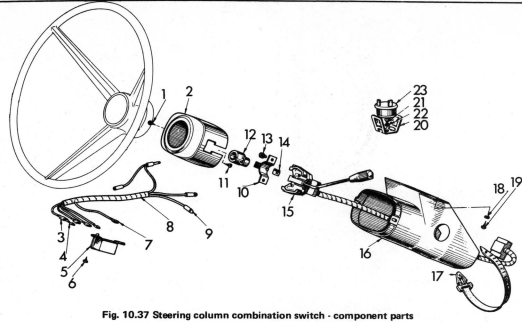

Fig. 10.37 Steering column combination switch - component parts

1 Screw	7 Terminal	13 Screw	19 Screw
2 Upper housing	8 Wiring loom	14 Screw clip	20 Bracket
3 Insulator	9 'Bullet' connector	15 Switch assembly	21 Washer
4 Lucar connector	10 Mounting bracket	16 Lower housing	22 Screw
5 Multi-pin connector	11 Screw	17 Strap	23 Flasher unit
6 Screw	12 Cancelling cam	18 Washer	

45 Headlamps - alignment

1   It is always advisable to have the headlamps aligned on proper optical beam setting equipment but if this is not available, the following procedure may be used.
2   Position the car on level ground 10 feet in front of a dark wall or board. The wall or board must be at right angles to the centre line of the car.
3   Draw a vertical line on the board in line with the centre line of the car.
4   Bounce the car on its suspension to ensure correct settlement and then measure the height between the ground and the centre of the headlamps.
5   Draw a horizontal line across the board at this measured height. On this horizontal line mark a cross 21.1 inch (536.2 mm) either side of the vertical centre line.
6   On early models, remove the radiator grille by removing the nine retaining screws and switch the headlamps onto full beam. (Removal of the grille is not necessary on later model vehicles.)
7   By carefully adjusting the horizontal and vertical adjusting screws on each lamp, align the centres of each beam onto the crosses which you have previously marked on the horizontal line.
8   Bounce the car again and check that the beams return to the correct positions. At the same time check the operation of the dip switch.

46 Front direction indicators (flashers) - bulb renewal

1   Remove the two lens retaining screws, lift off the lens and remove the bulb by pushing it in and turning it in an anticlockwise direction.
2   Refitting is a reversal of the removal procedure.

47 Rear direction indicators (flashers), stop and tail lamps - bulb renewal

1   Working inside the boot, remove the rear lamp assembly cover panel by unscrewing the single retaining nut.
2   Pull the bulb holder which needs attention from its socket in the light cluster and remove the bulb by depressing it and rotating it in an anticlockwise direction.
3   Refitting is a reversal of the removal procedure.
4   On estate cars and vans the rear bulbs are accessible after the lenses have been removed by unscrewing the retaining screws from outside the body (Figs 10.22 and 10.23).

48 Rear licence plate lamp - bulb renewal

1   Undo the two screws holding the lamp assembly to the car, then remove the two screws holding the lens to the lamp body.
2   Remove the lens and remove the bulb by depressing it and turning it in an anticlockwise direction.
3   Reassembly is a reversal of the above procedure.

49 Interior lamp - bulb renewal

1   Carefully prise the lamp assembly from the panel above the windscreen.
2   The bulb is held in position by a spring retainer.

50 Courtesy light switch - servicing

1   These switches are pressed into holes in the front door pillars and the interior lamp whenever the front doors are opened.
2   The switches are very susceptible to dampness and in the event of non-operation, prise them from their locations and clean the contacts by scraping. It is a good idea to apply petroleum jelly to the switch interior before refitting to protect them against further corrosion.

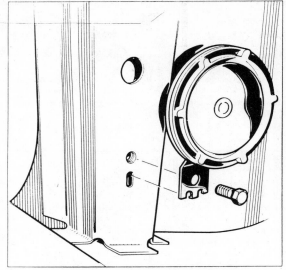

Fig. 10.38 Position for fitting dual horn

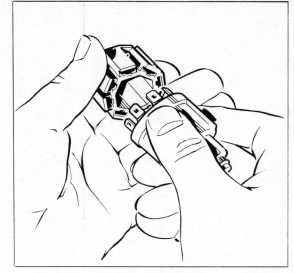

Fig. 10.39 Ignition switch and terminal plug

Fig. 10.40 Cigar lighter illumination connection

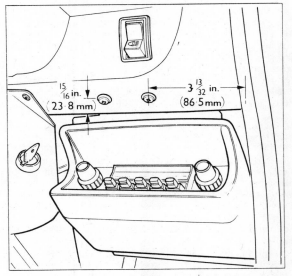

Fig. 10.40A Suggested radio receiver location

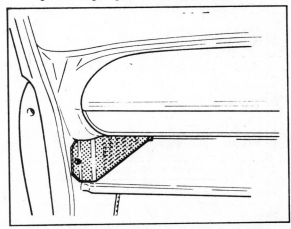

Fig. 10.41 Radio loudspeaker location on parcels shelf

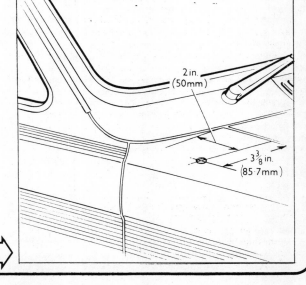

Fig. 10.41A Suggested location for radio aerial

51 Light switch - removal and refitting

1   Disconnect the battery by removing the negative earth lead.
2   From the back of the switch under the dashboard, pull off the wiring plug, then depress the top spring retaining lug and with the other hand pull the top of the switch away from the dash into the car.
3   Depress the lower retaining lug from under the dashboard and then withdraw the switch. Refitting is a reversal of the above procedure.

52 Ignition switch - removal and refitting

1   Two types of ignition switch may be encountered.

a) Early vehicles without a steering lock
2   To remove the switch, disconnect the lead from the battery negative terminal. Unscrew the bezel which holds the switch in position and withdraw the switch from under the facia panel.
3   The lock barrel may be removed from the switch once the multi-pin connector has been detached.

b) Later vehicles with combined ignition/steering lock switch
4   Disconnect the lead from the battery negative terminal.
5   Remove the steering wheel and shrouds as described in Section 56.
6   Unscrew the ignition switch block from the main steering column lock assembly.
7   The lock barrel and steering lock assembly may be removed from the steering column as described in Chapter 11.
8   Refitting of either type is a reversal of removal.

53 Stop lamp switch - adjustment

1   The stop lamp switch operates on the plunger principle. With the brake pedal arm fully back against its stop, the plunger is depressed and the switch contacts are open. Immediately the footbrake is depressed, the plunger moves outward by means of its return spring and the switch contacts close to complete the circuit and illuminate the stop lamps.
2   Adjustment is carried out by the nut and locknut on the switch bracket to alter the effective length of the plunger. The switch should operate at the slightest depression of the footbrake when the switch is correctly set. The ignition must be switched on before the switch will operate.

54 Speedometer cable - disconnection and renewal

1   The speedometer cable may be disconnected from the rear of the speedometer head simply by reaching under the instrument panel and either unscrewing the knurled retaining nut or by depressing the snap connector plunger, according to type.
2   The lower end of the speedometer may be disconnected from the speedometer drive by removing the retaining circlip (manual gearbox) or the bolt and clip (automatic transmission) from the extension housing of the gearbox or transmission housing.
3   When fitting a new inner cable, lightly grease the lower two-thirds of its length before sliding it into the outer conduit.
4   Refitting is a reversal of removal but ensure that the squared end of the inner cable is fully engaged with the speedometer head before tightening the retaining nut or engaging the snap connector whichever method is used.

55 Instrument panel, instruments and warning lamps - removal and refitting

1   Disconnect the lead from the battery negative terminal.
2   Disconnect the speedometer cable under the instrument panel

as described in the preceding Section.
3   Unscrew the four screws which retain the instrument panel to the facia and pull the panel forward.
4   The warning lamp holders may now be removed from the rear of the panel for bulb renewal.
5   Individual instruments including the speedometer may be removed from the instrument panel once the bezel securing screws have been removed and the bezel, glasses and sealing O rings have been withdrawn.
6   Refitting is a reversal of removal.

56 Combination switch - removal and refitting

1   This switch combines the functions of the headlamp flasher, dipper, direction indicator and horn switches in one unit, attached to the upper part of the steering column.
2   Disconnect the battery by removing the negative earth lead, then from under the steering wheel, pull off the multi-pin wiring connector from the switch.
3   Prise out the emblem in the centre of the steering wheel, knock back the locking tab on the steering wheel centre nut, undo the nut and remove the steering wheel.
4   Undo the two small screws retaining the upper portion of the steering column shroud and remove the shroud.
5   Remove the switch assembly by undoing the two screws holding it to the steering column. If faulty, the switch will have to be renewed as it is not a serviceable item.
6   Refitting is a direct reversal of the removal procedure.

57 Accessories - guide to fitting

1   This Section indicates briefly the method and recommended location of additional electrical accessories which the owner may wish to fit.
2   The descriptions given are based upon Ford approved accessories but they will prove useful for other makes with slight adaptation.

a) Dual horn
3   A hole with captive nut is located directly opposite the single horn on the bodyframe side member within the engine compartment.
4   Bolt the second horn in this position using the setscrew supplied with the horn (7/16 AF).
5   Disconnect the electrical supply lead from the existing horn and connect it to a wire which will connect between both old and new horn terminals. A proprietary cable jointer is ideal for this purpose.

b) Fog and pass lamps
6   The location of these lamps must be such that their centres are 24 inches (0.6096 m) from the ground otherwise their use will be legally limited to use in conditions of fog or falling snow only.
7   Connections should be made to a spare position on the fuse block or to No 5 terminal on the rear of the ignition switch.

c) Cigar lighter
8   Disconnect the lead from the battery negative terminal.
9   Prise the blanking disc from below the choke control knob.
10 Fit the cigar lighter to the facia panel.
11 Connect the terminal on the cigar lighter inner component to No 4 terminal at the back of the ignition switch.
12 Connect the outer barrel to a good earth and the cigar lighter illuminating bulb to the spare position on the loom plug which is located at the junction of the windscreen pillar and the facia panel (Fig 10.40).

d) Radio, loudspeaker and aerial
13 The best position for the radio receiver is to the right of the steering column, slung below the facia panel or located centrally

below the ashtray.

14 The loudspeeker may be fixed in the left hand corner of (or suspended above) the parcel shelf, or in the case of saloons, fitted below the rear parcel shelf.

15 The aerial should be positioned on the front wing on the same side as the steering wheel, the fitting diagram (Fig 10.41A) will indicate its location.

16 It is unusual for modern ignition systems to cause radio interference but where a dynamo is fitted as opposed to an alternator, pull the blade connector from the large terminal at the rear of the unit and fit a suppressor by slipping its terminal clip under the plastic cover of the blade connector and then refitting the blade connector. Secure the suppressor to the small hole in the dynamo end plate using a self-tapping screw.

58 Fault finding chart

Symptom	Reason/s	Remedy
STARTER MOTOR FAILS TO TURN ENGINE		
No electricity at starter motor	Battery discharged	Charge battery.
	Battery defective internally	Fit new battery.
	Battery terminal leads loose or earth lead not securely attached to body	Check and tighten leads.
	Loose or broken connections in starter motor circuit	Check all connections and tighten any that are loose.
	Starter motor switch or solenoid faulty	Test and replace faulty components with new.
Electricity at starter motor: faulty motor	Starter motor pinion jammed in mesh with flywheel gear ring	Disengage pinion by turning squared end of armature shaft.
	Starter brushes badly worn, sticking, or brush wires loose	Examine brushes, replace as necessary, tighten down brush wires.
	Commutator dirty, worn, or burnt	Clean commutator, recut if badly burnt.
	Starter motor armature faulty	Overhaul starter motor, fit new armature.
	Field coils earthed	Overhaul starter motor.
STARTER MOTOR TURNS ENGINE VERY SLOWLY		
Electrical defects	Battery in discharged condition	Charge battery.
	Starter brushes badly worn, sticking or, brush wires loose	Examine brushes, replace as necessary, tighten down brush wires.
	Loose wires in starter motor circuit	Check wiring and tighten as necessary.
STARTER MOTOR OPERATES WITHOUT TURNING ENGINE		
Dirt or oil on drive gear	Starter motor pinion sticking on the screwed sleeve	Remove starter motor, clean starter motor drive.
Mechanical damage	Pinion or flywheel gear teeth broken or worn	Fit new gear ring to flywheel, and new pistons to starter motor drive.
STARTER MOTOR NOISY OR EXCESSIVELY ROUGH ENGAGEMENT		
Lack of attention or mechanical damage	Pinion or flywheel gear teeth broken or worn	Fit new gear teeth to flywheel, or new pinion to starter motor drive.
	Starter drive main spring broken	Dismantle and fit new main spring.
	Starter motor retaining bolts loose	Tighten starter motor securing bolts. Fit new spring washer if necessary.
BATTERY WILL NOT HOLD CHARGE FOR MORE THAN A FEW DAYS		
Wear or damage	Battery defective internally	Remove and fit new battery.
	Electrolyte level too low or electrolyte too weak due to leakage	Top up electrolyte level to just above plates.
	Plate separators no longer fully effective	Remove and fit new battery.
	Battery plates severely sulphated	Remove and fit new battery.
Insufficient current flow to keep battery charged	Fan/dynamo belt slipping	Check belt for wear, replace if necessary, and tighten.
	Battery terminal connections loose or corroded	Check terminals for tightness, and remove all corrosion.
	Dynamo or alternator not charging properly	Remove and overhaul generator.
	Short in lighting circuit causing continual battery drain	Trace and rectify.
	Regulator unit not working correctly	Check setting, clean, and renew if defective.
IGNITION LIGHT FAILS TO GO OUT, BATTERY RUNS FLAT IN A FEW DAYS		
Dynamo or alternator not charging	Fan belt loose and slipping, or broken	Check, renew and tighten as necessary.
	Brushes worn, sticking, broken, or dirty	Examine, clean, or renew brushes as necessary.
	Brush springs weak or broken	Examine and test. Renew as necessary.
	Commutator dirty, greasy, worn, or burnt	Clean commutator and undercut segment separators.

Symptom	Reason/s	Remedy
	Armature badly worn or armature shaft bent	Fit new or reconditioned armature.
	Commutator bars shorting	Undercut segment separations.
	Dynamo bearings badly worn	Overhaul dynamo, fit new bearings.
	Dynamo field coils burnt, open, or shorted	Remove and fit rebuilt dynamo.
	Commutator no longer circular	Recut commutator and undercut segment separators.
	Pole pieces very loose	Strip and overhaul dynamo. Tighten pole pieces.
Regulator or cut-out fails to work correctly	Regulator incorrectly set	Adjust regulator correctly.
	Cut-out incorrectly set	Adjust cut-out correctly.
	Open circuit in wiring of cut-out and regulator unit	Remove, examine, and renew as necessary.

Failure of individual electrical equipment to function correctly is dealt with alphabetically, item by item, under the headings listed below:

FUEL GAUGE

Symptom	Reason/s	Remedy
Fuel gauge gives no reading	Fuel tank empty!	Fill fuel tank.
	Electric cable between tank sender unit and gauge earthed or loose	Check cable for earthing and joints for tightness.
	Fuel gauge case not earthed	Ensure case is well earthed.
	Fuel gauge supply cable interrupted	Check and renew cable if necessary.
	Fuel gauge unit broken	Renew fuel gauge.
Fuel gauge registers full all the time	Electric cable between tank unit and gauge broken or disconnected	Check over cable and repair as necessary.

HORN

Symptom	Reason/s	Remedy
Horn operates all the time	Horn push either earthed or stuck down	Disconnect battery earth. Check and rectify source of trouble.
	Horn cable to horn push earthed	Disconnect battery earth. Check and rectify source of trouble.
Horn fails to operate	Blown fuse	Check and renew if broken. Ascertain cause.
	Cable or cable connection loose, broken or disconnected	Check all connections for tightness and cables for breaks.
	Horn has an internal fault	Remove and overhaul horn.
Horn emits intermittent or unsatisfactory noise	Cable connections loose	Check and tighten all connections.
	Horn incorrectly adjusted	Adjust horn until best note obtained.

LIGHTS

Symptom	Reason/s	Remedy
Lights do not come on	If engine not running, battery discharged	Push-start car, charge battery.
	Light bulb filament burnt out or bulbs broken	Test bulbs in live bulb holder.
	Wire connections loose, disconnected or broken	Check all connections for tightness and wire cable for breaks.
	Light switch shorting or otherwise faulty	By-pass light switch to ascertain if fault is in switch and fit new switch as appropriate.
Lights come on but fade out	If engine not running battery discharged	Push-start car, and charge battery.
Lights give very poor illumination	Lamp glasses dirty	Clean glasses.
	Reflector tarnished or dirty	Fit new units.
	Lamps badly out of adjustment	Adjust lamps correctly.
	Incorrect bulb with too low wattage fitted	Remove bulb and replace with correct grade.
	Existing bulbs old and badly discoloured	Renew bulb units.
	Electrical wiring too thin not allowing full current to pass	Rewire lighting system.
Lights work erratically - flashing on and off, especially over bumps	Battery terminals or earth connection loose	Tighten battery terminals and earth connection.
	Lights not earthing properly	Examine and rectify.
	Contacts in light switch faulty	By-pass light switch to ascertain if fault is in switch and fit new switch as appropriate.

WIPERS

Symptom	Reason/s	Remedy
Wiper motor fails to work	Blown fuse	Check and renew fuse.
	Wire connections loose, disconnected, or broken	Check wiper wiring. Tighten loose connections.

Symptom	Reason/s	Remedy
	Brushes badly worn	Remove and fit new brushes.
	Armature worn or faulty	If electricity at wiper motor remove and overhaul and fit replacement armature.
	Field coils faulty	Purchase reconditioned wiper motor.
Wiper motor works very slowly and takes excessive current	Commutator dirty, greasy, or burnt	Clean commutator thoroughly.
	Drive to wheelboxes too bent or unlubricated	Examine drive and straighten out severe curvature. Lubricate.
	Wheelbox spindle binding or damaged	Remove, overhaul, or fit replacement.
	Armature bearings dry or unaligned	Renew with new bearings correctly aligned.
	Armature badly worn or faulty	Remove, overhaul, or fit replacement armature.
Wiper motor works slowly and takes little current	Brushes badly worn	Remove and fit new brushes.
	Commutator dirty, greasy, or burnt	Clean commutator thoroughly.
	Armature badly worn or faulty	Remove and overhaul armature or fit replacement.
Wiper motor works but wiper blades remain static	Driving cable rack disengaged or faulty	Examine and if faulty, renew.
	Wheelbox gear and spindle damaged or worn	Examine and if faulty, renew.
	Wiper motor gearbox parts badly worn	Overhaul or fit new gearbox.

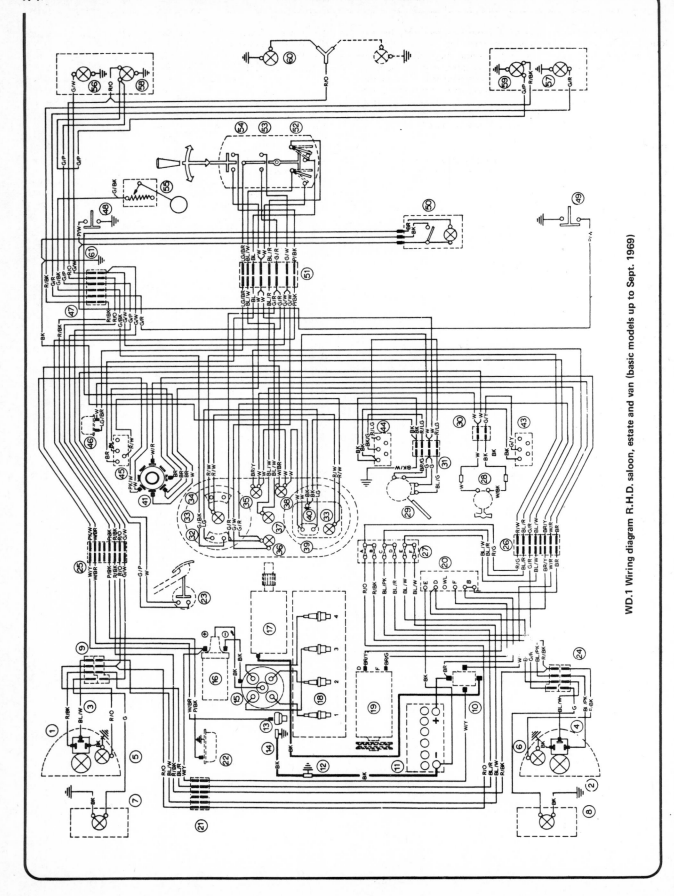

WD.1 Wiring diagram R.H.D. saloon, estate and van (basic models up to Sept. 1969)

The fully fused wiring loom is broken into sections, the rear loom running from the rear lamps up to the facia.

The main instrument loom runs behind the facia panel and connects with the rear loom and the engine compartment loom(s).

All the loom connections to the various electrical components are fitted with non-reversible plugs. This system ensures that the loom can only be fitted to a component the right way round, thus avoiding 'blowing' a fuse.

A fuse block, holding either six or seven fuses, is located on the engine compartment rear bulkhead. The six-fuse type provides protection for all the exterior lighting with the exception of the direction indicators, while the seven-fuse type protects all lighting circuits, the heater and wiper motors and the cigar lighter. Provision is also made for connecting accessories if required.

The wiring diagrams are grouped in six-fuse block and seven-fuse block categories. First ascertain whether the vehicle is fitted with a six- or a seven-fuse block and then refer to the required diagram under the relevant heading.

SIX-FUSE BLOCK

The wiring diagrams shown in this category have the wiring colour identified by alphabetical letters and the individual components in the diagrams by numbers which correspond to the numbers shown below.

1 R.H. headlamp
2 L.H. headlamp
3 R.H. headlamp connector
4 L.H. headlamp connector
5 R.H. side lamp (front)
6 L.H. side lamp (front)
7 R.H. direction indicator lamp (front)
8 L.H. direction indicator lamp (front)
9 R.H. lighting connector (front)
10 Starter solenoid
11 Battery
12 Body earth
13 Oil pressure sender unit
14 Engine earth
15 Distributor
16 Ignition coil
17 Starter motor
18 Spark plugs
19 Generator
20 Regulator
21 L.H. to R.H. loom connector
22 Horn
23 Brake light switch
24 L.H. lighting connector (front)
25 R.H. bulkhead multi-way connector
26 L.H. bulkhead multi-way connector
27 Fuse block
28 Heater motor
29 Windscreen wiper motor
30 Heater motor connector
31 Windscreen wiper motor connector
32 Fuel gauge
33 Panel light
34 Temperature gauge
35 Generator warning light

36 Direction indicator light
37 Main beam indicator light
38 Oil pressure warning light
39 Instrument voltage stabilizer
40 Instrument earth
41 Ignition switch
42 Oil pressure gauge
43 Heater motor switch
44 Windscreen wiper switch
45 Head/side light switch
46 Flasher unit
47 Rear loom connector
48 R.H. courtesy light switch
49 L.H. courtesy light switch
50 Interior light
51 Headlamp flasher/direction indicator, horn switch connector
52 Headlamp flasher switch
53 Direction indicator switch
54 Horn switch
55 Fuel gauge sender unit
56 R.H. direction indicator lamp
57 L.H. direction indicator lamp
58 R.H. stop/side lamp (rear)
59 L.H. stop/side lamp (rear)
60 Rear number plate light
61 Body earth
62 Ignition lock
63 Cigar lighter
64 Cigar lighter illumination lamp
65 Heater motor resistor (two-speed)
66 Water temperature sender unit
67 Battery condition indicator
68 Tachometer
69 Water temperature gauge
70 Automatic transmission illuminating lamp

Wiring Colour Code

R	Red	W	White	Y	Yellow	O	Orange
Bk	Black	Br	Brown	LG	Light green	Pk	Pink
Bl	Blue	G	Green	P	Purple		

WD.2 Wiring diagram L.H.D. saloon, estate and van

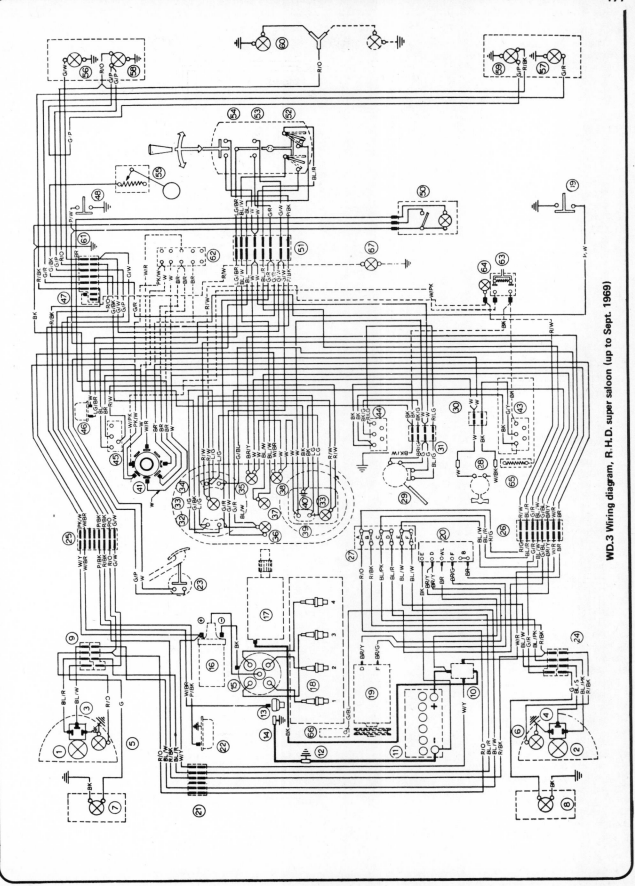

WD.3 Wiring diagram, R.H.D. super saloon (up to Sept. 1969)

SEVEN-FUSE BLOCK

The wiring diagram retains the alphabetical and numerical identification system used in the six-fuse block diagrams. Refer to tables below for relevant coding.

Actual wiring can be traced and is coded by both letters and/or numbers e.g. 15—3 or R2.1.

Wiring Colour Code

Bk	Black	G	Green	P	Purple	W	White
Bl	Blue	LG	Light green	Pk	Pink	Y	Yellow
Br	Brown	O	Orange	R	Red	S	Slate

Component Codes

1 R.H. turn signal lamp (front)
2 L.H. turn signal lamp (front)
3 R.H. side light (front)
4 L.H. side light (front)
5 R.H. headlamp
6 L.H. headlamp
7 R.H. headlamp connector
8 L.H. headlamp connector
9 R.H. side flasher (R.P.O.)
10 L.H. side flasher (R.P.O.)
11 Not applicable
12   ''   '''
13 Horn
14 Not applicable
15   ''   ''
16   ''   ''
17   ''   ''
18 Battery
19 Ignition coil
20 Distributor
21 Oil pressure switch
22 Temperature sender unit
23 Generator
24 Not applicable
25 Starter solenoid (automatic transmission)
26 Starter solenoid (manual transmission)
27 Not applicable
28   ''   ''
29 Inertial starter motor
30 Pre-engaged starter motor
31 Regulator
32 Fuse block
33 Not applicable
34 L.H. Bulkhead wiring connectors
35 Stop switch lamp
36 Brake fluid low pressure switch (R.P.O.)
36a Brake fluid low pressure warning lamp test switch (R.P.O.)
37 Windscreen wiper motor
38 Windscreen wiper motor 2 speed
39 Heater motor
40 Not applicable
41 Reversing lamp switch - manual transmission (R.P.O.)
42 Reversing lamp and park inhibitor switch - automatic transmission (R.P.O.)
43 Turn signal warning lamp
44 Instrument voltage regulator
45 Instrument panel earth
46 Brake fluid low pressure warning lamp (R.P.O)
47 R.H. courtesy switch
48 L.H. courtesy switch
49 Side/head lamp switch
50 Fuel gauge
51 Temperature gauge
52 Instrument illumination lamp
53 Speedometer
54 Tachometer
55 Speedometer illumination lamp
56 Tachometer illumination lamp
57 Battery condition indicator
58 Oil pressure gauge
59 Generator warning lamp
60 Oil pressure warning lamp
61 Main beam warning lamp
62 Turn signal flasher unit
63 Not applicable
64   ''   ''
65   ''   ''
66 Windscreen wiper switch
67 Heater switch
68 Not applicable
69 Radio (R.P.O.)
70 Not applicable
71 Accessory connector
72 Ignition switch
73 Rear wiring loom connector
74 Emergency flasher unit (R.P.O.)
75 Emergency flasher indicator lamp (R.P.O.)
76 Steering column connector
77 Not applicable
78 Emergency flasher switch (R.P.O.)
79 Not applicable
80   ''   ''
81 Not applicable
82   ''   ''
83   ''   ''
84   ''   ''
85 Horn switch
86 Direction indicator switch
87 Column dip switch
88 Headlamp flasher switch
89 Interior light
90 Fuel gauge sender unit
91 Not applicable
92 R.H. turn signal lamp (rear)
93 L.H. turn signal lamp (rear)
94 R.H. stop lamp
95 L.H. stop lamp
96 R.H. side lamp (rear)
97 L.H. side lamp (rear)
98 R.H. reversing lamp
99 L.H. reversing lamp
100 Licence plate lamp
101 Not applicable
102 Cigar lighter
103 Not applicable
104   ''   ''
105   ''   ''
106   ''   ''
107   ''   ''
108   ''   ''
109 Connector

Wiring Code

Wire No.	From	To
R1	73	92
R2	76	Wire R2.1
R2.1	Wire R2	43
R4	78/5	Wire R2

Wire No.	From	To
15	72	Soldered joint 22
15	Soldered joint 22	104
15	104	34
15	34	Soldered joint 20
15-3	Soldered joint 22	76
15-3	76	86
15-3.1	76	86
15-4	Soldered joint 22	32/15/54
15-5	86/H	76
15-5	76	43
15-5	34	13
15a	Soldered joint 20	19/15
16	26/16	19/15
16	30/16	19/15
16	26/30	29
30	18/+ve	26/30/51
30	18/+ve	30/30/51
30-1	31	34
30-1	34	72
30-2	Soldered joint 2	32/30
30-3	Soldered joint 2	49
30-4	32/1	71
30-4	71	89
30-4.1	71	89
30-5	71	102
30-9	71	74
30-9.1	7	75
30-9.2	Wire 30-9.2	Wire 30-10
30-10	Car earth	46
31	Car earth	Engine earth
31	7	18/+ve
31-2	8	Earth
31-3	89	Wire 31-7.1 & 31-7.2
31-7	Wire 31-7	61
31-7.1	Wire 31-7	47
31-7.2	37	Wire 31-12.3 & 31-23
31-12	Wire 31-12.2	37
31-12.1	66	Wire 31-12.1
31-12.2	68/4	Wire 31-12.1
31-12.2	Wire 31-12	Casing earth
31-12.3	45	Casing earth
31-13	102	Wire 31-25
31-14	Wire 13-14	Wire 31-25
31-14.1	36	46
31-16	36	36a
31-17	39	67
31-19	Wire 31-12.3	67
31-23	67	Wire 31-12
31-24	67	40
31-25	89	Wire 31-25.1
31-25.1	Wire 31-25	Casing earth
31-25.2	89	41
31-26	99	73

Wire No.	From	To
31-26.1	Wire 31-26	41
31-26.2	98	Wire 31-26
31-26.3	Wire 31-26	42
31-30	42	Casing earth
31-31	36a	Casing earth
31-32	Wire 31-32	93
31-33	Wire 31-33	Casing earth
31-34	Wire 31-35	92
31-35	Wire 31-34	Casing earth
31-40	80	43
31b2	37	Wire 31b2
31b2	Wire 31b1	66/2
31b2	Wire 31b1	68/2
49	Wire 54-5	62/49
49	Wire 54-5	Wire 49-1
49-1	Wire 49	78/1
49-2	78/4	62
49a	62	76
49a	76	86/49a
49a1	74	78/3
49a1.1	74	75
50	72	26
50	34	30/50
50-1	Wire 50	89
50-2	42	89
51	31/B+	74
51	31/B+	26/30/51
53	37	30/30/51
53	37	66
53b	68/8	68/6
54-1	32/6	37
54-3	32/7	39
54-3	Wire 54-3	Wire 54-3.3
54-3.1	Wire 54-3	37
54-3.3	Wire 54-3	37
54-4	Soldered joint 4	44/IGN
54-4.1	Soldered joint 4	59
54-9.2	Soldered joint 4	60
54-4.2	32/6	10
54-4.3	35	57
54-5	73	35
54-6	Wire 54-6	73
54-6.1	35	95
54-8	73	94
54-8	99	73
54-9	44	99
54-9.1	44	98
54-10	60	51
54-10	34	50
54-11	50	34
54-11	73	21
54-11	50	73

Wire No.	From	To
54-11	73	90
54-11.1	Wire 54-11	90
54-11.1	Wire 54-11	34
54-12	51	22
54-12	34	34
54-12	51	76
56	49	86/56
56	76	76
56a	86/56a	32/56a
56a	76	7
56a1	32/4	61
56a2	32/4	76
56b	86/56b	32/56b
56b	76	7
56b	32/5	32/58
56b1	32/5	73
58	49	96
58-2	Wire 58-2	Wire 58-2.1
58-2	32/2	96
58-2.1	73	73
58-3	73	97
58-3	73	97
58-3	32/3	3
58-4	32/3	4
58-5	32/3	Wire 58-8
58-6	Wire 58-6	52
58-8	Soldered joint 3	102
58-8.1	Soldered joint 3	52
58-8.1	Soldered joint 3	52
58-8.2	Soldered joint 3	52
58-8.3	80	Wire 58-6
58-16	Wire 58-16	102
58-16.1	31/D+	34
61	34	59
61	72	69
75	31/D+	23/D+
D+	31/D+	23/D+
D-	31/D-	23/D-
DF	31/DF	23/DF
L	86/L	76
L	76	34
L	34	2
L1	L	10
L1	34	73
L2	73	93
L2.1	Wire L2	Wire L2.1
L4	78/6	43
R	86/R	34
R	76	1
R	Wire R	9
R1	34	73

Fuse connections

Wire No.	Fuse	Connection	Amp.
30	1	Interior lamps	
		Cigar lighter	8
		Four way hazard flashers	
58	2	Tail light—LH	8
		Licence plate lamp	
		Side light—LH	8
	3	Tail light—RH	
		Instrument illumination	8
		Side light—RH	
56a	4	Main beam	8
56b	5	Dip beam	8
	6	Stop light	
		Reversing lamp	8
		Indicator warning light	
		Fan motor	
15/54	7	Windscreen wiper motor	8

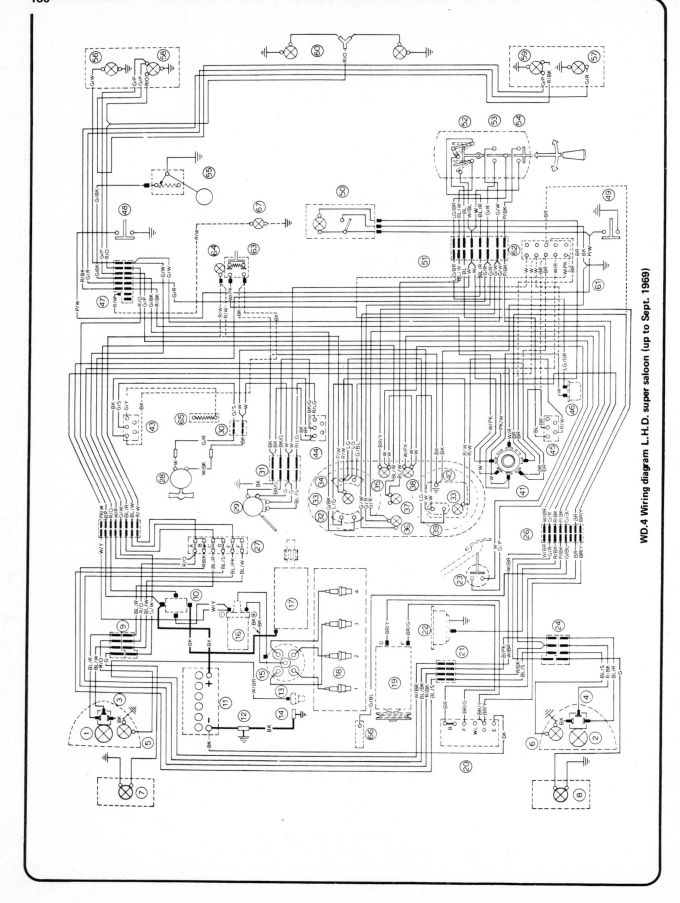

WD.4 Wiring diagram L.H.D. super saloon (up to Sept. 1969)

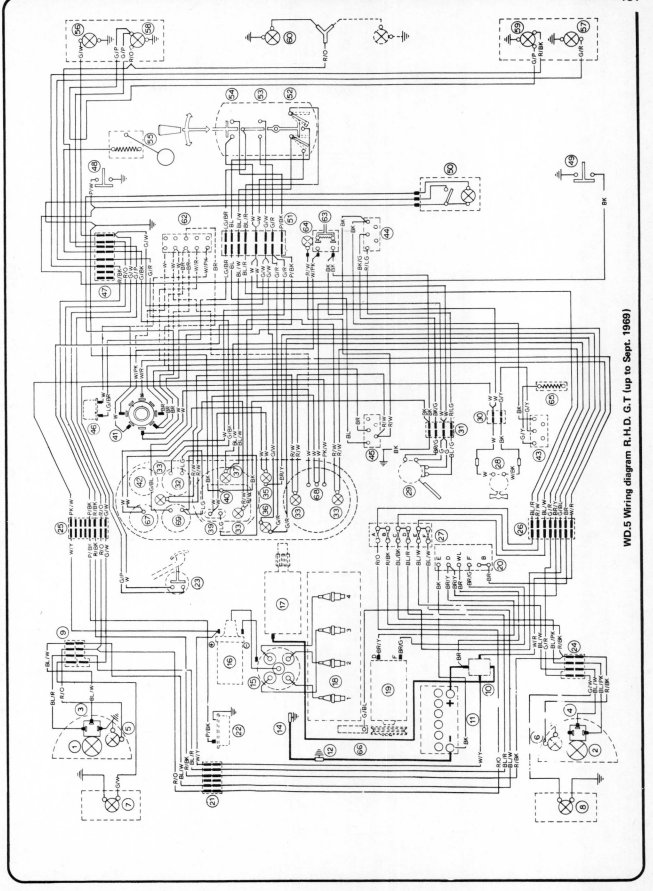

WD.5 Wiring diagram R.H.D. G.T (up to Sept. 1969)

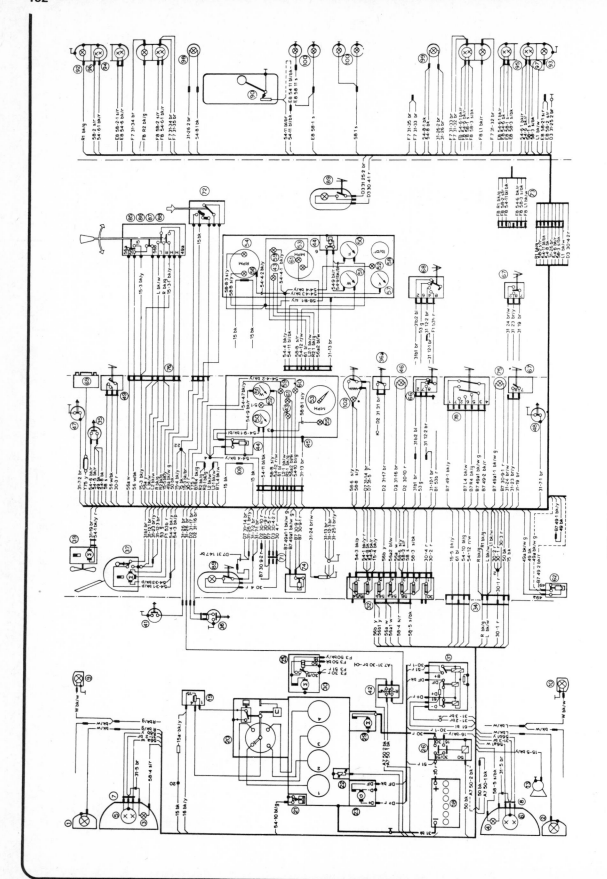

WD6. Wiring diagram. All models RHD 1969 onward

Chapter 11 Suspension and steering

Contents

Specifications

Front suspension

Type ... ...   Independent MacPherson strut.
Vehicles produced after September 1969 incorporate an anti-roll bar.

Coil spring application:

A Saloons and estates up to September 1969
   Saloons and estates (heavy duty) up to September 1970
   6 cwt vans up to September 1970
B G.T. and 8 cwt vans up to September 1969
   G.T. (heavy duty) and 8 cwt vans up to September 1970
C Saloons and estates September 1969 to September 1970
D G.T. after September 1969
E Saloons and estates (heavy duty) after September 1970
   6 cwt vans after September 1970
   6 cwt vans (heavy duty) after September 1970
F G.T. (heavy duty) 8 cwt vans after September 1970
G Saloons and estates after September 1970
H G.T./Sport/1300E after September 1970

All springs are right hand coil type

Refer to the following table for individual spring specification.

Vehicle Application	A	B	C	D	E	F	G	H
Mean load	512 lb 232.2 kg	512 lb 232.2 kg	512 lb 232.2 kg	512 lb 232.2 kg	512 lb 232.2 kg	512 lb 232.2 kg	512 lb 232.2 kg	512 lb 232.2 kg
Mean rate	115 lb/in 20.4 kg/cm	135 lb/in 23.9 kg/cm	85 lb/in 15.2 kg/cm	100 lb/in 17.8 kg/cm	115 lb/in 20.4 kg/cm	135 lb/in 23.9 kg/cm	85 lb/in 15.2 kg/cm	100 lb/in 17.8 kg/cm
Coil diameter ...	4.36 in 110.7 mm	4.32 in 109.7 mm	4.37 in 110.5 mm	4.30 in 109.2 mm	4.36 in 110.7 mm	4.32 in 109.7 mm	4.37 in 110.0 mm	4.30 in 109.2 mm
Wire diameter ...	0.439 in 11.15 mm	0.452 in 11.5 mm	0.420 in 10.66 mm	0.430 in 10.92 mm	0.439 in 11.15 mm	0.452 in 11.5 mm	0.420 in 10.66 mm	0.430 in 10.92 mm
Colour Code ...	Red/white	Red/blue	Red	Blue	Red/white	Red/blue	Red	Blue

Shock absorbers

Type ... ...   Double acting
Fluid capacity ... ...   260 cc

Steering

Type ... ...   Rack and pinion (Burman or Cam gears)

	Cam Gears	Burman
Rack travel (lock to lock)	5.27 in. (13.5 cm)	5.26 in. (13.3 cm)
Number of pinion teeth	5	6
Ratio (steering wheel to road wheel movement)	16.63 : 1	16.35 : 1
	(After September 1970 17.5 : 1 both types)	

Number of turns of steering wheel (lock to lock) 3½
Lubricant capacity ... ...   ¼ pint (0.15 litre)
Steering wheel diameter ... ...   15 in. (38.1 cm)
Adjustment method ... ...   Shims

Steering angles:	Standard	Heavy duty
Castor	0º 35' to 1º 35'	0º 40' to 1º 40'
Camber	0º 10' to 1º 10'	0º 50' to 1º 50'
King pin inclination	8º 05' to 9º 05'	7º 25' to 8º 25'
Toe-in	0 to 0.25 in. (0 to 6.4 mm)	
Turning circle (saloon and estate car)	29.0 ft (8.85 m)	
Turning circle (van)	29.7 ft (9.05 m)	

Rear suspension

Spring type ... ...   Semi-elliptical leaf

Up to September 1969	No. of leaves	Colour Code
Saloons	3	Salmon pink
Saloons (heavy duty)	3	Battleship grey
Estate cars	3	Blue
Estate cars (heavy duty)	4	White
6 cwt van	3	Green
6 cwt van (heavy duty)	3	Orange
8 cwt van	4	Yellow
8 cwt van (heavy duty)	4	None

From September 1969		
Saloons	4	Grey/Green
Saloons (heavy duty)	4	Grey
Estate cars	3	Blue
Estate cars (heavy duty)	4	Grey/Orange
6 cwt vans	3	Green
6 cwt vans (heavy duty)	3	Orange
8 cwt vans	4	White/Yellow
8 cwt vans (heavy duty)	4	None

Width of spring leaves ... ...   2 in. (51 mm)
Spring length ... ...   47 in. (1144 mm) between eye centres

Rate: - Saloons	97 lb/in. (17.3 kg/cm)
Estate cars	115 lb/in. (20.5 kg/cm)
6 cwt vans	147 lb/in. (26.2 kg/cm)
8 cwt vans	190 lb/in. (33.9 kg/cm)
Estate cars (heavy duty)	137 lb/in. (24.6 kg/cm)

Shock absorbers

Type ... ...   Double acting, hydraulic telescopic

Wheels and Tyres

Wheel size - 1100, 1300 Saloons	3.5c x 12
- G.T. and Saloon option	4.5c x 12
- Estate cars and vans	4.5c x 12

Pressure recommendations:
These are shown according to date of vehicle manufacture. Due to changes in suspension and tyre design the pressures for vehicles built after September 1970 have been modified in comparison with those recommended for earlier models.

Up to September 1970

Tyre size and application	Normal pressure		High speed pressure		Full load pressure	
	Front	Rear	Front	Rear	Front	Rear
1100 Saloon - 5.50 x 12 crossply ...	24 (1.7)	24 (1.7)	28 (2.0)	28 (2.0)	24 (1.7)	26 (1.85)
- 155 x 12 radial	24 (1.7)	28 (2.0)	24 (1.7)	28 (2.0)	24 (1.7)	28 (2.0)
1300 Saloon - 5.50 x 12 crossply ...	24 (1.7)	24 (1.7)	28 (2.0)	28 (2.0)	24 (1.7)	26 (1.85)
- 155 x 12 radial	24 (1.7)	28 (2.0)	24 (1.7)	28 (2.0)	24 (1.7)	28 (2.0)
G.T. - 155 x 12 radial	24 (1.7)	28 (2.0)	24 (1.7)	28 (2.0)	24 (1.7)	28 (2.0)
Estate cars - 6.00 x 12 crossply ...	24 (1.7)	24 (1.7)	28 (2.0)	28 (2.0)	24 (1.7)	30 (2.1)
- 155 x 12 radial	24 (1.7)	28 (2.0)	24 (1.7)	28 (2.0)	24 (1.7)	28 (2.0)
6 cwt vans - 5.50 x 12 light van ...	24 (1.7)	24 (1.7)	28 (2.0)	28 (2.0)	24 (1.7)	43 (3.0)

8 cwt vans	- 6.00 x 12 light van	...	24 (1.7)	24 (1.7)	28 (2.0)	28 (2.0)	24 (1.7)	43 (3.0)

After September 1970

			2 passengers + luggage		3/4 passengers + luggage	
			Front	Rear	Front	Rear
1100 cc	550 x 12 crossply	... ...	24 (1.7)	24 (1.7)	24 (1.7)	30 (2.1)
	155SR x 12 radial	... ...	20 (1.4)	27 (1.9)	22 (1.6)	28 (2.0)
1300 cc	550S x 12 crossply	... ...	27 (1.9)	27 (1.9)	27 (1.9)	30 (2.1)
	155SR x 12 radial	... ...	20 (1.4)	27 (1.9)	22 (1.6)	28 (2.0)
G.T./Sport	155SR x 12 radial	... ...	20 (1.4)	27 (1.9)	24 (1.7)	28 (2.0)
Estate car	600 x 12 crossply	... ...	20 (1.4)	27 (1.9)	22 (1.6)	30 (2.1)
	155SR x 12 radial	... ...	20 (1.4)	27 (1.9)	22 (1.6)	28 (2.0)
6/8 cwt van	550 x 12 crossply	... ...	24 (1.7)	24 (1.7)	24 (1.7)	43 (3.1)
	600 x 12 crossply	... ...	24 (1.7)	24 (1.7)	24 (1.7)	43 (3.1)
	155 x 12 radial	... ...	22 (1.6)	28 (1.7)	24 (1.7)	36 (2.5)

All pressures are shown in lb/in^2 with equivalent kg/cm^2 in brackets.
Pressure readings to be taken with tyres cold

Torque wrench settings

	lb ft	kg m
Compression strut to mounting bracket	25 to 30	(3.5 to 4.1)
Compression strut mounting bracket to sidemember	25 to 30	(3.5 to 4.1)
Track control arm inner bushing	25 to 30	(3.5 to 4.1)
Compression strut to track control arm	35 to 40	(4.9 to 5.5)
**Spindle to top mount assembly	28 to 32	(3.9 to 4.4)
Track control arm ball stud	30 to 35	(4.2 to 4.8)
Suspension top mount assembly to body	15 to 18	(2.1 to 2.5)
*Track control arm inner bushing	25 to 30	(3.5 to 4.1)
Anti-roll bar bracket to side frame	20 to 25	(2.8 to 3.5)
Anti-roll bar to front panel	20 to 25	(2.8 to 3.5)
*Anti-roll bar clamp to bracket	15 to 18	(2.1 to 2.5)
*Anti-roll bar to track control arm	25 to 30	(3.5 to 4.1)
Rear shock absorber upper mounting bracket to body	15 to 18	(2.1 to 2.5)
*Shock absorber to mounting bracket	25 to 30	(3.5 to 4.1)
Shock absorber to spring plate	25 to 30	(3.5 to 4.1)
*Rear spring 'U' bolts	20 to 25	(2.8 to 3.5)
*Rear spring front hanger	22 to 27	(3.04 to 3.73)
*Rear spring rear shackle nuts	12 to 15	(1.66 to 2.0)
Spring centre bolt	15 to 18	(2.1 to 2.5)
Steering arm to suspension unit	30 to 34	(4.2 to 4.7)
Steering gear to crossmember	12 to 15	(1.7 to 2.0)
Track rod end to steering arm	18 to 22	(2.5 to 3.0)
Coupling to pinion spline	7 to 7	(0.7 to 1.0)
Coupling to steering shaft spline	5 to 7	(0.7 to 1.0)
Steering wheel to steering shaft	20 to 25	(2.8 to 3.4)
Roadwheel nuts	50 to 65	(7.0 to 8.9)

*Tighten with vehicle weight on roadwheels
**Tighten with vehicle weight on roadwheels and steering in 'straight ahead' position.

1 General description

Each of the independent front suspension Macpherson strut units consists of a vertical strut enclosing a double acting shock absorber surrounded by a coil spring.

The upper end of each strut is secured to the top of the wing valance under the bonnet by rubber mountings.

The wheel spindle (stub axle) carrying the brake assembly and wheel hub is forged integrally with the suspension unit foot.

The steering arms are connected to each unit which are in turn connected to track rods and thence to the rack and pinion steering gear.

The lower end of each suspension unit is located by a track control arm. On models produced before September 1969 a compression strut runs from the outer end of each track control arm to a strengthened mounting on the side members. On models produced after September 1969 a stabilising torsion bar (anti-roll bar) is fitted between the outer ends of each track control arm and secured at the front to mountings on the body front member.

On all models a rubber rebound stop is fitted inside the suspension unit. This prevents the spring becoming over-extended and jumping out of its mounting plates.

On Escorts with heavy duty suspension prior to September 1969 and on all models after that date a rubber bump stop is fitted around the suspension unit piston rod. This comes into operation before the spring is fully compressed.

Whenever repairs have been carried out on a suspension unit it is essential to check the wheel alignment as the linkage could be altered which would affect the correct front wheel settings.

Every time the car goes over a bump vertical movement of a front wheel pushes the damper body upward against the combined resistance of the coil spring and the shock absorber piston.

Hydraulic fluid in the shock absorber is displaced and it is then forced through the compression valve into the space between the inner and outer cylinder. On the downward movement of the suspension, the road spring forces the shock absorber body downward against the pressure of the hydraulic fluid which is forced back again through the rebound valve. In this way the natural oscillations of the spring are damped out and a comfortable ride is obtained.

On the front uprights there is a shroud inside the coil spring which protects the machined surface of the piston rod from road dirt.

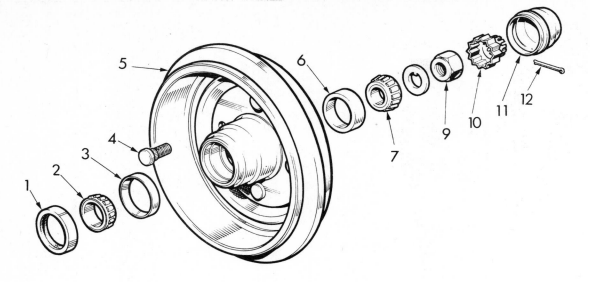

Fig. 11.1 Hub/drum assembly

1	Grease seal	7	Outer bearing
2	Inner roller bearing	9	Nut
3	Track	10	Nut retainer
4	Road wheel stud	11	Dust cap
5	Drum/hub assembly	12	Split pin
6	Outer bearing track		

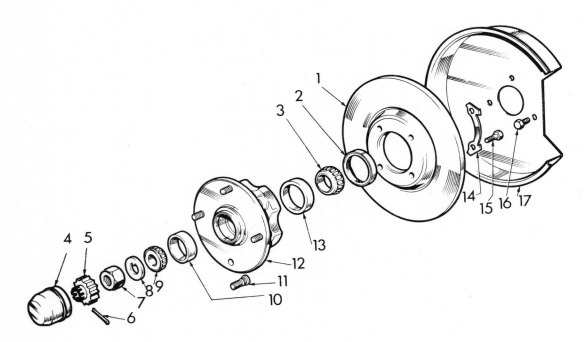

Fig. 11.2 Hub/disc assembly

1	Disc	9	Outer bearing
2	Grease seal	10	Outer bearing track
3	Inner roller bearing	11	Road wheel stud
4	Dust cap	12	Hub
5	Nut retainer	13	Inner bearing track
6	Split pin	14	Lock plate
7	Nut	15,16	Bolts
8	Thrust washer	17	Splash shield

Fig. 11.3 Checking disc run-out with a dial gauge

Fig. 11.4 Compressing a front road spring

The upper mounting assembly consists of a steel sleeve with a rubber bush bonded to it. The steering gear on the Escort is rack and pinion and can be of either cam gears or Burman manufacture. These two units are interchangeable on any Escort, but the parts within them are not, the Burman type having a six tooth pinion whilst the cam gears type has a five tooth pinion.

The steering gear is located on the front crossmember by two U shaped clamps. The pinion is connected to the steering column by a flexible coupling.

Turning the steering wheel thus causes the rack to move in a lateral direction and the track rods attached to either end of the rack pass this movement to the steering arms on the suspension/axle units thereby moving the road wheels.

Two adjustments are possible on the steering gear, namely rack damper adjustment and pinion bearing pre-load adjustment, but the steering gear must be removed from the car to carry out these adjustments. Both adjustments are made by varying the thickness of shim packs. The cam gears steering unit has the pinion bearing pre-load shim pack and cover plate facing upward whilst the Burman type has the shim pack and cover plate on the underside.

The rear axle is located by two inverted U bolts at each end of the casing to underslung semi-elliptical leaf springs which provide both lateral and longitudinal location.

Double acting telescopic shock absorbers are fitted between the spring plates on the axle and reinforced mountings in the floor pan. These shock absorbers work on the same principle as the front shock absorbers.

In the interests of lessening noise and vibration, the springs and shock absorbers are mounted on rubber bushes. Later Escort models also incorporate a rubber spacer between the axle and the springs.

After September 1973 a rear anti-roll bar is incorporated in the rear suspension of all saloon models in conjunction with rear road springs and shock absorbers of revised ratings.

2 Suspension and steering - maintenance and inspection

1 Every 6000 miles (9600 km) brush the rear road springs free from dirt and apply either penetrating oil or engine oil to the leaves with a spray or brush. Do not allow oil to come in contact with the rubber bushes at the spring eyes.

2 Check the torque setting of the U bolts and shackle bolts.

3 Inspect the rubber bushes for deterioration or wear and renew if necessary as described later in this Section.

4 At a similar mileage interval, check the condition of the rubber bellows at both ends of the steering rack. Renew them if

they are split or perished.

5 Check the condition of the rubber gaiters on all the steering ball joints and renew them if they are split or perished. It is unlikely that the gaiters themselves can be obtained without purchasing a complete ball joint.

6 Check all suspension securing bolts and nuts for correct tightening torque in accordance with the figures specified in the Specifications Section.

3 Front hub/drum assemblies - maintenance, removal and refitting

1 Jack up the front of the car, remove the road wheel, the dust cap, split pin, nut retainer, nut, thrust washer, outer bearing and hub/drum assembly.

2 From the back of the drum/hub carefully prise out the grease seal and remove the inner tapered bearing.

3 Carefully clean out the hub and wash the bearings with petrol, making sure no grease or oil is allowed to get onto the brake drum.

4 Working the grease well into the bearings fully pack the bearing cages and rollers with Castrolease LM or any suitable lithium based grease. **Note**: Leave the hub and grease seal empty to allow for subsequent expansion of the grease.

5 To reassemble the hub, first fit the inner bearing and then gently tap the grease seal back into the hub. If the seal was at all damaged during removal, a new one must be fitted.

6 Replace the hub and drum assembly on the stub axle and slide on the outer bearing and thrust washer.

7 Tighten down the centre adjusting nut to a torque of 27 lb ft (3.73 kg m) whilst rotating the drum to ensure free movement, then slacken the nut off 90° and fit the nut retainer and a new split pin.

8 Bend the ends of the split pin, refit the dust cap.

9 Check the adjustment of the front brakes (Chapter 9), refit the road wheel and then lower the vehicle to the ground.

4 Front hub/disc assemblies - maintenance, removal and refitting

1 Jack up the front of the vehicle, remove the road wheel and disconnect the brake pipe at the suspension leg bracket. Plug the pipe to prevent loss of fluid.

2 Knock back the locking tabs on the two caliper unit securing bolts, unscrew and remove the bolts and the caliper unit.

3 Knock the dust cap from the end of the hub and then withdraw the split pin, nut retainer, nut, thrust washer and

outer bearing.
4   Pull the hub/disc assembly from the stub axle.
5   From the back of the hub assembly, carefully prise out the grease seal and remove the inner tapered bearing.
6   Carefully clean out the hub and wash the bearings with petrol, making sure that no grease or oil is allowed to get onto the brake disc.
7   Working the grease well into the bearings, fully pack the bearing cages and rollers with Castrolease LM or any suitable lithium based grease. **Note**: Leave the hub and grease seal empty to allow for subsequent expansion of the grease.
8   To reassemble the hub, first fit the inner bearing and then gently tap the grease seal back into the hub. If the oil seal was at all damaged during removal, a new one must be fitted.
9   Replace the hub and disc assembly on the stub axle and slide on the outer bearing and thrust washer.
10 Tighten down the centre adjusting nut to a torque of 27 lb ft (3.73 kg m) whilst rotating the hub and disc to ensure free movement, then slacken the nut off 90º and fit the nut retainer and new split pin but do not bend back the split pin.
11 At this stage it is advisable, if a dial gauge is available, to check the disc for run-out. The measurement should be taken as near to the edge of the worn, smooth part of the disc as possible and must not exceed 0.004 inch (0.10 mm). If this figure is found to be excessive, check the mating surfaces of the disc and hub for dirt or damage and check the bearings and cups for excessive wear or damage. Renew the disc if the run-out is excessive or it appears deeply scored.
12 Bend the ends of the split pin and refit the dust cap.
13 Reconnect the hydraulic brake pipe and bleed the brakes (Chapter 9).

5   Front hub bearings - checking for wear and renewal

1   To check the condition of the hub bearings, jack up the front end of the car and grasp the road wheel at two opposite points to check for any rocking movement in the wheel hub. Watch carefully for any movement in the steering gear, which can easily be mistaken for hub movement. If movement is observed in the ball joints, they must be renewed.
2   If a front wheel hub has excessive movement, this is adjusted by removing the hub cap and then levering off the small dust cap. Remove the split pin through the stub axle and take off the adjusting nut retainer.
3   If a torque wrench is available, tighten the centre adjusting nut down to a torque of 27 lb ft (3.73 kg m) and then slacken it off 90º and replace the nut retainer and a new split pin.
4   Where this action does not remove the rocking or if a grinding or grating sound can be heard when the hub is rotated, then the bearings must be renewed.
5   Remove the hub/drum or hub/disc assembly as previously described. Remove the outer bearing.
6   Prise out the grease seal from the back of the hub and remove the inner bearing.
7   Drift out the bearing outer tracks from each end of the hub and then thoroughly clean the grease from the hub interior.
8   It is essential to keep the new bearings in their individual packs until required for fitting. Do not open them and mix the roller races and tracks but keep them as matched pairs.
9   Drift in the new bearing outer tracks using a suitable piece of tubing. Ensure that they are fully home in their recesses. Fit a new grease seal.
10 Fill the intervening space between the two bearings with recommended grease but not by more than 1/3 of the available capacity.
11 Refitting is a reversal of removal. Adjust the bearings as described in Sections 3 or 4 and in the case of disc assemblies; bleed the brakes.

6   Front coil spring - removal and installation

1   Before commencing operations, the spring must be compressed.

Fig. 11.5 Cut-away view of front suspension unit top mounting (later vehicles have double cranked retainer at top)

This can be carried out by having an assistant sit on the front wing and then fitting clips over two or three adjacent coils or by using the screw type compressors. Either item is available from most good accessory stores.
2   With the spring compressed, jack up the front of the vehicle and support the bodyframe and crossmember adequately on stands.
3   Working under the bonnet, measure the distance that the threads on the top of the piston rod protrude above the nut, then remove the nut and the cranked retainer.
4   Undo and remove the three bolts securing the top of the suspension unit to the side panel.
5   Push the piston rod downward as far as it will go. It should now be possible to remove the top mounting assembly, the dished washer and the upper spring seat from the top of the spring.
6   The spring can now be lifted off its bottom seat and removed over the piston assembly.
7   If a new spring is being fitted, check extremely carefully that it is of the same rating as the spring on the other side of the car. The colour coding of the springs can be found in the Specifications at the beginning of this Chapter.
8   Before fitting a new spring, it must be compressed with the adjustable restrainers and make sure that the clips are placed on the same number of coils, and in the same position as on the spring which has been removed.
9   Place the new spring over the piston and locate it on its bottom seat, then pull the piston upward and fit the upper spring seat so that it locates correctly on the flats cut on the piston rod.
10 Fit the dished washer to the piston rod, ensuring that the convex side faces upward.
11 Now fit the top mount assembly. With the steering in the straight ahead position, fit the cranked retainer facing inward at 90º to the wheel angles and the piston rod nut having previously applied Loctite or similar compound to the thread. Do not fully tighten down the nut at this stage.
12 If necessary, pull the top end of the unit upward until it is possible to locate correctly the top mount bracket and fit the three retaining bolts from under the bonnet. These nuts must be tightened down to a torque of 15 to 18 lb ft (2.1 to 2.5 kg m).
13 Remove the spring clips, fit the road wheel and lower the car to the ground.
14 Finally, slacken off the piston rod nut, get an assistant to hold the upper spring seat to prevent it turning, and retighten the nut to a torque of 28 to 30 lb ft (3.9 to 4.4 kg m). Check that the same amount of thread is protruding above the nut as was measured in paragraph 3 of this Section. If this is not the same,

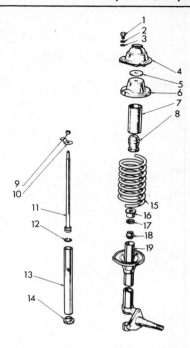

Fig. 11.6 Front suspension unit

1 Mounting bolt	11 Piston rod
2 Spring washer	12 Piston ring
3 Washer	13 Cylinder
4 Upper mounting	14 Compression valve
5 Spring seat retainer	15 Coil spring
6 Spring upper seat	16 Gland cap
7 Spacer	17 Oil seal
8 Rebound stop	18 Bush
9 Nut	19 Strut/stub axle assembly
10 Cranked retainer	

it is probable that the upper spring seat is not correctly located or alternatively, that the spring itself is not properly seated.

7 Front suspension unit - removal and installation

1   Compress the coil spring (Section 6).
2   Jack up the front of the vehicle and remove the road wheel.
3   Remove the hub/drum or hub/disc assembly (Section 3 or 4).
4   Disconnect the track control arm from the base of the suspension unit after removal of the split pin and castellated nut.

On cars equipped with drum type front brakes
5   Free the steering arm from the unit by undoing the two securing bolts, then remove the brake backplate from the hub by undoing the single remaining bolt.
6   Move the backplate and brake assembly to one side and support it on a block of wood or similar object, taking care not to place any strain on the flexible hydraulic hose.

On cars equipped with disc type front brakes
7   Remove the outer end of the track control arm from the base of the suspension unit by pulling out the split pin and undoing the castellated nut.

On all vehicles
8   Working under the bonnet, unscrew and remove the three bolts on the side apron holding the top of the suspension unit in place and then lower the unit away from the car.
9   Replacement is a direct reversal of the removal procedure, but remember to use a new split pin on the track control arm to suspension unit castellated nut.
10 The steering arm to suspension unit nuts must be tightened to a torque of 30 to 34 lb ft (4.2 to 4.7 kg m), the track control arm to suspension unit nut to a torque of 30 to 35 lb ft (4.2 to 4.8 kg m), and the top mounting bolts to a torque of 15 to 18 lb ft (2.1 to 2.5 kg m).

8 Compression strut (early vehicles) - removal and refitting

1   Jack up the front of the vehicle and remove the road wheel.
2   From on top of the track control arm, remove the nut holding the forward end of the compression strut to the arm and then lift off the recessed washer and the nylon washer.

3   From the rear of the compression strut remove the single nut holding the strut to the mounting bracket on the bodyframe side member.
4   After removing the nut, take off the dished washer and the rubber bush carefully noting the way in which they are fitted.
5   Remove the front end of the strut from the track control arm and take off the nylon washer from the stud on the track control arm.
6   Pull the rear end of the strut from its mounting bracket and remove the remaining rubber bush and dished washer from the strut once again noting the correct fitting positions. Remove the strut from the car.
7   Refitting is a direct reversal of the removal procedure, but the following points should be noted.
8   Always fit a new nylon washer on either side of the compression strut on the track control arm stud.
9   Take great care to ensure that the dished washers and rubber bushes are correctly fitted at the rear end of the strut.
10 Once refitting of the strut is completed and the car has been lowered to the ground, the single nut at the rear of the strut should be tightened to a torque of 25 to 30 lb ft (3.5 to 4.1 kg m) and the nut retaining the strut to the track control arm to a torque of 34 to 40 lb ft (4.9 to 5.5 kg m).

9 Anti-roll bar (later vehicles) - removal and refitting

1   Jack up the front of the vehicle, support the vehicle on suitable stands and remove both front road wheels.
2   Working under the car at the front, knock back the locking tabs on the four bolts securing the two front clamps which hold the torsion bar to the frame and then undo the four bolts and remove the clamps and rubber insulators.
3   Remove the split pins from the castellated nuts retaining the anti-roll bar to the track control arms then undo the nuts and pull off the large washers, carefully noting the way in which they are fitted.
4   Pull the anti-roll bar forward out of the two track control arms and remove it from the vehicle.
5   With the anti-roll bar out of the car, remove the sleeve and large washer from each end of the bar, again noting the correct fitting positions.
6   Reassembly is a reversal of this procedure, but new locking tabs must be used on the front clamp bolts and new split pins on the castellated nuts. The nuts on the clamps and the

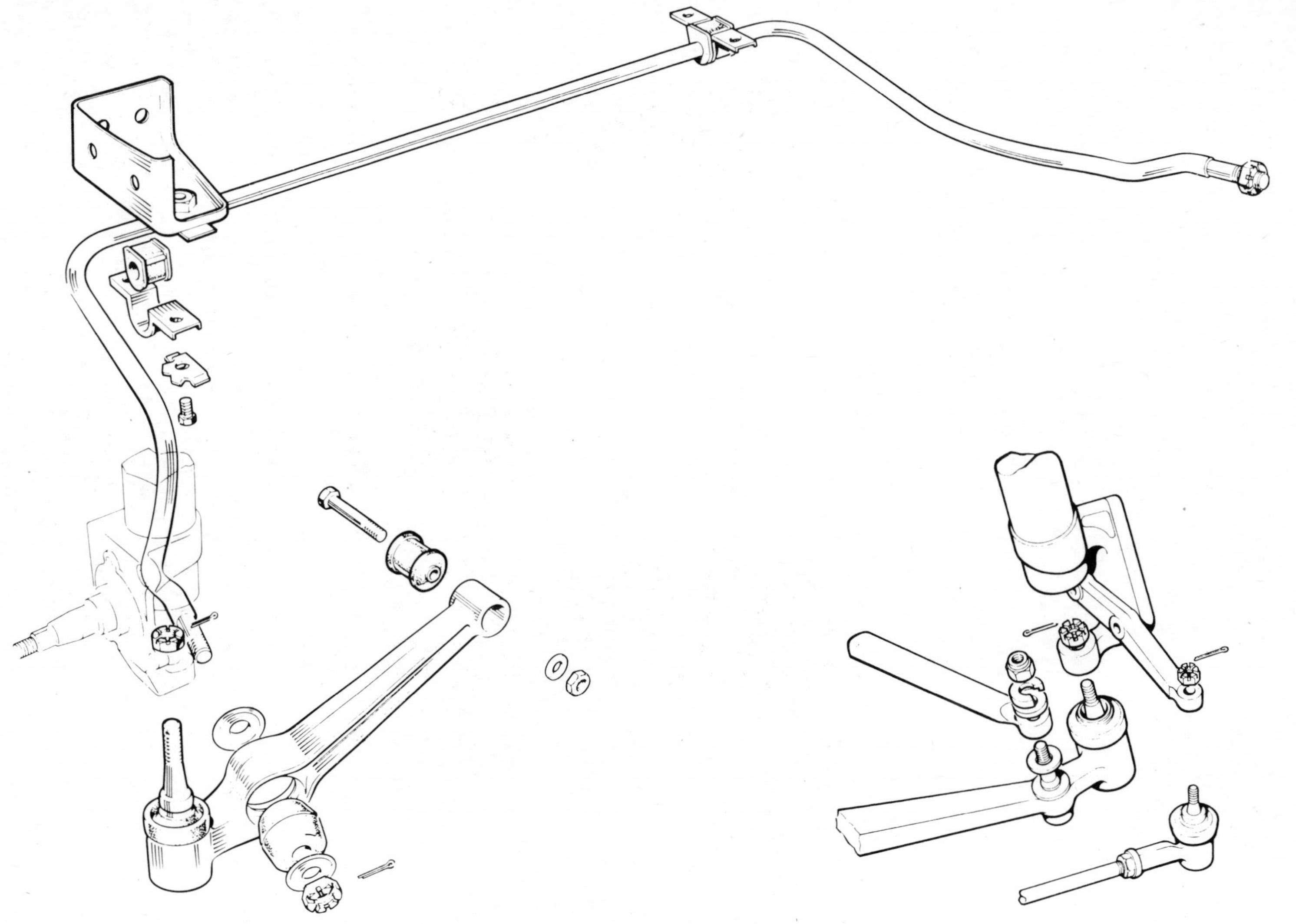

Fig. 11.7 Later type track control arm with anti-roll bar (inset) early type with compression strut

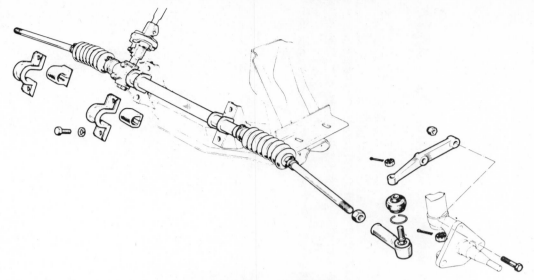

Fig. 11.8 Steering gear - components

Fig. 11.9 Steering column flexible coupling

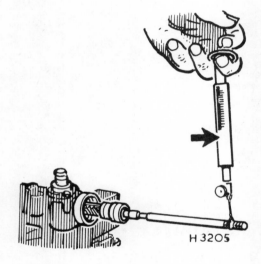

H 3205

Fig. 11.10 Measuring track rod to rack ball joint pre-load

castellated nuts on each end of the anti-roll bar must not be fully tightened down until the vehicle is resting on its wheels.

7 Once the vehicle is on its wheels the castellated nuts on the ends of the anti-roll bar should be tightened down to a torque of 25 to 30 lb ft (3.46 to 4.15 kg m) and the new split pins fitted. The four clamp bolts on the front mounting points must be tightened down to a torque of 15 to 18 lb ft (2.07 to 2.47 kg m) and the locking tabs knocked up.

10 Steering gear - removal and installation

1 Before starting this job set the front wheels in the straight ahead position. Then jack up the front of the vehicle and place blocks under the wheels; lower the vehicle slightly on the jack so that the track rods are in a near horizontal position.

2 Remove the nut and bolt from the clamp at the front of the flexible coupling on the steering column. This clamp holds the coupling to the pinion splines (Fig 11.9).

3 Working on the front crossmember, knock back the locking

tabs on the two nuts on each U clamp, undo the nut and remove the locking tabs and clamps.

4 Remove the split pins and castellated nuts from the ends of each track rod where they join the steering arms. Separate the track rods from the steering arms using a ball joint extractor or wedges and lower the steering gear downward out of the car.

5 Before replacing the steering gear, make sure that the wheels have remained in the straight ahead position. Also check the condition of the mounting rubbers round the housing and if they appear worn or damaged, renew them.

6 Check that the steering gear is also in the straight ahead position. This can be done by ensuring that the distances between the ends of both track rods and the steering gear housing on both sides are the same.

7 Place the steering gear in its location on the crossmember and at the same time mate up the splines on the pinion with the splines in the clamp on the steering column flexible coupling.

8 Replace the two U clamps using new locking tabs under the bolts, tighten down the bolts to a torque of 12 to 15 lb ft (1.7 to 2.0 kg m) and bend up the locking tabs.

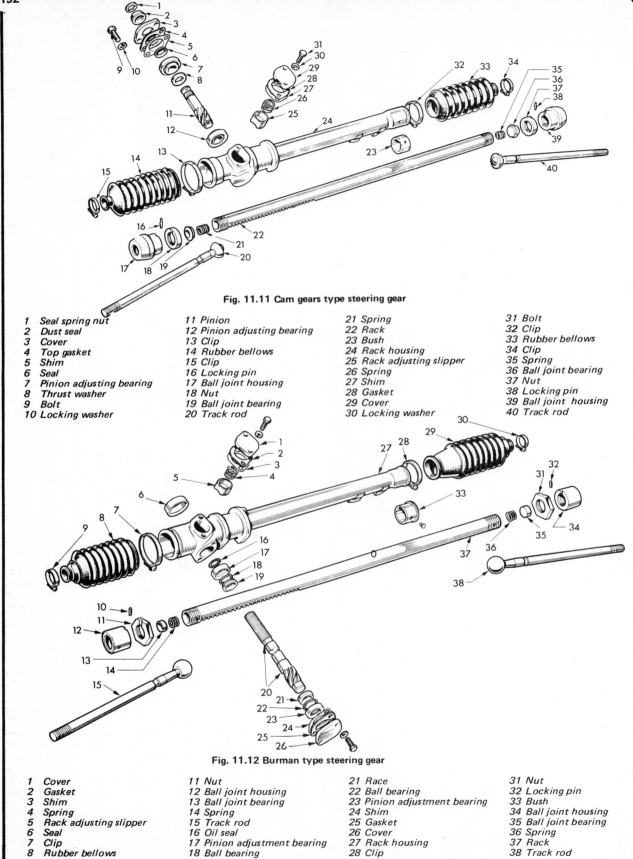

Fig. 11.11 Cam gears type steering gear

1 Seal spring nut	11 Pinion	21 Spring	31 Bolt
2 Dust seal	12 Pinion adjusting bearing	22 Rack	32 Clip
3 Cover	13 Clip	23 Bush	33 Rubber bellows
4 Top gasket	14 Rubber bellows	24 Rack housing	34 Clip
5 Shim	15 Clip	25 Rack adjusting slipper	35 Spring
6 Seal	16 Locking pin	26 Spring	36 Ball joint bearing
7 Pinion adjusting bearing	17 Ball joint housing	27 Shim	37 Nut
8 Thrust washer	18 Nut	28 Gasket	38 Locking pin
9 Bolt	19 Ball joint bearing	29 Cover	39 Ball joint housing
10 Locking washer	20 Track rod	30 Locking washer	40 Track rod

Fig. 11.12 Burman type steering gear

1 Cover	11 Nut	21 Race	31 Nut
2 Gasket	12 Ball joint housing	22 Ball bearing	32 Locking pin
3 Shim	13 Ball joint bearing	23 Pinion adjustment bearing	33 Bush
4 Spring	14 Spring	24 Shim	34 Ball joint housing
5 Rack adjusting slipper	15 Track rod	25 Gasket	35 Ball joint bearing
6 Seal	16 Oil seal	26 Cover	36 Spring
7 Clip	17 Pinion adjustment bearing	27 Rack housing	37 Rack
8 Rubber bellows	18 Ball bearing	28 Clip	38 Track rod
9 Clip	19 Race	29 Rubber bellows	
10 Locking pin	20 Pinion	30 Clip	

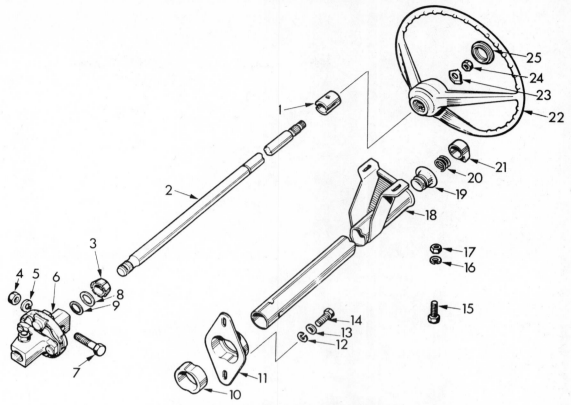

Fig. 11.13 Steering column (without steering lock)

1 Shaft collar	10 Column opening seal	19 Upper bearing
2 Steering gear shaft	11 Lower mounting	20 Spring
3 Lower bearing	12 Locking washer	21 Indicator cancelling cam
4 Nut	13 Washer	22 Steering wheel
5 Locking washer	14 Bolt	23 Tab washer
6 Flexible coupling	15 Bolt	24 Nut
7 Clamp bolt	16 Locking washer	25 Emblem
8 Washer	17 Nut	
9 Circlip	18 Column tube assembly	

9 Refit the track rod ends into the steering arms, replace the castellated nuts and tighten them to a torque of 18 to 22 lb ft (2.5 to 3.0 kg m). Use new split pins to retain the nuts.

10 Tighten the clamp bolt on the steering column flexible coupling to a torque of 5 to 7 lb ft (0.7 to 1.0 kg m), having first made sure that the pinion is correctly located in the splines.

11 Jack up the car, remove the blocks from under the wheels and lower the car to the ground. It is advisable at this stage to take your car to your local Ford dealer and have the toe-in checked (Section 16).

11 Steering gear - dismantling and reassembly

1 Remove the steering gear from the car (Section 10).

2 Unscrew the ball joints and locknuts from the end of each track rod, having previously marked the threads to ensure correct positioning on reassembly. Alternatively, the number of turns required to undo the ball joint can be counted and noted.

3 Slacken off the clips securing the rubber bellows to each track rod and the steering gear housing then pull off the bellows. Have a quantity of rag handy to catch the oil which will escape when the bellows are removed.

4 To dismantle the steering gear, it is only necessary to remove the track rod which is furthest away from the pinion on either right or left hand drive cars.

5 To remove the track rod place the steering gear in a soft jawed vice. Working on the track rod ball joint, carefully drill out

the pin which locks the ball housing to the locknut. Great care must be taken not to drill too deeply or you will drill into the threads on the rack thus causing irrepairable damage. The hole on cam gears steering should be ¼ inch (6.35 mm) deep and on Burman steering 3/8 inch (9.5 mm) deep.

6 Using two pairs of mole wrenches firmly grip the locknut and undo the ball housing from the end of the rack. On Burman steering it is possible to hold the locknut with a spanner.

7 Take out the spring and ball seat from the recess in the end of the rack and then unscrew the locknut from the threads on the rack. The spring and ball seat must be replaced by new components on reassembly.

8 On the cam gears steering remove the pinion bearing pre-load cover plate together with the gasket and shim pack.

9 On both types of steering now withdraw the pinion together with the top pinion bearing assembly. The cam gears assembly has a caged bearing, but the Burman assembly uses bearing tracks and loose balls (eleven in each bearing) so care must be taken not to lose any of the balls, or drop them inside the steering gear on reassembly.

10 With the pinion removed, withdraw the complete rack assembly with one track rod still attached from the pinion end of the casing, having first removed the rack damper cover, gasket, shims, springs and yoke by unscrewing the two cover retaining bolts. Also remove the two small springs and the recessed yoke which bears on the rack.

11 Now remove the remaining pinion bearing and thrust washer

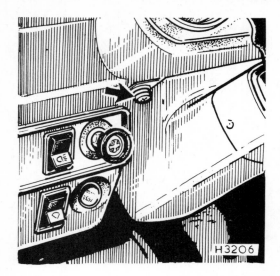

Fig. 11.14 Location of steering column shroud screws

Fig. 11.15 Removing steering wheel and direction indicator cancelling cam

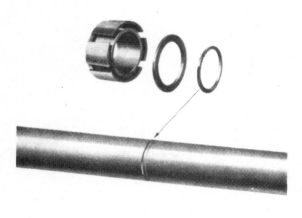

Fig. 11.16 Components of the steering shaft lower bearing

from the steering gear casing.

12 Carefully examine all parts for signs of wear or damage. Check the condition of the rack support bush at the opposite end of the casing from the pinion. If this is worn, renew it. If the rack or pinion teeth are in any way damaged, a completely new steering gear will have to be fitted.

13 In the case of Burman steering, take the pinion oil seal off the top of the casing and replace it with a new seal. The cam gears pinion oil seal is located in the cover plate and must be renewed in the same way.

14 To commence reassembly, fit the lower pinion bearing and thrust washer into their recess in the casing. The loose balls of the Burman bearing can be held in place by a small amount of grease.

15 Replace the rack in the casing from the pinion end and position it in the straight ahead position by equalising the amount it protrudes at either end of the casing.

16 Replace the remaining pinion bearing and thrust washer onto the pinion and fit the pinion into the casing so that the larger master spline on the pinion shaft is parallel to the rack and on the right hand side of the pinion. This applies to both right and left hand drive cars.

17 In the case of the cam gears assembly, replace the cover plate, gasket and shim pack, then replace the rack damper yoke, springs,

shims, gasket and cover plate.

18 To replace the track rod which has been removed, start by fitting a new spring and ball seat to the recess in the end of the rack shaft and replace the locknut onto the threads of the rack.

19 Lubricate the ball, ball seat and ball housing with a small amount of SAE 90 EP oil. Then slide the ball housing over the track rod and screw the housing onto the rack threads, keeping the track rod in the horizontal position until the track rod starts to become stiff to move.

20 Using a normal spring balance hook it round the track rod half an inch (12.7 mm) from the end and check the effort required to move it from the horizontal position (Fig 11.10).

21 By adjusting the tightness of the ball housing on the rack threads the effort required to move the track rod must be set at 5 lb (2.8 kg).

22 Tighten the locknut up to the housing and then re-check that the effort required to move the track rod is still correct at 5 lb (2.8 kg).

23 On the line where the locknut and ball housing meet, drill a 1/8 inch (3.18 mm) diameter hole which must be ¼ inch (6 35 mm) deep on cam gears steering and 3/8 inch (9.52 mm) deep on Burman steering. Even if the two halves of the old hole previously drilled out align, a new hole must still be drilled.

24 Tap a new retaining pin into the hole and peen the end over to secure it.

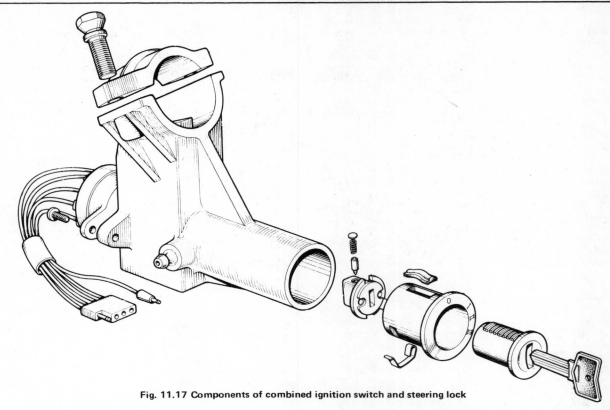

Fig. 11.17 Components of combined ignition switch and steering lock

25 Replace the rubber bellows and the track rod ends ensuring that they are replaced in exactly the same position from which they were removed.
26 Remove the cover plate and pour in ¼ pint (0.15 litre) of EP 90 grade oil.
27 Carry out both the adjustments described in the following Section.
28 Refit the steering gear (Section 10) and then have the toe-in checked at your Ford dealers or refer to Section 16.

12 Steering gear - adjustments

1 For the steering gear to function correctly, two adjustments must be carried out whenever the unit is dismantled or reassembled and the settings must be maintained when wear calls for further adjustment.
2 To carry out these adjustments, remove the steering gear from the car (Section 11), then mount the steering gear in a soft jawed vice so that the pinion is in a horizontal position and the rack damper cover plate to the top.
3 Remove the rack damper cover plate by undoing the two retaining bolts, then take off the gasket and shims from under the plate. Also remove the two small springs and the recessed yoke which bears on the rack.
4 Move to the pinion bearing pre-load cover plate. On the Burman type of steering it is on the base of the pinion and on cam gears steering on the top of the pinion.
5 On cam gears steering only remove the dust seal from the pinion shaft by gently prising off its retainer and then pulling the seal off up the pinion shaft.
6 On both types of steering, now remove the cover plate by undoing the two retaining bolts, then lift off the gasket and shims.
7 To correctly set the pinion bearing pre-load, replace the cover plate without the gasket and shims and tighten down the bolts evenly until the cover plate is just touching the pinion bearing.

8 Using feeler gauges measure the gap between the cover plate and the steering gear casing. To be sure that the cover plate has been evenly tightened, take a reading adjacent to each bolt. These readings should be the same.
9 Assemble a shim pack to include a gasket which must be located next to the cover plate. In the case of Burman type units, the shim pack must measure between 0.002 and 0.004 inch (0.05 and 0.10 mm) less than the gap measured in the previous paragraph. With cam gear units, the shim pack should be between 0.001 and 0.003 inch (0.03 and 0.07 mm) less than the gap measured. Shims are available in the following thicknesses:

Cam gears	
Steel	0.020 inch (0.508 mm)
	0.015 inch (0.381 mm)
	0.010 inch (0.254 mm)
	0.005 inch (0.127 mm)
	0.002 inch (0.051 mm)
Paper	0.005 inch (0.127 mm)
Burman	
Steel	0.010 inch (0.254 mm)
	0.005 inch (0.127 mm)
	0.002 inch (0.051 mm)
Paper	0.005 inch (0.127 mm)

10 Fit the assembled shim pack and paper gasket next to the cover plate. Refit the cover plate with Loctite applied to the securing bolt threads. Tighten them to a torque of between 6 and 8 lb ft (0.9 to 1.1 kg m).
11 To set the rack damper adjustment, replace the yoke in its location on the rack and make sure it is fully home. Then measure the distance between the bottom of the recess in the yoke and the top of the steering gear casing. On cam gears steering, two recesses will be found in the yoke, the measurement must be taken from the deeper central recess.
12 Assemble a shim pack and gasket which, when added to the measurement obtained in the previous paragraph, will equal 0.33 inch (9.38 mm) in the case of Burman steering or 0.37 (9.4

mm) for cam gears steering. Shim thicknesses available in similar thicknesses and materials are as listed for pinion bearing adjustment.

13 Refit the springs into their recesses in the yoke and position the new shim pack so that the gasket is next to the cover plate. Replace the cover plate having first applied Loctite or similar sealing compound to the bolt threads. Then tighten down the bolts to a torque of 6 to 8 lb ft (0.9 to 1.1 kg m). On the cam gears assembly only, replace the pinion dust seal and its retainer.

13 Steering wheel and column - removal and refitting

1 Place the vehicle with the wheels in the straight ahead position, disconnect the battery by removing the negative earth lead, then disconnect the lower end of the steering shaft from the flexible coupling by removing the nut and bolt on the top clamp of the coupling.

2 Prise out the centre emblem on the steering wheel, knock back the locking tab on the centre nut, undo the nut, remove the locking plate and lift off the steering wheel.

3 Take off the upper half of the steering column shroud by removing the two small screws holding it to the lower half, then lift the indicator cancelling cam and its spring off the steering shaft, noting the position in which they were fitted in relation to the indicator switch.

4 Pull off the multi-pin connectors to the indicator switch and the ignition switch, then remove the indicator switch assembly from the top of the column by undoing the two retaining screws.

5 Fold back the carpet from around the area where the steering column passes through the floor, then undo the two bolts and washers which hold the steering column lower support bracket to the floor.

6 Remove the lower half of the steering column shroud by undoing the two screws holding it to the underside of the facia panel and lift it off the column.

7 Undo the two nuts and bolts holding the upper steering column bracket to the underside of the facia panel, then lift the complete steering column assembly into the car.

8 To replace the steering column in the car, pass it through the hole in the floor and mate up the splines on the shaft with the clamp on the flexible coupling and tighten the nut to a torque of 5 to 7 lb ft (0.7 to 1.0 kg m).

9 Secure the top bracket on the column to the underside of the facia panel with the nuts and bolts, but do not tighten them down at this stage.

10 Secure the column lower support bracket to the floor and tighten down the bolts. Now return to the upper bracket and tighten down the nuts and bolts. This order of procedure ensures correct alignment of the steering column.

11 The remainder of the replacement procedure is a direct reversal of the removal sequence. The centre steering wheel nut should be tightened down to a torque of 29 to 25 lb ft (2.8 to 3.4 kg m).

14 Steering column - servicing

1 Withdraw the steering shaft from the lower end of the steering column.

2 Pull the shaft lower support bearing in an upward direction from the shaft. Renew the retaining washer and circlip if they are at all suspect.

3 Remove the upper bearing from its location at the top of the steering column by drifting it out from below using a long rod.

4 Check that the splines at both ends of the steering shaft are in good order.

5 Reassembly is a reversal of dismantling.

15 Steering column lock - removal and refitting

1 Refer to Chapter 10, Section 52.

2 Disconnect the lead from the battery negative terminal.

3 Remove the two screws which secure the ignition switch to the rear of the lock assembly.

4 The steering column lock assembly is clamped to the steering column by two shear bolts and the only means of removing them is to drill them out.

5 When the lock is being refitted, tighten the shear bolts finger tight and check for smooth and positive engagement of the locking pawl with the cut-out in the steering shaft. Do this by operating the ignition key.

6 Tighten the bolts fully to shear their heads and refit the ignition switch and battery lead.

16 Front wheel alignment

1 Accurate front wheel alignment is essential to provide good steering and slow tyre wear. Before considering the steering angles, check that the tyres are correctly inflated, that the road wheels are not buckled, that the hub bearings are not worn or incorrectly adjusted and that the steering gear and linkage is in good order without slackness or wear at the joints.

2 Wheel alignment consists of four factors:

Camber — the angle at which the front wheels are set from the vertical when viewed from the front of the car. Positive camber is the angle that the wheels are tilted outward at the top of their vertical centre line.

Castor — the angle between the steering axis and a vertical line when viewed from each side of the vehicle. Positive castor is when the steering axis is inclined rearward at the top.

Steering axis inclination — the angle, when viewed from the front of the vehicle, between the vertical and an imaginary line drawn between the upper and lower suspension/steering pivots.

Toe-in — the amount by which the distance between the front inside edges of the road wheels (measured at hub height) is less than that measured between the rear inside edges of the wheels.

3 The only steering adjustment which can be made by the home mechanic is for toe-in (tracking) the rest of the geometry having been set in production. It is recommended that the toe-in of the front wheels should be checked and adjusted by a service station having modern wheel alignment gauges but where this is not possible, carry out the following procedure.

4 Place the vehicle on level ground with the wheels in the straight ahead position.

5 Obtain one of the proprietary tracking gauges or make one from a length of tubing, suitably cranked to clear the engine sump and bellhousing and having an adjustment nut and setscrew at one end.

6 With the gauge, measure the distance between the two inner wheel rims at hub height at the front of the road wheel.

7 Roll the vehicle forward or backward so that a chalk mark made on the tyre wall will move through 180° (½ a turn). Now (without altering the setting previously obtained on the gauge) place the gauge between the inner wheel rims at hub height at the rear of the road wheel. This measurement should be greater by up to ¼ inch (6.4 mm). This represents the required toe-in for the front wheels.

8 Where the toe-in is found to be incorrect, slacken both track rod end locknuts and the outer clips on the rubber steering rack gaiters and ensure that the gaiters are not sticking to the track rods.

9 Rotate both track rods equally until the correct toe-in is obtained. Do not rotate the track rods more than ¼ of a turn at a time before re-checking with the gauge.

10 Tighten the track rod end locknuts ensuring that the track rod end ball joints are held in the centre of their arc of travel during tightening. Tighten the gaiter clips

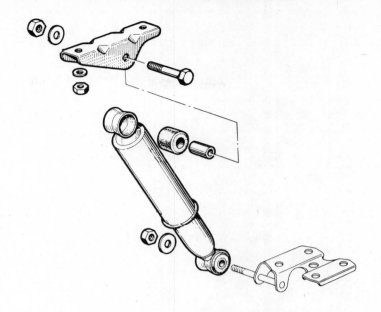

Fig. 11.18 Rear shock absorber mounting (early vehicles)

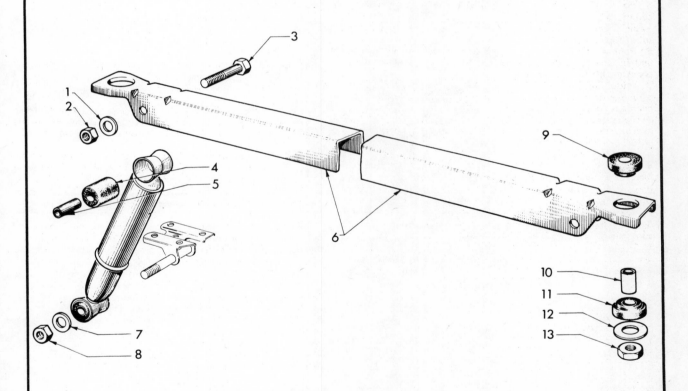

Fig. 11.19 Rear shock absorber mounting (later vehicles)

1 Washer
2 Locknut
3 Bolt
4 Bush

5 Sleeve
6 Crossmember
7 Washer

8 Locknut
9 Insulator
10 Spacer

11 Insulator
12 Special washer
13 Locknut

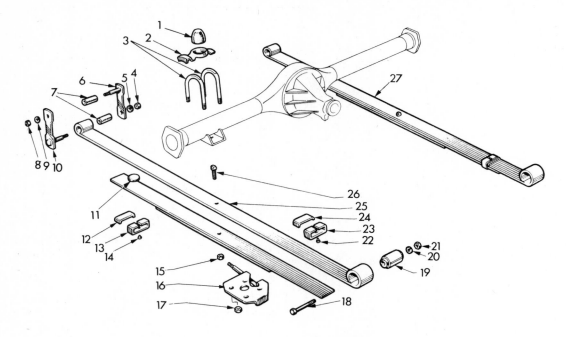

Fig. 11.20 Components of rear road leaf springs

1 Rubber bump stop	8 Nut	15 Nut	22 Rivet
2 Bump stop bracket	9 Locking washer	16 'U' bolt plate	23 Clamp
3 'U' bolts	10 Shackle bar and stud	17 Nut	24 Clamp insulator
4 Nut	11 Insert	18 Bolt	25 Spring leaf
5 Locking washer	12 Clamp insulator	19 Bush	26 Special bolt
6 Shackle bar and stud	13 Clamp	20 Locking washer	27 Spring assembly
7 Bushes	14 Rivet	21 Nut	

17 Rear shock absorbers - removal and refitting

1 Chock the front wheels and jack up the rear of the vehicle. The road wheels need not be removed but it will be more convenient to do so.

2 Remove the upper mounting eye bolt and then disconnect the lower mounting.

3 Refitting is a reversal of removal.

18 Rear shock absorbers - testing

1 Once removed, the shock absorber should be secured vertically in a vice, the jaws of which grip the lower mounting eye.

2 Fully extend and contract the shock absorber ten or twelve times and observe if there is strong resistance in both directions. If this is so, then the unit is operating satisfactorily and can be refitted. If there is no resistance or the unit jumps erratically during its movement, it must be renewed as it is not repairable.

3 Examine the shock absorber body for fluid leakage, also the rubber mounting bushes for wear or deterioration. If there is evidence of these, renew the unit.

19 Rear road springs - removal and installation

1 Chock the front wheels to prevent the car moving, then jack up the rear of the car and support it on suitable stands. To make the springs more accessible, remove the road wheels.

2 Then place a trolley jack underneath the differential housing to support the rear axle assembly when the springs are removed. Do not raise the jack under the differential housing so that the springs are flattened, but raise it just enough to take the full weight of the axle with the springs fully extended.

3 Undo the rear shackle nuts and remove the combined shackle bolt and plate assemblies. Then, if fitted, remove the small rubber bushes from the body aperture.

4 Undo the nut from the front mounting and take out the bolt running through the mounting.

5 Undo the nuts on the ends of the four U bolts and remove the U bolts together with the attachment plate and rubber spring insulators found on later models. Also remove the bump stops from the top of the U bolts.

6 Replacement is a direct reversal of the above procedure. The nuts on the U bolts, spring front mounting and rear shackles must be torqued down to the figures given in the Specifications at the beginning of this Chapter but only **after** the car has been lowered onto its wheels.

7 Saloons built after September 1973 incorporate a rear anti-roll bar and this must be disconnected before removing the rear road springs.

20 Fault finding chart

Symptom	Reason/s	Remedy
STEERING FEELS VAGUE, CAR WANDERS AND FLOATS AT SPEED		
General wear or damage	Tyre pressures uneven	Check pressures and adjust as necessary.
	Shock absorbers worn or require topping up	Top up shock absorbers, test, and replace if worn.
	Spring clips broken	Renew spring clips.
	Steering gear ball joints badly worn	Fit new ball joints.
	Suspension geometry incorrect	Check and rectify.
	Steering mechanism free play excessive	Adjust or overhaul steering mechanism.
	Front suspension and rear axle pick-up points out of alignment	Normally caused by poor repair work after a serious accident. Extensive rebuilding necessary.
STIFF AND HEAVY STEERING		
Lack of maintenance or accident damage	Tyre pressures too low	Check pressures and inflate tyres.
	Front wheel toe-in incorrect	Check and reset toe-in.
	Suspension geometry incorrect	Check and rectify.
	Steering gear incorrectly adjusted too tightly	Check and readjust steering gear.
	Steering column badly misaligned	Determine cause and rectify (Usually due to bad repair after severe accident damage and difficult to correct)
WHEEL WOBBLE AND VIBRATION		
General wear or damage	Wheel nuts loose	Check and tighten as necessary.
	Front wheels and tyres out of balance	Balance wheels and tyres and add weights as necessary.
	Steering ball joints badly worn	Replace steering gear ball joints.
	Hub bearings badly worn	Remove and fit new hub bearings.
	Steering gear free play excessive	Adjust and overhaul steering gear.
	Front springs loose, weak or broken	Inspect and overhaul as necessary.

Chapter 12 Bodywork and underframe

Contents

Specifications

Wheelbase (all models)	...	...	...	...	...	...	94.5 in. (231.5 cm)
Overall length	- Saloon	...	...	...	...	...	156.6 in. (397.8 cm)
	- Estate car	...	...	...	...	...	160.8 in. (408.4 cm)
	- Van	...	...	...	...	...	160.8 in. (408.4 cm)
Overall width (all models)	...	...	...	...	...	...	61.8 in. (157.0 cm)
Overall height	- Saloon	...	...	...	...	...	54.8 in. (139.2 cm)
	- Estate car	...	...	...	...	...	55.9 in. (123.0 cm)
	- Van	...	...	...	...	...	61.8 in. (157.0 cm)

1 General description

The combined body and underframe is of welded, all steel unit construction. Models are available in two and four door saloon, estate car and van versions. The GT Sport and 1300E variations have minor body modifications such as slightly flared wing arches. The interior treatment of the range of Escort models has varied over the years since its introduction and the De Luxe, XL and 1300E versions are the most luxurious and completely equipped.

Two door versions of the saloon and estate cars and vans have door hinges which are welded to the door frame and the body pillar, the four door saloons have bolted type hinges.

'Aeroflow' ventilation is installed as standard and opening quarterlight ventilator may be specified as an option.

Toughened safety glass is fitted all round although the safer type of laminated screen may be specified as an option.

All models are fitted with bucket seats at the front and bench seats at the rear.

2 Maintenance - bodywork and underframe

1 The condition of your car's bodywork is of considerable importance as it is on this that the secondhand value of the car will mainly depend. It is very much more difficult to repair neglected bodywork than to renew mechanical assemblies. The hidden portions of the body, such as the wheel arches and the underframe and the engine compartment, are equally important, though obviously not requiring such frequent attention as the immediately visible paintwork.

2 Every two or three years it is a worthwhile scheme to either pressure hose or steam clean the underbody and particularly the under wing surfaces. When all traces of dirt and mud have been removed, check carefully for rust, particularly on rigid hydraulic brake pipes. Where there is evidence of rusting, renew the brake pipes and treat other areas with an anti-rust product. The opportunity may then be taken to paint the underside with an undersealing compound or black bitumastic paint.

3 The wheel arches should be given particular attention as underscaling can easily come away here and stones and dirt thrown up from the road wheels can soon cause the paint to chip and flake, and so allow rust to set in.

4 At the same time the engine compartment should be cleaned in the same manner. If steam cleaning facilities are not available, then brush Gunk or a similar cleanser over the whole engine and engine compartment with a stiff paintbrush, working it well in where there is an accumulation of oil and dirt. Do not paint the ignition system but protect it with polythene sheeting when the Gunk is washed off. As the Gunk is washed away, it will take with it all traces of oil and dirt, leaving the engine looking clean and bright.

5 The bodywork should be washed once a week or when dirty. Thoroughly wet the car to soften the dirt and then wash the car down with a soft sponge and plenty of clean water. If the

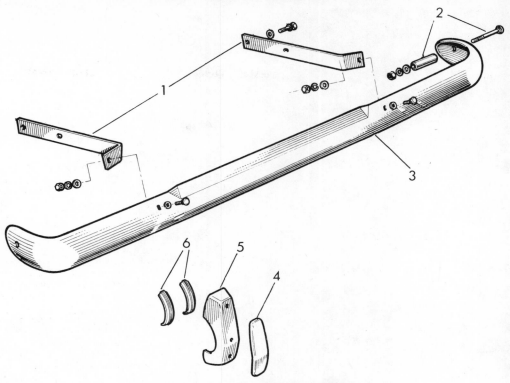

Fig. 12.1 Components of the front bumper

1 Support brackets	4 Rubber insert
2 End bolt and spacer	5 Over-rider
3 Bumper bar	6 Plastic insulator

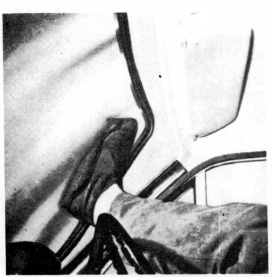

Fig. 12.2 Removing windscreen

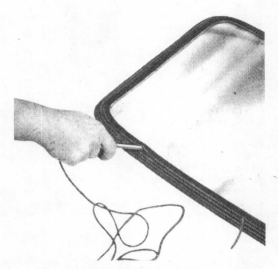

Fig. 12.3 Inserting windscreen fitting cord

dirt is not washed off very gently, in time it will wear the paint down as surely as wet and dry paper. It is best to use a hose if this is available. Give the car a final washdown and then dry with a soft chamois leather to prevent the formation of spots.
6 Spots of tar and grease thrown up from the road can be removed with a rag dampened with fuel.
7 Once every six months, or every three months if wished, give the bodywork and chromium trim a thoroughly good wax polish.

3 Maintenance - upholstery and carpets

1 Remove the carpets and thoroughly vacuum clean the interior of the car every three months or more frequently if necessary.
2 Beat out the carpets and vacuum clean them if they are very dirty. If the headlining or upholstery is soiled apply an upholstery cleaner with a damp sponge and wipe off with a clean dry cloth.

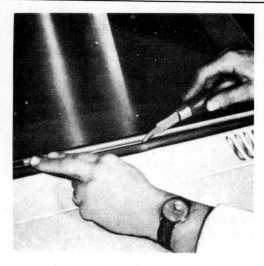

Fig. 12.4 Fitting trim to rubber surround of screen

Fig. 12.5 Door striker plate (early models)

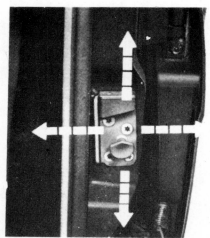

Fig. 12.6 Door striker plate (later models)

Fig. 12.7 Removing door trim panel

4 Minor body repairs

1   At some time during your ownership of your car, it is likely that it will be bumped or scraped in a mild way, causing some slight damage to the body.

2   Major damage must be repaired by your local Ford agent, but there is no reason why you cannot successfully beat out, repair and respray minor damage yourself. The essential items which the owner should gather together to ensure a really professional job are:

a) A plastic filler such as Holts Cataloy
b) Paint whose colour matches exactly that of the bodywork, either in a can for application by a spray gun, or in an aerosol can
c) Fine cutting paste
d) Medium and fine grade wet and dry paper

3   Never use a metal hammer to knock out small dents as the blows tend to scratch and distort the metal. Knock out the dent with a mallet or rawhide hammer and press on the underside of the dented surface a metal dolly or smooth wooden block roughly contoured to the normal shape of the damaged area.

4   After the worst of the damaged area has been knocked out, rub down the dent and surrounding area with medium wet and

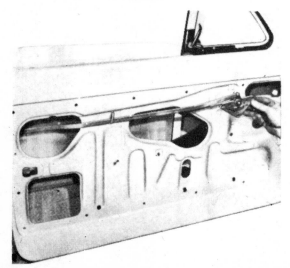

Fig. 12.8 Removing door lock remote control (early models)

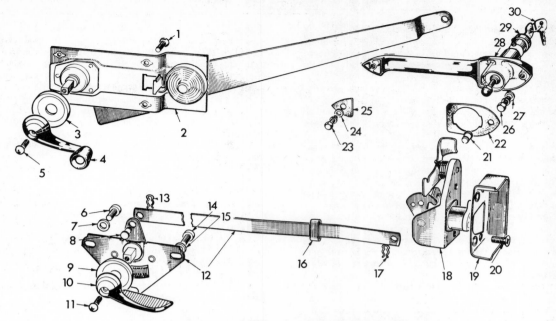

Fig. 12.9 Door lock and window winder mechanism (early models)

1 Screw	9 Escutcheon	17 Clip	25 Gasket
2 Window actuating mechanism	10 Handle	18 Door catch mechanism	26 Bolt
3 Escutcheon	11 Screw	19 Door catch exterior plate	27 Washer
4 Winder handle	12 Lock actuating mechanism	20 Screw	28 Exterior handle
5 Screw	13 Clip	21 Clevis pin	29 Lock barrel
6 Screw	14 Screw	22 Gasket	30 Keys
7 Washer	15 Washer	23 Bolt	
8 Clevis pin	16 Clip	24 Washer	

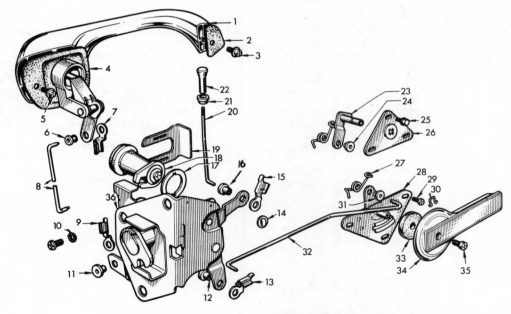

Fig. 12.10 Front door lock mechanism (later models)

1 Exterior handle	11 Bush	21 Escutcheon	30 Clip
2 Gasket	12 Bush	22 Interior lock button	31 Bush
3 Screw	13 Clip	23 Remote control lever	32 Connecting rod
4 Gasket	14 Clip	24 Bush	33 Pad
5 Screw	15 Clip	25 Bolt	34 Interior handle
6 Bush	16 Bush	26 Plate	35 Screw
7 Connecting rod retaining clip	17 Locking ring	27 Spring	36 Door catch assembly
8 Connecting rod	18 Lock assembly	28 Door catch actuating lever assembly	
9 Connecting rod clip	19 Lock barrel securing clip	29 Screw	
10 Shakeproof washer	20 Connecting rod		

dry paper and thoroughly clean away all traces of dirt.

5   The plastic filler comprises a paste and a hardener which must be thoroughly mixed together. Mix only a small portion at a time as the paste sets hard within five to fifteen minutes, depending on the amount of hardener used.

6   Smooth on the filler with a knife or stiff plastic to the shape of the damaged portion and allow to thoroughly dry - a process which takes about six hours. After the filler has dried it is likely that it will have contracted slightly so spread on a second layer of filler if necessary.

7   Smooth down the filler with fine wet and dry paper wrapped around a suitable block of wood and continue until the whole area is perfectly smooth and it is impossible to feel where the filler joins the rest of the paintwork.

8   Spray on from an aerosol can, or with a spray gun, an anti-rust undercoat, smooth down with wet and dry paper, and then spray on two coats of the final finishing using a circular motion.

9   When thoroughly dry, polish the whole area with a fine cutting paste to smooth the resprayed area into the remainder of the wing and to remove the small particles of spray paint which will have settled round the area.

10 This will leave the wing looking perfect with not a trace of the previous unsightly dent.

5 Major body repairs

1   Because the body is built on the unitary principle and is integral with the underframe, major damage must be repaired by competent mechanics with the necessary welding and hydraulic straightening equipment.

2   If the damage has been serious, it is vital that the body is checked for correct alignment, as otherwise the handling of the car will suffer and many other faults such as excessive wear in the tyres, transmission and steering may occur.

6 Maintenance - hinges and locks

Once every six months or 6000 miles (9600 km) the door, bonnet and boot hinges should be oiled with a few drops of engine oil from an oil can. The door striker plates can be given a thin smear of grease to reduce wear and ensure free movement.

7 Front bumper - removal and refitting

1   Undo the single retaining bolt from inside the front wings of the car on each side.

2   Undo the two chrome headed bolts from the centre of the bumper and remove the bumper.

3   Replacement is a reversal of the above procedure, but before replacing the two bolts from inside the wings, ensure that the bumper is straight and firm. To make sure that this is correct, it is not advisable to tighten the centre bolts fully down until the end bolts have been located.

8 Rear bumper - removal and refitting

1   Working inside the boot, take out the spare wheel and undo the bolt at each end of the bumper bar with their washers and spring washers.

2   Undo the chrome headed bolts and nuts in the centre of the bumper and take off the bumper with its spacer tubes.

3   To replace the bumper, position the spacer tubes over the end bolts and loosely replace the washers and nuts.

4   Replace the two chrome headed nuts and bolts in the centre of the bumper and after checking that the bumper is correctly positioned, tighten down all four bolts and nuts.

9 Windscreen glass - removal and installation

1   If you are unfortunate enough to have a windscreen shatter

or should you wish to renew your present windscreen, fitting a replacement is one of the few jobs which the average owner is advised to leave to a professional. For the owner who wishes to do the job himself the following instructions are given.

2   Cover the bonnet with a blanket or cloth to prevent accidental damage and remove the windscreen wiper blades and arms.

3   If the screen has shattered, cover the facia demister slots and then knock the crystals out of the rubber frame. Withdraw the rubber surround and clean the glass channel free from mastic or glass crystals. If it is cut or hardened, renew it.

4   If the screen is intact, put on a pair of soft shoes and sit in one of the front seats. With a piece of soft cloth between the soles of your shoes and the windscreen glass, place both feet in one top corner of the windscreen and push firmly.

5   When the rubber surround has freed itself from the body flange in that area, repeat the process at frequent intervals along the top edge of the windscreen until, from outside the car, the glass and rubber surround can be removed together.

6   Gently prise out the clip which covers the joint of the chromium finisher strip and pull the finisher strip out of the rubber surround. Then remove the rubber surround from the glass.

7   To fit a new windscreen, start by fitting the rubber surround around the new windscreen glass.

8   Apply a suitable sealer such as Expandite SR-51-B to the rubber to body groove. In this groove fit a fine but strong piece of cord right the way round allowing an overlap of about 6 inches (152.4 mm) at the joint.

9   From outside the car, place the windscreen in its correct position, making sure the loose end of the cord is inside the car.

10 With an assistant pressing firmly on the outside of the windscreen get into the car and pull out the cord thus drawing the lip of the rubber surround over the body flange.

11 Apply a further layer of sealer to the underside of the rubber glass groove from outside the car.

12 Replace the chromium finisher strip into its groove in the rubber surround and replace the clip which covers its joint.

13 Carefully clean off any surplus sealer from the windscreen glass before it has a chance to harden and then replace the windscreen wiper arms and blades.

10 Door rattles - tracing and rectification

1   The most common cause of door rattle is a misaligned, loose or worn striker plate, but other causes may be:

a) Loose door handles or window winder handles
b) Loose, or misaligned door lock components
c) Loose or worn remote control mechanism

2   It is quite possible for door rattles to be the result of a combination of the above faults so a careful examination must be made to determine the cause of the fault.

3   If the nose of the striker plate is worn and as a result the door rattles, renew and then adjust the plate as described in Section 11.

4   Should the inner door handle rattle, this is easily cured by fitting a rubber washer between the escutcheon and the handle.

5   If the door lock is found to be worn and rattles as a consequence, then fit a new lock (Section 11).

11 Door striker plate - removal, refitting and adjustment

1   Mark the position of the striker plate on the door pillar using a soft pencil.

2   On early models, unscrew and remove the three crosshead securing screws and lift the striker plate away.

3   On later models fitted with anti-burst door locks, a special type of screwdriver bit is required to loosen the securing screws and this is obtainable from your Ford main dealer.

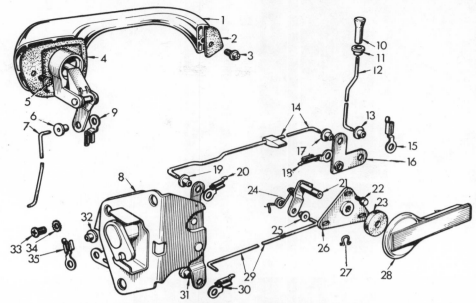

Fig. 12.11 Rear door lock components (later models)

1	Exterior handle	10	Interior lock button	19	Bush	28	Interior handle
2	Gasket	11	Escutcheon	20	Clip	29	Connecting rod
3	Screw	12	Connecting rod	21	Remote control lever	30	Clip
4	Gasket	13	Bush	22	Bolt	31	Bush
5	Screw	14	Connecting rod	23	Pad	32	Bush
6	Bush	15	Clip	24	Spring	33	Screw
7	Connecting rod	16	Lock actuating lever	25	Bush	34	Shakeproof washer
8	Door catch assembly	17	Bush	26	Plate	35	Clip
9	Clip	18	Clip	27	Clip		

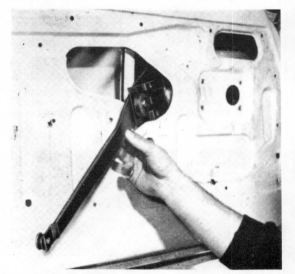

Fig. 12.12 Removing window regulator (two door early models)

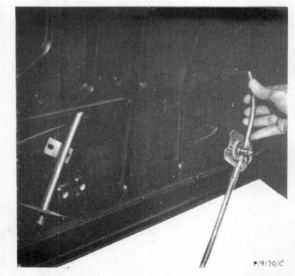

Fig. 12.13 Removing cable type window regulator (four door model)

4 To adjust the striker plate, slightly loosen the screws and move the plate so that the dovetail on the door frame engages correctly with the striker plate and when the door is fully closed, the outer surface of the door panel is flush with the external body surface.

5 When adjustment is correct, fully tighten the securing screws.

12 Door locks - removal and refitting

1 Wind up the window and remove the door remote control

handle and the window regulator handle by undoing their centre screws and lifting off the washers, handles and escutcheon plates in that order. On four door models, the window regulator handle is retained by a clip which is accessible after inserting a screwdriver between the handle boss and the escutcheon plate.

2 Remove the combined arm rest and door pull by undoing its two retaining screws.

3 Insert a thin strip of metal with all the sharp edges removed between the recessed trim panel and the door. This will release one or two of the trim panel clips without damaging the trim and the panel can then be gently eased off by hand. A short

This sequence of photographs deals with the repair of the dent and scratch (above rear lamp) shown in this photo. The procedure will be similar for the repair of a hole. It should be noted that the procedures given here are simplified - more explicit instructions will be found in the text

In the case of a dent the first job - after removing surrounding trim - is to hammer out the dent where access is possible. This will minimise filling. Here, the large dent having been hammered out, the damaged area is being made slightly concave

Now all paint must be removed from the damaged area, by rubbing with coarse abrasive paper. Alternatively, a wire brush or abrasive pad can be used in a power drill. Where the repair area meets good paintwork, the edge pf the paintwork should be 'feathered', using a finer grade of abrasive paper

In the case of a hole caused by rusting, all damaged sheet-metal should be cut away before proceeding to this stage. Here, the damaged area is being treated with rust remover and inhibitor before being filled

Mix the body filler according to its manufacturer's instructions. In the case of corrosion damage, it will be necessary to block off any large holes before filling - this can be done with zinc gauze or aluminium tape. Make sure the area is absolutely clean before ...

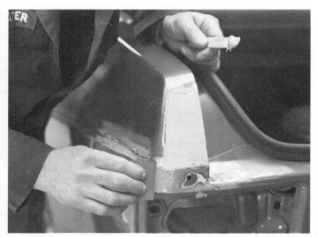

... applying the filler. Filler should be applied with a flexible applicator, as shown, for best results: the wooden spatula being used for confined areas. Apply thin layers of filler at 20-minute intervals, until the surface of the filler is slightly proud of the surrounding bodywork

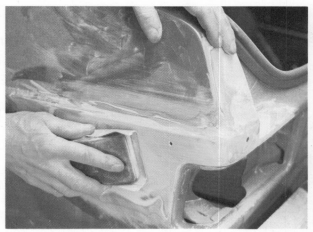

Initial shaping can be done with a Surform plane or Dreadnought file. Then, using progressively finer grades of wet-and-dry paper, wrapped around a sanding block, and copious amounts of clean water, rub-down the filler until really smooth and flat. Again, feather the edges of adjoining paintwork

The whole repair area can now be sprayed or brush-painted with primer. If spraying, ensure adjoining areas are protected from over-spray. Note that at least one-inch of the surrounding sound paintwork should be coated with primer. Primer has a 'thick' consistency, so will fill small imperfections

Again, using plenty of water, rub down the primer with a fine grade of wet-and-dry paper (400 grade is probably best) until it is really smooth and well blended into the surrounding paint-work. Any remaining imperfections can now be filled by carefully applied knifing stopper paste

When the stopper has hardened, rub-down the repair area again before applying the final coat of primer. Before rubbing-down this last coat of primer, ensure the repair area is blemish-free - use more stopper if necessary. To ensure that the surface of the primer is really smooth use some finishing compound

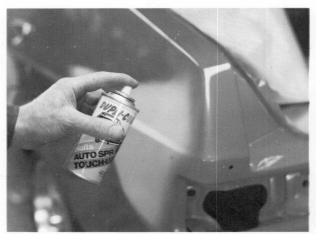

The top coat can now be applied. When working out of doors, pick a dry, warm and wind-free day. Ensure surrounding areas are protected from over-spray. Agitate the aerosol thoroughly, then spray the centre of the repair area, working outwards with a circular motion. Apply the paint as several thin coats.

After a period of about two-weeks, which the paint needs to harden fully, the surface of the repaired area can be 'cut' with a mild cutting compound prior to wax polishing. When carrying out bodywork repairs, remember that the quality of the finished job is proportional to the time and effort expended

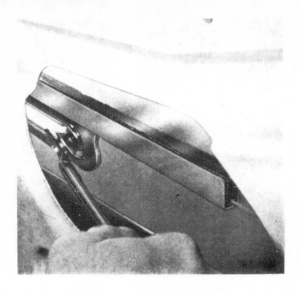

Fig. 12.14 Disconnecting window regulator arm from glass carrier

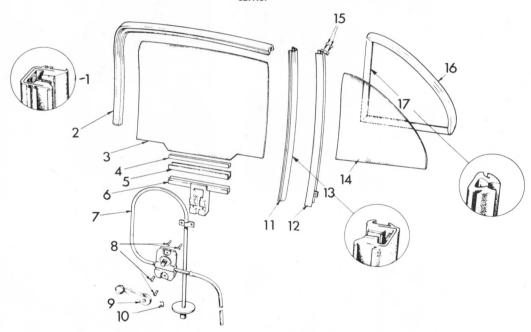

Fig. 12.15 Rear door windows and operating cable mechanism (four door models)

1 Weather strip section	6 Glass carrier	10 Clip	14 Glass
2 Weather sealing strip	7 Cable tube	11 Guide strip	15 Screws
3 Glass	8 Screws	12 Glass guide	16 Sealing strip
4 Grip	9 Winder handle	13 Guide strip section	17 Sealing strip section
5 Insulator			

metal ruler is ideal for this job. Then remove the waterproof sheet which is found inside the trim panel.

4   Take off the spring clip which secures the door remote control operating arm to the lock mechanism and disconnect the operating arm.

5   To remove the outside door handle, remove from inside the door panel the screw and washer holding the rear of the handle to the door, then through the door access hole, undo and remove the screw and washer securing the front of the handle. Withdraw the handle and sealing gaskets. On later vehicles,

remove the spring clip which retains the separately mounted door cylinder lock.

6   From the rear end of the door remove the single screw and washer which secure the bottom of the door window glass rear lower run in position. Pull the run downward to free the metal backing channel from the window frame.

7   Undo the three screws which hold the lock to the door and having moved the rear lower run to one side, withdraw the lock assembly through the door access hole.

8   Reassembly is a direct reversal of this procedure.

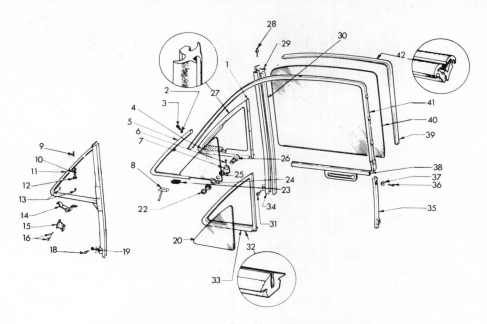

Fig. 12.16. Front door windows (early two door models)

1	Quarter light sealing rubber	11	Quarter light frame	23	Rubber insulator	33	Fixed quarterlight sealing strip
2	Washer	12	Hinge pin	24	Washer	34	Window guide
3	Screw	13	Rivets	25	Washer	35	Guide
4	Quarter light glass	14	Swivel bracket	26	Catch swivel pin	36	Screw
5	Glass frame	15	Bracket	27	Section of sealing rubber	37	Washer
6	Screw	16	Rivets	28	'Pop' rivet	38	Glass carrier
7	Catch bracket	18	Screw	29	Screw	39	Weather sealing strip
8	Swivel	19	Washer	30	Window guide strip	40	Glass
9	Pin	20	Fixed quarterlight glass	31	Screw	41	Window frame
10	Washer	22	Split washer	32	Rubber sealing strip section	42	Sealing strip section

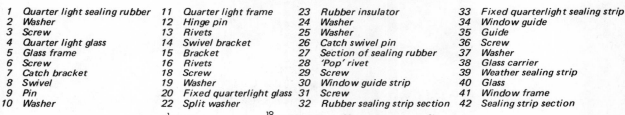

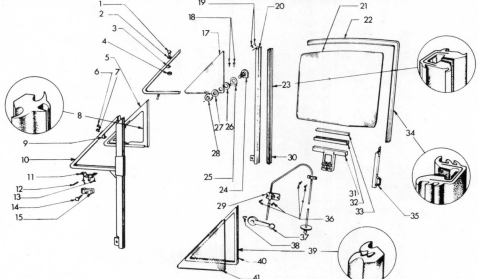

Fig. 12.17. Front door windows (four door models)

1	Hinge pin	12	Pin	23	Glass guide strip section	33	Grip
2	Washer	13	Screws	24	Catch swivel pin	34	Weather strip section
3	Glass frame	14	Screw	25	Plate	35	Guide
4	Pin retainer	15	Clip	26	Washer	36	Screws
5	Quarterlight sealing strip	17	Quarterlight glass	27	Washer	37	Window handle
6 & 7	Rivets	18	Rivets	28	Pin retainer	38	Clip
8	Sealing strip section	19	Rivets	29	Clip	39	Sealing strip section
9	Hinge	20	Window guide	30	Glass guide strip	40	Fixed quarterlight sealing strip
10	Quarterlight frame	21	Glass	31	Glass carrier	41	Quarterlight glass
11	Swivel bracket	22	Weather sealing strip	32	Insulator		

Fig. 12.18. Removing window glass (two door model)

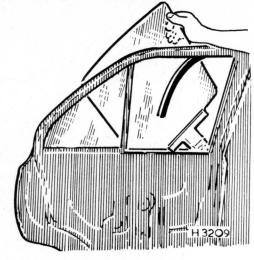

Fig. 12.19. Removing window glass (four door model)

Fig. 12.20. Drilling out ventilator 'pop' rivet

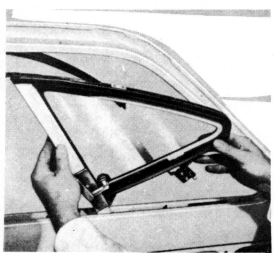

Fig. 12.21. Removing opening type ventilator

Fig. 12.22. Removing rear side window (two door model)

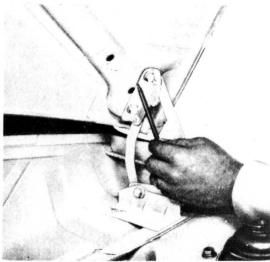

Fig. 12.23. Marking bonnet hinges before removal

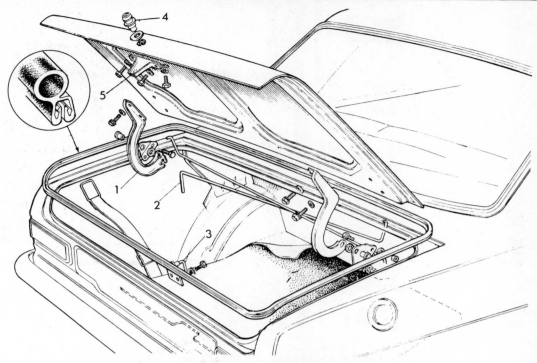

Fig. 12.24. Luggage boot lid components

| 1 Hinge | 2 Torsion bar to counterbalance lid | 3 Striker plate 4 Lock barrel | 5 Lock mechanism |

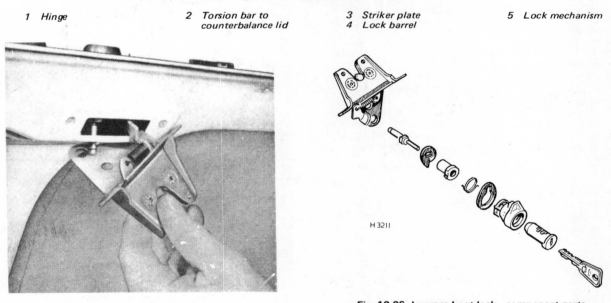

Fig. 12.25. Removing luggage boot lock

H 3211

Fig. 12.26. Luggage boot lock - component parts

13 Door glass and winder mechanism - removal and refitting

1 Wind the window down and remove the door remote control handle, the window regulator handle, the arm rest/door pull and trim panel (Section 12).

2 Undo the screws and washers which secure the window regulator assembly to the door panel.

3 On two door models, pull the regulator towards the rear of the door and disconnect the operating arm and its grooved wheel from the window glass carrier. On four door models, remove the two screws holding the regulator mechanism to the glass carrier.

4 Push the window up by hand and support it to prevent it falling back, then remove the regulator assembly through the door access hole.

5 Rotate the window glass through 90º and then withdraw it upwards out of the top of the door panel. Replacement is a reversal of this procedure.

14 Ventilation or fixed quarterlights - removal and refitting

1 Commence removal of these components from the front door by first removing the inner and outer weather sealing strips and their clips.

2 Drill out the top two pop rivets which secure the top of the main window sliding channel to the door frame.

Fig. 12.27. Estate car tailgate lock and handle

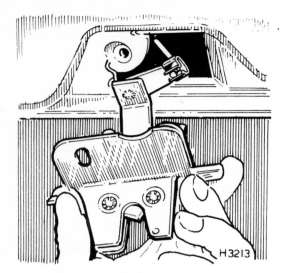

Fig. 12.28. Withdrawing lock from estate tailgate

3   Remove the door interior trim panel as previously described and then remove the screw and washer securing the bottom of the sliding channel.

4   With an opening type ventilator, remove the three screws which secure the forward sloping edge of its frame to the door frame.

5   Pull the sliding channel down and then incline it toward the rear of the vehicle. The ventilator or fixed quarterlight may now be lifted from the door frame.

6   Removal of quarterlights from the rear doors of four door models is similar except that the top of the dividing sliding channel is secured by screws.

7   Removal of the rear quarter window from two door bodies is simply a matter of prising the lip of the rubber surround and pushing the glass from the inside of the vehicle.

8   Refitting is a reversal of removal. If the opening type ventilator is too loose on its swivel, this may be rectified by adjusting the clamp plate bolts. The use of a pop riveter will be required when refitting the upper end of the sliding channel to front door frames.

15   Bonnet - removal and refitting

1   Open the bonnet lid and prop it open with the strut provided.

2   With a pencil, draw a line round the hinge plates on the bonnet lid to ensure correct alignment when refitting.

3   Remove the bolts and washers on each side and carefully lift the bonnet from the car.

4   When replacing the bonnet, loosely retain it with the bolts and then carefully line up the hinge plates with the pencil lines before finally tightening down the bolts.

5   Check the closure of the bonnet catch and adjust the length of the conical striker bolt if necessary to provide positive closure without rattling.

16   Luggage boot lid and lock - removal and refitting

1   Open the boot lid and mark the position of the hinge plates using a sharp pencil.

2   Release the cranked end of the torsion bar (used to counterbalance the lid) from its retaining bracket. Disconnect the double cranked end from the hinge and withdraw the torsion bar.

3   Remove the hinge securing bolts and their washers and lift the lid away.

4   The boot lock can be removed without removing the luggage boot lid.

5   To remove the lock assembly from 2 door models, remove the spring clip from the end of the lock spindle and remove the three bolts which secure the lock to the boot lid.

6   On four door models, the method of removal is similar but a spring clip is not used on the lock spindle.

7   To remove the lock barrel from two door models, insert a pair of long nosed pliers through the aperture left after withdrawal of the lock mechanism, and compress the legs of the lock barrel retaining clip.

8   To remove the lock barrel from four door models, insert a screwdriver between the lock housing and the rubber sealing gasket. Lever up the housing to expose the retaining clip. Compress the legs of the clip and withdraw the lock barrel.

9   Refitting of all components is a reversal of removal but if necessary adjust the lock striker by slightly loosening its retaining bolts to provide positive closure of the boot lid without any rattling.

17   Estate car tailgate lock - removal and refitting

1   Remove the tailgate trim panel in a similar manner to that described for doors (Section 12).

2   Disconnect the operating rod from the tailgate handle.

3   Unscrew and remove the three screws which retain the lock assembly to the tailgate and withdraw the lock complete with its operating rod through the small aperture in the tailgate panel.

4   Refitting is a reversal of removal.

18   Estate car tailgate - removal and refitting

1   Open the tailgate door to its full extent. Remove the trim panel from the hinge assemblies.

2   Mark the position of the hinge plates on the tailgate and then unscrew and remove the two bolts from each hinge plate and lift the tailgate away.

3   Refitting is a reversal of removal.

19   Estate car tailgate hinge and torsion bar assembly - removal and installation

1   Remove the tailgate (Section 18).

2   Unscrew and remove the four bolts which retain each of the hinge/torsion bar assemblies to the body. **On no account remove the nut from the torsion bar locking plate bolt.**

Fig. 12.29. Estate tailgate handle

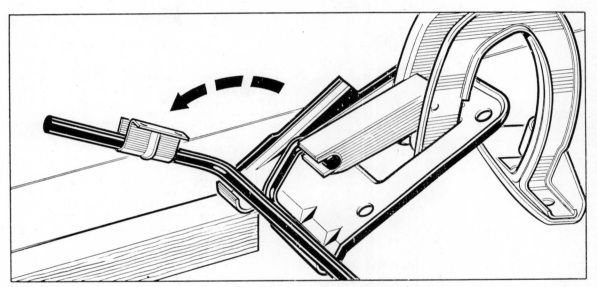

Fig. 12.30. Releasing estate tailgate torsion bar

Fig. 12. 31. Withdrawing van rear door lock

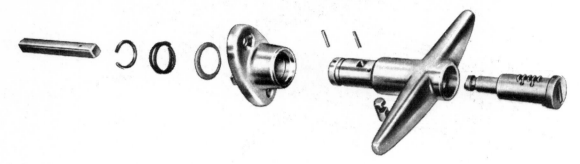

Fig. 12.32. Rear door lock components - van

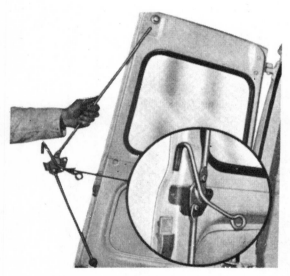

Fig. 12.33. Removing van rear door lock bar

Fig. 12.34. Withdrawing heater control bezel from fascia panel

3   If further dismantling is essential, lay the assembly upside down (to its normal location in the vehicle) on a block of wood positioned under the locking plate of one hinge.

4   Obtain the help of an assistant to stand on the hinge baseplate and unscrew the torsion bar locking plate bolt of this particular hinge. Gradually release the tension of the torsion bar by allowing the hinge and baseplate to rise against the combined weights of yourself and your assistant.

5   Remove the other torsion bar locking plate, the two locating spacers and then withdraw the torsion bars from the hinges.

6   To reassemble the hinge/torsion bar assemblies, position the baseplate on the floor with the hinge arms uppermost at approximately the correct distance apart.

7   Locate the torsion bar which has a single right angled bend at one end in the baseplate and secure it with a locking plate and bolt.

8   Fit the other end of the torsion bar in the opposite baseplate and position a spacer between the short section of the torsion bar (which is parallel to the main bar) and the hinge arm pin.

9   Locate the end of the torsion bar which has a double right angled bend in the baseplate to which the torsion bar with the single right angled bend was first connected.

10 Position the second spacer between the hinge arm pin and the end of the torsion bar. The remaining unattached end of the

second torsion bar should now be at an angle of about 120° to the baseplate to which it is to be attached. Should it be only about 15° however, the torsion bars will have to be dismantled and reversed.

11 Turn the hinge and torsion bar assembly over and support the unattached end of the torsion bar on a block of wood.

12 Locate the remaining locking plate under the unattached end of the torsion bar.

13 Turn the baseplate over and then with the combined weights of two people standing on it, bolt the locking plate into position. It is imperative that the foregoing instructions are rigidly adhered to otherwise personal injury can be caused by the sudden release of the torsion bar tension.

20 Van rear door lock and lock bar - removal and refitting

1   Remove the trim panel from the right hand door.

2   Unscrew and remove the three lock securing screws and withdraw the lock through the door aperture (Fig 12.31).

3   The exterior handle is withdrawn after removal of the two escutcheon plate securing screws (Fig 12.32).

4   To remove the locking bar from the opposing door, unscrew and remove the screws from the pivot plate and pull the lock bar

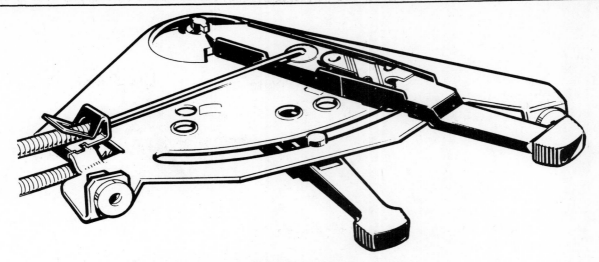

Fig. 12.35. Heater control lever mounting plate

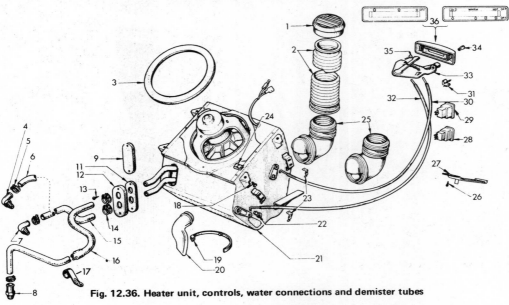

Fig. 12.36. Heater unit, controls, water connections and demister tubes

1	Grille	11	Gasket	20	Drain tube (air intake)
2	Hose	12	Plate	21	Heater body
3	Gasket	13	Screw	22	Nipple (cable)
4	Elbow union	14	Clip	23	Cable clip
5	Clip	15	Hose	24	Screw clip
6	Hose	16	Hose	25	Elbows
7	Elbow union	17	Clip	26	Screw
8	Union	18	Screw	27	Resistor assembly
9	Blanking gasket	19	Hose clip	28	Switch

29	Switch
30	Control cable
31	Cable clip
32	Control cable
33	Actuating lever assembly
34	Bezel clip
35	Screw
36	Control bezels

outward to free the ends of the bars from their guides (Fig 12.33).

5   Refitting is a reversal of removal.

21 Heater unit - removal and refitting

1   Disconnect the battery by removing the negative earth lead and drain the radiator.

2   Remove the three trim clips securing the front parcel shelf to its support bracket on the cowl side trim panel, then undo the two bolts holding the shelf to the heater and lift the shelf away.

3   Open the bonnet and disconnect the choke cable from the carburettor. This cable must be released in order to remove the heater control panel bezel.

4   Take off the spring clips holding the top edge of the heater control panel bezel to the dashboard. If a cigar lighter is fitted, it will be necessary to disconnect the wiring at this stage.

5   Undo the three screws securing the bottom of the panel and lift the panel away to one side, taking care not to damage the choke outer cable.

6   Carefully disconnect the inner heater control cables from their slots on the two arms on the heater, then remove the clips on the heater body holding the outer cables in place. Tuck the cables out of harms way.

7   Pull the two ventilator louvres out of the top of the crash pad, then by pulling down on the flexible pipes leading to the louvres, disconnect them from the crash pad.

8   Pull the lower ends of these pipes off the heater mechanism and remove the pipes.

216

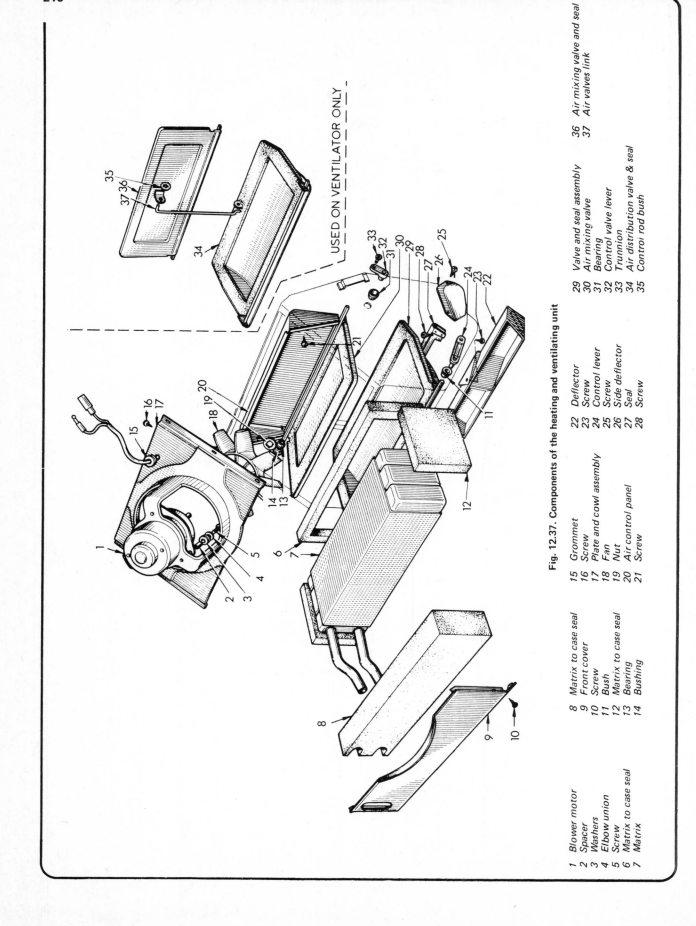

USED ON VENTILATOR ONLY

Fig. 12.37. Components of the heating and ventilating unit

1 Blower motor
2 Spacer
3 Washers
4 Elbow union
5 Screw
6 Matrix to case seal
7 Matrix

8 Matrix to case seal
9 Front cover
10 Screw
11 Bush
12 Matrix to case seal
13 Bearing
14 Bushing

15 Grommet
16 Screw
17 Plate and cowl assembly
18 Fan
19 Nut
20 Air control panel
21 Screw

22 Deflector
23 Screw
24 Control lever
25 Screw
26 Side deflector
27 Seal
28 Screw

29 Valve and seal assembly
30 Air mixing valve
31 Bearing
32 Control valve lever
33 Trunnion
34 Air distribution valve & seal
35 Control rod bush

36 Air mixing valve and seal
37 Air valves link

217

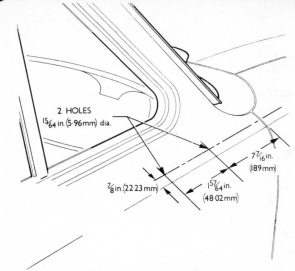

Fig. 12.38. Door mirror fitting diagram

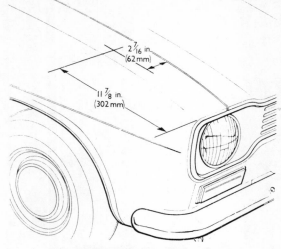

Fig. 12.39. Wing mirror fitting diagram

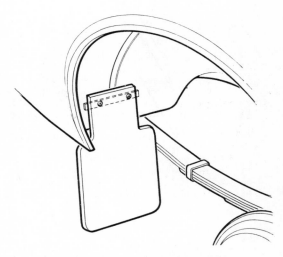

Fig. 12.40. Location of rear mud flaps

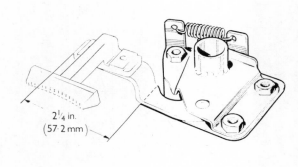

Fig. 12.41. Diagram for shortening bonnet lock hand lever

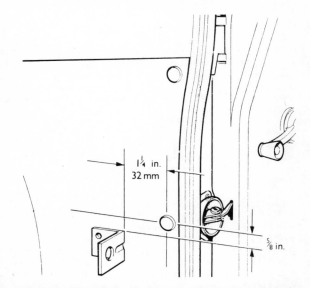

Fig. 12.42. Fitting diagram for remote control bonnet lock release

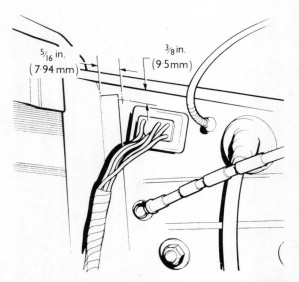

Fig. 12.43. Hole drilling diagram (rear engine bulkhead) for remote control bonnet lock

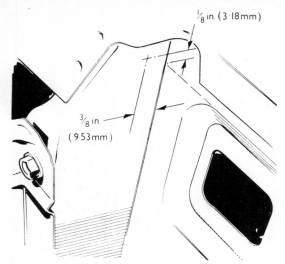

1/8 in. (3·18mm)

3/8 in. (9·53mm)

Fig. 12.44. Hole drilling diagram (radiator support panel) for remote control bonnet lock

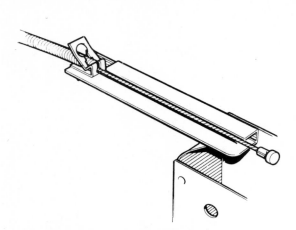

Fig. 12.46. Method of securing bonnet lock release cable to lock operating arm

5   Refitting is a reversal of removal.

23 Heater matrix - removal, servicing and refitting

1   Withdraw the heater assembly (Section 21).
2   Unscrew and remove the screw which holds the matrix cover panel in position, remove the panel and then lift off the matrix insulating pad and finally withdraw the matrix from the heater.
3   Flush the unit through with cold water. If it is clogged, try reverse flushing it with a hose. If this does not clear it, exchange it for a reconditioned unit. Do not be tempted to use chemical cleansers as they will only loosen deposits which will in turn cause further clogging of the fine cooling tubes. If the matrix leaks, do not attempt to solder it as this work seldom proves satisfactory.

24 Accessories - guide to fitting

The following information is applicable to Ford approved accessories but with slight modification it will normally apply to products of other manufacturers.

Exterior mirrors

Door or wing mounted mirrors may be installed in accordance with Figs 12.38 and 12.39. When drilling the door or wing, stick a piece of masking tape on the spot where the hole is to be made; this will stop the drill slipping. Make a pilot hole first and then open it out with a hole cutter or file. Always paint the bare metal edge of the hole to prevent rusting before installing the mirror.

Mudflaps

These may be fitted at the rear of the front or rear wheel arches. A typical rear wheel installation is shown in Fig 12.40.

Bonnet lock

1   Disconnect the battery and remove the four radiator mounting bolts. Pull the radiator to the rear.
2   Unscrew and remove the bonnet catch retaining bolts and withdraw the lock from below the radiator mounting panel.
3   With a hacksaw cut off the operating arm from the lock assembly (Fig 12.41).
4   Fit the lock release handle bracket (Fig 12.42).
5   Drill a 3/8 inch (9.5 mm) hole in the engine rear bulkhead (Fig 12.43) and another of similar diameter in the side of the radiator support panel (Fig 12.44).

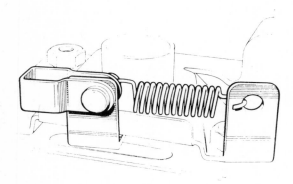

Fig. 12.45. Bonnet lock release cable location at lock cover plate

9   Disconnect the leads to the heater, at their snap connectors, then remove the single screw holding the windscreen wiper motor to the scuttle panel.
10   Working under the bonnet, slacken off the two cable clips on the heater water pipes and then pull the pipes off the bulkhead. Remove the heater pipe sealing plate and gasket from the bulkhead by undoing the two retaining screws.
11   Undo the four bolts holding the heater mechanism to the bulkhead and remove the heater from the car.
12   Replacement of the complete mechanism is a direct reversal of the above procedure.
13   Remember to refill the cooling system with the heater control lever set to full on.

22 Heater motor - removal and refitting

1   Remove the heater assembly from the car (Section 21).
2   Undo the thirteen small screws securing the blower motor to the heater and remove the blower motor and mounting plate as an assembly from the heater.
3   Undo the three screws holding the blower motor to the mounting plate and remove the motor.
4   Remove the three rubber insulators from the blower motor flange, then remove the single spring clip and pull the fan off the motor spindle.

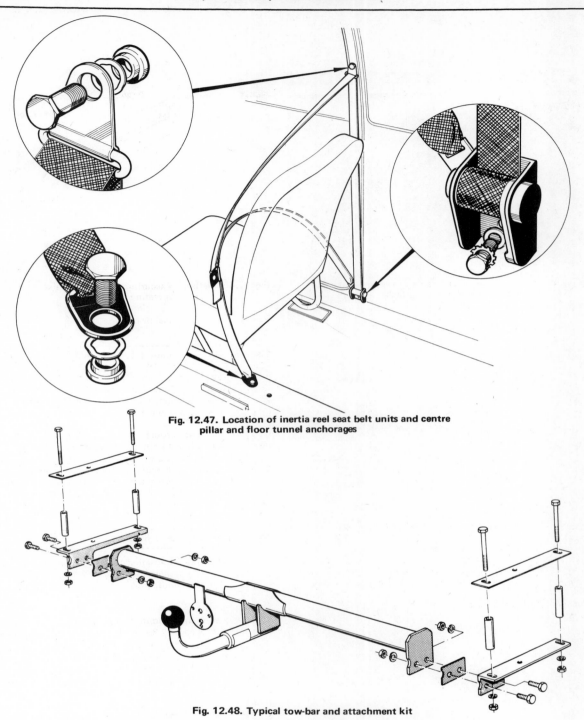

Fig. 12.47. Location of inertia reel seat belt units and centre pillar and floor tunnel anchorages

Fig. 12.48. Typical tow-bar and attachment kit

6   Feed the control cable between the release handle and the lock assembly using the grommets and support plates supplied. Attach the inner cable to the clevis and then connect the lock tension spring to the hole in the clevis pin (Fig 12.46).
7   Fit the radiator grille blanking plate and then refit the radiator.
8   Check the operation of lock; adjusting the centre striker bolt length if necessary to obtain smooth yet positive operation.

Inertia reel seat belts
    These may be fitted in place of the normal static type belts to provide greater freedom of movement for driver or passenger.

Installation is simply a matter of removing the original seat belts from their anchorages and installing the inertia reel type. Note carefully the sequence of fitting the attachment components (Fig 12.47). **The top of the inertia reel must be perfectly horizontal to ensure correct operation of the internal locking mechanism under impact or heavy braking.**

Towing bracket
    Many types of proprietary towing brackets are available with full fitting kits and instructions. A typical product for bolting to the bodyframe side members is shown in Fig 12.48.

Metric conversion tables

Inches	Decimals	Millimetres
1/64	0.015625	0.3969
1/32	0.03125	0.7937
3/64	0.046875	1.1906
1/16	0.0625	1.5875
5/64	0.078125	1.9844
3/32	0.09375	2.3812
7/64	0.109375	2.7781
1/8	0.125	3.1750
9/64	0.140625	3.5719
5/32	0.15625	3.9687
11/64	0.171875	4.3656
3/16	0.1875	4.7625
13/64	0.203125	5.1594
7/32	0.21875	5.5562
15/64	0.234375	5.9531
1/4	0.25	6.3500
17/64	0.265625	6.7469
9/32	0.28125	7.1437
19/64	0.296875	7.5406
5, 16	0.3125	7.9375
21/64	0.328125	8.3344
11/32	0.34375	8.7312
23/64	0.359375	9.1281
3/8	0.375	9.5250
25/64	0.390625	9.9219
13/32	0.40625	10.3187
27/64	0.421875	10.7156
7/16	0.4375	11.1125
29/64	0.453125	11.5094
15/32	0.46875	11.9062
31/64	0.484375	12.3031
1/2	0.5	12.7000
33/64	0.515625	13.0969
17/32	0.53125	13.4937
35/64	0.546875	13.8906
9/16	0.5625	14.2875
37/64	0.578125	14.6844
19/32	0.59375	15.0812
39/64	0.609375	15.4781
5/8	0.625	15.8750
41/64	0.640625	16.2719
21/32	0.65625	16.6687
43/64	0.671875	17.0656
11/16	0.6875	17.4625
45/64	0.703125	17.8594
23/32	0.71875	18.2562
47/64	0.734375	18.6531
3/4	0.75	19.0500
49/64	0.765625	19.4469
25/32	0.78125	19.8437
51/64	0.796875	20.2406
13/16	0.8125	20.6375
53/64	0.828125	21.0344
27/32	0.84375	21.4312
55/64	0.859375	21.8281
7/8	0.875	22.2250
57/64	0.890625	22.6219
29/32	0.90625	23.0187
59/64	0.921875	23.4156
15/16	0.9375	23.8125
61/64	0.953125	24.2094
31/32	0.96875	24.6062
63/64	0.984375	25.0031

Millimetres to Inches

mm	Inches
0.01	0.00039
0.02	0.00079
0.03	0.00118
0.04	0.00157
0.05	0.00197
0.06	0.00236
0.07	0.00276
0.08	0.00315
0.09	0.00354
0.1	0.00394
0.2	0.00787
0.3	0.01181
0.4	0.01575
0.5	0.01969
0.6	0.02362
0.7	0.02756
0.8	0.03150
0.9	0.03543
1	0.03937
2	0.07874
3	0.11811
4	0.15748
5	0.19685
6	0.23622
7	0.27559
8	0.31496
9	0.35433
10	0.39370
11	0.43307
12	0.47244
13	0.51181
14	0.55118
15	0.59055
16	0.62992
17	0.66929
18	0.70866
19	0.74803
20	0.78740
21	0.82677
22	0.86614
23	0.90551
24	0.94488
25	0.98425
26	1.02362
27	1.06299
28	1.10236
29	1.14173
30	1.18110
31	1.22047
32	1.25984
33	1.29921
34	1.33858
35	1.37795
36	1.41732
37	1.4567
38	1.4961
39	1.5354
40	1.5748
41	1.6142
42	1.6535
43	1.6929
44	1.7323
45	1.7717

Inches to Millimetres

Inches	mm
0.001	0.0254
0.002	0.0508
0.003	0.0762
0.004	0.1016
0.005	0.1270
0.006	0.1524
0.007	0.1778
0.008	0.2032
0.009	0.2286
0.01	0.254
0.02	0.508
0.03	0.762
0.04	1.016
0.05	1.270
0.06	1.524
0.07	1.778
0.08	2.032
0.09	2.286
0.1	2.54
0.2	5.08
0.3	7.62
0.4	10.16
0.5	12.70
0.6	15.24
0.7	17.78
0.8	20.32
0.9	22.86
1	25.4
2	50.8
3	76.2
4	101.6
5	127.0
6	152.4
7	177.8
8	203.2
9	228.6
10	254.0
11	279.4
12	304.8
13	330.2
14	355.6
15	381.0
16	406.4
17	431.8
18	457.2
19	482.6
20	508.0
21	533.4
22	558.8
23	584.2
24	609.6
25	635.0
26	660.4
27	685.8
28	711.2
29	736.6
30	762.0
31	787.4
32	812.8
33	838.2
34	863.6
35	889.0
36	914.4

Castrol GRADES

Castrol Engine Oils

Castrol GTX

An ultra high performance SAE 20W/50 motor oil which exceeds the latest API MS requirements and manufacturers' specifications. Castrol GTX with liquid tungsten† generously protects engines at the extreme limits of performance, and combines both good cold starting with oil consumption control. Approved by leading car makers.

Castrol XL 20/50

Contains liquid tungsten†; well suited to the majority of conditions giving good oil consumption control in both new and old cars.

Castrolite (Multi-grade)

This is the lightest multi-grade oil of the Castrol motor oil family containing liquid tungsten†. It is best suited to ensure easy winter starting and for those car models whose manufacturers specify lighter weight oils.

Castrol Grand Prix

An SAE 50 engine oil for use where a heavy, full-bodied lubricant is required.

Castrol Two-Stroke-Four

A premium SAE 30 motor oil possessing good detergency characteristics and corrosion inhibitors, coupled with low ash forming tendency and excellent anti-scuff properties. It is suitable for all two-stroke motor-cycles, and for two-stroke and small four-stroke horticultural machines.

Castrol CR (Multi-grade)

A high quality engine oil of the SAE-20W/30 multi-grade type, suited to mixed fleet operations.

Castrol CRI 10, 20, 30

Primarily for diesel engines, a range of heavily fortified, fully detergent oils, covering the requirements of DEF 2101-D and Supplement 1 specifications.

Castrol CRB 20, 30

Primarily for diesel engines, heavily fortified, fully detergent oils, covering the requirements of MIL-L-2104B.

Castrol R 40

Primarily designed and developed for highly stressed racing engines. Castrol 'R' should not be mixed with any other oil nor with any grade of Castrol.
†*Liquid Tungsten is an oil soluble long chain tertiary alkyl primary amine tungstate covered by British Patent No. 882,295.*

Castrol Gear Oils

Castrol Hypoy (90 EP)

A light-bodied powerful extreme pressure gear oil for use in hypoid rear axles and in some gearboxes.

Castrol Gear Oils (continued)

Castrol Hypoy Light (80 EP)

A very light-bodied powerful extreme pressure gear oil for use in hypoid rear axles in cold climates and in some gearboxes.

Castrol Hypoy B (90 EP)

A light-bodied powerful extreme pressure gear oil that complies with the requirements of the MIL-L-2105B specification, for use in certain gearboxes and rear axles.

Castrol Hi-Press (140 EP)

A heavy-bodied extreme pressure gear oil for use in spiral bevel rear axles and some gearboxes.

Castrol ST (90)

A light-bodied gear oil with fortifying additives

Castrol D (140)

A heavy full-bodied gear oil with fortifying additives.

Castrol Thio-Hypoy FD (90 EP)

A light-bodied powerful extreme pressure gear oil. This is a special oil for running-in certain hypoid gears.

Automatic Transmission Fluids

Castrol TQF
(Automatic Transmission Fluid)

Approved for use in all Borg-Warner Automatic Transmission Units. Castrol TQF also meets Ford specification M2C 33F.

Castrol TQ Dexron®
(Automatic Transmission Fluid)

Complies with the requirements of Dexron® Automatic Transmission Fluids as laid down by General Motors Corporation.

Castrol Greases

Castrol LM

A multi-purpose high melting point lithium based grease approved for most automotive applications including chassis and wheel bearing lubrication.

Castrol MS3

A high melting point lithium based grease containing molybdenum disulphide.

Castrol BNS

A high melting point grease for use where recommended by certain manufacturers in front wheel bearings when disc brakes are fitted.

Castrol Greases (continued)

Castrol CL

A semi-fluid calcium based grease, which is both waterproof and adhesive, intended for chassis lubrication.

Castrol Medium

A medium consistency calcium based grease.

Castrol Heavy

A heavy consistency calcium based grease.

Castrol PH

A white grease for plunger housings and other moving parts on brake mechanisms. *It must NOT be allowed to come into contact with brake fluid when applied to the moving parts of hydraulic brakes.*

Castrol Graphited Grease

A graphited grease for the lubrication of transmission chains.

Castrol Under-Water Grease

A grease for the under-water gears of outboard motors.

Anti-Freeze

Castrol Anti-Freeze

Contains anti-corrosion additives with ethylene glycol. Recommended for the cooling systems of all petrol and diesel engines.

Speciality Products

Castrol Girling Damper Oil Thin

The oil for Girling piston type hydraulic dampers.

Castrol Shockol

A light viscosity oil for use in some piston type shock absorbers and in some hydraulic systems employing synthetic rubber seals. It must not be used in braking systems.

Castrol Penetrating Oil

A leaf spring lubricant possessing a high degree of penetration and providing protection against rust.

Castrol Solvent Flushing Oil

A light-bodied solvent oil, designed for flushing engines, rear axles, gearboxes and gearcasings.

Castrollo

An upper cylinder lubricant for use in the proportion of 1 fluid ounce to two gallons of fuel.

Everyman Oil

A light-bodied machine oil containing anti-corrosion additives for both general use and cycle lubrication.

Index

Printed by
Haynes Publishing Group
Sparkford Yeovil Somerset
England